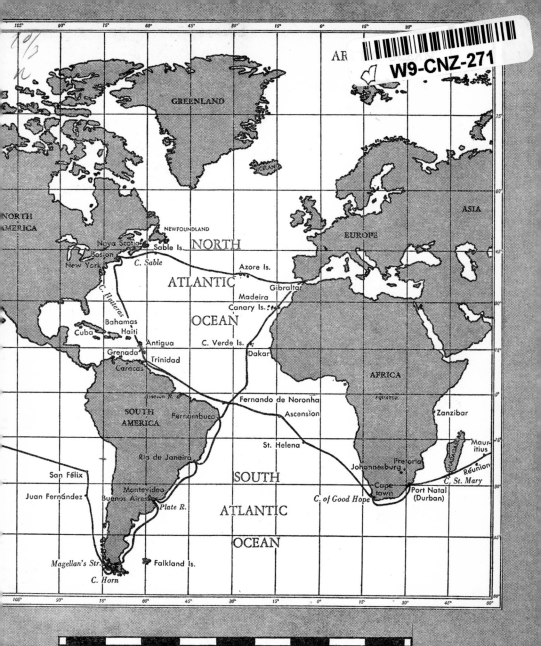

Chart of

THE "SPRAY'S" VOYAGE
AROUND THE WORLD

24th April, 1895 – 27th June, 1898

The Voyages of

JOSHUA SLOCUM

The Voyages of
JOSHUA SLOCUM

————◆————

Collected and Introduced by

WALTER MAGNES TELLER

•

VOYAGE OF THE LIBERDADE

VOYAGE OF THE DESTROYER FROM NEW YORK TO BRAZIL

SAILING ALONE AROUND THE WORLD

RESCUE OF SOME GILBERT ISLANDERS

RUTGERS UNIVERSITY PRESS

New Brunswick   *New Jersey*

Preface

Joshua Slocum was one of the breed who struggle against the world's arrangements. As the first man to sail his way alone around the earth, he made an immortal gesture. And in the account which he gave of that solo voyage he wrote not only a classic of literature and sailing but also, perhaps unawares, a parable of the human condition.

One can never say till fifty years afterwards just what will stick in the minds and hearts of men. But that number of years and more have gone by since *Sailing Alone Around the World* first hove up on the horizon. The statistics of copies published, sold, translated, and still being read are a verdict in themselves for the lovely story of the small boat venture and the strange Yankee odyssey of the spirit. Van Wyck Brooks calls it a "nautical equivalent" to *Walden.* And, indeed, one discovers Slocum the way one discovers Thoreau, a key example in literary history of a man determined to gain possession of himself.

While Slocum's masterpiece gathers momentum, his two earlier books have hardly got under way. Practically unobtainable for many years, they are virtually unknown to present-day readers. *Voyage of the Liberdade*, which Slocum first published himself in 1890, has not been in print in America since 1894, when Roberts Brothers issued 1,000 copies. As for *Voyage of the Destroyer from New York to Brazil,* it narrowly missed oblivion. The Library of Congress does not own a copy, probably because at the time Slocum wrote it he could not afford the copyright fee. It was printed in 1893, also at the captain's expense, and bound in paper. The paper, however, was such poor stuff that most of the edition has certainly crumbled away. In years of searching for copies I have seen only three. Speaking strictly, *Voyage of the Destroyer* has only now found a publisher.

And only here does *Sailing Alone Around the World* appear in contemporary dress. The text is cut loose from the nineteenth-century style illustrations which till now have clung to it. The old-fashioned chapter headings, not written by Slocum, of course, have been left behind.

This first ingathering then of the works of Joshua Slocum includes his three books as well as excerpts from his letters and early writing. The assembling of it began in a casual way—at Martha's Vineyard, where, in the summer of 1952, I happened to be told Slocum once had his only dwelling ashore. Having some time before read *Sailing Alone Around the World,* and ever since desired to know more about its author, I went to see that quondam home. I also learned that his widow, his second wife, still lived nearby, in West Tisbury. I called on her and was delighted to meet a charming lady in her ninetieth year. Thereafter, one thing, one person, led to the next. I visited around with old men and women, many of them gathered to their fathers since, and listened to their memories of Captain Slocum. I looked for documentary evidence, too. "The Spray tied to a palm-tree at Keeling Cocos Islands Aug 20th 1897" was the heading on the first Slocum letter I held and read. Little by little, data came to hand, and eventually more than I dreamed existed; for when Joshua Slocum went missing nearly half a century ago, boat, books, logs, and papers—all had disappeared with him.

In 1953, in "Any Word of Captain Slocum?" an article for the Martha's Vineyard *Gazette,* I cast my first notes and impressions on the waters. They brought fresh leads to further information. The next year, in a new introduction for a reprint of *Sailing Alone Around the World,* I wrote a brief notice of Slocum's life and work, setting down what I thus far knew and dimly comprehended. At the same time, fortified and encouraged by a Guggenheim Foundation fellowship, I began a book-length study of him, and this was published in 1956 as *The Search for Captain Slocum: A Biography.* Inevitably, this book also brought new material to light. I put it into an article: "Postscripts to *The Search for Captain Slocum,*" *American Neptune,* July 1958.

Preface

The introductory pieces in the present volume, while drawing of course and necessity on preceding work, also offer still further new material. In fact it was only last year that I found the clue to the Slocum letters and related consular dispatches in the National Archives; and these are now published for the first time. In the main, the purpose of *The Voyages of Joshua Slocum* is to make available in one volume Slocum's writing, to let his story speak for itself: not to provide conclusions but rather what may lead to conclusions, for in the final analysis this is the captain's book.

WALTER MAGNES TELLER

Summer 1958
Lahaska, Pennsylvania

Acknowledgments

I thank William Sloane for aid and comfort throughout the making of this book. And I thank Barbara Rex, Helen Stewart and Katherine Morgan for skillful and sympathetic reading and editing. Once again I wish to thank every one of the many persons who helped unfold the story of Joshua Slocum.

W. M. T.

Contents

Joshua Slocum: Navigator
and Writer

Joshua Slocum: Navigator and Writer

Joshua Slocum, navigator and writer, was born 20 February 1844 and declared legally dead as of 14 November 1909, the date on which he last set sail.

He was born to seafaring, for his birthplace was Nova Scotia on a trap ridge farm in Annapolis County by the shore of the Bay of Fundy. From the start he heard the rolling of the tidal waters and smelled the salt smell of the ocean. He was raised amid tall-masted ships, since in those days the maritime province of Nova Scotia was one of the leading shipbuilding centers of the world.

Slocum was a naturalized Yankee. His forefathers were English and spelled the family name Slocomb. They went to Massachusetts early in the seventeenth century, but after the War of Independence, along with other colonists who had taken the British side, they were exiled. They settled in Nova Scotia, then by the second half of the nineteenth century began drifting back; and when Joshua later won his personal independence and became a Massachusetts man, it was, in a sense, as a native returning.

Though his forebears, by and large, were sailors, Joshua's father was a farmer. John Slocomb was a tall, heavy, muscular man, a deacon in his church, and, according to his son, was not afraid of a gale of wind; but he had a hard time making a living.

3

Joshua's mother, Sarah Jane Southern, was the daughter of the keeper of the Southwest Point Light at Westport, on Brier Island, off Digby Neck. She was a fine-featured, gentle woman, and Joshua was said to have looked like her and to have inherited her exceptional eyes. She married early, and thereafter her life was the familiar experience of a country woman of her time: pregnancies, births, infant diseases and deaths. Joshua was the fifth of her eleven children. From the beginning he was a competitor in the struggle for existence.

When he was eight, the family left "the old clay farm," as he spoke of it, without love, long afterwards. They moved down country to the little village of Westport, and for extremely serious reasons. The father had failed at farming; and now the mother's health was giving way. She was weary and needed to be near her kin. In Westport, Joshua went to school for a couple of years, and this seems to have been the extent of his formal education. At age ten he went to work. It is not surprising that the future writer never learned to spell or punctuate.

John Slocomb tried a new line: making fishermen's leather boots. He put Josh to work beside him, tending the soaking vats and whittling pegs. Josh hated it. From the wharfside shack where he worked he watched the ships in the bay. Whenever he could, he went sailing, with chances, as he said, "greatly in favor of being drowned," for, like country boys and seafaring men of those days, he could not swim; nor in a lifetime at sea, did he learn. He had no fear of the water. He was fatalistic about it in a way that the swimmer, who really fights against it, is not. He knew that the sea would claim him if it meant to. But he did learn very early how to sail and manage a boat, and, what was perhaps of equal importance for a coming ship's captain, how to use his fists.

So from very early on, Joshua knew what he wanted. "Next in attractiveness, after seafaring, came shipbuilding. I longed to be master in both professions . . . ," he wrote. On one occasion, when he was twelve, his father found him in the cellar, painstakingly putting the finishing touches to a ship's model he was making. Enraged by this evidence of what he considered idleness and the workings of Beelzebub, with whom he daily wrestled, John Slocomb seized the model and smashed it to the ground. But the violent end of the boy's first ship did not demolish the dream of building or sailing. On the contrary it was thereby compressed and intensified.

Navigator and Writer

One must try to imagine what Joshua's boyhood was like: the father, irritable and defeated, holding him to a hated task; the fine-grained mother worn out by life and dying before young Joshua's eyes. As long as his mother lived, he made only one attempt to escape, and that was at fourteen as cook on a fishing schooner—a task he was unequal to. But when, in 1860, she died at age forty-six, he left for good, and was ever thereafter wholly committed to the sea.

Josh was sixteen when he made his first voyage, on a British ship bound for Liverpool. He next sailed to China via the Cape of Good Hope. By the time he was eighteen, he was made second mate, for he had a natural taste for reading and learning and in spare hours practiced with the sextant and taught himself navigation.

For a number of years he sailed on British ships. However, in San Francisco, in 1869, he was offered command of an American coasting schooner, and so decided to be an American citizen. At age twenty-five, he became Captain Slocum. It was a young age at which to win command but not unusual in his time and profession.

His next ship was a larger craft and thus was another step upward. In the bark *Washington* he sailed from San Francisco with a mixed cargo for Sydney, Australia; and there, all unforeseen, in the words of their marriage certificate, "Marriage between Joshua Slocum, Bachelor, Master Mariner of Massachusetts, United States, and Virginia Albertina Walker, Spinster, of 19 Buckingham Street, Strawberry Hill, Sydney," was celebrated in the Bathhurst Street Baptist Church, 31 January 1871. If it was a quite typical sea captain's romance—first sight, courtship, and marriage all pressed into a space of two or three weeks while the vessel was unloading and loading again—it proved to be a meeting of a man and woman supremely right for each other.

Virginia, twenty-one at the time she married, was born in New York City, 22 August 1849. It was the year of the gold rush, and her father, William Walker, joined the stampede. From California, he took his family still further west, to New South Wales, and it was in and around Sydney that Virginia grew to womanhood. Virginia claimed a dash of American Indian blood, and lingering over her photograph, one easily believes it. Her flashing yellow-gold eyes, as one of her sons described them, had the steady gaze of an eagle.

Regal in bearing, but light-hearted, too, she was a splendid horse-woman and an excellent shot. Though she dearly loved the land where she was raised and was used to freedom outdoors, and elbow room, after her marriage she packed up, kissed her parents good-bye, and followed her new husband into the tiny quarters which a vessel such as the *Washington* offered its captain and captain's lady. It was a rarely courageous wife who accompanied her husband on more than one voyage. But Virginia, for the rest of her life, sailed wherever Captain Joshua went.

A voyage from down under and across the Pacific—from Australia to Alaska—accompanied by a rough crew bent on taking in a cargo of salmon, was the honeymoon trip of Joshua and Virginia. It was only four years since the United States had acquired Alaska from Russia, and Alaskan waters had hardly been fished or charted. The fishing was splendid, but in a gale one night, the *Washington* drove on a bar and stuck. Thereupon Slocum built a whaleboat and boated his cargo of fish to the holds of a couple of empty sealers nearby. The bride was taken off by revenue cutter. So though Slocum lost his ship, he managed to land the catch in San Francisco, a feat of personal self-reliance bordering on genius.

The owners of the *Washington*, despite the accident, retained their confidence in their young captain and gave him another command, this time a San Francisco to Honolulu packet, the barkentine *Constitution*. On board the *Constitution*, in San Francisco harbor, Virginia gave birth to their first child, Victor, early in 1872.

The next year, Slocum went to work for Aymar & Company of New York. With Virginia and the baby, he changed his shipbound residence, moving now to the captain's cabin of the square-rigger, *B. Aymar*. In December 1873, a second son was born on board and, in honor of the ship, named Benjamin Aymar. A third child, Jessie, was born as the ship lay in Philippine waters in the summer of 1875.

In the Philippines, Slocum took time out to work at his second profession: shipbuilding. He contracted to build a steamship hull. Though a master mariner, he was no master carpenter, as the head of a shipyard was termed. But jack of all nautical trades, he knew the rule-of-thumb methods, and that was enough for constructing a vessel in an outport. In a jungle village on Subic Bay he set up a primitive boatyard, and there, with his wife and family, lived in a nipa-thatched hut on stilts for about a year. At the end of that time

6

he seems not to have received the expected pay. Apparently the people for whom he was building failed, and all he got for his trouble was the 45-ton schooner *Pato*, Spanish for "duck," as he explained, which had neither deck nor cabin. Slocum, however, soon remedied those deficiencies, and keeping his family with him, as usual, went to live on board. They then made a few inter-island trips before starting out on a voyage.

Now Slocum was owner as well as master. In his new command, a vessel halfway in size between the *Pinta* and the *Niña*, the captain with Virginia and their children, ages two, four and five, crossed the South China Sea to Hong Kong. There, in 1877, he decided to go fishing again. Getting together a crew of sea-hunters and fishers, he set sail for Yokohama, thence to the peninsula of Kamchatka and Petropavlovsk-Kamchatski, where Virginia, thousands of ocean miles away from all she had known, gave birth to twins. They were four days old when, as Slocum wrote, "we began to take in fish."

The newly discovered North Pacific cod banks were teeming. Though Slocum had not brought salt enough to cure a bonanza catch, luck was with him. In that far-off corner of the world he, sailor-like, met up with an old friend, the *Constitution*, chockablock with fish and about to jettison her unused salt, but instead it was shoveled into the *Pato's* hold. "Yes sir, we had a stirring voyage and altogether a delightful time on the fishing grounds, for every cod-fish that came in over the rail was a quarter of a dollar—clear," Slocum recalled. In two weeks' time the *Pato*, loaded to her marks, hoisted sail for an American West Coast port.

The twins, who later died in infancy, were two months old when the *Pato* sailed into Portland, Oregon, with what Slocum claimed was the first cargo of salt cod to enter the state. After selling the fish, he sailed the family to Honolulu, where he disposed of the schooner for $5,000 in gold. So ended a cruise of more than 8,000 miles. "The whole voyage was a great success," Slocum, in one of his nobler understatements, concluded. Actually, the voyage of the *Pato* might have made an extraordinary book. However, all that survives, firsthand, on the subject is a rather telegraphic account Slocum gave years later to a business acquaintance.

Returning to San Francisco by steamer, the captain now bought an ancient full-rigged vessel, his largest to date, the *Amethyst*, 350 tons. On his first voyage out, to Manila, he took along a brother as cook, and a sister to help his wife. Raising her family on the wild ocean was proving a strenuous life for Virginia. She taught the children their school and Sunday school lessons, played the piano and sang to them. She sewed, embroidered, and also displayed some unusual and, in her case, fortunate abilities. One of her sons, B. Aymar, recalled how he and his mother used to hunt in mid-ocean. "It was my job," he said, "to get the shark interested in coming close up. I used a new tin can with a string on it to attract the shark close under the stern where Mother dispatched it with her .32 cal. revolver with which she never needed but one shot. How I loved to see her do it—and without any signs on her part of showing superior skill." Quite untypical memories for a boy to have of his mother, but Virginia was quite untypical even among captain's wives.

For several years the *Amethyst* carried all manner of freight, timber from the hardwood forests of the Philippines, coal from Nagasaki to Vladivostok and Shanghai, natural ice from Hakodate to Hong Kong, gunpowder from Shanghai to Tainan. Somewhere in all this voyaging, and sometime in 1879, Virginia gave birth to another daughter, but the infant died soon after. Late in the following year the Slocums returned to Hong Kong. And in Hong Kong harbor, on board the *Amethyst,* flying the American flag, another child, the seventh, was born. It was 3 March 1881. The parents named him James Garfield Slocum.

Along with many other vessels at that time in the ten-square-mile harbor was an 1,800-ton windjammer, *Northern Light*—not to be confused with the earlier clipper of the same name, for clipper ship days, which had marked the zenith of sail, were now well past. However, this later *Northern Light* was a splendid tall-masted ship with round stern and a figurehead. She was five times the size of the *Amethyst* and as beautiful to Slocum as her name.

So far, what Slocum wanted, he got. Now in the great East Asian entrepôt, he worked out his biggest deal. The captain of the *Northern Light* was also part owner. By buying out his interest, after first selling the *Amethyst,* Slocum succeeded him as master of the larger ship. Slocum was now in command of what he believed to be one of the finest American sailers afloat. With Virginia by his side, he had struggled to the top of the tree. And he was not yet forty.

So the family moved into still larger quarters, this time a truly

luxurious home afloat. Victor, the oldest son, recalled that one of
the cabins had a library of five hundred volumes and that, with its
built-in bookshelves, it "looked very much like the study of a literary worker or a college professor." Proudly and with a profitable
cargo of sugar loaded at Manila, Captain Slocum sailed for New
York via the Cape of Good Hope. It was a June day in 1882 when
the *Northern Light* came up New York harbor and glided to her
East River berth. Her rig was so lofty that part of it had to be
struck to let her pass under the Brooklyn Bridge, then being built.
Did Slocum see that the bridge was designed to accommodate
not sailers but steamers, and that ships like the *Northern Light*
would have no place in the future?

In New York, Slocum summoned his father from Nova Scotia to
come and behold his son and the ship he commanded. He sent the
money for the trip, and the old man came. John Slocomb had not
seen Josh for twenty-two years, had never met Virginia or the grand-
children. All that Slocum had set out to win, he had won. As master,
husband, father, and son, it was Joshua Slocum's finest hour. But
the brief surcease from travel ended. Two months later the ship was
outward bound with a cargo of case oil for Yokohama.

Once again Slocum had embarked on a course which well might
have been the subject of a book. But the only thing we have from
his hand concerning the voyage of the *Northern Light* is a brief
account of an incident on the way, *Rescue of Some Gilbert Islanders*,
the endpiece to the present volume.

Very soon after leaving New York the *Northern Light* had rudder
trouble and put into New London to make repairs. The crew, or
some members of it, tried to make this a pretext to call the voyage
off. After all, they had been paid in advance, as was the custom.
Suddenly it was mutiny. In trying to seize the ringleader, the chief
officer was fatally stabbed, while Virginia, a pistol in either hand,
covered her captain husband. In reply to the signal for help, the
coast guard steamed out, and the mutiny ended—at least for the time
being.

When the ship was ready to sail again, Slocum faced a difficult
situation. A good crew was hard to come by. For some years the
American merchant marine had grown faster than the seafaring
part of the population. Foreign sailors were being employed for
want of enough Americans. With their employment all the pleas-

anter relations between cabin and forecastle vanished. In fact, life in American ships was becoming unbearable at the very moment when opportunities ashore, notably in the westward expansion, were becoming increasingly attractive. In this situation, Slocum decided to keep the same crew with which he had left New York. It proved an unfortunate decision, for the *Northern Light* was to sail around the world, and the captain to have a hard time all the way. During one of the more peaceful interludes Slocum rescued a party of Gilbert Islanders who had been adrift forty days in an open boat.

After discharging cargo and castaways in Yokohama, the *Northern Light* sailed to Manila, where she loaded sugar and hemp to be carried to Liverpool. From Manila, she sailed across the South China Sea and through Sunda Strait, passing by Krakatau just a few days before that volcanic island blew up in August 1883. As the vessel approached the Cape of Good Hope, heavy seas loosened her planking and twisted her rudderhead off. She began to leak in the topsides. Water got below and melted the sugar; the hemp had to be jettisoned. Under jury steering gear she somehow made Port Elizabeth, where the remains of the cargo were discharged, an officer released on account of sickness, and the ship laid up two months.

Before getting under way again, Slocum shipped a new officer, a certain Henry A. Slater, an ex-convict who seems to have been in league with some of the crew. In any case, soon after Slocum put to sea again there was trouble, and the captain, perhaps at his wit's end, had Slater imprisoned and bound in irons and kept so for fifty-three days, the balance of the voyage to New York. At the end, Slocum and Virginia and the children were older by almost a year and a half than when they had started out.

The voyage of the *Northern Light,* together with its sequel, was disastrous. Early in 1884, Slocum was hailed into court, and on Slater's testimony convicted of charges of false and cruel imprisonment. He was fined $500, a sum which his underwriters paid. The ship herself needed overhauling, but with steam cutting further and further into sail, it was not economically feasible. Slocum sold his share, and his proud ship was eventually converted to a coal barge. By 24 January 1884, Slocum was no longer listed as either an owner or master. He was never again so prosperous as when he had sent for his father, nor did he ever again command so imposing a vessel. The high point of his merchant career was past. The long downgrade now began.

While Slocum went in search of another ship, Virginia and the children took lodging near Boston with one and another of his married sisters; for since her marriage Virginia had had no home ashore. It was a welcome change from life at sea, which by now had undermined her health. One of the relatives described Virginia as "a handsome woman," and added that she and the captain "were deeply in love and could be completely oblivious of everyone and everything if they could be together."

Though many masters and owners were switching to steam, Slocum was determined to continue in the way he knew and loved. In Baltimore he found "a little bark which of all men's handiwork" was to him "the nearest to perfection of beauty." This was the *Aquidneck*, owned by Thos. Whittridge, and she was about the size of Slocum's old *Amethyst*. With the last of his *Pato* money, Slocum bought her, and by spring had her ready to make her first voyage. He ordered his family to Baltimore, loaded the *Aquidneck* with flour for Pernambuco, Brazil, and set sail.

Victor, the oldest son, recalled the bark as being "as close to a yacht as a merchantman could be." It was the first home Garfield, the youngest, could remember. The square piano bolted to the deck, the handsome saloon, the livestock in pens on the roof of the deckhouse, the canary, and the many books were unforgettable. The voyage to Pernambuco was pleasant. From there, the Slocums sailed south for Buenos Aires. But soon after passing Santa Catarina, Brazil, Virginia was taken ill. No longer was she able to go on deck, as she often had, to help the captain take his observations at noon, nor, in the evenings, could she now read aloud. Very likely her heart had been damaged. Garfield recalled the piece of embroidery his mother was making. "She left her needle where she stopped," he said.

Virginia was in bed as the bark approached Buenos Aires and anchored in the Plata River. Slocum hurried ashore to try to get cargo for Sydney as Virginia wished; for she longed to lay eyes on her people again. But not many hours later, the captain saw flying from the masthead of his vessel the flag letter J—J for Joshua—which signaled that he was needed. Hastily, he returned. That evening, 25 July 1884, in the presence of her husband, and with her children kneeling by her bedside, Virginia, not yet thirty-five, died. Slocum had now lost the signifying women of his life: his mother when he was sixteen, his sea-wife when he was forty.

Virginia was buried in the English Cemetery in Buenos Aires, and a few days after, Slocum, in his own words, "got crazy," and ran the *Aquidneck* on shore. At considerable financial cost, he managed to bring her off and then sailed for Boston with his motherless brood. Many years later, when himself an old man, B. Aymar, the second son, said of that terrible time: "Father's days were done with the passing of mother. . . ." Garfield summed it up this way: "When she died, then father never recovered. He was like a ship with a broken rudder."

For almost two years Slocum sailed alone in the captain's cabin, carrying freights between Baltimore and Pernambuco. Then, on a visit to Massachusetts, where his children were parceled out among his sisters, he met a first cousin fresh from Nova Scotia. Her name was Henrietta Elliott—Hettie, she was called. She was a seamstress and pretty, and only twenty-four years old. Slocum was forty-two and finding it a lonely life. So they were married, in Boston, on Washington's Birthday in 1886. Six days later they set sail on their wedding trip. Garfield, five, was taken along, and Victor, fourteen, sailed as mate.

The voyage which Slocum now began is the subject of his first book. Instead of *Voyage of the Liberdade,* he might have called it *Voyage of the Aquidneck,* and, in fact, when a version of the story was printed in *Outing* magazine in April 1903, it was called "Voyage of the *Aquidneck* and Its Varied Adventures in South American Waters." Actually, the book tells about a voyage in which the passage out was made in one ship, the passage home in another.

The complex of events surrounding this voyage will be taken up in a commentary antecedent to *Voyage of the Liberdade.* All that need be said here is that while freighting along the east coast of South America in 1886-1887, Slocum became involved in a strange and extraordinary series of passages which finally led to Paranaguá Bay and a sandbar. There the *Aquidneck* "stranded broadside on, where, open to the sea, a strong swell came in that raked her fore and aft, for three days, the waves dashing over her groaning hull the while till at last her back was broke and—why not add 'heart' as well! for she lay now undone." She also lay uninsured.

Saving what he could from the wreck, Slocum, with a kit of hand tools, built on the beach a 35-foot craft which he called a canoe. *Liberdade,* he named it, because it was launched on the day the Brazilian slaves were freed. In that boat, wearing the sails that Hettie sewed, Slocum and Hettie and Victor and Garfield sailed 5,500 miles in fifty-three days, from Paranaguá Bay to Washington, D.C., where they arrived in December 1888. It was voyage enough for Hettie for the rest of her life; she never made another. As for Slocum, it had, perhaps, carried him further than he knew, adumbrating the still greater voyage to come, on the downhill course to fame.

After spending the winter in Washington, Slocum with Hettie and the children returned to Massachusetts in the summer of 1889, and took up temporary quarters with relatives in East Boston. In five years Slocum had lost Virginia, his ship, and his worldly fortune. Now his profession was gone as well. The age of steam had fully arrived, and there were not enough sailing ships to go round. Perhaps he knew that never again would he be in command of a merchant vessel. It was at this point, when everything had been taken from him, that he turned to writing.

The shipmaster of little schooling, but of wide reading, sat down and wrote his first book, and had it printed at his own expense. It was a slim, trim volume, 176 pages bound in dark green, and in 1890 Slocum tried to sell it at $1 a copy. He peddled it in Boston and New York but without success, until finally, his financial situation desperate, he had to take whatever work he could get: odd jobs on boats fitting out, or helping in shipyards. While many a master, as Slocum remarked, went into Sailors' Snug Harbor, he himself felt compelled to keep on. Times were indeed hard. The panic of 1893 impended.

On a winter day of 1892, at loose ends on the Boston waterfront, Slocum met an old friend, a prosperous retired whaler named Captain Eben Pierce. "Come to Fairhaven, and I'll give you a ship," the ex-whaler said to the ex-merchant captain. "But," he added, "she wants some repairs."

The very next day Slocum arrived in Fairhaven, on the eastern shore of New Bedford harbor, only to find that his friend had, as he later wrote, "something of a joke" on him. The ship in question was an ancient oysterman called *Spray* and was lying high and dry in a pasture along the Acushnet River.

A Yankee shipmaster does not wear his heart on his sleeve, and what Slocum felt at that moment he has not described. But the sight of the sloop, whose sailing days, like his own, seemed done for, stirred him deeply. The meeting on the beach of Slocum and the *Spray* was the start of one of the world's love affairs. From that hour, and for all remaining existence, Slocum and the *Spray* were never really to be parted.

Early in *Sailing Alone Around the World,* Slocum tells how he reshaped the *Spray's* silvered bones. He began in the spring of 1893, and the job took thirteen months of his labor. When launched, the *Spray* was 37 feet long, measured 9 tons net, and, according to Slocum, "sat on the water like a swan." However, before the rejuvenation was completed he unexpectedly received and accepted the offer of a place on a ship, his first in almost six years.

It was not a captain's position, nor was it on board a merchantman. Rather, the contract was for "navigator in command" on the iron gunboat, *Destroyer,* the invention of John Ericsson, who had died four years before. While Slocum was quietly going about his business in his pasture shipyard, civil war had erupted in Brazil. The insurrection was led by Brazilian naval officers in ports on the coast Slocum knew so well. In consequence, Brazilian government agents were out buying up whatever warships they could find. The background of the war was complicated, but Slocum's interest in it relatively simple: the promise of wartime wages for taking the gunboat down, and perhaps the chance to square old scores with the Brazilian government—which he blamed for the loss of the *Aquidneck.*

Though the fantastic and extremely hazardous voyage which began in New York, 7 December 1893, provided Slocum with the subject for his second book, it was a digression from the main current of his life. Confessing, as he wrote, his "own frailty," as a soldier of fortune, he delivered the vessel and then promptly returned to his calling.

Back in Massachusetts in the spring of 1894, and without any part of the promised pay, Slocum went home—not to Hettie and their relations, nor to his children, who, except for Garfield, were now quite grown—but to his cabin on the *Spray*. There he wrote his story. Once again he footed the printer's bill, but instead of trying to sell the book, he gave the copies away. Next, he tried his hand at catching fish, but though years before with Virginia he had done very well in this occupation, he found that he now "had not the cunning properly to bait a hook." He took out a few charter fishing parties, and then went back to selling books. In the fall of that year, in time for the holiday trade, Roberts Brothers, a Boston publishing house, brought out a new edition of *Voyage of the Liberdade*, but at the old price: $1.

Just when or how Slocum got the idea of sailing around the world alone can only be guessed at. His own explanation, that it was the outcome of lifelong experience, is all right as far as it goes. But one must know what that lifelong experience had been. Certainly the circumstances of his life, compounded with his natural disposition, had been driving him relentlessly to it. The central motives of his life were building to a climax; only some pretext to satisfy the world, and possibly his more conventional self, was needed. He found one: The voyage should be undertaken for the sake of making money by writing and syndicating travel letters. It was not at all a new idea. Newspaper-sponsored accounts of travel were very much the thing in the 1890's. Two of Slocum's favorite authors, Robert Louis Stevenson and Mark Twain, had done it. Slocum talked it over with Roberts Brothers, and they agreed to act as his agents. They also helped him fit out by stocking his cabin with books—one of his prime considerations in planning for the voyage alone.

Well-wishers supplied the captain with stores, and also the rather primitive equipment he took along. He had been five times around the world and still had his charts, compass and sextant, rifles, revolvers, and medicines. He described to reporters, who watched him preparing, the route he proposed to follow; it was very different from the one he actually took. He thought he might be away for two years, but the circumnavigation required more than three.

He was ready and waiting for the wind to blow fair when a lady went to the pier to see him. She was Mabel Wagnalls, the twenty-four-year-old daughter of Adam Wagnalls, encyclopedist and publisher. Adam Wagnalls and Slocum were old acquaintances, and Wagnalls, as a bon voyage present, had sent the captain a box of books. Now his daughter brought Slocum one more, a copy of her own first literary effort, a romantic "musical story," in which she had pasted her visiting card inscribed with good wishes; and she asked him to take it around the world and bring it to her again. The lady whispered to the bearded seafarer: "The *Spray* will come back." They were deeply important words to Slocum, and later, when the *Spray* did indeed come back, he dedicated his book to "the one" who had said them.

And so at last the moment arrived when the pieces of life fell into place. Slocum was fifty-one when, amid modest fanfare, he set sail from Boston, 24 April 1895, with a dollar and a half in his pocket. According to a reporter on the scene, he was 5 feet 9½ inches tall, weighed 146 pounds, and was "spry as a kitten and nimble as a monkey."

A southward course had been plotted, but the sloop sailed eastward instead, as though both boat and passenger were reluctant to take the plunge. Hugging his familiar coast, Captain Slocum went as far as Gloucester, twenty miles away, where he asked himself again "whether it were best to sail beyond the ledge and rocks at all." He moved on to Nova Scotia, his native land which he had not seen for thirty-five years, and there he tarried six weeks. Finally, on 2 July, he let go, as he said, his last hold on America.

Slocum crossed the Atlantic to Gibraltar, but warned of pirates in the Mediterranean, he turned around and recrossed, this time following Magellan's southwestward course. By skill and strength and the grace of God, he survived the vicissitudes of the Strait. He traversed the vastness of the South Pacific and visited the land where he had found Virginia. Thence he made his way through the Coral Sea, the Arafura Sea, and the Indian Ocean. Then rounding the Cape of Good Hope, he crossed the Atlantic a third time, and dropped anchor at Newport, Rhode Island, three years, two months, two days, and 46,000 miles after setting out. Still he had a strong urge to return to the place of beginning, and apparently the *Spray* did, too; for shortly afterward, "not quite satisfied . . . she waltzed beautifully round the coast and up the Acushnet River to Fairhaven, where I secured her to the cedar spile driven in the bank to hold her when she was launched. I could bring her no nearer home." So Slocum wrote at the end of *Sailing Alone.*

Navigator and Writer

From New York, Mabel Wagnalls hurried to Newport to greet her warrior, and got there ahead of Hettie coming from Boston. But not many others shared the ardor of these ladies. Some refused to believe a story of single-handed circumnavigation, some hinted Slocum was a diamond smuggler; to others he was just an old fossil cast up from the age of sail. Mostly his news was not heard at all, but was lost in the hubbub of the Spanish-American War. It began to seem he had gone around only to find himself back where he started—on the land where he did not belong, with his land-wife with whom he had no deep connection. Yet there was one important difference: Almost upon arrival a telegram came requesting his story. It was from Richard Watson Gilder, poet, and editor of the *Century Illustrated Monthly Magazine.*

However, from such a successful sea journey, Slocum could not easily shift to the rhythm of writing. Almost from the minute the voyage was over he longed to put his sailorly gifts to work. Perhaps he could serve as a gunboat pilot in the Philippine waters he had known long ago. But hardly had he expressed the thought when the Spanish-American War was over.

By autumn of 1898 the captain was proposing another course: a college ship, wind-driven, certainly, to accommodate three hundred student-passengers, both men and women, for his ideas had not changed since the days when he wanted Virginia with him on board. Instruction would be given not only in seamanship and in engineering but also in the liberal arts. He would give lessons in celestial navigation, the subject he had taught himself so well. But the plan never got on the stocks.

So Slocum settled down to his story. His preparatory letters to *Century* editors show his intensity and vivid talent as well as his limitations of punctuation and spelling. "Without saying Slocum Slocum all the time—that I do not care for I know that the whole story will be hard to beat— My ship, essentially mine, is as tight today as the best ship afloat; her pump is dry enough for matchwood; not wormed not worn, my ship is as good or better than she was the day I launched her and I myself, I am ten years younger than I was the day I fell the first tree for the construction of my bark. . . ." At first he wrote in East Boston, where he and Hettie were again doubling up with relatives. But as soon as winter was

17

over, he went to New York to finish his book in the cabin of the *Spray,* tied up at Erie Basin Drydocks, Brooklyn. Early in the summer of 1889 he delivered the manuscript, then cast off his mooring lines and went for a cruise in New England waters, correcting proof and corresponding with his editors from various Massachusetts ports he put into.

Sailing Alone Around the World was first published in monthly installments in the *Century* from September 1899 through March 1900. The unheard-of feat became an accepted fact. For one thing, Slocum had the consular endorsements on the *Spray's* yacht license from places he had visited to prove it. But some still questioned the captain's statement that with the wheel lashed, the *Spray* steered herself while he sat below, cooking, reading, mending his sails or clothes, or sleeping. Strangely, it did not seem obvious that no man could go around the world standing or sitting at a wheel. One such critic challenged him in the columns of the *New York Times.* Slocum replied:

The Sloop Spray

To the Editor of the New York Times:

I am honored by a criticism from an old salt in THE TIMES of Nov. 7. It is possible that things occured on the voyage of the Spray inexplicable to some mariners, even of vast experience, and I can only regret not having met them before the articles referred to in The Century Magazine were written so that I might have taken them on a sail in the Spray to demonstrate her prowess. As the matter stands, it is now out of my power to further elucidate. I am not aware that the charge of boasting may be laid at my gangway. But while I claim to be only the poorest of Anglo-Saxon sailors, I will say that possibly there are better men, even in our merchant marine, than your navigating officer has yet met.

Thanking the same kind mariner for his thought of the story, may I venture to call his attention to the Spray herself, now in Winter quarters at Erie Basin dry docks, South Brooklyn?

This unpretentious sloop, built by one pair of hands, after circumnavigating the globe, is sound and snug and tight. She does not leak a drop. This would be called a great story by some; nevertheless it is a hard fact.

The story of the voyage is constructed on the same seaworthy lines; that is, it remains waterproof which your navigating officer will discover, I trust, if only he exercise to the end that patience necessary on a voyage around the world.

JOSHUA SLOCUM

New York, Nov. 8, 1899

That the *Spray*, taught by her master, was able to steer herself is no longer doubted, though yachtsmen still enjoy debating her model and rig. There are many who think that the captain succeeded, not because of the *Spray*, but in spite of her. Built along the lines of a fisherman, she was not in the first place designed for around-the-world sailing, or for sailing alone. Her mainsail and gaff were exceedingly heavy for a man to raise by himself, and she was altogether a very large, beamy boat for any one man to handle.

In March 1900 the book was published by the Century Company, somewhat revised from the magazine pieces, and later in the same year *Sailing Alone* made its first appearance in England. Reviews were favorable, and within twelve months, sales were approaching the 10,000 mark. That meant, according to the terms of his contract, about $2,000 for Slocum in addition to pay for the magazine rights. Concerning the latter, he wrote Clarence C. Buel, the *Century* editor who had worked closely with him: "No one knows how much I have been paid. When they ask me I say 'double the amount agreed upon'—which is so— They say 'how much is that?'—I say enough to buy me a house—which is also true. . . . All the old women will be sending in sea stories . . . when they hear of my amazing success (financial)."

Another resource of the ever-resourceful captain was a by-product of his travels. He had started when halfway around the world—in Australia—to reap a harvest from lecturing with lantern slides and charging admission to come aboard. "Had to do something for expenses of the voyage," he wrote. "Other captains might draw bottomry bonds but I lectured the *Spray* around the world." He took to the pulpit whenever and wherever the chance arose or could be made to arise, though lecturing, as he very well knew, was not his true function or purpose.

From circling the world in the way Slocum had, where does a man go next? With the voyage now two years behind him, the captain did not know which way to turn. He wanted to exhibit the *Spray* and himself at the Universal Exhibition in Paris, in 1900, but was not invited. He thought of a voyage to Iceland. Prince Luigi Amedeo, Duke of the Abruzzi, had thrust farther north than Nansen. Arctic fever was at its height. He thought of under-water exploration, or, perhaps, he could find the action he craved in the air. While he had been on the voyage around, Samuel P. Langley had invented the first power-driven, heavier-than-air machine, and sent it on a successful, though unmanned, flight. Slocum mailed a copy of *Sailing Alone* to an acquaintance who was also a colleague of Langley's at the Smithsonian Institution, and from the office of the Century Company wrote him this letter:

11 E. 17 St
New York N. Y.
Feb 27 1901

Dear Professor Mason

I am sending by this post, a book of some account of a voyage alone. I am not the old fossil that some take me for and I am not for old ideas when new are better

I was hoping that Professor Langly or some one else would have launched a successful flying ship before this and that I could have a second mate's position on it, to soar I felt sure that when you have time to scan my poor story you will find that I consider the human mind above all else that we know of in this world. You will see that at any rate I could trust even my poor head to find my way about independent of the machine we call chronometer. I sailed scientiffically, too, I was in touch with nature as few have ever been. I was aware of it all the time and had never a doubt of the outcome of my voyage.

With great respect
Joshua Slocum

But instead of adventure Parisian, Icelandic, submarine, or airborne, Slocum went on his way in the mode in which he began. By sail and by tow he now proceeded up the Hudson River and through the Erie Canal to Buffalo, where, at the Pan American Exposition, from May to November 1901, the world-circling *Spray* rode at anchor on the fair grounds lake, Gala Water. There he exhibited himself and the boat, and Hettie and Garfield; sold his books and answered the tourists' questions. Like Buffalo Bill, a fellow-exhibitor at the Exposition, and some others who played heroic parts, he was finishing up in side-shows.

With earnings from the Exposition, royalties, lecturing, and book-selling, Slocum was able at last to buy the thing he had some-times dreamed of at sea, and believed that he wanted. Certainly it was what Hettie wanted and had waited many years for: a home of her own in a small New England village. And so in the spring of 1902 he bought a farm at West Tisbury, in the center of the island of Martha's Vineyard, off the Massachusetts coast where he had often visited. *Fag End,* he called the place where he thought he was settling down with Hettie to farming. The next year he bought more ground, planted fruit trees and hops, but by summer he was back with his old love the *Spray,* cruising in New England waters. Long ago he had made the discovery that a ship is the ideal habi-tation, the only kind that enables its owner to retain independence and movement. The Vineyard paper published a report that he might yet return to Australia.

Slocum was adrift, wandering in and out of Vineyard harbors and relatives' and neighbors' lives. In November 1905 he sailed again, alone in the *Spray,* from Menemsha, Massachusetts, bound for warmer waters. He spent the winter in Jamaica and Grand Cayman, and by the time he was ready to sail north again had shipped a thousand conch shells and other curiosities, and agreed to deliver a cargo of orchid plants to President Theodore Roosevelt.

About 1 April 1906 he left the Caribbean and headed for his Vineyard home. On the way he detoured up the Delaware River to lecture at the Riverton, New Jersey, yacht club. While at Riverton, just above Camden, the parents of a twelve-year-old girl made a charge against him which caused his arrest and imprisonment. Many papers reported the incident. "Capt. Slocum in Trouble./ Accused of Maltreating A Girl on His Famous Yacht Spray," read one headline. Another wrote: "Capt. Slocum Held on Girl's Charge./ Famous Sailor is Arrested While Club's Guest./ He Protests Inno-cence." Some papers said Slocum ridiculed the accusation, others that he said he had no recollection of the matter and that if anything had occurred, it must have been during one of the mental lapses to which he was subject. In the course of the voyage around, Slo-cum had suffered blows on the head, once from a heavy line heaved from a dock at Newcastle, New South Wales, and again, from the *Spray's* mainsail boom.

But the only facts are that the charge, which at first was rape but later changed to "a misdemeanor," was not proved. Medical examination established the point that there had been no rape, but that the child had been "greatly agitated" by what her father, in a public letter, called "indecent action." Slocum was held in jail at Mt. Holly, New Jersey, forty-two days. Apparently the authorities did not know what to do. In finally disposing of the case, Judge Joseph Gaskill was reported as saying: "I am very sorry to be obliged to administer reproof to a man of your experience and years, and I am glad, and no doubt you are, too . . . there was no attempt made to injure the person of the girl. . . ."

In *Mardi,* Melville wrote of the "heart-loneliness which overtakes most seamen, as they grow aged, impelling them to fasten on some chance object of regard." Old man that he was now becoming, Slocum may have been, as he sometimes was, negligently unbuttoned. Such a condition could have been misunderstood by a girl nearing adolescence.

Whatever the truth was, Slocum was discharged 6 July 1906 after a plea of *non vult contendere,* literally, he will not contest. The *non vult* plea, when accepted by the court, is an implied admission of guilt, but only implied. There is no record of why Slocum made it, who advised him, or to what extent he understood or cared for the niceties of the law. But after the rather extended delay—for either he could not or would not post bail—one can be sure that his main concern was to get on with the voyage. And, in fact, within a matter of hours he was on his way with the orchids. In less than a month he navigated from the New Jersey jail to Sagamore Hill, where the President cordially received him.

Early in August, Slocum delivered the orchids. And after that, young Archibald Roosevelt went for a sail on the *Spray* while his father wrote to a friend, 6 August: ". . . Archie is off for a week's cruise with Captain Joshua Slocum—that man who takes his little boat, without any crew but himself, all around the world."

After seeing Archie home, Slocum went home himself, for the first time in nine months or so. What he then said to Hettie, or she to him, is not known, but apparently the reunion was not a success. In reporting West Tisbury news, the *Vineyard Gazette,* 16 August 1906,

22

said: "Capt. Joshua Slocum master of the Spray, was in town on Monday." A few weeks later the *New Bedford Standard* stated he was "tied up on the south side of Merrill's Wharf . . . before starting for the south. . . ." Toward the end of September, Slocum slid into Bristol, Rhode Island. There he met his youngest son, now twenty-five, and gave him, finally, a copy of the book which told of the voyage they had made together so many years before. He inscribed it:

To James G. Slocum

One of the crew of *Liberdade*
This is the last copy of the Capt's poor efforts at a sea story
It is to appear however in better form by the author

Your Father
Joshua Slocum

Bristol R I Sept 30th 1906

But what those strange and cryptic words intended to say remains a mystery.

So the captain sailed south again, alone again, and spent a second winter in the Caribbean. A Philadelphia newspaperwoman, Louise B. Ward, saw him in Kingston not long after the earthquake of January 1907 destroyed the city. "I went on the *Spray*," she wrote, "and talked with him. He seemed well. I remember he said to me—'I can patch up the *Spray* but who will patch up Captain Slocum?'" When spring returned, he spread his gray wings for the north, and from Washington, D.C., 26 May, he wrote his second son, B. Aymar.

Dear Ben:

I was glad to get your letter. . . .

I am going ahead some again, with a vessel full of stuff worth something My books are selling rather better than at first

I "lecture" Friday 31st at a fine hall here, and am promised a good house.

The president sent down for me yesterday to meet him in the Red Room, White House Archie came and brought me in their market wagon

Archie will join me again at Oyster Bay and come further east this summer, perhaps to Falmouth or Woods Hole. You must find time to meet us in Aug

Your father
Joshua Slocum

And then by way of explanation he added a postscript: "The old market wagon is reserved for best friends always."

The story is told that when the captain and the President shook hands in the White House, the ex-rancher and Rough Rider said: "Captain, our adventures have been a little different." To which the ex-merchant captain and sailor replied: "That is true, Mr. President, but I see you got here first."

However, Archie did not join the captain in the summer of 1907, nor, apparently, did Benjamin Aymar; and Slocum spent the summer, not on the farm, but on the *Spray*, selling books and souvenirs and shells to the tourists at Martha's Vineyard. That fall he made his third single-handed voyage south.

In January 1908, Slocum was seen in Miami by a yachtsman from West Chester, Pennsylvania, Vincent Gilpin, who bought from the captain a copy of *Sailing Alone* and went to hear his travel talk. In a letter to the present writer, Gilpin recalled how the captain lived in Miami, which at that time was a very small town.

I rather think he lived on the *Spray*. . . . He was thrifty and usually hard up—which didn't bother him for his wants were few. *Spray* . . . was very simply fitted out, rather bare, and very damp from many soakings with salt water, and Slocum kept a little wood-stove going to help dry her out. I remember seeing him lunching one day on what looked like a half-baked potato from which he sliced pieces with his jack-knife. He was rather shabbily dressed in civilian clothes, with a ragged black felt hat. . . . On the whole, I felt him a good example of the old-line Yankee skipper, competent, self-reliant, not talkative, but perfectly friendly and ready to answer questions. He was obviously a first-class boat-handler—which is something quite different from being a ship-captain; apparently he was both, beside being a shipwright. A very capable man; and a lonely, unhappy man.

That winter Slocum was in the Bahamas and not in a very communicative mood, at least, not so far as Hettie was concerned. Two or three times in the course of the circumnavigation she had given him up for lost. Now, on 11 May 1908, from West Tisbury, she wrote to Buel, his editor friend: "Have just heard that the 'Spray' is reported lost in the Maritime Register. . . . Personally have not heard from Captain Slocum since Nov. 1st 1907. A Vineyard man reports that he saw Captain Slocum in Jamaica a few weeks ago. I have doubts about the truth of the report at this time. Will you kindly let

24

me know if you have heard from him or of him of late. . . ." But Buel had not heard anything, either.

And then the very next month, the tenth anniversary of the *Spray's* return, Slocum sailed into New York harbor with a 2-ton piece of coral aboard consigned to the American Museum of Natural History. Museum scientists had found it in the Bahamas and engaged the captain to freight it home. This seems to have been his last cargo.

On 30 July, the *Vineyard Gazette* reported: "Captain Joshua Slocum of the sloop Spray is on the Island and has been a recent guest of Mrs. Slocum at West Tisbury." By now he was recognized for the alien on land that he was. His visits were becoming short and far between. Vineyarders said he would plant his bones in that boat.

For another year life played at will-o'-the-wisp with Slocum. Then from Quincy, Massachusetts, 4 September 1909, he wrote to his oldest:

> *Dear Victor:*
> Your letter . . . received just as I was leaving W Tisbury
> . . . We are pulling out of it for the winter at least and would sell if a purchaser should turn up. . . .
> I am on the Spray hustling for a dollar
> Just where I will be next I don't know. . . .

Captain Slocum, sixty-five now, was once again plotting a sensational voyage. His plan was to sail to South America, up the Orinoco River, and into the Río Negro, and from there to the Amazon's unknown beginning. He would then sail down that greatest of rivers to the ocean, and so on home. Vineyarders watched him getting ready. Captain Ernest Mayhew of Menemsha said that the *Spray* had been moored by two stakes, and that high tide had lifted her bowsprit onto one of them. When the tide fell, the bowsprit hung on one of the stakes and was forced up several inches. Slocum then took an axe, Captain Mayhew said, and simply drove the bowsprit into place.

The late Ernest Dean of Chilmark thought that Slocum and his boat had grown old together. "When I first met him and the *Spray,*" he said, "they both were neat, trim, and seaworthy, but as the years rolled along I noticed signs of wear and exposure." Captain Donald Poole, also of Chilmark, said of the *Spray* that "her rigging was slack and in need of tarring, and Irish pennants were much in evidence."

Joshua Slocum:

From Menemsha, Slocum set sail for Vineyard Haven, and from Vineyard Haven, which used to be known as Tisbury, he set sail again, but he does not seem to have made his port of call. Hettie's petition to the court a few years later said: ". . . that Joshua Slocum . . . *disappeared, absconded* and absented himself on the 14th day of November A.D. 1909; . . . that said absentee . . . a Master Mariner by occupation . . . disappeared on the date above-named under the following circumstances, to wit: He sailed from Tisbury, Massachusetts in the Sloop 'Spray' of about nine tons burden only . . . encountered a very severe gale shortly afterwards and has never been heard from since. . . ." In its formality and inevitability, it was a classical ending.

There were and are, of course, all sorts of theories as to where he was at the time, or what might have happened. But wherever he went or how, he remains knight and squire of the spirit of sea-going Yankeeism. Slocum was heart and fiber of the New England people of the sea, and his old-fashioned Yankee temperament and nature were as tough and flinty and poetic as his native coast. A courageous and tenacious confronter of life, a resolute battler with the elements, an asserter against a world he did not make, he had led, not a comfortable life, perhaps, but one from which he demanded meaning.

Voyage of the "Liberdade"

Foreword

Something about his first book troubled Slocum. Though four years after he had published it himself, in 1890, Roberts Brothers of Boston was reprinting and gift-binding 1,000 copies and he himself planning to retail half that number, he nevertheless, from Pemaquid Beach, Maine, wrote his newly found publisher, 18 September 1894:

> *Dear Sirs:*
> Referring to the book "Voyage of the Liberdade," I believe I would like to take 500 copies when published. . . .
> I would dearly love to revise the little book throughout. Have tried to do so but as often as I have tried I have fallen into the same faults of style: too earnestly in the fight on deck: Too gloriously free in the boat on the broad ocean
> Let anyone reading the story put himself in my place if he can, bringing his family around him, and he will see better, maybe, how it should be told
> The best that may be done I fear will be to let it go as a sailors book. . . .

Eight years later he was still worrying. From New London, Connecticut, 13 April 1902, he wrote the Century Company editor who had helped him with *Sailing Alone.*

> *Dear Mr. Buel:*
> The Liberdade book should find its way to your office Monday Morning.
> The story in manuscript does not tally with the book It has

29

been twice written since the scratching was made. I know it will stand another to advantage. . . .

Perhaps it was a certain incompleteness that bothered the captain, or a continuing emotional involvement in the events of his story. As Slocum wrote it, the narrative divides in two: the passage out in the ill-fated bark *Aquidneck*—in which he drew a vivid self-portrait of a sailing shipmaster in the twilight of sail; the passage home in the *Liberdade* canoe—a superb account of resourcefulness and nerve and self-sufficiency at sea. But there was also a kind of third part which Slocum did not or could not get into the book, yet which he succeeded very well in recounting in letters. Published now for the first time, they tell the rest of the story: how he, a sailor ashore, was haunted by the loss of his ship, and how by virtue of literary gifts he transformed an obsession into a creation.

Before embarking with the captain and Hettie, Victor and Garfield, in 1886—on a voyage which happened to be a wedding trip as well as a matter of business—it may be well to note briefly the general situation of shipmasters such as Slocum. By the fourth quarter of the nineteenth century most sailing ships were tramps, going anywhere, though actually most American sailers, especially the wood ones, had gone with the Civil War. The opening of the Suez Canal in 1869, eliminating for steamers the long run around the Cape of Good Hope, made it still harder for sailing ships under any flag to compete world-wide. Thus, by 1884, when Slocum invested his savings in the *Aquidneck*, small single-deckers of her sort had little chance for employment in foreign trade except in the carriage of mineral oils, mostly between the United States, the West Indies, and South America; in the coasting business they served chiefly as carriers of coarse freights such as lumber or coal. The cream of the traffic, and higher rates to carry it, went to steamers which could calculate their time of arrival. As every merchant knew, the time of even the swiftest sailing ship might be extended for weeks by adverse winds.

So when on 28 February 1886, Slocum sailed for Montevideo with a cargo of case oil, probably kerosene in 5-gallon cans, two cans to a case, he was performing in the quite typical risk-taking manner of men of that time and profession. On the very first page of his book he wrote that the "crew mustered ten, all told; twelve had been the complement, when freights were good." Undermanned crews were becoming a common practice as masters and owners tried to economize, and, in fact, some of the toughest conditions of life in the merchant marine prevailed as the age of sail shut down.

Once his crew was on board, Slocum was anxious to begin the voyage. In spite of predicted storms, he sailed. On 1 March the *New York Times* reported a gale blowing off the coast and the temperature down to zero. For the first time in years the North River was frozen over; one could cross on the ice from shore to shore. Two vessels were reported aground on the nearby coast, and in Gravesend Bay five garbage scows broke from their moorings. Next day a hurricane blew up, and the *Aquidneck* was battered severely. Nevertheless, Slocum kept her on course, and after riding out the storm, made a fast run to Montevideo. On 5 May, sixty-six days after leaving New York, he dropped her hook and discharged her cargo.

From Montevideo, on the north side of the entrance to the Plata River, he sailed north nine hundred miles up the coast to Antonina in Brazil. There he took in a cargo of maté, which he carried south to Buenos Aires, where Virginia had been buried two years earlier. From Buenos Aires, he made a shift up the Plata to salve a cargo of wine, which he then carried to Rosario, an Argentine river port two hundred miles northwest of Buenos Aires. At Rosario, he was chartered to load baled alfalfa for Rio de Janeiro. However, there was at the time an epidemic of cholera at Rosario and other Plata River ports, and so the Brazilian consul ordered him to proceed instead to Ilha Grande, the Brazilian quarantine station some sixty miles outside of Rio. In mid-December 1886 Slocum was cleared from Rosario, had a narrow escape from grounding on a bar in the Plata as he sailed downstream, and arrived at Ilha Grande about 7 January 1887.

Before his cargo could be discharged, even though he had conformed to port regulations at Rosario and had proper documents, he was ordered, at gun point, to leave, and to keep clear of all Brazilian ports since all were now closed to vessels coming from the plague-stricken ports on the Plata. What to do with the cargo was a ticklish problem. "One person suggested that the case required me to pitch the whole cargo into the sea! This friend, I may mention, was from Boston," the captain wrote. He did not, however, follow the Tea Party precedent, but stuck to the terms of the charter party.

He returned all the way to Rosario with the hay, where he understood he had the right to discharge it. However, he did not do so. Hopeful that quarantine restrictions would soon be lifted, he elected to lay there with the cargo in. But it was not until 9 April, after the epidemic had run its course, that the ports of Brazil were open again. For a second time Slocum sailed from Rosario. He made Ilha Grande 29 April, went into Rio harbor 11 May, and there rid his bark of a cargo loaded six months before. The business was a terrible loss.

It was now more than a year since the *Aquidneck* had sailed from New York. At this point Slocum might have sailed north and home with Hettie and the two boys, but he did not, perhaps because he had no northbound cargo. A most important feature of successful freighting is to carry cargo both ways. In June, Slocum sailed from Rio heading south for Paranaguá and Antonina, "partly laden with flour, kerosene, pitch, tar, rosin and wine, three pianos . . . and one steam engine and boiler, all as ballast. . . ." On the way down a sudden storm caught the bark unprepared and carried away her topgallant masts, but not before throwing her on her beam-ends and shaking up the nonpaying cargo. To stow a general cargo correctly requires a considerable knowledge of stowage; however, in due course, the pianos, "fearfully out of tune," and the other goods were landed safely.

For a while thereafter the bark lay at anchor in Antonina harbor. Then one night "between the hours of 11 and 12 P.M. . . . ," as Slocum wrote later, "I was called instantly to defend my life and all that is dear to a man." At the time of the cholera in Rosario the jails had been opened so that when Slocum sailed from there a second time, it was with a crew of pirates, not sailors. Now, on 23 July 1887, those Rosario hands tried to murder and rob their captain. Hettie's wakefulness, however, checked them. Then Slocum's courage and carbine brought order. In a fight on deck he shot two of his four assailants, killing one. "It is idle to say what I would or would not have given to have the calamity averted," he wrote, ". . . however . . . I had but one course to pursue. . . . A man will defend himself and his family to the last, for life is sweet, after all."

In *Voyage of the Liberdade,* the narrative breaks at the point where Slocum, in consequence of the fight, was arrested and tried. Like most sailing shipmasters, he aimed to keep clear of the shore. On the waves he coped with whatever came along in an expert, even magical way. All his best thoughts and writing were profoundly related to the sea. But out of his element, he was out of step. He does not seem interested in writing of events ashore. Fortunately, though, consular dispatches tell the rest of this story.

Not long after, the *Aquidneck* was loaded, and sailed south for Montevideo with a Spanish master in charge, and Victor, the mate, representing his father as owner. Slocum, on parole, had to stay in Antonina. A month later, on 23 August, he was tried in Municipal Court, acquitted, and freed. Leaving Hettie and Garfield behind, he at once went to Montevideo by steamer to rejoin his ship. It was probably from there that he wrote an undated letter to President Grover Cleveland complaining of the "ruinous loss" caused by the rejection of his cargo when he first sailed to Ilha Grande, and asking for damages from Brazil.

At Montevideo, cargo was discharged, other cargo taken aboard. The fact that there had been a change of master owing to Slocum's detention in Antonina led to a dispute with the crew and red tape with consular officials which resulted in the crew's being paid off, then reshipped. However, in the interval ashore, the men were exposed to smallpox. And so the bark sailed north again, homeward bound, but with an infected crew.

A very few days later, after what Slocum called the most dismal of all his nights at sea, the bark had to be turned south again. Some of the crew had "already gone on that voyage which somehow seems so far away." The *Aquidneck* returned to Montevideo, where the remaining sick were removed, the ship disinfected, Slocum relieved of more than a thousand dollars in costs, and a new crew shipped. After that, Slocum sailed a second time for Antonina, where Hettie and Garfield were waiting.

"Breathing once more the fresh air of the sea, we set all sail . . . ," Slocum wrote two years later. "Fine weather prevailed. . . . One day, however, coming to an island, one that was inhabited only by birds, we came to a stand, as if it were impossible to go further on the voyage; a spell seemed to hang over us. I recognized the place as one that I knew well; a very dear friend had stood by me on deck, looking at this island, some years before. It was the last land that my friend ever saw. . . ."

This island of birds, the last land which his dear friend standing on deck beside him had seen some three and a half years before, was one of the little places off Santa Catarina, Brazil. The friend was, of course, Virginia, and the hidden reference to her a typical Slocum reticence.

At Antonina, where "sorrows of the past took flight, or were locked in the closet at home, the fittest place for past misfortunes," the captain plunged into new business. This time he bought and loaded a cargo of hardwood logs. The *Aquidneck* was shifted to another part of Paranaguá Bay and moored in the lee of a stand of timber, whence the logs, lashed to canoes, were floated out to her. Shortly after Christmas 1887, the bark, fully loaded, was proceeding across the bay when "currents and wind caught her foul," and she took the ground and was wrecked.

A castaway now, Slocum might have applied for help for himself and his family from the nearest United States consul, one of whose duties is the repatriation of citizen mariners in distress. Such a course, however, did not seem suitable to Captain Joshua Slocum. How, instead, he built and sailed his own canoe is, of course, the sprightly subject of the happier half of the book. ". . . sailing near the line," Slocum wrote, "we saw the constellations of both hemispheres, but heading north, we left those of the south at last, with the Southern Cross—most beautiful in all the heavens—to watch over a friend."

While building the new boat, the family Slocum seems to have lived on the stranded old one, for the captain's letter to "The Honorable F. Bayard, Secretary of State" is date-lined *Aquidneck*, Paranaguá, 24 March 1888. To the loss of freights which followed his having been turned away from Ilha Grande some fourteen months before, Slocum now added the loss of the vessel, and this, of course, very much increased the amount of his quixotic claim on Brazil. Built at Mystic, Connecticut, in 1865, the *Aquidneck* was issued Permanent Register No. 65 at Baltimore, 4 March 1884, when Slocum became her sole owner and master. At the time of her stranding four years later, it would have cost more to refit her than she was worth, even if Slocum had had the money to do so, which he did not. Nothing could be done but accept the offer of Rs2,000$000, about $1,000, from a certain Gaspar Pinto de Sousa, of Santos, who saw in the *Aquidneck* a possible pontoon.

Like variations on a theme, Slocum told his "chapter of disasters," and with each repetition gained clarity. From Norfolk, Virginia, 12

Voyage of the "Liberdade"

December 1888, when homeward bound in "the present command"
—that would have been the 35-foot canoe—he wrote Bayard a second
time. And then in Washington, D.C., 17 January 1889, where the
Liberdade had tied up a year after the wreck of the *Aquidneck,* he
wrote to A. P. Gorman, "my senator from Baltimore . . ." concerning his case against Brazil. He had already called at the State Department and received no satisfaction.

Summer came, and Slocum and Hettie returned to East Boston,
where the captain, with his claim still unrecognized, wrote his book.
After having it printed, he packed up some copies with the idea of
selling them in New York. From that place, 11 March 1890, he
wrote again to the Secretary of State—it was now James G. Blaine—
and asked the Department "to examine the case of the Aquidneck
presented some time ago." Almost a month later, an Assistant Secretary, William F. Wharton, answered. In answer to the answer, Slocum sent a copy of the *Voyage,* just off the press. Wharton replied,
"Very interesting," which remark was so significant to the captain
that in a circular advertisement he got up for *Voyage of the Liberdade,* he printed those very words.

Later that year, on 15 November, Wharton sent the captain a copy
of a translation of the Brazilian government's reply to the State Department's inquiry on his behalf. The next month Slocum made a
further protest. Three years went by, and then on 27 November
1893, just as Slocum was about to start for Brazil with the *Destroyer,*
he wrote again. "I hope at last to satisfy the Department of State
. . . that my cause is a just one." A few days later his six-year battle
with economic laws, red tape, and the vagaries of political history
came to a close—as far as the State Department was concerned.
"This Department . . . ," read the official letter, "does not feel warranted in taking any further action."

As for the *Liberdade,* the craft which Slocum designed as half
Cape Ann Dory, half Japanese sampan, she went to the Smithsonian
Institution. Slocum just left her there; apparently he had no further
use for her until ten years later, after he had sailed around the world
on the *Spray.* Then, on 9 October 1900, Slocum wrote from New
York to a friend and Smithsonian ethnologist, Otis Tufton Mason,
that the *Liberdade* as well as the *Spray* was invited to the forthcoming Pan American Exposition. "I'll be along soon," he wrote, "to

refit her at least for rivers lakes and canals. I bought an engine for her the other day. With power, she will tow the Spray next spring through the canals, to Buffalo . . . a friend in need once may be a friend once more." But Slocum did not show up in Washington at that time, and the *Liberdade* did not get to Buffalo.

So the *Liberdade* gathered dust in the Annex another five years. By this time the Smithsonian Institution was eager indeed to see her sail again, for it was a period when Smithsonian collections of all kinds were expanding rapidly. Mason wrote Slocum several times, and then from Boothbay, Maine, where he was living aboard the *Spray*, the captain replied, 21 June 1905:

> The Liberdade, as a boat, has gone— Her planks however and her ribs would be worth saving Her sides are cedar—long lengths—I intended to have been in Washington long before this with a hacksaw and cut all the nails and bundle the old boat up for some reconstruction; perhaps one in which my old friend and Curator might sail at least a little way about the world. . . .
>
> I understand how much in need you are of room
>
> If the old thing might be all sawd apart and bundled in some corner I would gladly send the amout of the cost and as soon as possible get the bundles away If not, let the executioner do his work I think you have been exceedingly patient and have been a friend. . . .

But instead of going to Washington to bundle her up, the captain returned to his island home, Martha's Vineyard, where he made a deal to trade her off—for a piece of an adjacent island called Nomans Land. The boat which a few months before seemed worthless, now appeared in another light. From Menemsha, Massachusetts, 7 November 1905, he wrote one of the Smithsonian staff:

> The plan is to put power in the old Brazil boat and run her as packet between Nomans and New Bedford— She will want some repairs I know, but one week on her will make things look different. . . .

But like so many of his post-periplus plans, it misfired, and eleven months later, on 13 October 1906, the captain was writing again, this time from the *Spray*, Goffs Wharf, Point Street, Providence, Rhode Island.

Voyage of the "Liberdade"

My dear Professor Mason:

If it is not asking too much I would very much like to have Liberdad hauled away to some lot or down to the Potomac if any of your people know a place for her there or most any where. I would chance her, turned bottom up, under a tree, or alongside of a stone wall or fence. And will gladly pay for the trouble in the matter.

I have written Archie Roosevelt about Liberdade. If Archie cares for her please deliver to him. Otherwise she might be hauled inland to some farm yard. I headed for Washington last spring but was blown off shore and couldn't fetch the capes of the Chessapeake. . . .

Now the old craft at a farm house, if Archie dont want her, would be all right.

I feel guilty for not having carted this boat away and after you have been so kind I have no right to ask it but if your people can lodge her somewhere for me till next Spring! Anyhow she must go from the present place.

Very Sincerely,

Joshua Slocum

So the *Liberdade* went, at last and for good, and nobody seems to know how or where. Both the voyage she made and the book about it had foreshadowed the still greater voyage and book to come; and even in vanishing, as she did, the *Liberdade* was prophetic.

Voyage of the "Liberdade"

GREETING

This literary craft of mine, in its native model and rig, goes out laden with the facts of the strange happenings on a home afloat. Her constructor, a sailor for many years, could have put a whole cargo of salt, so to speak, in the little packet: but would not so wantonly intrude on this domain of longshore navigators. Could the author and constructor but box-haul, club-haul, tops'l-haul and catharpin like the briny sailors of the strand, ah me!—and hope to be forgiven!

Meterological data of the voyage is used only for small stowage in the general cargo, statistics being left entirely to the works of scientists, where they more properly belong. Your author would not abuse fickle weather by the hour, or berate the Gulf Stream, if it should for a moment go astray, knowing, as all do, that it is the law of all things on earth to err. Believing, nevertheless, that a great Power will regulate all under one law, and make all happy, he would fain sail always free with the wind. For whither wafted are joys and sorrows!

Be the current against us, what matters it? Be it in our favor, we are carried hence, to what place or for what purpose? Our plan of the whole voyage is so insignificant that it matters little, maybe, whither we go, for the "grace of a day" is the same! Is it not a recognition of this which makes the old sailor happy, though in the storm; and hopeful even on a plank out in mid-ocean? Surely it is this! for the spiritual beauty of the sea, absorbing man's soul, permits of no infidels on its boundless expanse.

THE AUTHOR.

Chapter I

To get underweigh, it was on the 28th of February, 1886, that the bark *Aquidneck,* laden with case-oil, sailed from New York for Montevideo, the capital of Uruguay, the strip of land bounding the River Platte on the east, and called by the natives "Banda Oriental." The *Aquidneck* was a trim and tidy craft of 326 tons' register, hailing from Baltimore, the port noted for clippers, and being herself high famed above them all for swift sailing, she had won admiration on many seas.

Her crew mustered ten, all told; twelve had been the complement, when freights were good. There were, beside the crew with regular stations, a little lad, aged about six years, and his mamma, (age immaterial,) privileged above the rest, having "all nights in"—that is, not having to stand watch. The mate, Victor, who is to see many adventures before reaching New York again, was born and bred on shipboard. He was in perfect health, and as strong as a windlass. When he first saw the light and began to give orders, he was at San Francisco on the packet *Constitution,* the vessel lost in the tempest at Samoa, just before the great naval disaster at the same place in this year of 1889. Garfield, the little lad above mentioned, Victor's brother, in this family ship, was born in Hong Kong harbor, in the old bark *Amethyst,* a bona-fide American citizen, though first seeing the light in a foreign port, the stars and stripes standing sponsors for his nationality. This bark had braved the wind and waves for fifty-eight years, but had not, up to that date, so far as I know, experienced so lively a breeze as the one which sprung up about her old timbers on that eventful 3d of March, 1880.

41

Voyage of the "Liberdade"

Our foremast hands on the *Aquidneck*, six in number, were from as many nations, strangers to me and strangers to each other; but the cook, a negro, was a native American—to the manner born. To have even so many Americans in one ship was considered exceptional.

Much or little as matters this family history and description of the crew: the day of our sailing was bitter-cold and stormy, boding no good for the coming voyage, which was to be, indeed, the most eventful of my life of more than five-and-thirty years at sea. Studying the morning weather report, before sailing, we saw predicted a gale from the nor'west, and one also approaching from the sou'west at the same time. "The prospect," said the New York *Tribune,* "is not encouraging." We were anxious, however, to commence the voyage, having a crew on board, and, being all ready, we boldly sailed, somewhat against our better judgment. The nor'wester blowing, at the time, at the rate of forty miles an hour, increased to eighty or ninety miles by March 2d. This hurricane continued through March 3d, and gave us serious concern for the ship and all on board.

At New York, on those days, the wind howled from the north, with the "storm centre somewhere on the Atlantic," so said the wise seamen of the weather bureau, to whom, by the way, the real old salt is indebted, at the present day, for information of approaching storms, sometimes days ahead. The prognostication was correct, as we can testify, for out on the Atlantic our bark could carry only a mere rag of a foresail, somewhat larger than a table-cloth, and with this storm-sail she went flying before the tempest, all those dark days, with a large "bone in her mouth," * making great headway, even under the small sail. Mountains of seas swept clean over the bark in their mad race, filling her decks full to the top of the bulwarks, and shaking things generally.

Our men were lashed, each one to his station; and all spare spars not doubly lashed were washed away, along with other movables that were broken and torn from their fastenings by the wild storm.

The cook's galley came in for its share of the damage, the cook himself barely escaping serious injury from a sea that went thundering across the decks, taking with it doors, windows, galley stove, pots, kettles and all, together with the culinary artist; landing the whole wreck in the leescuppers, but, most fortunately, with the

* The white foam at the bows produced by fast sailing is, by sailors, called, "a bone in her mouth."

professor on top. A misfortune like this is always—felt. It dampens one's feelings, so to speak. It means cold hash for a time to come, if not even worse fare.

The day following our misfortune, however, was not so bad. In fact, the tremendous seas boarding the bark latterly were indications of the good change coming, for it meant that her speed had slackened through a lull of the gale, allowing the seas to reach her too full and heavy.

More sail was at once crowded on, and still more was set at every stage of the abatement of the gale, for the craft should not be lazy when big seas race after her. And so, on we flew, like a scud, sheeting home sail after sail, as required, till the 5th of March, when all of her white wings were spread, and she fairly "walked the waters like a thing of life." There was now wind enough for several days, but not too much, and our swift-sailing craft laughed at the seas trying to catch her.

Cheerily on we sailed for days and days, pressed by the favoring gale, meeting the sun each day one hour's span earlier, making daily four degrees of longitude. It was the time, on these bright days, to forearm with dry clothing against future stormy weather. Boxes and bags were brought on deck, and drying and patching went on by wholesale in the watch below, while the watch on deck bestirred themselves putting the ship in order. "Chips," the carpenter, mended the galley; the cook's broken shins were plastered up; and in a few days all was well again. And the sailors moving cheerfully about once more in their patched garments of varied hues, reminded me of the spotted cape pigeons, pecking for a living, the pigeons, I imagined, having the best life of the two. A panican of hot coffee or tea by sailors called "water bewitched," a "sea-biscuit" and "bit of salt-horse," had regaled the crew and restored their voices. Then "Reuben Ranzo" was heard on the breeze, and the main tack was boarded to the tune of "Johnny Boker." Other wondrous songs through the night-watch could be heard in keeping with the happy time. Then what they would do and what they wouldn't do in the next port was talked of, when song and yarn ran out.

Hold fast, shipmate, hold fast and belay! or the crimps of Montevideo will wear the new jacket you promise yourself, while you will be off Cape Horn, singing "Haul out to leeward," with a wet stocking on your neck, and with the same old "lamby" on, that long since was "lamby" only in name, the woolly part having given way to a cloth worn much in "Far Cathay;" in short, you will dress in dungaree, the same as now, while the crimps and land-sharks divide your scanty earnings, unless you "take in the slack" of your feelings, and "make all fast and steady all."

Ten days out, and we were in the northeast "trades"—porpoises were playing under the bows as only porpoises can play; dolphins were racing alongside, and flying-fish were all about. This was, indeed, a happy change, and like being transported to another world. Our hardships were now all forgotten, for "the sea washes off all the woes of men."

One week more of pleasant sailing, all going orderly on board, and Cape Verde Islands came in sight. A grand and glorious sight they were! All hail, *terra firma!* It is good to look at you once again! By noon the islands were abeam, and the fresh trade-wind in the evening bore us out of sight before dark.

Most delightful sailing is this large, swinging motion of our bark over the waves, with the gale abaft the beam, driving her forward till she fairly skips from billow to billow, as if trying to rival her companions, the very flying-fish. When thwarted by a sea, at such times, she strikes it with her handsome bows, sending into the sunlight countless thousand sprays, that shine like a nimbus of glory. The tread on her deck-plank is lighter then, and the little world afloat is gladsome fore and aft.

Cape Frio (cold cape) was the next landfall. Upon reaching that point, we had crossed the Atlantic twice. The course toward Cape Verde Islands had been taken to avail ourselves of a leading wind through the southeast trades, the course from the islands to Frio being southwesterly. This latter stretch was spanned on an easy bow-line; with nothing eventful to record. Thence our course was through variable winds to the River Platte, where a "*pampeiro*" was experienced that blew "great guns," and whistled a hornpipe through the rigging.

These *pampeiros* (winds from the *pampas*), usually blow with great fury, but give ample warning of their approach: the first sign being a spell of unsurpassed fine weather, with small, fleecy clouds floating so gently in the sky that one scarcely perceives their movements, yet they do move, like an immense herd of sheep grazing undisturbed on the great azure field. All this we witnessed, and took

44

into account. Then gradually, and without any apparent cause, the clouds began to huddle together in large groups; a sign had been given which the elements recognized. Next came a flash of fire from behind the accumulating masses, then a distant rumbling noise. It was a note of warning, and one that no vessel should let pass unheeded. "Clew up, and furl!" was the order. To hand all sail when these fierce visitors are out on a frolic over the seas, and entertain them under bare poles, is the safest plan, unless, indeed, the best storm sails are bent; even then it is safest to goose-wing the tops'ls before the gale comes on. Not till the fury of the blast is spent does the ship require sail, for it is not till then that the sea begins to rise, necessitating sail to steady her.

The first onslaught of the storm, levelling all before it, and sending the would-be waves flying across in sheets—sailor sheets, so to speak—lends a wild and fearful aspect; but there is no dread of a lee-shore in the sailor's heart at these times, for the gale is off from the land, as indicated by the name it bears.

After the gale was a calm; following which came desirable winds, that carried us at last to the port we sought—Montevideo; where we cast anchor on the 5th of May, and made preparations, after the customs' visit, for discharging the cargo, which was finally taken into lighters from alongside to the piers, and thence to the warehouses, where ends the ship's responsibility to the owner of the goods. But not till then ceases the ship's liabilities, or the captain's care of the merchandise placed in his trust. Clearly the captain has cares on sea and on land.

Chapter II

Montevideo, sister city to Buenos Ayres, is the fairer of the two to look upon, from the sea, having a loftier situation, and, like Buenos Ayres, boasts of many fine mansions, comely women, liberal schools, and a cemetery of great splendor.

It is at Montevideo that the "beggar a-horseback" becomes a verity (horses are cheap); galloping up to you the whining beggar will implore you, saying: "For the love of Christ, friend, give me a coin to buy bread with."

From "the Mont," we went to Antonina, in Brazil, for a cargo of mate, a sort of tea, which, prepared as a drink, is wholesome and refreshing. It is partaken of by the natives in a highly sociable manner, through a tube which is thrust into the steaming beverage in a silver urn or a calabash, whichever may happen to be at hand when "draughty neebors neebors meet;" then all sip and sip in bliss, from the same tube, which is passed from mouth to mouth. No matter how many mouths there may be, the *bombelia,* as it is called, must reach them all. It may have to be replenished to make the drink go around, and several times, too, when the company is large. This is done with but little loss of time. By thrusting into the urn or gourd a spoonful of the herb, and two spoonfuls of sugar to a pint of water, which is poured, boiling, over it, the drink is made. But to give it some fancied extra flavor, a live coal (*carbo vegetable*) is plunged into the potion to the bottom. Then it is again passed around, beginning where it left off. Happy is he, if a stranger, who gets the first sip at the tube, but the initiated have no prejudices. While in that country I frequently joined in the social rounds at *mate,* and finally rejoiced in a *bombelia* of my own.

The people at Antonina (in fact all the people we saw in Brazil), were kind, extremely hospitable, and polite; living in thrift generally, their wants were but few beyond their resources. The mountain scenery, viewed from the harbor of Antonina, is something to gloat over; I have seen no place in the world more truly grand and pleasing. The climate, too, is perfect and healthy. The only doctor of the place, when we were there, wore a coat out at the elbows, for lack of patronage. A desirable port is Antonina.

We had musical entertainments on board, at this place. To see the display of beautiful white teeth by these Brazilian sweet singers was good to the soul of a sea-tossed mariner. One nymph sang for the writer's benefit a song at which they all laughed very much. Being in native dialect, I did not understand it, but of course laughed with the rest, at which they were convulsed; from this, I supposed it to be at my expense. I enjoyed that, too, as much, or more, than I would have relished *areytos* in my favor.

With *mate* we came to Buenos Ayres, where the process of discharging the cargo was the same as at Montevideo—into lighters.

But at Buenos Ayres we lay four times the distance from the shore, about four miles.

The herb, or *herva mate*, is packed into barrels, boxes, and into bullock-hide sacks, which are sewed up with stout hide thongs. The contents, pressed in tightly when the hide is green and elastic, becomes as hard as a cannon ball by the contraction which follows when it dries. The first load of the *soroes*, so-called, that came off to the bark at the port of loading, was espied on the way by little Garfield. Piled in the boat, high above the gunwales, the hairy side out, they did look odd. "Oh, papa," said he, "here comes a load of cows! Stand by, all hands, and take them in."

Chapter III

From Buenos Ayres, we proceeded up the River Platte, near the confluence of the Parena and Paraguay, to salve a cargo of wine from the stranded brig *Neovo San Pascual*, from Marseilles.

The current of the great river at that point runs constantly seaward, becoming almost a sea of itself, and a dangerous one to navigate; hence the loss of the *San Pascual*, and many others before her.

If, like the "Ancient Mariner," we had, any of us, cried, "water, water all around, and not a drop to drink," we forgot it now, in this bountiful stream. Wine, too, we had without stint. The insurance agent, to leave no excuse for tampering with the cargo, rolled out a cask of the best, and, like a true Hans Briterman, "knocked out der bung." Then, too, cases were broken in the handling, the contents of which drenched their clothes from top to toe, as the sailors carried them away on their heads.

The diversity of a sailor's life—ah me! The experience of Dana and his shipmates, for instance, on a sunburnt coast, carrying dry hides on their heads, if not a worse one, may be in store for us, we cried, now fairly swimming in luxuries—water and wine alike free. Although our present good luck may be followed by times less cheerful, we preferred to count this, we said, as compensation for past misfortunes, marking well that "it never rains but it pours."

The cargo of wine in due course, was landed at Rosario, with but small loss, the crew, except in one case, remaining sober enough to help navigate even the difficult Parana. But one old sinner, the case I speak of, an old Labrador fisherman, became a useless, drunken swab, in spite of all we could do. I say "we" for most of the crew were on my side, in favor of a fair deal and "regular supplies."

The hold was barred and locked, and every place we could think of, for a time, was searched; still Dan kept terribly drunk. At last his mattress was turned out, and from it came—a dozen or more bottles of the best liquor. Then there was a row, but all on the part of Dan, who swore blue vengeance on the man, if he could but find him out, who had stowed that grog in his bunk, "trying to get" him "into trouble;" some of those "young fellows would rue it yet!"

The cargo of wine being discharged, I chartered to load alfalfa, packed in bales, for Rio. Many deaths had occurred about this time, with appalling suddenness; we soon learned that cholera was staring us all in the face, and that it was fast spreading through the country, filling towns and cities with sickness and death.

Approaching more frightfully near, it carried our pilot over the bar: his wife was a widow the day after he brought our bark to the loading berth. And the young man who commenced to deliver us the cargo was himself measured the day after. His ship had come in!

Many stout men, and many, many women and children succumbed to the scourge: yet it was our high privilege to come through the dark cloud without losing a loved one, while thousands were cast down with bereavements and grief. At one time it appeared that we were in the centre of the cloud which zig-zagged its ugly body, serpent-like, through districts, poisoning all that it touched, and leaving death in its wake. This was indeed cholera in its most terrible form!

One poor fellow sat at the Widow Lacinas' hotel, bewildered. "Forty-eight hours ago," said he, "I sat at my own hearth, with wife and three children by my side. Now I am alone in the world! Even my poor house, such as it was, is pulled down." This man, I say, had troubles; surely was his "house pulled down"!

There was no escaping the poison or keeping it off, except by disinfectants, and by keeping the system regular, for it soon spread over all the land and the air was full of it. Remedies sold so high that many must have perished without the test of medicinal aid to cure their disease. A cry went up against unprincipled druggists who were overcharging for their drugs, but nothing more was done to check their greed. Camphor sold as high as four dollars a pound, and the druggist with a few hundred drops of laudanum and as much chlorodyne could travel through Europe afterwards on the profits of his sales.

It was at Rosario, and at this time, that we buried our young friend, Captain Speck, well loved of young and old. His friends did not ask whether it was cholera or not that he died of, but performed the last act of friendship as became men of heart and feeling. The minister could not come that day, but Captain Speck's little friend, Garfield, said: "The flags were set for the angels to come and take the Captain to Heaven!" Need more be said?

And the flags blew out all day.

Then it became us to erect a memorial slab, and, hardest of all, to write to the widow and orphans. This was done in a homely way, but with sympathetic, aching hearts away off there in Santa Fè.

Our time at Rosario, after this, was spent in gloomy days that dragged into weeks and months, and our thoughts often wandered from there to a happy past. We preferred to dwell away from there and in other climes, if only in thought. There was, however, one happy soul among us—the child whose face was a sunbeam in all kinds of weather and at all times, happy in his ignorance of the evils that fall to the lot of man.

Our sailing-day from Rosario finally came; and, with a feeling as of casting off fetters, the lines were let go, and the bark hauled out into the stream, with a full cargo on board; but, instead of sailing for Rio, as per charter, she was ordered by the Brazilian consul to Ilha Grande [Great Island], the quarantine station of Brazil, some sixty-two miles west of Rio, there to be disinfected and to discharge her cargo in quarantine.

A new crew was shipped and put aboard, but while I was getting my papers, about noon, they stole one of the ship's boats and scurried off down the river as fast, no doubt, as they could go. I have not seen them or my boat since. They all deserted,—every mother's son of them! taking, beside the boat, a month's advance pay from a Mr. Dutch Harry, a sailor boarding master, who had stolen my inward crew that he might, as he boasted afterward, "ship new hands in their places." In view of the fact that this vilest of crimps was the loser of the money, I could almost forgive the "galoots" for the theft of my boat. (The ship is usually responsible for advance wages twenty-four hours after she has sailed, providing, too, that the sailors proceed to sea in her.) Seeing, moreover, that they were of that stripe, unworthy the name of sailor, my vessel was the better without them, by at least what it cost to be rid of them, namely, the price of my boat.

However, I will take back what I said about Dutch Harry being the "vilest crimp." There came one to Rosario worse than he, one "Pete the Greek," who cut off the ears of a rival boarding-master at the Boca, threw them into the river, then, making his escape to Rosario, some 180 miles away, established himself in the business in opposition to the Dutchman, whom he "shanghied" soon after, then "reigned peacefully in his stead."

A captain who, like myself, had suffered from the depredations of this noted gentry, told me, in great glee, that he saw Harry on a bone-laden Italian bark outward bound,—"even then nearly out of the river." The last seen of him by my friend, the captain, was "among the branches," with a rope around his neck—they hanged him, maybe—I don't know what else the rope was for, or who deserved more to be hanged. The captain screamed with delight:— "he'll get bone soup, at least, for a while, instead of Santa Fè good mutton-chops at our expense."

My second crew was furnished by Mr. Pete, before referred to, and on the seventeenth of December we set sail from that country of revolutions. Things soon dropped into working order, and I found reason to be pleased with the change of crew. We glided smoothly along down the river, thence wishing never again to see Rosario under the distressing circumstances through which she had just passed.

On the following day, while slipping along before a light, rippling breeze, a dog was espied out in the current, struggling in the whirlpools, which were rather strong, apparently unable to extricate himself, and was greatly exhausted. Coming up with him our main-tops'l was laid to the mast, and as we ranged by the poor thing, a sailor, plunging over the side in a bowline, bent a rope on to doggy, another one hauled him carefully on board, and the rescue was made. He proved to be a fine young retriever, and his intelligent signs of thankfulness for his escape from drowning were scarcely less eloquent of gratitude than human spoken language.

This pleasant incident happening on
course, the name we should give him. Hi
was Garfield, who at once said, "I guess †
I get home, with my new suit—and a dog!"
thenceforth, early and late. It was goo
"Friday" "barkit wi' joy."

Our pets were becoming numerous
till a stow-a-way cat, one day, killed
For ten years or more we had listened to
in many countries and climes. Sweetest of sweet singe..,
in the great Atlantic at last. A strange cat, a careless steward, ..
its tiny life was ended—and the tragedy told. This was indeed a great
loss to us all, and was mourned over,—almost as the loss of a child.

A book that has been read at sea has a near claim on our friendship, and is a thing one is loth to part with, or change, even for a
better book. But the well-tried friend of many voyages is, oh! so
hard to part with at sea. A resting-place in the solemn sea of same-
ness—in the trackless ocean, marked only by imaginary lines and
circles—is a cheerless spot to look to; yet how many have treasures
there!

Returning to the voyage and journal: Our pilot proved incompetent, and we narrowly escaped shipwreck in consequence at
Martin Garcia Bar, a bad spot in the River Platte. A small schooner
captain, observing that we needlessly followed in his track, and being anything but a sailor in principle, wantonly meditated mischief
to us. While I was confidently trusting to my pilot, and he (the pilot)
trusting to the schooner, one that could go over banks where we
would strike, what did the scamp do but shave close to a dangerous
spot, my pilot following faithfully in his wake. Then, jumping upon
the taffrail of his craft, as we came abreast the shoal, he yelled, like
a Comanche, to my pilot to: "Port the helm!" and what does my
mutton-headed jackass do but port hard over! The bark, of course,
brought up immediately on the ground, as the other had planned,
seeing which his whole pirate crew—they could have been little less
than pirates—joined in roars of laughter, but sailed on, doing us no
other harm.

By our utmost exertions the bark was gotten of, not a moment too
soon, however, for by the time we kedged her into deep water a
pampeiro was upon us. She rode out the gale safe at anchor, thanks

ve crew. Our water tanks and casks were then refilled,
een emptied to lighten the bark from her perilous position.
t evening the storm went down, and by mutual consent our
-pilot left, taking passage in a passing river craft, with his pay
d our best advice, which was to ship in a dredging-machine, where
his capabilities would be appreciated.

Then, "paddling our own canoe," without further accident we
reached the light-ship, passing it on Christmas Day. Clearing thence,
before night, English Bank and all other dangers of the land, we set
our course for Ilha Grande, the wind being fair. Then a sigh of relief
was breathed by all on board. If ever "old briny" was welcomed, it
was on that Christmas Day.

Nothing further of interest occurred on the voyage to Brazil,
except the death of the little bird already spoken of, which loss
deeply affected us all.

We arrived at Ilha Grande, our destination, on the 7th day of
January, 1887, and came to anchor in nine fathoms of water, at about
noon, within musket-range of the guard-ship, and within speaking
distance of several vessels riding quarantine, with more or less communication going on among them all, through flags. Several ships,
chafing under the restraint of quarantine, were "firing signals" at the
guard-ship. One Scandinavian, I remember, asked if he might be
permitted to communicate by *cable* with his owners in Christiana.
The guard gave him, as the Irishman said, "an evasive answer," so
the cablegram, I suppose, laid over. Another wanted police assistance; a third wished to know if he could get fresh provisions—ten
mil-reis' ($5) worth (he was a German)—naming a dozen or more
articles that he wished for, "and *the balance in onions!*" Altogether,
the young fellows on the guard-ship were having, one might say, a
signal practice.

On the next day, Jan. 8th, the officers of the port came alongside
in a steam launch, and ordered us to leave, saying the port had been
closed that morning. "But we have made the voyage," I said. "No
matter," said the guard, "leave at once you must, or the guard-ship
will fire into you." This, I submit, was harsh and arbitrary treatment.
A thunderbolt from a clear sky could not have surprised us more or
worked us much greater harm—to be ruined in business or struck by
lightning, being equally bad!

Then pointing something like a gun, Dom Pedro said, said he,

"*Vaya Homem*" (hence, begone), "Or you'll give us cholera." So back we had to go, all the way to Rosario, with that load of hay—and trouble. But on our arrival there we found things better than they were when we sailed. The cholera had ceased—it was on the wane when we sailed from Rosario, and there was hardly a case of the dread disease in the whole country east of Cordova when we returned. That was, indeed, a comfort, but it left our hardship the same, and led, consequently, to the total loss of the vessel after dragging us through harrowing trials and losses, as will be seen by subsequent events.

Chapter IV

This Ilha Grande decree, really a political movement, brought great hardships on us, notwithstanding that it was merely intended by the Brazilians as retaliation for past offences by their Argentine neighbors; not only for quarantines against Rio fevers, but for a discriminating duty as well, on sugar from the empire; a combination of hardships on commerce—more than the sensitive Brazilians could stand—so chafing them, that a retaliation fever sprung up reaching more than the heat of *febre marello*, and they decided to teach their republican cousins a wholesome lesson. However, their wish was to retaliate without causing war, and it was done. In fact, closing ports as they did at the beginning of Argentine's most valuable season of exports to Brazil, and with the plausible excuse, namely, fear of pain in the stomach, so filled the Argentines with admiration of their equals in strategy that they on the earliest opportunity proclaimed two public holidays in honor of bright Brazil. So the matter of difference ended, to the delight of all—in firecrackers and champagne!

To the delight of all except the owner and crew of the *Aquidneck*. For our bark there was no way but to return where the cargo came from, at a ruinous loss, too, of time and money. We called at the first open port and wired to the owner of the cargo, but got no answer. Thence we sailed to Buenos Ayres, where I telegraphed again for instructions. The officers of the guard ship, upon receiving my report from Brazil, were convulsed with laughter, while I! I confess it—could not see the joke. After waiting two days, this diplomatic reply came from the owner of the cargo: "Act as the case may require." Upon this matter I had several opinions. One person suggested that the case required me to pitch the whole cargo into the sea! This friend, I may mention, was from Boston.

I have ever since regretted, however, that I did not take his advice. There seemed to be no protection for the vessel, the law that a ship must be allowed to live was unheeded, in fact this law was reversed and there were sharpers and beechcombers at every turn ready to take advantage of one's misfortunes or even drive one to despair. I concluded, finally, to shake the lot of them, and proceeding up the Parena, moored again at the berth where, a few weeks before, we had taken in the cargo. Spans and tackle were rigged, and all was made ready to discharge. It was now, "Come on, McCarthy, or McCarthy, come on!" I didn't care which, I had one *right* on my side, and I kept that always in view; namely, the right to discharge the cargo where I had first received it; but where the money to buy ballast and pay other charges was to come from I could not discover.

My merchant met me in great concern at my "misfortunes," but "carramba!" [zounds] said he, "my own losses are great." It required very little reasoning to show me that the least expensive course was the safest one for me to adopt, and my merchant offering enough to pay the marketing, I found it wisest not to disturb the cargo, but to lay up instead with it in the vessel and await the reopening of the Brazilian ports. This I did.

My merchant, Don Manuel, is said to be worth millions of *pesos*. The foundation of his wealth was laid by peddling charcoal, carrying it at first, to his credit be it said, on his back, and was then a good fellow. Many a hard bargain has he waged since, and is now a "Don," living in a $90,000 house. The Don doesn't peddle charcoal any more, but he's got a glass eye!

Moored at Rosario, waiting, waiting; but all of us well in body, and myself finally less agitated in mind. My old friend, Don Manuel, seems better also; he "may yet purge and live clean like a gentleman."

I found upon our return to Rosario that some of the old hands were missing; laid low by the scourge, to make room for others, and some were spared who would have been less lamented. Among all the ship brokers that I knew at Rosario, and I knew a great many, not one was taken away. They all escaped, being, it was thought, epidemic-proof. There was my broker, Don Christo Christiano—called by Don Manuel "El Sweaga" (the Swede)—whom nothing could strike with penetrative force, except a commission.

At last, April 9th, 1887, news came that the Brazilian ports were open. Cholera had long since disappeared in Santa Fè and Buenos Ayres. The Brazilians had established their own beef-drying factories, and could now afford to open their ports to competition. This made a great stir among the ships. Crews were picked up here and there, out of the few brothels that had not been pulled down during the cholera, and out of the street or from the fields. Some, too, came in from the bush. Mixed among them were many that had been let out of the prisons all over the country, so that the scourge should not be increased by over-crowded jails. Of six who shipped with me, four had been so released from prison, where they had been serving for murder or highway robbery; all this I learned when it was too late. I shall have occasion before long to speak of these again!

Well, we unmoored and dropped down the river a few miles the first day; with this crew, the hardest looking set that ever put foot on a ship of mine, and with a swarthy Greek pilot that would be taken for a pirate in any part of the world. The second mate, who shipped also at Rosario, was not less ill-visaged, and had, in addition to his natural ugly features, a deep scar across his face, suggestive of a heavy sabre stroke; a mark which, I thought upon further acquaintance, he had probably merited. I could not make myself easy upon the first acquaintance of my new and decidedly ill-featured crew. So, early the first evening I brought the bark to anchor, and made all snug before dark for prudent reasons. Next morning, the Greek, instead of getting the bark underweigh, as I expected him to do, came to me, demanding more pay for his services, and thinking, may-be, that I could not do without him, demanded unless I chose to pay considerably in excess of his regular dues, to be put on shore. I took the fellow at his first bounce. He and his grip-sack were landed on the bank there and then, with but little "palaver" over it. It was then said, so I learned after, that "old S——" would drop into the wake of some ship, and save his pilotage; in fact, they didn't know "what else he could do," as the pilots were then all engaged for other vessels.

Voyage of the "Liberdade"

The money was taken care of all right, and so was the *Aquidneck!* By daylight of the following morning she was underweigh, and under full sail at the head of a fleet of piloted vessels, and, being the swiftest sailer, easily kept the lead, and was one of the vessels that did *not* "*rompe el banco,*" as was predicted by all the pilots, while they hunched their shoulders above their ears, exclaiming, "No *practico,* no *possebla!*" This was my second trip down the Parana, it is true, and I had been on other rivers as wonderful as this one, and, had moreover, read Mark Twain's "Life on the Mississippi," which gives no end of information on river currents, wind-reefs, sand-reefs, alligator-water, and all that is useful to know about rivers, so that I was confident of my ability; all that had been required was the stirring-up that I got from the impertinent pilot, or buccaneer, whichever is proper to call him—one thing certain, he was no true sailor!

A strong, fair wind on the river, together with the current, in our favor, carried us flying down the channel, while we kept the lead, with the Stars and Stripes waving where they ought always to be seen; namely, on the ship in the van! So the duffers followed us, instead of our following them, and on we came, all clear, with the good wishes of the officers and the crews. But the pilots drawing their shoulders up, and repeating the refrain, "No *practico,* no *possebla!*" cursed us bitterly, and were in a vile mood, I was told, cursing more than usual, and that is saying a great deal, for all will agree who have heard them, that the average "Dago" pilot is the most foul-mouthed thing afloat.

Down the river and past the light-ship we came once more, this time with no halt to make, no backing sails to let a pilot off, nothing at all to stop us; we spread all sail to a favorable breeze, and reached Ilha Grande eight days afterward, beating the whole fleet by two days. Garfield kept strict account of this. He was on deck when we made the land, a dark and foggy night it was! nothing could be seen but the dimmest outline of a headland through the haze. I knew the place, I thought, and Garfield said he could smell land, fog or coal-tar. This, it will be admitted, was reassuring. A school of merry porpoises that gamboled under the bows while we stood confidently in for the land, diving and crossing the bark's course in every direction, also guarded her from danger. I knew that so long as deep-sea porpoises kept with us we had nothing to fear of the ground. When the lookout cried, "Porpoises gone," we turned the bark's head off shore, backed the main-tops'l, and sent out the "pigeon" (lead). A few grains of sand and one soft, delicate white shell were brought up out of fourteen fathoms of water. We had but to heed these warnings and guides, and our course would be tolerably clear, dense and all as the fog and darkness was.

The lead was kept constantly going as we sailed along in the intense darkness, till the headland of our port was visible through the haze of gray morning. What Garfield had smelled, I may mention, turned out to be coal-tar, a pot of which had been capsized on deck by the leadsman, in the night.

By daylight in the morning, April 29, we had found the inner entrance to Ilha Grande, and sailed into the harbor for the second time with this cargo of hay. It was still very foggy, and all day heavy gusts of wind came down through the gulches in the mountains, laden with fog and rain.

Two days later, the weather cleared up, and our friends began to come in. They found us there all right, anchored close under the highest mountain.

Eight days of sullen gloom and rain at this place; then brimstone smoke and fire turned on to us, and we were counted healthy enough to be admitted to *pratique* in Rio, where we arrived May 11th, putting one more day between ourselves and our friendly competitors, who finally arrived safe, all except one, the British bark *Dublin*. She was destroyed by fire between the two ports. The crew was rescued by Captain Lunt, and brought safe into Rio next day.

At the fort entrance to the harbor of Rio we were again challenged and brought to, all standing, on the bar; the tide running like a mill race at the time brought the bark aback on her cables with a force, nearly cutting her down.

The *Aquidneck* it would seem had outsailed the telegram which should have preceded her; it was nevertheless, my imperative duty to obey the orders of the port authorities which, however, should have been tempered with reason. It was easy for them in the fort to say, "Come to, or we'll sink you," but we in the bark, between two evils, came near being sunk by obeying the order.

Formerly, when a vessel was challenged at this fort, one, two or three shots, if necessary to bring her to, were fired, at a cost to the ship, if she were not American, of fifteen shillings for the first shot, thirty for the second, and sixty for the third; but, for American ships, the sixty shilling shot was fired first—Americans would always have the best!

After all the difficulties were cleared away, the tardy telegram received, and being again identified by the officers, we weighed anchor for the last time on this voyage, and went into our destined port, the spacious and charming harbor of Rio.

Chapter V

The cargo was at last delivered, and no one made ill over it. A change of rats also was made; at Rio those we brought in gave place to others from the Dom Pedro Docks where we moored. Fleas, too, skipped about in the hay as happy as larks, and nearly as big; and all the other live stock that we brought from Rosario—goodness knows of what kind and kith, arrived well and sound from over the water, notwithstanding the fumigations and fuss made at the quarantine.

Had the little microbes been with us indeed, the Brazilians would not have turned us away as they did, from the doors of an hospital! for they are neither a cruel or cowardly people. To turn sickness away would be cruel and stupid, to say the least! What we were expelled for I have already explained.

After being so long in gloomy circumstances we felt like making the most of pleasant Rio! Therefore on the first fine day after being docked, we sallied out in quest of city adventure, and brought up first in Ouvidor—the Broadway of Rio, where my wife bought a tall hat, which I saw nights looming up like a dreadful stack of hay, the innocent cause of much trouble to me, and I declared, by all the great islands—in my dreams—that go back with it I would not, but would pitch it, first, into the sea.

I get nervous on the question of quarantines. I visit the famous Botanical Gardens with my family, and I tremble with fear lest we are fumigated at some station on the way. However, our time at Rio is pleasantly spent in the main, and on the first day of June, we set sail once more for Paranagua and Antonina of pleasant recollections; partly laden with flour, kerosene, pitch, tar, rosin and wine, three pianos, I remember, and one steam engine and boiler, all as ballast; "freight free," so the bill of lading read, and further, that the ship should "not be responsible for leakage, breakage, or rust." This clause was well for the ship, as one of those wild *pampeiros* overtook her, on the voyage, throwing her violently on her beam-ends, and shaking the motley cargo into a confused and mixed-up mess. The vessel remaining tight, however, no very serious damage was done, and she righted herself after awhile, but without her lofty topgallantmasts, which went with a crash at the first blast of the tempest.

This incident made a profound impression on Garfield. He happened to be on deck when the masts were carried away, but managed to scamper off without getting hurt. Whenever a vessel hove in sight after that having a broken spar or a torn sail, it was "a *pampeiroed* ship."

The storm, though short, was excessively severe, and swept over Paranagua and Antonina with unusual violence. The owner of the pianos, I was told, prayed for us, and regretted that his goods were not insured. But when they were landed, not much the worse for their tossing about, old Strichine, the owner (that was his name or near that, strychnine the boys called him, because his singing was worse than "rough on rats," they said, a bit of juvenile wit that the artist very sensibly let pass unheeded), declared that the ship was a good one, and that her captain was a good pilot; and, as neither freight nor insurance had been paid, he and his wife would feast us on music; having learned that I especially was fond of it. They had screeched operas for a lifetime in Italy, but I didn't care for that. As arranged, therefore, I was on deck at the appointed time and place, to stay at all hazards.

The pianos, as I had fully expected, were fearfully out of tune— suffering, I should say, from the effects of seasickness!

So much so that I shall always believe this opportunity was seized upon by the artist to avenge the damage to his instruments, which, indeed, I could not avert, in the storm that we passed through. The good Strichine and his charming wife were astonished at the number of opera airs I could name. And they tried to persuade me to sing Il Trovatore; but concluding that damage enough had already been done, I refrained, that is, I refracted my song.

And all parties finally seemed satisfied and happy.

Chapter VI

July 23d, 1887, brings me to a sudden and shocking point in the history of the voyage that I fain would forget, but that will not be possible. Between the hours of 11 and 12 P.M. of this day I was called instantly to defend my life and all that is dear to a man.

The bark, anchored alone in the harbor of Antonina, was hid from the town in the darkness of a night that might well have covered the blackest of tragedies. My pirates thought their opportunity had surely come to capture the *Aquidneck,* and this they undertook to do. The ringleader of the gang was a burly scoundrel, whose boast was that he had "licked" both the mate and second mate of the last vessel he had sailed in, and had "busted the captain in the jaw" when they landed in Rio, where the vessel was bound, and where, of course, the captain had discharged him. It was there the villain shipped with me, in lieu of one of the Rosario gang who had been kindly taken in charge by the guard at Ilha Grande and brought to Rio to be tried before the American Consul for insubordination. Said he, one day when I urged him to make haste and help save the top-sails in a squall, "Oh, I'm no soft-horn to be hurried!" It was the time the bark lost her topgallant-mast and was cast on her beam-ends on the voyage to Antonina, already told; it was, in fact, no time for loafing, and this braggart at a decisive word hurried aloft with the rest to do his duty. What I said to him was meant for earnest, and it cowed him. It is only natural to think that he held a grudge against me forever after, and waited only for his opportunity; knowing, too, that I was the owner of the bark, and supposed to have money. He was heard to say in a rum-mill a day or two before the attack that he would find the —— money and his life, too. His chum and bosom friend had come pretty straight from Palermo penitentiary at Buenos Ayres when he shipped with me at Rosario.

It was no secret on board the bark that he had served two years for robbing, and cutting a ranchman's throat from ear to ear. These records, which each seemed to glory in, were verified in both cases.

Voyage of the "Liberdade"

I met the captain afterwards who had been "busted in the jaw"—Captain Roberts, of Baltimore, a quiet gentleman, with no evil in his heart for any one, and a man, like myself, well along in years.

Two of the gang, old Rosario hands, had served for the lesser offence of robbery alone—they brought up in the rear! The other two of my foremast hands—one a very respectable Hollander, the other a little Japanese sailor, a bright, young chap—had been robbed and beaten by the four ruffians, and then threatened so that they deserted to the forest instead of bringing a complaint of the matter to me, for fear, as the Jap expressed it afterwards, when there was no longer any danger,—for fear the "la-la-long mans (thieves) would makee killo mi!"

The ringleader bully, had made unusual efforts to create a row when I came on board early in the evening; however, as he had evidently been drinking, I passed it off as best I could for the natural consequence of rum, and ordered him forward; instead of doing as he was bid, when I turned to hand my wife to the cabin he followed me threateningly to the break of the poop. What struck me most, however, was the conduct of his chum, who was sober, but in a very unusual high, gleeful mood. It was knock-off time when I came along to where he was seizing off the mizzen topgallant backstay, the last of the work of refitting the late *pampeiro* damage; and the mate being elsewhere engaged, I gave the usual order to quit work. "Knock off," I said to the man, "and put away your tools. The bark's rigging looks well," I added, "and if to-morrow turns out fine, all will be finished;" whereupon the fellow laughed impertinently in my face, repeating my words, "All will be finished!" under his breath, adding, "before to-morrow!" This was the first insult offered by the "Bloodthirsty Tommy," who had committed murder only a short time before; but I had been watched by the fellow, with a cat-like eye at every turn.

The full significance of his words on this occasion came up to me only next morning, when I saw him lying on the deck with a murderous weapon in his hand! I was not expecting a cowardly, night attack, nevertheless I kept my gun loaded. I went to sleep this night as usual, forgetting the unpleasant episode as soon as my head touched the pillow; but my wife, with finer instincts, kept awake. It was well for us all that she did so. Near midnight, my wife, who had heard the first footstep on the poop-deck, quietly wakened me, saying, "We must get up, and look out for ourselves! Something is going wrong on deck; the boat tackle has been let go with a great deal of noise, and— O! don't go that way on deck. I heard some one on the cabin steps, and heard whispering in the forward entry."

"You must have been dreaming," I said.

"No, indeed!" said she; "I have not been asleep yet; don't go on deck by the forward companion-way; they are waiting there; I am sure, for I heard the creaking of the loose step in the entry."

If my wife has not been dreaming, thought I, there can be no possible doubt of a plot.

Nothing justifies a visit on the poop deck after working hours, except a call to relieve sickness, or for some other emergency, and then secrecy or stealth is non-permissible.

It may be here explained to persons not familiar with ships, that the sailors' quarters are in the forward part of the ship where they (the sailors) are supposed to be found after working hours, in port, coming never abaft the mainmast; hence the term "before the mast."

My first impulse was to step on deck in the usual way, but the earnest entreaties of my wife awoke me, like, to a danger that should be investigated with caution. Arming myself, therefore, with a stout carbine repeater, with eight ball cartridges in the magazine, I stepped on deck abaft instead of forward, where evidently I had been expected. I stood rubbing my eyes for a moment, inuring them to the intense darkness, when a coarse voice roared down the forward companion-way to me to come on deck. "Why don't ye come on deck like a man, and order yer men forid?" was the salute that I got, and was the first that I heard with my own ears, and it was enough. To tell the whole story in a word, I knew that I had to face a mutiny.

I could do no less than say: "Go forward there!"

"Yer there, are ye?" said the spokesman, as with an oath, he bounded toward me, cursing as he came.

Again I ordered him forward, saying, "I am armed,—if you come here I will shoot!" But I forbore to do so instantly, thinking to club him to the deck instead, for my carbine was a heavy one. I dealt him a blow as he came near, sufficient I thought, to fell an ox; but it had, apparently, no effect, and instantly he was inside of my guard. Then grasping me by the throat, he tried to force me over the taffrail, and cried, exultingly, as he felt me give way under his brute strength,

"Now, you damn fool, shoot!" at the same time drawing his knife to strike.

I could not speak, or even breathe, but my carbine spoke for me, and the ruffian fell with the knife in his hand which had been raised against me! Resolution had proved more than a match for brute force, for I then knew that not only my own life but also the lives of others depended on me at this moment. Nothing daunted, the rest came on, like hungry wolves. Again I cried, "Go forward!" But thinking, maybe, that my rifle was a single shooter, or that I could not load it so quick, the order was disregarded.

"What if I don't go forward?" was "Bloody Tommy's" threatening question, adding, as he sprang toward me, "I've got this for you!" but fell instantly as he raised his hand; and there on the deck, was ended, his misadventure! and like the other he fell with deadly knife in his hand. I was now all right. The dread of cold steel had left me when I freed myself from the first would-be assassin, and I only wondered how many more would persist in trying to take my life. But recollecting there were only two mutineers left, and that I had still six shots in the magazine of my rifle, and one already in the chamber, I stood ready with the hammer raised, and my finger on the trigger, confident that I would not be put down.

There was no further need of extreme measures, however, for order was now restored, though two of the assailants had skulked away in the dark.

How it was that I regained my advantage, after once losing it, I hardly know; but this I am certain of, that being down I was not to be spared. Then desperation took the place of fear, and I felt more than a match for all that could come against me. I had no other than serene feelings, however, and had no wish to pursue the two pirates that fled.

Immediately after the second shot was fired, and I found myself once more master of my bark, the remaining two came aft again, at my bidding this time, and in an orderly manner, it may be believed.

It is idle to say what I would or would not have given to have the calamity averted, or, in other words, to have had a crew of sailors, instead of a gang of cut-throats.

However, when the climax came, I had but one course to pursue, this I resolutely followed. A man will defend himself and his family to the last, for life is sweet, after all.

It was significant, the court thought afterwards, that while my son had not had time to dress, they all had on their boots except the one who fell last, and he was in his socks, with no boots on. It was he who had waited for me as I have already said, on the cabin steps that I usually passed up and down on, but this time avoided. Circumstantial evidence came up in abundance to make the case perfectly clear to the authorities. There are few who will care to hear more about a subject so abhorrent to all, and I care less to write about it. I would not have said this much, but for the enterprise of a rising department clerk, who, seeing the importance of telling to the world what he knew, and seeing also some small emolument in the matter, was, I believe prompted to augment the consular dispatches, thus obliging me to fight the battle over. However, not to be severe on the poor clerk, I will only add that no indignities were offered me by the authorities through all the strict investigation that followed the tragedy.

The trial being for justice and not for my money the case was soon finished.

I sincerely hope that I may never again encounter such as those who came from the jails to bring harm and sorrow in their wake.

The work of loading was finished soon after the calamity to my bark, and a Spanish sailing-master was engaged to take her to Montevideo; my son Victor going as flag captain.

I piloted the *Aquidneck* out of the harbor, and left her clear of the buoy, looking as neat and trim as sailor could wish to see. All the damage done by the late *pampeiro* had been repaired, new topgallant masts rigged, and all made ataunto. I saw my handsome bark well clear of the dangers of the harbor limits, then in sorrow I left her and paddled back to the town, for I was on parole to appear, as I have said, for trial! That was the word; I can find no other name for it—let it stand!

Chapter VII

As soon as the case was over I posted on for Montevideo by steamer, where the bark had arrived only a few days ahead of me. I found her already stripped to a gantline though, preparatory to a long stay in port. I had given Victor strict orders to interfere in no way with the Spaniard, but to let him have full charge in nearly everything. I could have trusted the lad with full command, young as he was; but there was a strange crew of foreigners which might, as often happens, require maturer judgment to manage than to sail the vessel. As it proved, however, even the *cook* was in many ways a better man than the sailing-master.

Victor met me with a long face, and the sailors wore a quizzical look as I came over the vessel's side. One of them, in particular, whom I shall always remember, gave me a good-humored greeting, along with his shake of the head, that told volumes; and next day was aloft, crossing yards, cheerfully enough. I found my Brazilian crew to be excellent sailors, and things on board the *Aquidneck* immediately began to assume a brighter appearance, aloft and alow.

Cargo was soon discharged, other cargo taken in, and the bark made ready for sea. My crew, I say, was a good one; but, poor fellows, they were doomed to trials—the worst within human experience, many of them giving up to grim death before the voyage was ended. Too often one bit of bad luck follows another. This rule brought us in contact with one of these small officials at Montevideo, better adapted to home life; one of those knowing, perhaps, more than need a cow-boy, but not enough for consul. This official, managing to get word to my crew that a change of master dissolved their contract, induced them to come on shore and claim pay for the whole voyage and passage home on a steamer besides, the same as though the bark had been sold.

What overwhelming troubles may come of having incompetent officials in places of trust, the sequel will show. This unwise, even stupid interference, was the indirect cause of the sufferings and deaths among the crew which followed.

I was able to show the consul and his clerk that sailors are always engaged for the ship, and never for the master, and that a change of master did not in any way affect their contract. However, I paid the crew off, and then left it to their option to re-ship or not, for they were all right, they had been led to do what they did, and I knew that they wanted to get home, and it was there that the bark was going, direct.

All signed the articles again, except one, a long-haired Andalusian, whom I would not have longer at any price. The wages remained the same as before, and all hands returned to their duty cheerful and contented—but pending the consul's decision, (which, by the way, I decided for him) they had slept in a contagioned house, where, alas, they contracted small-pox of the worst type.

We were now homeward bound. All the "runaway rum" that could be held out by the most subtle crimps of Montevideo could not induce these sober Brazilian sailors to desert their ship.

These "crimps" are land-sharks who get the sailors drunk when they can, and then rob them of their advance money. The sailors are all paid in advance; sometimes they receive in this way most of their wages for the voyage, which they make after the money is spent, or wasted, or stolen.

We all know what working for dead horse means—sailors know too well its significance.

As sailing day drew near, a half-day liberty to each watch was asked for by the men, who wanted to make purchases for their friends and relatives at Paranagua. Permission to go on shore was readily granted, and I was rewarded by seeing every one return to his ship at the time promised, and every one sober. On the morrow, which was sailing day, every man was at his post and all sang "Cheerily, ho!" and were happy; all except one, who complained of slight chills and a fever, but said that he had been subject to this, and that with a dose of quinine he would soon be all right again.

It appeared a small matter. Two days later though, his chills turned to something which I knew less about. The next day, three more men went down with rigor in the spine, and at the base of the brain. I knew by this that small-pox was among us!

We bore up at once, for Maldonado, which was the nearest port, the place spoken of in "Gulliver's Travels," though Gulliver, I think, is mistaken as to its identity and location, arriving there before a gathering storm that blew wet and cold from the east. Our signals of distress, asking for immediate medical aid were set and flew thirty-six hours before any one came to us; then a scared Yahoo, the country was still inhabited by Yahoos, in a boat rowed by two other animals, came aboard, and said, "Yes, your men have got small-pox." "*Vechega,*" he called it, but I understood the lingo of the Yahoo very well, I could even speak a few words of it and comprehend the meanings. "*Vechega!*" he bellowed to his mates alongside, and, turning to me, he said, in Yahoo: "You must leave the port at once," then jumping into his boat he hurried away, along with his scared companions.*

To leave a port in our condition was hard lines, but my perishing crew could get no succor at Maldonado, so we could do nothing but leave, if at all able to do so. We were indeed short-handed, but desperation lending a hand, the anchor was weighed and sufficient sail set on the bark to clear the inhospitable port. The wind blowing fair out of the harbor carried us away from the port toward Flores Island, for which we now headed in sore distress. A gale, long to be remembered, sprung suddenly up, stripping off our sails like autumn leaves, before the bark was three leagues from the place. We hadn't strength to clew up, so her sails were blown away, and she went flying before the mad tempest under bare poles. A snow-white sea-bird came for shelter from the storm, and poised on the deck to rest. The incident filled my sailors with awe; to them it was a portentious omen, and in distress they dragged themselves together and prostrate before the bird, prayed the Holy Virgin to ask

---

* In our discourse, Yahoo was spoken, but I write it in English because many of my readers would not understand the original. The signals that we used were made by universal code symbols. For example, two flags hoisted representing "P" "D" signified "want (or wants) immediate medical assistance." And so on, by hoists of two, three or four flags representing the consonants, our wants and wishes could be made known, each possessing the key to the code.

Our commercial code of signals is so invented and arranged that no matter what tongues may meet, perhaps those utterly incomprehensible by word of mouth, yet by these signs communications may be carried on with great facility. The whole system is so beautifully simple that a child of ordinary intelligence can understand it. Even the Yahoos were made to comprehend—when not color-blind. And, lest they should forget their lesson, a gunboat is sent out every year or two, to fire it into them with cannon.

God to keep them from harm. The rain beat on us in torrents, as the bark tossed and reeled ahead, and day turned black as night. The gale was from E. S. E., and our course lay W. N. W. nearly, or nearly before it. I stood at the wheel with my shore clothes on, I remember, for I hadn't yet had time to change them for waterproofs; this of itself was small matter, but it reminds me now that I was busy with other concerns. I was always a good helmsman, and I took in hand now, the steering of the bark in the storm—and I gave directions to Victor and the carpenter how to mix disinfectants for themselves, and medicines for the sick men. The medicine chest was fairly supplied.

Flores, when seen, was but a few ship's lengths away. Flashes of lightning revealed the low cliffs, amazingly near to us, and as the bark swept by with great speed, the roar of the breakers on the shore, heard above the din of the storm, told us of a danger to beware. The helm was then put down, and she came to under the lee of the island like a true, obedient thing.

Both anchors were let go, and all the chain paid out to both, to the bitter end, for the gale was now a hurricane. She walked away with her anchors for all that we could do, till, hooking a marine cable, one was carried away, and the other brought her head to the wind, and held her there trembling in the storm.

Anxious fear lest the second cable should break was on our minds through the night; but a greater danger was within the ship, that filled us all with alarm.

Two barks not far from us that night, with pilots on board, were lost, in trying to come through where the *Aquidneck*, without a pilot and with but three hands on deck to work her, came in. Their crews, with great difficulty, were rescued and then carried to Montevideo. When all had been done that we three could do, a light was put in the rigging, that flickered in the gale and went out. Then wet, and lame and weary, we fell down in our drenched clothes, to rest as we might—to sleep, or to listen to groans of our dying shipmates.

When daylight came (after this, the most dismal of all my nights at sea), our signals went up telling of the sad condition of the crew, and begging for medical assistance. Toward night the gale went down; but, as no boat came off, a gloom darker than midnight settled over the crew of the pest-ridden bark, and in dismay they again prayed to be spared to meet the loved ones awaiting them at home.

Our repeated signals, next day, brought the reply, "Stand in." *Carramba!* Why, we could hardly stand at all; much less could we get the bark underway, and beat in against wind and current. No one knew this better than they on the island, for my signals had told the whole story, and as we were only a mile and a half from the shore, the flags were distinctly made out. There was no doubt in our minds about that!

Late in the day, however, a barge came out to us, ill-manned and ill-managed by as scared a set of "galoots" as ever capsized a boat, or trembled at a shadow! The coxswain had more to say than the doctor, and the Yahoo—I forgot to mention that we were still in Yahoodom, but one would see that without this explanation—the Yahoo in the bow said more than both; and they all took a stiff pull from a bottle of *cachazza,** the doctor having had the start, I should say, of at least one or two pulls before leaving the shore, insomuch as he appeared braver than the crew.

The doctor, having taken an extra horn or two, with Dutch courage came on board, and brought with him a pound of sulphur, a pint of carbolic acid, and some barley—enough to feed a robin a few times, for all of which we were thankful indeed, our disinfectants being by this time nearly exhausted; then, glancing at the prostrate men, he hurried away, as the other had done at Maldonado. I asked what I should do with the dead through the night—bury them where we lay? "Oh, no, no!" cried the Yahoo in the bow; but the doctor pointed significantly to the water along side! I knew what he meant!

That night we buried Josè, the sailor whose honest smile had welcomed me to my bark at Montevideo. I had ordered stones brought on deck, before dark, ostensibly to ballast the boat. I knew they would soon be wanted! About midnight, the cook called me in sore distress, saying that Josè was dying without confession!

So poor Josè was buried that night in the great river Platte! I listened to the solemn splash that told of one life ended, and its work done; but gloomy, and sad, and melancholy as the case was, I had to smile when the cook, not having well-secured the ballast, threw

---

* This *cachazza* is said to be death to microbes, or even to larger worms; it will kill anything, in fact, except a Yahoo!

it over after his friend, exclaiming, "Good-bye, José, good-bye!" I added, "Good-bye, good shipmate, good-bye! I doubt not that you rest well!"

Next day, the signal from the shore was the same as the day before, "Stand in," in answer to my repeated call for help. By this time my men were demoralized and panic-stricken, and the poor fellows begged me, if the doctor would not try to cure them, to get a priest to confess them all. I saw a padre pacing the beach, and set flags asking him to come on board. No notice was taken of the signal, and we were now left entirely to ourselves.

After burying one more of the crew, we decided to remain no longer at this terrible place. An English telegraph tender passing, outward-bound, caught up our signals at that point, and kindly reported to her consul at Maldonado, who wired it to Montevideo.

The wind blowing away from the shore, as may it always blow when friend of mine nears that coast, we determined to weigh anchor or slip cable without further loss of time, feeling assured that by the telegraph reports some one would be on the look-out for us, and that the *Aquidneck* would be towed into port if the worst should happen—if the rest of her crew went down. Three of us weighed one anchor, with its ninety fathoms of chain, the other had parted on the windlass in the gale. The bark's prow was now turned toward Montevideo, the place we had so recently sailed from, full of hope and pleasant anticipation; and here we were, dejected and filled with misery, some of our number already gone on that voyage which somehow seems so far away.

At Montevideo, things were better. They *did* take my remaining sick men out of the vessel, after two days' delay; my agent procuring a tug, which towed them in the ship's boat three hundred fathoms astern. In this way they were taken to Flores Island, where, days and days before, they had been refused admittance! They were accompanied this time by an order from the governor of Montevideo, and at last were taken in. Two of the cases were, by this time, in the favorable change. But the poor old cook, who stood faithfully by me, and would not desert his old shipmates, going with them to the Island to care for them to the last, took the dread disease, died of it, and was there buried, not far from where he himself had buried his friend José, a short time before. The death of this faithful man occurred on the day that the bark finally sailed seaward, by the

Island. She was in sight from the hospital window when his phantom ship, that put out, carried him over the bar! His widow, at Paranagua, I was told, on learning the fate of her husband, died of grief.

The work of disinfecting the vessel, at Montevideo, after the sick were removed, was a source of speculation that was most elaborately carried on. Demijohns of carbolic acid were put on board, by the dozen, at $3.00 per demijohn, all diluted ready for use; and a *guardo* was put on board to use it up, which he did religiously over his own precious self, in my after-cabin, as far from the end of the ship where the danger was as he could get. Some one else disinfected *el proa*, not he! Abundant as the stuff was, I had to look sharp for enough to wash out forward, while aft it was knee-deep almost, at three dollars a jar! The harpy that alighted on deck at Maldonado sent in his bill for one hundred dollars—I paid eighty.

The cost to me of all this trouble in money paid out, irrelevantly to mention, was over a thousand dollars. What it cost me in health and mental anxiety cannot be estimated by such value. Still, I was not the greatest sufferer. My hardest task was to come, you will believe, at the gathering up of the trinkets and other purchases which the crew had made, thoughtful of wife and child at home. All had to be burned, or spoiled with carbolic acid! A hat for the little boy here, a pair of boots for his mamma there, and many things for the *familia* all around—all had to be destroyed!

Chapter VIII

After all this sad trouble was over, a new crew was shipped, and the *Aquidneck's* prow again turned seaward. Passing out by Flores, soon after, we observed the coast-guard searching, I learned, for a supposed sunken bark, which had appeared between squalls in the late gale with signals of distress set. I was satisfied from the account that it was our bark which they had seen in the gale, and the supposed flags were our tattered sails, what there was left of them, streaming in the storm. But we did not discourage the search, as it could do no harm, and I thought that they might perhaps find something else worth knowing about. This was the day, as I have said, on which my faithful cook died, while the bark was in sight from the window of his sick ward. It was a bright, fine day to us. We cannot say that it was otherwise than bright to him.

Breathing once more the fresh air of the sea, we set all sail for Paranagua, passing the lights on the coast to leave them flickering on the horizon, then soon out of sight. Fine weather prevailed, but with much head wind; still we progressed, and rarely a day passed but something of the distance toward our port was gained. One day, however, coming to an island, one that was inhabited only by birds, we came to a stand, as if it were impossible to go further on the voyage; a spell seemed to hang over us. I recognized the place as one that I knew well; a very dear friend had stood by me on deck, looking at this island, some years before. It was the last land that my friend ever saw. I would fain have sailed around it now, but a puff of fair wind coming sent us on our course for the time some leagues beyond. At sunset, though, this wind went down, and with the current we drifted back so much that by the next day we were farther off on the other side. However, fair wind coming again, we passed up inside, making thus the circuit of the island at last.

More or less favorable winds thenceforth filled our sails, till at last our destined port was gained.

The little town of Antonina, where my wife and Garfield had remained over during this voyage, twelve miles up the bay from Paranagua, soon after our arrival, was made alive with the noise of children marching to children's own music, my "Yawcob" heading the band with a brand-new ninety-cent organ, the most envied fellow of the whole crowd. Sorrows of the past took flight, or were locked in the closet at home, the fittest place for past misfortunes.

A truly hard voyage for us all was that to Montevideo! The survivors reached home after a while. Their features were terribly marked and disfigured; so much so that I did not know them till they accosted me when we met.

I look back with pleasure to the good character of my Brazilian sailors, regretting the more their hard luck and sad fate! We may meet again! *Quiem sabe!*

Getting over all this sad business as best we could, we entered on the next venture, which was to purchase and load a cargo of the famous Brazilian wood. The *Aquidneck* was shifted to an arm of the bay, where she was moored under the lee of a virgin forest, twenty minutes' canoe ride from the village of Guarakasava, where she soon began to load.

The timber of this country, generally very heavy, is nevertheless hauled by hand to the water, where, lashed to canoes, it is floated to the ship.

These canoes, formed sometimes from mammoth trees, skillfully shaped and dug out with care, are at once the carriage and *cariole* of the family to the *citio*, or the rice to mill. Roads are hardly known where the canoe is available; men, women and children are consequently alike, skilled in the art of canoeing to perfection, almost. There are no carriages to speak of in such places, even a saddle horse about the waterfront is a *rara avis*. There was, indeed one horse at Guarakasava—the owner of it was very conspicuous.

The family canoe just spoken of, has the capacity, often, of several tons, is handsomely decorated with carvings along the topsides, and is painted, as the "Geordie" would say, "in none o' your gaudy colors, but in good plain red or blue"—sometimes, however, they are painted green.

The cost of these handsome canoes are, say, from $250 down in price and size, from the grand turnout to the one man craft which may be purchased for five mil reis ($2.50).

From the greatest to the smallest they are cared for, with almost an affectionate care, and are made to last many years.

One thing else which even the poorest Brazilian thinks much of is his affectionate wife who literally and figuratively is often in the same boat with her husband, pulling against the stream. Family ties are strong in Brazil and the sweet flower of friendship thrives in its sunny clime. The system of land and sea breezes prevail on the coast from Cape Frio to Saint Catherine with great regularity most of the year; the sail is therefore used to good advantage by the almost amphibious inhabitants along the coast who love the water and take to it like ducks and natural born sailors.

The wind falling light they propel their canoes by paddle or long pole with equal facility. The occupants standing, in the smaller ones, force them along at a great speed. The larger ones, when the wind does not serve, are pulled by banks of oars which are fastened to stout pegs in the gunwail with grummits, that fit loosely over the oars so as to allow them free play in the hand of the waterman.

Curling the water with fine, shapely prows as they dart over the smooth waters of the bays and rivers, these canoes present a picture of unrivalled skill and grace.

I find the following entry in my diary made near the close of transactions at Guarakasava which in the truthful word of an historian I am bound to record, if only to show my prevailing high opinion of the natives while I was among them:—

"GUARAKASAVA, Dec. 20th.

Heretofore I have doted on native Brazilian honesty as well as national seamanship and skill in canoes but my dream of a perfect paradise is now unsettled forever. I find, alas! that even here the fall of Adam is felt: Taking in some long poles to-day the negro tallyman persisted in counting twice the same pole. When the first end entered the port it was *"umo"* (one); when the last end disappeared into the ship he would sing out *"does"* (two).

I had no serious difficulty over the matter, but left Guarakasava with that hurt feeling which comes of being over pursuaded that one and one make four.

We spent Christmas of 1887 at Guarakasava. The bark was loaded soon after, and when proceeding across the bay where currents and wind caught her foul, near a dangerous sand bar, she misstayed and went on the strand. The anchor was let go to club her. It wouldn't hold in the treacherous sands; so she dragged and stranded broadside on, where open to the sea, a strong swell came in that raked her fore and aft, for three days, the waves dashing over her groaning hull the while till at last her back was broke and—why not add "heart" as well! for she lay now undone. After twenty-five years of good service the *Aquidneck* here ended her days!

I had myself carried load on load, but alas! I could not carry a mountain; and was now at the end where my best skill and energy could not avail. What was to be done? What could be done? We had indeed the appearance of shipwrecked people, away, too, from home.

This was no time to weep, for the lives of all the crew were saved; neither was it a time to laugh, for our loss was great.

But the sea calmed down, and I sold the wreck, which floated off at the end of the storm. And after paying the crew their wages out of the proceeds had a moiety left for myself and family—a small sum.

Then I began to look about for the future, and for means of escape from exile. The crew (foreign) found shipping for Montevideo, where they had joined the *Aquidneck,* in lieu of the stricken Brazilian sailors. But for myself and family this outlet was hardly available, even if we had cared to go farther from home,—which was the least of our thoughts; and there were no vessels coming our way.

Chapter IX

> Away, away, no cloud is lowering o'er us,
>   Freely now we stem the wave;
> Hoist, hoist all sail, before us
>   Hope's beacon shines to cheer the brave.
>   —*Massaneillo.*

When all had been saved from the wreck that was worth saving, or that could be saved, we found ourselves still in the possession of some goods soon to become of great value to us, especially my compass and charts which, though much damaged, were yet serviceable and suggested practical usefulness; and the chronometer being found intact, my course was no longer undecided, my wife and sons agreeing with what I thought best.

The plan, in a word, was this: We could not beg our way, neither would we sit idle among the natives. We found that it would require more courage to remain in the far-off country than to return home in a boat, which then we concluded to build and for that purpose.*

My son Victor, with much pride and sympathy, entered heartily into the plan, which promised a speedy return home. He bent his energies in a practical direction, working on the boat like an old builder.

Before entering on the project, however, all responsibilities were considered. Swift ocean currents around capes and coral reefs were taken into account; and above all else to be called dangerous we

* This alternative I was obliged to accept, or bring my family home as paupers, for my wealth was gone—need I explain more? This explanation has been forced from me.

75

knew would be the fierce tropical storms which surely we would encounter.

But a boat should be built stout and strong, we all said, one in which we should not be afraid to trust our lives even in the storm.

And with the advantage of experience in ships and boats of various sizes and in many seas, I turned to the work of constructing, according to my judgment and means, a craft which would be best adapted to all weathers and all circumstances. My family with sympathetic strength pulling hard in the same direction.

Seaworthiness was to be the first and most prominent feature in our microscopic ship; next to this good quality she should sail well; at least before free winds, for we counted on favorable winds; and so they were experienced the greater part of the voyage that followed.

Long exposures and many and severe disappointments by this time, I found, had told on health and nerve, through long quarantines, expensive fumigations, and ruinous doctors' visits, which had swept my dollars into hands other than mine. However, with still a "shot in the locker," and with some feelings of our own in the matter of how we should get home, I say, we set to work with tools saved from the wreck—a meagre kit—and soon found ourselves in command of another ship, which I will describe the building of, also the dimensions and the model and rig, first naming the tools with which it was made.

To begin with, we had an axe, an adze and two saws, one 1-2 inch auger, one 6-8 and one 3-8 auger-bit; two large sail-needles, which we converted into nailing bits; one roper, that answered for a punch; and, most precious of all, a file that we found in an old sail-bag washed up on the beach. A square we readily made. Two splints of bamboo wood served as compasses. Charcoal, pounded as fine as flour and mixed in water, took the place of chalk for the line; the latter we had on hand. In cases where holes larger than the 6-8 bit were required, a piece of small jack-stay iron was heated, and with this we could burn a hole to any size required. So we had, after all, quite a kit to go on with. Clamps, such as are used by boat builders, we had not, but made substitutes from the crooked guava tree and from *massaranduba* wood.

Trees from the neighboring forest were felled when the timber from the wrecked cargo would not answer. Some of these woods that we sought for special purposes had queer sounding names, such as *arregebah, guanandee, batetenandinglastampai,* etc. This latter we did not use the saw upon at all, it being very hard, but hewed it with the axe, bearing in mind that we had but one file, whereas for the edged tools we had but to go down to a brook hard by to find stones in abundance suitable to sharpen them on.

The many hindrances encountered in the building of the boat will not be recounted here. Among the least was a jungle fever, from which we suffered considerably. But all that, and all other obstacles vanished at last, or became less, before a new energy which grew apace with the boat, and the building of the craft went rapidly forward. There was no short day system, but we rested on the Sabbath, or surveyed what we had done through the week, and made calculations of what and how to strike on the coming week.

The unskilled part of the labor, such as sawing the cedar planks, of which she was mostly made, was done by the natives, who saw in a rough fashion, always leaving much planing and straightening to be done, in order to adjust the timber to a suitable shape. The planks for the bottom were of iron wood, 1 1-4 x 10 inches. For the sides and top red cedar was used, each plank, with the exception of two, reaching the whole length of the boat. This arrangement of exceedingly heavy wood in the bottom, and the light on top, contributed much to the stability of the craft.

The iron wood was heavy as stone, while the cedar, being light and elastic, lent buoyancy and suppleness, all that we could wish for.

The fastenings we gathered up in various places, some from the bulwarks of the wreck, some from the hinges of doors and skylights, and some were made from the ship's metal sheathing, which the natives melted and cast into nails. Pure copper nails, also, were procured from the natives, some ten kilos, for which I paid in copper coins, at the rate of two *kilos* of coin for one *kilo* of nails. The same kind of coins, called *dumps,* cut into diamond-shaped pieces, with holes punched through them, entered into the fastenings as burrs for the nails. A number of small eyebolts from the spanker-boom of the wreck were turned to account for lashing bolts in the deck of the new vessel. The nails, when too long, were cut to the required length, taking care that the ends which were cut off should not be wasted, but remelted, along with the metal sheathing, into other nails.

Some carriage bolts, with nuts, which I found in the country, came in very handy; these I adjusted to the required length, when too long, by slipping on blocks of wood of the required thickness to take up the surplus length, putting the block, of course, on the inside, and counter-sinking the nut flush with the planks on the outside; then screwing from the inside outward, they were drawn together, and there held as in a vise, the planks being put together "lap-streak" fashion, which without doubt is the strongest way to build a boat.

These screw-bolts, seventy in number, as well as the copper nails, cost us dearly, but wooden pegs, with which also she was fastened, cost only the labor of being made. The lashings, too, that we used here and there about the frame of the cabin, cost next to nothing, being made from the fibrous bark of trees, which could be had in abundance by the stripping of it off. So, taking it by and large, our materials were not expensive, the principal item being the timber, which cost about three cents per superficial foot, sawed or hewed. Rosewood, ironwood, cedar or mahogany, were all about the same price and very little in advance of common wood; so of course we selected always, the best, the labor of shaping being least, sometimes, where the best materials were used.

These various timbers and fastenings, put together as best we could shape and join them, made a craft sufficiently strong and seaworthy to withstand all the buffetings on the main upon which, in due course she was launched.

The hull being completed, by various other contrivances and makeshifts in which, sometimes, the "wooden blacksmith" was called in to assist, and the mother of invention also lending a hand, fixtures were made which served as well on the voyage as though made in a dockyard and at great cost.

My builders balked at nothing, and on the 13th day of May, the day on which the slaves of Brazil were set free, our craft was launched, and was named *Liberdade* (Liberty).

Her dimensions being—35 feet in length over all, 7 1-2 feet breadth of beam, and 3 feet depth of hold, who shall say that she was not large enough?

Her model I got from my recollections of Cape Ann dories and

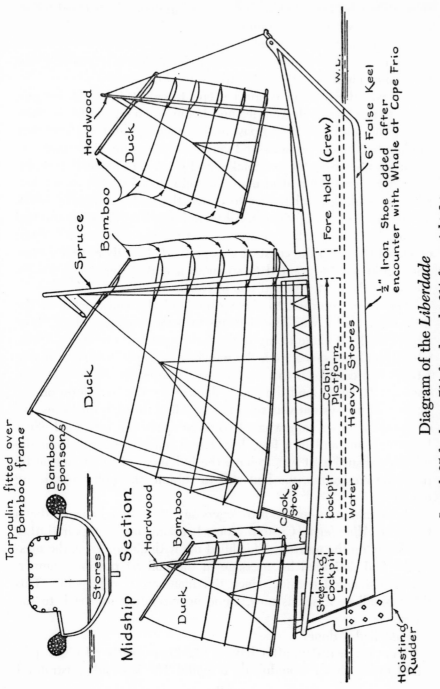

Tarpaulin fitted over Bamboo frame

Bamboo Sponsons

Stores

Midship Section

Hardwood

Bamboo

Duck

Spruce

Bamboo

Duck

Hardwood

Duck

Cook Stove

Steering Cockpit

Cockpit

Water

Heavy Stores

Cabin Platform

Fore Hold (Crew)

W.L.

6" False Keel

½" Iron Shoe added after encounter with Whale at Cape Frio

Hoisting Rudder

Diagram of the *Liberdade*

Length 35 ft, beam 7½ ft, draught 2½ ft, weight 6 tons.

from a photo of a very elegant Japanese *sampan* which I had before me on the spot, so, as it might be expected, when finished, she resembled both types of vessel in some degree.

Her rig was the Chinese *sampan* style, which is, I consider, the most convenient boat rig in the whole world.

This was the boat, or canoe I prefer to call it, in which we purposed to sail for North America and home. Each one had been busy during the construction and past misfortunes had all been forgotten. Madam had made the sails—and very good sails they were, too!

Victor, the carpenter, ropemaker and general roustabout had performed his part. Our little man, Garfield, too, had found employment in holding the hammer to clinch the nails and giving much advice on the coming voyage. All were busy, I say, and no one had given a thought of what we were about to encounter from the port officials further up the coast; it was pretended by them that a passport could not be granted to so small a craft to go on so long a voyage as the contemplated one to North America.

Then fever returned to the writer, and the constructor of the little craft, and I was forced to go to bed, remaining there three days. Finally, it came to my mind that in part of a medicine chest, which had been saved from the wreck, was stored some *arsenicum*, I think it is called. Of this I took several doses (small ones at first, you may be sure), and the good effect of the deadly poison on the malaria in my system was soon felt trickling through my veins. Increasing the doses somewhat, I could perceive the beneficial effect hour by hour, and in a few days I had quite recovered from the malady. Absurd as it was to have the judgment of sailors set on by pollywog navigators, we had still to submit, the pollywogs being numerous.

About this time—as the astrologers say—a messenger came down from the *Alfandega* (Custom House), asking me to repair thither at midday on the morrow. This filled me with alarm. True, the messenger had delivered his message in the politest possible manner, but that signified nothing, since Brazilians are always polite. This thing, small as it seems now, came near sending me back to the fever.

What had I done?

I went up next day, after having nightmare badly all night, prepared to say that I wouldn't do it again! The kind administrator I found, upon presenting myself at his office, had no fault to charge me with; but had a good word, instead. "The little *Liberdade*," he observed, had attracted the notice of his people and his own curiosity, as being "a handsome and well-built craft." This and many other flattering expressions were vented, at which I affected surprise, but secretly said, "I think you are right, sir, and you have good taste, too, if you are a customs officer."

The drift of this flattery, to make a long story short, was to have me build a boat for the *Alfandega*, or, his government not allowing money to build new—pointing to one which certainly would require new keel, planks, ribs, stem and stern-post—"could I not repair one?"

To this proposition I begged time to consider. Flattering as the officer's words were, and backed by the offer of liberal pay, so long as the boat could be "repaired," I still had no mind to remain in the hot country, and risk getting the fever again. But there was the old hitch to be gotten over; namely, the passport, on which, we thought, depended our sailing.

However, to expedite matters, a fishing license was hit upon, and I wondered why I had not thought of that before, having been, once upon a time, a fisherman myself. Heading thence on a new diplomatic course, I commenced to fit ostensibly for a fishing voyage. To this end, a fishing net was made, which would be a good thing to have, any way. Then hooks and lines were rigged and a cable made. This cable, or rope, was formed from vines that grow very long on the sandbanks just above tide water, several of which twisted together make a very serviceable rope, then being light and elastic, it is especially adapted for a boat anchor rope, or for the storm drag. Ninety fathoms of this rope was made for us by the natives, for the sum of ten milreis ($5.00).

The anchor came of itself almost. I had made a wooden one from heavy sinking timber, but a stalwart ranchman coming along, one day, brought a boat anchor with him which, he said, had been used by his slaves as a pot-hook. "But now that they are free and away," said he, "I have no further use for the crooked thing." A sewing-machine, which had served to stitch the sails together, was coveted by him, and was of no further use to us; in exchange for this the prized anchor was readily secured, the owner of it leaving us some boot into the bargain. Things working thus in our favor, the wooden anchor was stowed away to be kept as a spare bower.

These arrangements completed, our craft took on the appearance of a fishing smack, and I began to feel somewhat in my old element, with no fear of the lack of ways and means when we should arrive on our own coast, where I knew of fishing banks. And a document which translated read: "A license to catch fish inside and outside of the bar," was readily granted by the port authorities.

"How far outside the bar may this carry us?" I asked.

"*Quiem sabe!*" said the officer. (Literally translated, "Who knows?" but in Spanish or Portuguese used for, "Nobody knows, or I don't care.")

"Adieu, senor," said the polite official; "we will meet in heaven!"

This meant you can go since you insist upon it, but I must not officially know of it; and you will probably go to the bottom. In this he and many others were mistaken.

Having the necessary document now in our possession, we commenced to take in stores for the voyage, as follows: Sea-biscuits, 120 lbs.; flour, 25 lbs.; sugar, 30 lbs.; coffee, 9 lbs., which roasted black and pounded fine as wheaten flour, was equal to double the amount as prepared in North America, and afforded us a much more delicious cup.

Of tea we had 3 lbs.; pork, 20 lbs.; dried beef, 100 lbs.; *baccalao secca*, (dried codfish) 20 lbs.; 2 bottles of honey, 200 oranges, 6 bunches of bananas, 120 gallons of water; also a small basket of yams, and a dozen sticks of sugar-cane, by way of vegetables.

Our medicine chest contained Brazil nuts, pepper and cinnamon; no other medicines or condiments were required on the voyage, except table salt, which we also had.

One musket and a carbine—which had already stood us in good stead—together with ammunition and three cutlasses, were stowed away for last use, to be used, nevertheless, in case of necessity.

The light goods I stowed in the ends of the canoe, the heavier in the middle and along the bottom, thus economizing space and lending to the stability of the canoe. Over the top of the midship stores a floor was made, which, housed over by a tarpaulin roof reaching three feet above the deck of the canoe, gave us sitting space of four feet from the floor to roof, and twelve feet long amidships, supported by a frame of bamboo, made store-room and cabin. This arrangement of cabin in the centre gave my passengers a berth where the least motion would be felt: even this is saying but little, for best we could do to avoid it we had still to accept much tossing from the waves.

Precautionary measures were taken in everything, so far as our resources and skill could reach. The springy and buoyant bamboo was used wherever stick of any kind was required, such as the frame and braces for the cabin, yards for the sails, and, finally, for guard on her top sides, making the canoe altogether a self-righting one, in case of a capsize. Each joint in the bamboo was an air-chamber of several pounds buoyant capacity, and we had a thousand joints.

The most important of our stores, particularly the flour, bread and coffee, were hermetically sealed, so that if actually turned over at sea, our craft would not only right herself, but would bring her stores right side up, in good order, and it then would be only a question of baling her out, and of setting her again on her course, when we would come on as right as ever. As it turned out, however, no such trial or mishap awaited us.

While the possibility of many and strange occurrences was felt by all of us, the danger which loomed most in little Garfield's mind was that of the sharks.

A fine specimen was captured on the voyage, showing five rows of pearly teeth, as sharp as lances.

Some of these monsters, it is said, have nine rows of teeth; that they are always hungry is admitted by sailors of great experience.

How it is that sailors can go in bathing, as they often do, in the face of a danger so terrible, is past my comprehension. Their business is to face danger, to be sure, but this is a needless exposure, for which the penalty is sometimes a life. The second mate of a bark on the coast of Cuba, not long ago, was bitten in twain, and the portions swallowed whole by a monster shark that he had tempted in this way. The shark was captured soon after, and the poor fellow's remains taken out of the revolting maw.

Leaving the sharks where they are, I gladly return to the voyage of the *Liberdade*.

Chapter X

The efficiency of our canoe was soon discovered, for on the 24th of June, after having sailed about the bay some few days to temper our feelings to the new craft, and shake things into place, we crossed the bar and stood out to sea, while six vessels lay inside "bar-bound," that is to say by their pilots it was thought too rough to venture out, and they, the pilots, stood on the point as we put out to sea, crossing themselves in our behalf, and shouting that the bar was *crudo*. But the *Liberdade* stood on her course, the crew never regretting it.

The wind from the sou'west at the time was the moderating side of a *pampeiro* which had brought in a heavy swell from the ocean, that broke and thundered on the bar with deafening roar and grand display of majestic effort.

But our little ship bounded through the breakers like a fish—as natural to the elements, and as free!

Of all the seas that broke furiously about her that day, often standing her on end, not one swept over or even boarded her, and she finally came through the storm of breakers in triumph. Then squaring away before the wind she spread her willing sails, and flew onward like a bird.

It required confidence and some courage to face the first storm in so small a bark, after having been years in large ships; but it would have required more courage than was possessed by any of us to turn back, since thoughts of home had taken hold on our minds.

Then, too, the old boating trick came back fresh to me, the love of the thing itself gaining on me as the little ship stood out; and my crew with one voice said: "Go on." The heavy south Atlantic swell rolling in upon the coast, as we sped along, toppled over when it reached the ten fathom line, and broke into roaring combers, which forbade our nearer approach to the land.

Evidently, our safest course was away from the shore, and out where the swelling seas, though grand, were regular, and raced under our little craft that danced like a mite on the ocean as she

84

drove forward. In twenty-four hours from the time Paranagua bar was crossed we were up with Santos Heads, a run of 150 miles.

A squall of wind burst on us through a gulch, as we swept round the Heads, tearing our sails into shreds, and sending us into Santos under bare poles.

Chancing then upon an old friend, the mail steamship *Finance*, Capt. Baker, about to sail for Rio, the end of a friendly line was extended to us, and we were towed by the stout steamer toward Rio, the next day, as fast as we could wish to go. My wife and youngest sailor took passage on the steamer, while Victor remained in the canoe with me, and stood by, with axe in hand, to cut the tow-line, if the case should require it—and I steered.

"Look out," said Baker, as the steamer began to move ahead, "look out that I don't snake that canoe out from under you."

"Go on with your mails, Baker," was all I could say, "don't blow up your ship with my wife and son on board, and I will look out for the packet on the other end of the rope."

Baker opened her up to thirteen knots, but the *Liberdade* held on!

The line that we towed with was 1 1-3 inches in diameter, by ninety fathoms long. This, at times when the steamer surged over seas, leaving the canoe on the opposite side of a wave astern, would become as taut as a harp-string. At other times it would slacken and sink limp in a bight, under the forefoot, but only for a moment, however, when the steamer's next great plunge ahead would snap it taut again, pulling us along with a heavy, trembling jerk. Under the circumstances, straight steering was imperative, for a sheer to port or starboard would have finished the career of the *Liberdade,* by sending her under the sea. Therefore, the trick of twenty hours fell to me— the oldest and most experienced helmsman. But I was all right and not over-fatigued until Baker cast oil upon the "troubled waters." I soon got tired of that.

Victor was under the canvas covering, with the axe still in hand, ready to cut the line which was so arranged that he could reach it from within, and cut instantly, if by mischance the canoe should take a sheer.

I was afraid that the lad would become sleepy, and putting his head "under his wing" for a nap, would forget his post, but my frequent cry, "Stand by there, Victor," found him always on hand, though complaining some of the dizzy motion.

Heavy sprays dashed over me at the helm, which, however, seeming to wash away the sulphur and brimstone smoke of many a quarantine, brought enjoyment to my mind.

Confused waves rose about us, high and dangerous—often high above the ganwale of the canoe—but her shapely curves balanced her well, and she rode over them all in safety.

This canoe ride was thrilling and satisfactory to us all. It proved beyond a doubt that we had in this little craft a most extraordinary sea-boat, for the tow was a thorough test of her seaworthiness.

The captain of the steamer ordered oil cast over from time to time, relieving us of much spray and sloppy motion, but adding to discomforts of taste to me at the helm, for much of the oil blew over me and in my face. Said the captain to one of his mates (an old whaler by the way, and whalers for some unaccountable reason have never too much regard for a poor merchantman) "Mr. Smith."

"Aye, aye, sir," answered old Smith.

"Mr. Smith, hoist out that oil."

"Aye, aye, sir," said the old "blubberhunter," in high glee, as he went about it with alacrity, and in less than five minutes from the time the order was given, I was smothering in grease and our boat was oiled from keel to truck.

"She's all right now," said Smith.

"That's all right," said Baker, but I thought it all wrong. The wind, meanwhile, was in our teeth and before we crossed Rio Bar I had swallowed enough oil to cure any amount of consumption.

Baker, I have heard, said he wouldn't care much if he should "drown Slocum." But I was all right so long as the canoe didn't sheer, and we arrived at Rio safe and sound after the most exciting boat-ride of my life. I was bound not to cut the line that towed us so well; and I knew that Baker wouldn't let it go, for it was his rope.

I found at Rio that my fishing license could be exchanged for a pass of greater import. This document had to be procured through the office of the Minister of Marine.

Many a smart linguist was ready to use his influence in my behalf with the above-named high official; but I found at the end of a month that I was making headway about as fast as a Dutch galliot in a head sea after the wind had subsided. Our worthy Consul, General H. Clay Armstrong, gave me a hint of what the difficulty was and how to obviate it. I then went about the business myself as I should have done at first, and I found those at the various departments who were willing to help me without the intervention of outside "influence."

Commander Marquis of the Brazilian navy, recommended me to His Excellency, the Minister of Marine, "out of regard," he said, "for American seamen," and when the new document came it was *"Passe Especial,"* and had on it *a seal as big as a soup plate.* A port naval officer then presented me to the good *Administradore,* who also gave me a *passe especial,* with the seal of the *Alfandega.*

I had now only to procure a bill of health, when I should have papers enough for a man o' war. Rio being considered a healthy place, this was readily granted, making our equipment complete.

I met here our minister whose office, with other duties, is to keep a weather eye lifting in the interest of that orphan, the American ship—alas, my poor relation! Said he, "Captain, if your *Liberdade* be as good as your papers" (documents given me by the Brazilian officials), "you may get there all right;" adding, "well, if the boat ever reaches home she will be a great curiosity," the meaning of which, I could readily infer, was, "and your chances for a snap in a dime museum will be good." This, after many years of experience as an American shipmaster, and also ship owner, in a moderate way, was interesting encouragement. By our Brazilian friends, however, the voyage was looked upon as a success already achieved.

"The utmost confidence," said the *Journal Opiz,* of Rio, "is placed in the cool-headed, audacious American mariner, and we expect in a short time to hear proclaimed in all of the journals of the Old and New World the safe arrival of this wonderful little craft at her destination, ourselves taking part in the glory." "Temos confianca na pericia e sangue frio do audaciauso marinhero Americano por isso esperamos que dentro em pouco tempo veremos o seu nome proclamado por todos os jornaes do velho e novo mundo.

A nos tambem cabera parte da gloria."

With these and like kind expressions from all of our *friends,* we took leave of Rio, sailing on the morning of July 23d, 1888.

Chapter XI

July 23d, 1888, was the day, as I have said, on which we sailed from Rio de Janeiro.

Meeting with head winds and light withal, through the day we made but little progress; and finally, when night came on we anchored twenty miles east of Rio Heads, near the shore. Long, rolling seas rocked us as they raced by, then, dashing their great bodies against defying rocks, made music by which we slept that night. But a trouble unthought of before came up in Garfield's mind before going to his bunk: "Mamma," cried he as our little bark rose and fell on the heavy waves, tumbling the young sailor about from side to side in the small quarters while he knelt seriously at his evening devotion, "mamma, this boat isn't big enough to pray in!" But this difficulty was gotten over in time, and Garfield learned to watch as well as to pray on the voyage, and full of faith that all would be well, laid him down nights and slept as restfully as any Christian on sea or land.

By daylight of the second day we were again underway, beating to the eastward against the old head wind and head sea. On the following night we kept her at it, and the next day made Cape Frio where we anchored near the entrance to a good harbor.

Time from Rio, two days; distance, 70 miles.

The wind and tide being adverse, compelled us to wait outside for a favorable change. While comfortably anchored at this place, a huge whale, nosing about, came up under the canoe, giving us a toss and a great scare. We were at dinner when it happened. The meal, it is needless to say, was finished without dessert. The great sea animal—fifty to sixty feet long—circling around our small craft, looked terribly big. He was so close to me twice, as he swam round and round the canoe, that I could have touched him either time with a paddle. His flukes stirring the water like a steamer propeller appeared alarmingly close and powerful!—and what an ugly mouth the monster had! Well, we expected instant annihilation. The fate of the stout whale-ship *Essex* came vividly before me. The voyage of the *Liberdade,* I thought, was about ended, and I looked about for pieces of bamboo on which to land my wife and family. Just then, however, to the infinite relief of all of us, the leviathan moved off, without doing us much harm, having felt satisfied, perhaps, that we had no Jonah on board.

We lost an anchor through the incident, and received some small damage to the keel, but no other injury was done—even this, I believe, upon second thought, was unintentional—done in playfulness only! "A shark can take a joke," it is said, and crack one too, but for broad, rippling humor the whale has no equal.

"If this be a sample of our adventures in the beginning," thought I, "we shall have enough and to spare by the end of the voyage." A visit from this quarter had not been counted on; but Sancho Panza says, "when least aware starts the hare," which in our case, by the by, was a great whale!

When our breath came back and the hair on our heads settled to a normal level, we set sail, and dodged about under the lee of the cape till a cove, with a very enticing sand beach at the head of it, opened before us, some three miles northwest of where we lost the anchor in the remarkable adventure with the whale. The "spare bower" was soon bent to the cable. Then we stood in and anchored near a cliff, over which was a goat-path leading in the direction of a small fishing village, about a mile away. Sheering the boat in to the rocky side of the cove which was steep to, we leaped out, warp in hand, and made fast to a boulder above the tidal flow, then, scrambling over the cliff, we repaired to the village, first improvising a spare anchor from three sticks and a stone which answered the purpose quite well.

Judging at once that we were strangers the villagers came out to meet us, and made a stir at home to entertain us in the most hospitable manner, after the custom of the country, and with the villagers was a gentleman from Canada, a Mr. Newkirk, who, as we learned, was engaged, when the sea was smooth, in recovering treasure that was lost near the cape in the British war ship *Thetis,* which was wrecked there, in 1830. The treasure, some millions in silver coins and gold in bars, from Peru for England, was dumped in the cove, which has since taken the name of the ship that bore it there, and as I have said, came to grief in that place which is on the west shore near the end of the cape.

Some of the coins were given to us to be treasured as souvenirs of the pleasant visit. We found in Mr. Newkirk a versatile, roving genius; he had been a schoolmaster at home, captain of a lake schooner once, had practiced medicine, and preached some, I think; and what else I do not know. He had tried many things for a living, but, like the proverbial moving stone had failed to accumulate. "Matters," said the Canadian, "were getting worse and worse even, till finally to keep my head above water I was forced to go under the sea," and he had struck it rich, it would seem, if gold being brought in by the boat-load was any sign. This man of many adventures still spoke like a youngster; no one had told him that he was growing old. He talked of going home, as soon as the balance of the treasure was secured, "just to see his dear old mother," who, by the way, was seventy-four years old when he left home, some twenty years before. Since his last news from home, nearly two decades had gone by. He was "the youngest of a family of eighteen children, all living," he said, "though," added he, "our family came near being made one less yesterday, by a whale which I thought would eat my boat, diving-bell, crew, money and all, as he came toward us, with open mouth. By a back stroke of the oars, however, we managed to cheat him out of his dinner, if that was what he was after, and I think it was, but here I am!" he cried, "all right!" and might have added, "wealthy after all."

After hearing the diver's story, I related in Portuguese our own adventure of the same day, and probably with the same whale, the monster having gone in the direction of the diver's boat. The astonishment of the listeners was great; but when they learned of our intended voyage to *America do Norte*, they crossed themselves and asked God to lend us grace!

"Is North America near New York?" asked the village merchant, who owned all the boats and nets of the place.

"Why, America is *in* New York," answered the ex-schoolmaster.

"I thought so," said the self-satisfied merchant. And no doubt he thought some of us very stupid, or rude, or both, but in spite of manners I had to smile at the assuring air of the Canadian.

"Why did you not answer him correctly?" I asked of the ex-schoolmaster.

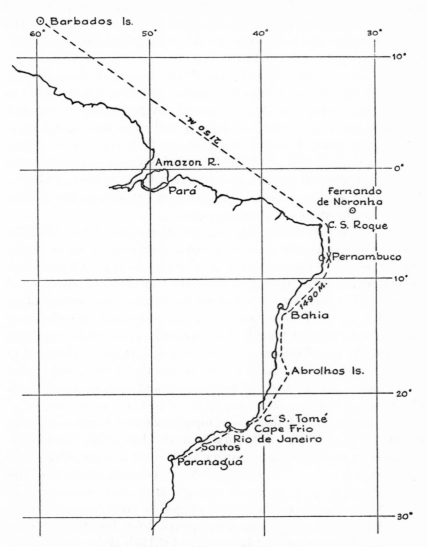

Course of the *Liberdade* from Paranaguá to Barbados

Voyage of the "Liberdade"

"I answered him," said Newkirk, "according to his folly. Had I corrected his rusty geography before these simple, impoverished fishermen, he would not soon forgive me; and as for the rest of the poor souls here, the knowledge would do them but little good."

I may mention that in this out-of-the-way place there were no schools, and except the little knowledge gained in their church, from the catchism, and from the fumbling of beads, they were the most innocent of this world's scheme, of any people I ever met. But they seemed to know all about heaven, and were, no doubt, happy.

After the brief, friendly chat that we had, coffee was passed around, the probabilities of the *Liberdade's* voyage discussed, and the crew cautioned against the dangers of the *balacna* (whale), which were numerous along the coast, and vicious at that season of the year, having their young to protect.

I realized very often the startling sensation alone of a night at the helm, of having a painful stillness broken by these leviathans bursting the surface of the water with a noise like the roar of a great sea, uncomfortably near, reminding me of the Cape Frio adventure; and my crew, I am sure, were not less sensitive to the same feeling of an awful danger, however imaginary. One night in particular, dark and foggy I remember, Victor called me excitedly, saying that something dreadful ahead and drawing rapidly near had frightened him.

It proved to be a whale, for some reason that I could only guess at, threshing the sea with its huge body, and surging about in all directions, so that it puzzled me to know which way to steer to go clear. I thought at first, from the rumpus made that a fight was going on, such as we had once witnessed from the deck of the *Aquidneck*, not far from this place. Our course was changed as soon as we could decide which way to avoid, if possible, all marine disturbers of the peace. We wished especially to keep away from infuriated swordfish, which I feared might be darting about, and be apt to give us a blind thrust. Knowing that they sometimes pierce stout ships through with their formidable weapons, I began to feel ticklish about the ribs myself, I confess, and the little watch below, too, got uneasy and sleepless; for one of these swords, they knew well, would reach through and through our little boat, from keel to deck. Large ships, have occasionally been sent into port leaky from the stab of a sword, but what I most dreaded was the possibility of one of us being ourselves pinned in the boat.

A swordfish once pierced a whale-ship through the planking, and through the solid frame timber and the thick ceiling, with his sword, leaving it there, a valuable plug indeed, with the point, it was found upon unshipping her cargo at New Bedford, even piercing through a cask in the hold.

Chapter XII

July 30th, early in the day, and after a pleasant visit at the cape, we sailed for the north, securing first a few sea shells to be cherished, with the *Thetis* relics, in remembrance of a most enjoyable visit to the hospitable shores of Cape Frio.

Having now doubled Cape Frio, a prominent point in our voyage, and having had the seaworthiness of our little ship thoroughly tested, as already told; and seeing, moreover, that we had nothing to fear from common small fry of the sea, (one of its greatest monsters having failed to capsize us,) we stood on with greater confidence than ever, but watchful, nevertheless, for any strange event that might happen.

A fresh polar wind hurried us on, under shortened sail, toward the softer "trades" of the tropics, but, veering to the eastward by midnight, it brought us well in with the land. Then, "Larboard watch, ahoy! all hands on deck and turn out reefs," was the cry. To weather Cape St. Thome we must lug on all sail. And we go over the shoals with a boiling sea and current in our favor. In twenty-four hours from Cape Frio, we had lowered the Southern Cross three degrees— 180 miles.

Sweeping by the cape, the canoe sometimes standing on end, and sometimes buried in the deep hollow of the sea, we sunk the light on St. Thome soon out of sight, and stood on with flowing sheet. The wind on the following day settled into regular south-east "trades," and our cedar canoe skipped briskly along, over friendly seas that were leaping toward home, doffing their crests onward and forward, but never back, and the splashing waves against her sides, then rippling along the thin cedar planks between the crew and eternity,

93

vibrated enchanting music to the ear, while confidence grew in the bark that was HOMEWARD BOUND.

But coming upon coral reefs, of a dark night, while we listened to the dismal tune of the seas breaking over them with an eternal roar, how intensely lonesome they were! no sign of any living thing in sight, except, perhaps, the phosphorescent streaks of a hungry shark, which told of bad company in our wake, and made the gloom of the place more dismal still.

One night we made shelter under the lee of the extensive reefs called the Paredes (walls), without seeing the breakers at all in the dark, although they were not far in the distance. At another time, dragging on sail to clear a lee shore, of a dark and stormy night, we came suddenly into smooth water, where we cast anchor and furled our sails, lying in a magic harbor till daylight the next morning, when we found ourselves among a maze of high reefs, with high seas breaking over them, as far as the eye could reach, on all sides, except at the small entrance to the place that we had stumbled into in the night. The position of this future harbor is South Lat. 16° 48', and West Long. from Greenwich 39° 30'. We named the place "PORT LIBERDADE."

The next places sighted were the treacherous Abrohles, and the village of Caravellas back of the reef where upon refitting, I found that a chicken cost a thousand reis, a bunch of bananas, four hundred reis; but where a dozen limes cost only twenty reis—one cent. Much whaling gear lay strewn about the place, and on the beach was the carcass of a whale about nine days slain. Also leaning against a smart-looking boat was a gray-haired fisherman, boat and man relics of New Bedford, employed at this station in their familiar industry. The old man was bare-footed and thinly clad, after the custom in this climate. Still, I recognized the fisherman and sailor in the set and rig of the few duds he had on, and the ample straw hat (donkey's breakfast) that he wore, and doffed in a seaman-like manner, upon our first salute. *"Filio do Mar do Nord Americano,"* said an affable native close by, pointing at the same time to that "son of the sea of North America," by way of introduction, as soon as it was learned that we, too, were of that country. I tried to learn from this ancient mariner the cause of his being stranded in this strange land. He may have been cast up there by the whale for aught I could learn to the contrary.

Voyage of the "Liberdade"

Choosing a berth well to windward of the dead whale—the one that landed "the old man of the sea" there, maybe!—we anchored for the night, put a light in the rigging and turned in. Next morning, the village was astir betimes; canoes were being put afloat, and the rattle of poles, paddles, bait boxes, and many more things for the daily trip that were being hastily put into each canoe, echoed back from the tall palm groves notes of busy life, telling us that it was time to weigh anchor and be sailing. To this cheerful tune we lent ear and hastening to be underweigh, were soon clear of the port. Then, skimming along near the beach in the early morning, our sails spread to a land breeze, laden with fragrance from the tropic forest and the music of many songsters, we sailed in great felicity, dreading no dangers from the sea, for there were none now to dread or fear.

Proceeding forward through this belt of moderate winds, fanned by alternating land and sea-breezes, we drew on toward a region of high trade winds that reach sometimes the dignity of a gale. It was no surprise, therefore, after days of fine-weather sailing, to be met by a storm, which so happened as to drive us into the indifferent anchorage of St. Paulo, thirty miles from Bahia, where we remained two days for shelter.

Time, three days from Caravellas; distance sailed, 270 miles.

A few fishermen lounged about the place, living, apparently, in wretched poverty, spending their time between waiting for the tide to go out, when it was in, and waiting for it to come in when it was out, to float a canoe or bring fish to their shiftless nets. This, indeed, seemed their only concern in life; while their ill-thatched houses, forsaken of the adobe that once clung to the wicker walls, stood grinning in rows, like emblems of our mortality.

We found at this St. Paulo anything but saints. The wretched place should be avoided by strangers, unless driven there for shelter, as we ourselves were, by stress of weather. We left the place on the first lull of the wind, having been threatened by an attack from a gang of rough, half-drunken fellows, who rudely came on board, jostling about, and jabbering in a dialect which, however, I happened to understand. I got rid of them by the use of my broken Portuguese, and once away I was resolved that they should stay away. I was not mistaken in my suspicions that they would return and try to come aboard, which shortly afterward they did, but my resolution to keep them off was not shaken. I let them know, in their own jargon this time, that I was well armed. They finally paddled back to the shore, and all visiting was then ended. We stood a good watch that night, and by daylight next morning, Aug. 12th, put to sea, standing out in a heavy swell, the character of which I knew better, and could trust to more confidently than a harbor among treacherous natives.

Early in the same day, we arrived at *Bahia do todos Santos* (All Saints' Bay), a charming port, with a rich surrounding country. It was from this port, by the way, that Robinson Crusoe sailed for Africa to procure slaves for his plantation, and that of his friend, so fiction relates.

At Bahia we met many friends and gentle folk. Not the least interesting at this port are the negro lasses of fine physique seen at the markets and in the streets, with burdens on their heads of baskets of fruit, or jars of water, which they balance with ease and grace, as they go sweeping by with that stately mien which the dusky maiden can call her own.

Chapter XIII

At Bahia we refitted, with many necessary provisions, and repaired the keel, which was found upon hauling out, had been damaged by the encounter with the whale at Frio. An iron shoe was now added for the benefit of all marine monsters wishing to scratch their backs on our canoe.

Among the many friends whom we met at Bahia was Capt. Boyd and his family of the Barque *H. W. Palmer*. We shall meet the *Palmer* and the Boyds again on the voyage. They were old traders to South America and had many friends at this port who combined to make our visit a pleasant one. And their little son Rupert was greatly taken with the *"Riberdade,"* as he called her, coming often to see us. And the officials of the port taking great interest in our voyage, came often on board. No one could have treated us more kindly than they.

The venerable *Administradore* himself gave us special welcome to the port and a kind word upon our departure, accompanied by a present for my wife in the shape of a rare white flower, which we cherished greatly as coming from a true gentleman.

Some strong abolitionists at the port would have us dine in an epicurean way in commemoration of the name given our canoe, which was adopted because of her having been put afloat on the thirteenth day of May, the day on which every human being in Brazil could say, "I have no master but one." I declined the banquet tendered us, having work on hand, fortifying the canoe against the ravaging worms of the seas we were yet to sail through, bearing in mind the straits of my great predecessor from this as well as other causes on his voyage over the Caribbean Seas. I was bound to be strengthened against the enemy.

The gout, it will be remembered, seized upon the good Columbus while his ship had worms, then both ship and admiral lay stranded among menacing savages; surrounded, too, by a lawless, threatening band of his own countrymen not less treacherous than the worst of cannibals. His state was critical, indeed! One calamity was from over high living—this I was bound to guard against—the other was from neglect on the part of his people to care for the ship in a seaman-like manner. Of the latter difficulty I had no risk to run.

Lazy and lawless, but through the pretext of religion the infected crew wrought on the pious feelings of the good Admiral, inducing him at every landing to hold mass instead of cleaning the foul ship. Thus through petty intrigue and grave neglects, they brought disaster and sorrow on their leader and confusion on their own heads. Their religion, never deep, could not be expected to keep *Terredo* from the ship's bottom, so her timbers were ravished, and ruin came to them all! Poor Columbus! had he but sailed with his son Diego and his noble brother Bartholomew, for his only crew and companions, not forgetting the help of a good woman, America would have been discovered without those harrowing tales of woe and indeed heart-rending calamities which followed in the wake of his designing people. Nor would his ship have been less well manned than was the *Liberdade*, sailing, centuries after, over the same sea and among many of the islands visited by the great discoverer—sailing too, without serious accident of any kind, and without sickness or discontent. Our advantage over Columbus, I say, was very great, not more from the possession of data of the centuries which had passed than from having a willing crew sailing without dissent or murmur—sailing in the same boat, as it were.

A pensive mood comes over one voyaging among the scenes of the New World's early play-ground. To us while on this canoe voyage of pleasant recollection the fancied experience of navigators gone before was intensely thrilling.

Sailing among islands clothed in eternal green, the same that Columbus beheld with marvelous anticipations, and the venerable Las Casas had looked upon with pious wonder, brought us, in the mind's eye, near the old discoverers; and a feeling that we should come suddenly upon their ships around some near headland took deep hold upon our thoughts as we drew in with the shores. All was there to please the imagination and dream over in the same balmy, sleepy atmosphere, where Juan Ponce de Leon would fain have tarried young, but found death rapid, working side by side with ever springing life. To live long in this clime one must obey great Nature's laws. So stout Juan and millions since have found, and so always it will be.

All was there to testify as of yore, all except the first owners of the land; they alas! the poor Caribbees, together with their camp fires, had been extinguished long years before. And no one of human sympathy can read of the cruel tortures and final extermination of these islanders, savages though they were, without a pang of regret at the unpleasant page in a history of glory and civilization.

Chapter XIV

From Bahia to Pernambuco our course lay along that part of the Brazilian coast fanned by constant trade winds. Nothing unusual occurred to disturb our peace or daily course, and we pressed forward night and day, as was our wont from the first.

Victor and I stood watch and watch at sea, usually four hours each.

The most difficult of our experiences in fine weather was the intense drowsiness brought on by constantly watching the oscillating compass at night; even in the daytime this motion would make one sleepy.

We soon found it necessary to arrange a code of signals which would communicate between the "wheel" and the "man forward." This was done by means of a line or messenger extending from one to the other, which was understood by the number of pulls given by it: three pulls, for instance, meant "Turn out," one in response, "Aye, aye, I am awake, and what is it that is wanted?" one pull in return signified that it was "Eight bells," and so on. But three quick jerks meant "Tumble out and shorten sail."

Victor, it was understood, would tie the line to his arm or leg when he turned in, so that by pulling I would be sure to arouse him, or bring him somewhat unceremoniously out of his bunk. Once, however, the messenger failed to accomplish its purpose. A boot came out on the line in answer to my call, so easily, too, that I suspected a trick. It was evidently a preconceived plan by which to gain a moment more of sleep. It was a clear imposition on the man at the wheel!

We had also a sign in this system of telegraphing that told of flying-fish on board—manna of the sea—to be gathered up for the *cuisine* whenever they happened to alight or fall on deck, which was often, and as often they found a warm welcome.

The watch was never called to make sail. As for myself, I had never to be called, having thoughts of the voyage and its safe completion on my mind to keep me always on the alert. I can truly say that I never, on the voyage, slept so sound as to forget where I was, but whenever I fell into a dose at all it would be to dream of the boat and the voyage.

Press on! press on! was the watchword while at sea, but in port we enjoyed ourselves and gave up care for rest and pleasure, carrying a supply, as it were, to sea with us, where sail was again carried on.

Though a mast should break, it would be no matter of serious concern, for we would be at no loss to mend and rig up spars for this craft at short notice, most anywhere.

The third day out from Bahia was set fine weather. A few flying-fish made fruitless attempts to rise from the surface of the sea, attracting but little attention from the sea-gulls which sat looking wistfully across the unbroken deep with folded wings.

And the *Liberdade* doing her utmost to get along through the common quiet, made but little progress on her way. A dainty fish played in her light wake, till temped by an evil appetite for flies, it landed in the cockpit upon a hook, thence into the pan, where many a one had brought up before. Breakfast was cleared away at an early hour; then day of good things happened—"the meeting of the ships."

> "When o'er the silent sea alone
>   For days and nights we've cheerless gone,
> Oh they who've felt it know how sweet,
>   Some sunny morn a sail to meet.
>
> "Sparkling at once is every eye,
>   'Ship ahoy! ship ahoy!' our joyful cry
> While answering back the sound we hear,
>   'Ship ahoy! ship ahoy! what cheer, what cheer.'
>
> "Then sails are backed, we nearer come,
>   Kind words are said of friends and home,
> And soon, too soon, we part with pain,
>   To sail o'er silent seas again."

On the clear horizon could be seen a ship, which proved to be our staunch old friend, the *Finance,* on her way out to Brazil, heading nearly for us. Our course was at once changed, so as to cross her bows. She rose rapidly, hull up, showing her lines of unmistakable beauty, the stars and stripes waving over all. They on board the great ship, soon discried our little boat, and gave sign by a deep whistle that came rumbling over the sea, telling us that we were recognized. A few moments later and the engines stopped. Then came the hearty hail, "Do you want assistance?" Our answer "No" brought cheer on cheer from the steamer's deck, while the *Liberdade* bowed and courtesied to her old acquaintance, the superior ship. Captain Baker, meanwhile, not forgetting a sailor's most highly prized luxury, had ordered in the slings a barrel of potatoes—new from home! Then dump they came, in a jiffy, into the canoe, giving her a settle in the water of some inches. This was a valuable addition to our stores. Some other fresh provisions were handed us, also some books and late papers.

In return for all of these goods we gave sincere thanks, about the only thing we could spare—above the shadow of the canoe—which was secured through a camera by the Rev. Doctor Hodge, the worthy missionary, then on his way to a field of labor in Brazil.

One gentleman passed us a bottle of wine, on the label of which was written the name of an old acquaintance, a merchant of Rio. We pledged Mr. Gudgeon and all his fellow passengers in that wine, and had some left long after, to the health of the captain of the ship, and his crew. There was but little time for words, so the compliments passed were brief. The ample plates in the sides of the Finance, inspiring confidence in American thoroughness and build, we had hardly time to scan, when her shrill whistle said "good-bye," and moving proudly on, the great ship was soon out of sight, while the little boat filling away on the starboard tack, sailed on toward home, perfumed with the interchange of a friendly greeting, tinged though, with a palpable lonesomeness. Two days after this pleasant meeting, the Port of Pernambuco was reached.

Tumbling in before a fresh "trade" wind that in the evening had sprung up, accompanied with long, rolling seas, our canoe came nicely round the point between lighted reef and painted buoy.

Spray from the breakers on the reef opportunely wetting her sails gave them a flat surface to the wind as we came close haul.

The channel leading up the harbor was not strange to us, so we sailed confidently along the lee of the wonderful wall made by worms, to which alone Pernambuco is indebted for its excellent harbor; which extending also along a great stretch of the coast, protects Brazil from the encroachment of the sea.

At 8 P.M., we came to in a snug berth near the *Alfandega*, and early next morning received the official visit from the polite port officers.

Time from Bahia, seven days; distance sailed, 390 miles.

Pernambuco, the principal town of a large and wealthy province of the same name, is a thriving place, sending out valuable cargoes, principally of sugar and cotton. I had loaded costly cargoes here, times gone by. I met my old merchant again this time, but could not carry his goods on the *Liberdade*. However, fruits from his orchards and a run among the trees refreshed my crew, and prepared them for the coming voyage to Barbadoes, which was made with expedition.

Voyage of the "Liberdade"

From Pernambuco we experienced a strong current in our favor, with, sometimes, a confused cross sea that washed over us considerably. But the swift current sweeping along through it all made compensation for discomforts of motion, though our "ups and downs" were many. Along this part of the coast (from Pernambuco to the Amazon,) if one day should be fine, three stormy ones would follow, but the gale was always fair, carrying us forward at a goodly rate.

Along about half way from Cape St. Roque to the Amazon, the wind which had been blowing hard for two days, from E. S. E., and raising lively waves all about, increased to a gale that knocked up seas, washing over the little craft more than ever. The thing was becoming monotonous and tiresome; for a change, therefore, I ran in toward the land, so as to avoid the ugly cross sea farther out in the current. This course was a mistaken one; we had not sailed far on it when a sudden rise of the canoe, followed by an unusually long run down on the slope of a roller, told us of a danger that we hardly dared to think of, then a mighty comber broke, but, as Providence willed, broke short of the canoe, which under shortened sail was then scudding very fast.

We were on a shoal, and the sea was breaking from the bottom! The second great roller came on, towering up, up, up, until nothing longer could support the mountain of water, and it seemed only to pause before its fall to take aim and surely gather us up in its sweeping fury.

I put the helm a-lee; there was nothing else to do but this, and say prayers. The helm hard down, brought the canoe round, bows to the danger, while in breathless anxiety we prepared to meet the result as best we could. Before we could say "Save us, or we perish," the sea broke over with terrific force and passed on, leaving us trembling in His hand, more palpably helpless than ever before. Other great waves came madly on, leaping toward destruction; how they bellowed over the shoal! I could smell the slimy bottom of the sea, when they broke! I could taste the salty sand!

In this perilous situation, buried sometimes in the foam of breakers, and at times tossed like a reed on the crest of the waves, we struggled with might and main at the helm and the sheets, easing her up or forcing her ahead with care, gaining little by little toward deep water, till at last she came out of the danger, shook her feathers

102

like a sea bird, and rode on waves less perilous. Then we had time and courage to look back, but not till then.

And what a sight we beheld! The horizon was illumined with phosphorescent light from the breakers just passed through. The rainstorm which had obscured the coast was so cleared away now that we could see the whole field of danger behind us. One spot in particular, the place where the breakers dashed over a rock which appeared awash, in the glare flashed up a shaft of light that reached to the heavens.

This was the greatest danger we had yet encountered. The elasticity of our canoe, not its bulk, saved it from destruction. Her light, springy timbers and buoyant bamboo guards brought her upright again and again through the fierce breakers. We were astonished at the feats of wonder of our brave little craft.

Fatigued and worn with anxiety, when clear of the shoal we hauled to under close reefs, heading off shore, and all hands lay down to rest till daylight. Then, squaring away again, we set what sail the canoe could carry, scudding before it, for the wind was still in our favor, though blowing very hard. Nevertheless the weather seemed fine and pleasant at this stage of our own pleased feelings. Any weather that one's craft can live in, after escaping a lee shore, is pleasant weather—though some may be pleasanter than other.

What we most wished for, after this thrilling experience, was sea room, fair wind, and plenty of it. That these without stint would suit us best, was agreed on all hands. Accordingly then I shaped the course seaward, clearing well all the dangers of the land.

The fierce tropical storm of the last few days turned gradually into mild trade winds, and our cedar canoe skipped nimbly once more over tranquil seas. Our own agitation, too, had gone down and we sailed on unruffled by care. Gentle winds carried us on over kindly waves, and we were fain to count fair days ahead, leaving all thoughts of stormy ones behind. In this hopeful mood we sailed for many days, our spirits never lowering, but often rising higher out of the miserable condition which we had fallen into through misfortunes on the foreign shore. When a star came out, it came as a friend, and one that had been seen by friends of old. When all the stars shone out, the hour at sea was cheerful, bright, and joyous. Welby saw, or had in the mind's-eye, a day like many that we experienced in the soft, clear "trades" on this voyage, when writing the pretty lines:—

> "The twilight hours like birds flew by,
> As lightly and as free,
> Ten thousand stars were in the sky,
> Ten thousand on the sea.

> "For every rippling, dancing wave,
> That leaped upon the air,
> Had caught a star in its embrace,
> And held it trembling there."

"The days pass, and our ship flies fast upon her way."

For several days while sailing near the line we saw the constellations of both hemispheres, but heading north, we left those of the south at last, with the Southern Cross—most beautiful in all the heavens—to watch over a friend.

Leaving these familiar southern stars and sailing towards constellations in the north, we hoist all sail to the cheery breeze that carried us on.

In this pleasant state of sailing with our friends all about us, we stood on and on, never doubting once our pilot or our ship.

A phantom of the stately *Aquidneck* appeared one night, sweeping by with crowning skysails set, that fairly brushed the stars. No apparition could have affected us more than the sight of this floating beauty, so like the *Aquidneck,* gliding swiftly and quietly by, from her mission to some foreign land—she, too, was homeward bound!

This incident of the *Aquidneck's* ghost, as it appeared to us, passing at midnight on the sea, left a pang of lonesomeness for a while.

But a carrier dove came next day, and perched upon the mast, as if to tell that we had yet a friend! Welcome harbinger of good! you bring us thoughts of angels.

The lovely visitor remained with us two days, off and on, but left for good on the third, when we reached away from Avis Island, to which, maybe, it was bound. Coming as it did from the east, and flying west toward the island when it left, bore out the idea of the lay of sweet singer Kingsley's "Last Buccaneer."

> "If I might but be a sea dove, I'd fly across the main
> To the pleasant Isle of Avis, to look at it once again."

Voyage of the "Liberdade"

The old Buccaneer, it may have been, but we regarded it as the little bird, which most likely it was, that sits up aloft to look out for poor "Jack." *

A moth blown to our boat on the ocean, found shelter and a welcome there. The dove! we secretly worshipped.

With utmost confidence in our little craft, inspired by many thrilling events, we now carried sail, blow high, blow low, till at times she reeled along with a bone in her mouth quite to the mind of her mariners. Thinking one day that she might carry more sail on the mast already bending hopefully forward, and acting upon the liberal thought of sail we made a wide mistake, for the mainmast went by the board, under the extra press and the foremast tripped over the bows. Then spars, booms and sail swung alongside like the broken wings of a bird but were grappled, however, and brought aboard without much loss of time. The broken mast was then secured and strengthened by "fishes" or splints after the manner in which doctors fish a broken limb.

Both of the masts were very soon refitted and again made to carry sail, all they could stand; and we were again bowling along as before. We made that day a hundred and seventy-five miles, one of our best days' work.

I protest here that my wife should not have cried "More sail! more sail!" when, as it has been seen the canoe had on all the sail that she could carry. Nothing further happened to change the usual daily events until we reached Barbadoes. Flying-fish on the wing striking our sails, at night, often fell on deck, affording us many a toothsome fry. This happened daily, while sailing throughout the trade-wind regions. To be hit by one of these fish on the wing, which sometimes occurs, is no light matter, especially if the blow be on the face, as it may cause a bad bruise or even a black eye. The head of the flying-fish being rather hard makes it in fact a night slugger to be dreaded. They never come aboard in the daylight. The swift darting bill-fish, too, is a danger to be avoided in the tropics at night. They are met with mostly in the Pacific Ocean. And the South Sea Islanders are loath to voyage during the "bill-fish season."

As to the flight of these fishes, I would estimate that of the flying-

* "There's a sweet little cherub that sits up aloft,
    To look out for a berth for poor Jack."—*Dibdin's Poems.*

fish as not exceeding fifteen feet in height, or five hundred yards of distance, often not half so much.

Bill-fish darting like an arrow from a bow, has, fortunately for sailors, not the power or do not rise much above the level of the waves, and can not dart further, say, than two hundred and fifty feet, according to the day for jumping. Of the many swift fish in the sea, the dolphin perhaps, is the most marvelous. Its oft told beauty, too, is indeed remarkable. A few of these fleet racers were captured, on the voyage, but were found tough and rank; notwithstanding some eulogy on them by other epicures, we threw the mess away. Those hooked by my crew were perhaps the tyrrhena pirates "turned into dolphins" in the days of yore.

On the 19th day from Pernambuco, early in the morning, we made Barbadoes away in the West. First, the blue, fertile hills, then green fields came into view, studded with many white buildings between sentries of giant wind-mills as old nearly, as the hills. Barbadoes is the most pleasant island in the Antilles; to sail round its green fringe of coral sea is simply charming. We stood in to the coast, well to windward, sailing close in with the breakers so as to take in a view of the whole delightful panorama as we sailed along. By noon we rounded the south point of the island and shot into Carlysle Bay, completing the run from Pernambuco exactly in nineteen days. This was considerably more than an hundred miles a day. The true distance being augmented by the circuitous route we adopted made it 2,150 miles.

Chapter XV

Many old friends and acquaintances came down to see us upon our arrival at Barbadoes, all curious to inspect the strange craft. While there our old friend, the *Palmer,* that we left at Bahia, came in to refit, having broken a mast "trying to beat us," so Garfield would have it. For all that we had beaten her time four days. Who then shall say that we anchored nights or spent much time hugging the shore? The *Condor* was also at Barbadoes in charge of an old friend, accompanied by a pleasant helpmeet and companion who had shared the perils of shipwreck with her husband the year before in a hurricane among the islands.

Meeting so many of this class of old friends of vast and varied experiences, gave contentment to our visit and we concluded to remain over at this port till the hurricane season should pass. Our old friend, the *Finance* too, came in, remaining but a few hours, however, she hurried away with her mails, homeward bound.

The pleasant days at Barbadoes with its enchantment flew lightly by; and on the 7th of October we sailed, giving the hurricane the benefit of eight days. The season is considered over on the 15th of that month.

Passing thence through the Antilles into the Caribbean Sea, a new period of our voyage was begun. Fair breezes filled the sails of the *Liberdade* as we glided along over tranquil seas, scanning eagerly the islands as they came into view, dwelling on each, in our thoughts, as hallowed ground of the illustrious discoverers—the same now as seen by them! The birds, too, of "rare plumage," were there, flying from island to island, the same as seen by the discoverers; and the sea with fishes teemed, of every gorgeous hue, lending enchantment to the picture, not less beautiful than the splendor on the land and in the air to thrill the voyager now, the same as then; we ourselves had only to look to see them.

Whether it was birds with fins or fishes with wings, or neither of these that the old voyagers saw, they discovered yet enough to make them wonder and rejoice.

"Mountains of sugar, and rivers of rum and flying-fish, is what I have seen, mother," said the son on his return home from a voyage to these islands. "John," said the enraptured mother, "you must be mistaken about the fish; now don't lie to me, John. Mountains of sugar, no doubt you saw, and even rivers of rum, my boy, but *flying-fish* could never be."

And yet the *fish* were there.

Among the islands of great interest which came in view, stretching along the Caribbean Sea, was that of Santa Cruz, the island famous for its brave, resolute women of days gone by, who, while their husbands were away, successfully defended home and happiness against Christian invaders, and for that reason were called fierce savages. I would fain have brought away some of the earth

107

of the island in memory of those brave women. Small as our ship was, we could have afforded room in it for a memento thus consecrated; but the trades hauling somewhat to the northward so headed us off that we had to forgo the pleasure of landing on its shores.

Pushing forward thence, we reached Porto Rico, the nearest land in our course from the island of Brave Women, standing well in with the southeast capes. Sailing thence along the whole extent of the south coast, in waters as smooth as any mill pond, and past island scenery worth the perils of ten voyages to see, we landed, on the 12th of October, at Mayaguez in the west of the island, and there shook the kinks out of our bones by pleasant walks in tropic shades.

Time, five days from Barbadoes; distance 570 miles.

This was to be our last run among the trees in the West Indies, and we made the most of it. "Such a port for mariners I'll never see again!" The port officials, kind and polite, extended all becoming courtesies to the quaint *"barco piquina."*

The American Consul, Mr. Christie, Danish Consul, Mr. Falby, and the good French Consul, vied in making our visit a pleasant one.

Photographers at Mayaguez desiring a picture of the canoe with the crew on deck at a time when we felt inclined to rest in the shade on shore, put a negro on board to take the place of captain. The photographs taken then found their way to Paris and Madrid journals where, along with some flattering accounts, they were published, upon which it was remarked that the captain was a fine-looking fellow, but "awfully tanned!" The moke was rigged all ataunto for the occasion, and made a picture indicative of great physical strength, one not to be ashamed of, but he would have looked more like me, I must say, if they had turned him back to.

We enjoyed long carriage drives over rich estates at Mayaguez. We saw with pain, however, that the atmosphere of the soldier hung over all, pervading the whole air like a pestilence.

Musketed and sabred, and uniformed in their bed-ticking suits; hated by the residents and despised by themselves, they doggedly marched, counter-marched and wheeled, knowing that they are loathsome in the island, and that their days in the New World are numbered. The sons of the colonies are too civil and Christianlike to be ruled always by sword and gun.

Voyage of the "Liberdade"

On the 15th of October, after three days' rest, we took in, as usual before sailing from ports, sufficient fresh supplies to carry us to the port steered for next, then set sail from pleasant Mayaguez, and bore away for the old Bahama Channel, passing east of Hayti, thence along the north coast to the west extremity of the island, from which we took departure for the headlands of Cuba, and followed that coast as far as Cardinas, where we took a final departure from the islands, regretting that we could not sail around them all.

The region on the north side of Cuba is often visited by gales of great violence, making this the lee shore; a weather eye was therefore kept lifting, especially in the direction of their source, which is from north to nor'west. However storms prevailed from other quarters, mostly from the east, bringing heavy squalls of wind, rain and thunder every afternoon, such as once heard will never be forgotten. Peal on peal of nature's artillery for a few hours, accompanied by vivid lightning, was on the cards for each day, then all would be serene again.

The nights following these severe storms were always bright and pleasant, and the heavens would be studded with constellations of familiar, guiding stars.

My crew had now no wish to bear up for port short of one on our own coast, but, impatient to see the North Star appear higher in the heavens, strung every nerve and trimmed every sail to hasten on.

Nassau, the place to which letters had been directed to us we forbore to visit. This departure from a programme which was made at the beginning was the only change that we made in the "charter party" throughout the voyage. There was no hap-hazard sailing on this voyage. Daily observations for determining latitude and longitude were invariably made unless the sun was obscured. The result of these astronomical observations were more reliable than one might suppose, from their being taken on a tittlish canoe. After a few days' practising, a very fair off-hand contact could be made, when the canoe rose on the crest of a wave, where manifestly would be found the best result. The observer's station was simply on the top of the cabin, where astride, like riding horseback, Victor and I took the "sights," and indeed became expert "snap observers" before the voyage ended.

One night in the Bahama Channel, while booming along toward the Banks to the nor'west of us before stiff trades, I was called in the first watch by Victor, to come up quickly, for signs of the dread "norther" were in the sky. Our trusty barometer had been low, but was now on the cheerful side of change. This phenomenon disturbed me somewhat, till the discovery was made, as we came nearer, that it was but the reflection of the white banks on the sky that we saw, and no cause at all for alarm.

Soon after this phenomenon the faint glimmer of Labos Light was descried flickering on the horizon, two points on the weather bow. I changed the course three points to windward, having determined to touch at the small Cay where the lighthouse stands; one point being allowed for leeway, which I found was not too much.

Three hours later we fetched in under the lee of the reef, or Cay, as it is commonly called, and came to in one and a half fathoms of water in good shelter.

We beheld then overhead in wonderful beauty what had awed us from the distance in the early night—a chart of the illuminating banks marked visibly on the heavens.

We furled sails and, setting a light in the rigging, turned in; for it lacked three hours yet of daylight. And what an interesting experience ours had been in the one short night! By the break of day my crew were again astir, preparing to land and fill water at a good landing which we now perceived farther around the point to leeward, where the surf was moderate.

On the Cay is stored some hundred thousand gallons of rain water in cisterns at the base of the iron tower which carries the light; one that we saw from the canoe at a distance of fourteen miles.

The keeper of the light, a hardy native of Nassau, when he discovered the new arrival at his "island," hoisted the British Board of Trade flag on a pole in the centre of this, his little world, then he came forward to speak us, thinking at first, he said, that we were shipwrecked sailors, which indeed we were, but not in distress, as he had supposed when hoisting the flag, which signified assistance for distressed seamen. On learning our story, however, he regarded us with grave suspicions, and refused water to Victor, who had already landed with buckets, telling him that the captain would have to bring his papers ashore and report. The mate's report would not be taken. Thus in a moment was transformed the friend in need to *governor of an island*. This amused me greatly, and I sent back word to my veritable Sancho Panza that in my many voyages to islands my mate had attended to the customs reports; at which his Excellency chafed considerably, giving the gunnels of his trousers a fitful tug up now and then as he paced the beach, waiting my compliance with the rules of the island. The governor, I perceived, was suspicious of smugglers and wreckers, apparently understanding their ways, if, indeed, even he were not a reformed pirate himself.

However, to humor the punctiliousness of his Excellency, now that he was governor of an island, I placed my papers in my hat, and, leaping into the surf, waded ashore, where I was received as by a monarch.

The document I presented was the original *Passe Especial*, the one with the big seal on it, written in Portuguese; had it been in Choctaw the governor would have read it with the same facility that he did this, which he stared at knowingly and said, "all right, take all the water you want; it is free."

I lodged a careful report of the voyage with the governor and explained to his Excellency the whereabouts of the "Island of Rio," as his grace persistently called Rio de Janeiro, whence dated my papers.

Conversing on the subject of islands, which was all the world to him, the governor viewed with suspicion the absence of a word in my documents, referring even to an islet; this, in his mind, was a reprehensible omission; for surely New York to which the papers referred was built on an island. Upon this I offered to swear to the truth of my clearance, "as far as known to me," after the manner of cheap custom-house swearing with which shipmasters, in some parts of the world, are made familiar. "Not on the island!" quickly exclaimed the governor, " 'for thou shalt not disglorify God's name,' is written in the Bible."

I assured the governor of my appreciation of his pious sentiment of not over-swearing, which the Chinese adopt as a policy—laudable however, and one that I would speak of on my return home, to the end that we all emulate the laws of the island; whereupon the governor, greatly pleased, urged me to take some more water, minding me again that it was free.

In a very few minutes I got all the water I wished for; also some aurora shells from the governor's lady, who had arisen with the sun to grace the day and of all things most appropriate held in her generous lap beautiful aurora shells for which—to spoil the poem—I bartered cocoanuts and rusty gnarly yams.

The lady was on a visit only to her lord and master, the monarch of all he surveyed. Beside this was their three children also on a visit, from Nassau, and two assistant keepers of the light which made up the total of this little world in the ocean.

It was the smallest kingdom I had ever visited, peopled by happy human beings and the most isolated by far.

The few blades of grass which had struggled into existence, not enough to support a goat, was all there was to look at on the island except the lighthouse, and the sand and themselves.

Some small buildings and a flagstaff had once adorned the place, but together with a coop of chickens, the only stock of the islanders— except a dog—had been swept away by a hurricane which had passed over the island a short time before. The water for which we had called being now in the canoe, and my people on board waiting for me, I bade the worthy governor good-bye, and, saluting his charming island queen in a seamanlike manner, hastened back to my own little world; and bore away once more for the north. Sailing thence over the Great Bahama Banks, in a crystal sea, we observed on the white marl bottom many curious living things, among them the conch in its house of exquisite tints and polished surface, the star-fish with radiated dome of curious construction, and many more denizens of the place, the names of which I could not tell, resting on the soft white bed under the sea.

"They who go down to the sea in ships, they see the wonders of the Lord," I am reminded by a friend who writes me, on receipt of some of these curious things which I secured on the voyage, adding: "For all these curious and beautiful things are His handiwork. Who can look at such things without the heart being lifted up in adoration?"

For words like these what sailor is there who would not search the caves of the ocean? Words too, from a lady.

Two days of brisk sailing over the white Bahama Banks brought us to Bimini. Thence a mere push would send us to the coast of our own native America. The wind in the meantime hauling from regular nor'east trade to the sou'west, as we came up to Bimini, promising a smooth passage across, we launched out at once on the great Gulf Stream, and were swept along by its restless motion, making on the first day, before the wind and current, two hundred and twenty miles. This was great getting along for a small canoe. Going at the same high rate of speed on the second night in the stream, the canoe struck a spar and went over it with a bound. Her keel was shattered by the shock, but finally shaking the crippled timber clear of herself she came on quite well without it. No other damage was done to our craft, although at times her very ribs were threatened before clearing this lively ocean river. In the middle of the current, where the seas were yet mountainous but regular, we went along with a wide, swinging motion and fared well enough; but on nearing the edge of the stream a confused sea was met with, standing all on end, in every which way, beyond a sailor's comprehension. The motion of the *Liberdade* was then far from poetical or pleasant. The wind, in the meantime, had chopped round to the nor'east, dead ahead; being thus against the current, a higher and more confused sea than ever was heaped up, giving us some uneasiness. We had, indeed, several unwelcome visitors come tumbling aboard of our craft, one of which furiously crashing down on her made all of her timbers bend and creak. However, I could partially remedy this danger by changing the course.

"Seas like that can't break this boat," said our young boatswain; "she's built strong." It was well to find among the crew this feeling of assurance in the gallant little vessel. I, too, was confident in her seaworthiness. Nevertheless, I shortened sail and brought her to the wind, watching the lulls and easing her over the combers, as well as I could. But wrathful Neptune was not to let us so easily off, for the next moment a sea swept clean over the helmsman, wetting him through to the skin and, most unkind cut of all, it put out our fire, and capsized the hash and stove into the bottom of the canoe. This left us with but a *damper* for breakfast! Matters mended, however, as the day advanced, and for supper we had a grand and glorious feast. Early in the afternoon we made the land and got into smooth water. This of itself was a feast, to our minds.

The land we now saw lying before us was hills of America, which we had sailed many thousands of miles to see. Drawing in with the coast, we made out, first the broad, rich forests, then open fields and villages, with many signs of comfort on every hand. We found it was the land about Bull's Bay on the coast of South Carolina, and night coming on, we could plainly see Cape Roman Light to the north of us. The wind falling light as we drew in with the coast, and finding a current against us, we anchored, about two miles from the shore, in four fathoms of water. It was now 8 P.M., October 28, 1888, thirteen days from Mayaguez, twenty-one days from Barbadoes, etc.

The following was the actual time at sea and distances in nautical miles from point to point on the courses steered, approximately:

	Days.	Distance.
From Paranagua to Santos - - - -	1	150
" Santos to Rio de Janeiro (towed by *Finance*) - - -	¾	200
" Rio to Cape Frio - - - - -	2	70
" Cape Frio to Carvellas - - -	4	370
" Carvellas to Saint Paulo - - -	3	270
" Saint Paulo to Bahia - - - -	½	40
" Bahia to Pernambuco - - - -	7	390
" Pernambuco to Barbadoes - - -	19	2,150
" Barbadoes to Mayaguez - - -	5	570
" Mayaguez to Cape Roman - -	13	1,300
	55¼	5,510

Computing all the distances of the ins and outs that we made would considerably augment the sum. To say, therefore, that the *Liberdade* averaged roundly a hundred miles a day for fifty-five days would be considerably inside the truth.

This was the voyage made in the boat which cost less than a hundred dollars outside of our own labor of building. Journals the world over have spoken not unkindly of the feat; encomiums in seven languages reached us through the newspapers while we lay moored in Washington. Should the same good fortune that followed the *Liberdade* attend this little literary craft, when finished, it would go safe into many lands. Without looking, however, to this mark of good fortune, the journal of the voyage has been as carefully constructed as was the *Liberdade*, and I trust, as conscientiously, by a hand, alas! that has grasped the sextant more often than the plane or pen, and for the love of doing. This apology might have been more appropriately made in the beginning of the journal, maybe, but it comes to me now, and like many other things done, right or wrong, but done on the impulse of the moment, I put it down.

Chapter XVI

No one will be more surprised at the complete success of the voyage and the speedy progress made than were we ourselves who made it, with incidents and events among which is the most prominent of a life at sea.

A factor of the voyage, one that helped us forward greatly, and which is worthy of special mention, was the ocean current spoken of as we came along in its friendly sway.

Many are the theories among fresh water philosophists respecting these currents, but in practical sailing, where the subject is met with in its tangible form, one cause only is recognized; namely, the action of the wind on the surface of the water, pushing the waves along. Out on the broad ocean the effect at first is hardly perceptible, but the constant trades sending countless millions of waves in one direction, cause at last a mighty moving power, which the mariner meets sometimes as an enemy to retard and delay, sometimes as a friend, as in our case, to help him on his way. These are views from a practical experience with no theory to prove.

By daylight on the twenty-ninth, we weighed anchor and set sail again for the north. The wind and current was still adverse but we kept near the land making short boards off and on through the day where the current had least effect. And when night came on again came to once more close in with Cape Roman light. Next day we worked up under the lee of the Roman shoals and made harbor in South Santee, a small river to the north of Cape Roman, within range of the light, there to rest until the wind should change, it being still ahead.

Next morning, since the wind had not changed, we weighed anchor and stood farther into the river looking for inhabitants, that we might listen to voices other than our own. Our search was soon rewarded, for, coming around a point of woodland, a farmhouse stood before us on the river side. We came alongside the bank and jumped ashore, but had hardly landed when, as out of the earth a thousand dogs so it seemed, sprung up threatening to devour us all. However, a comely woman came out of the house and it was explained to the satisfaction of all, especially to a persistent cur, by a vigorous whack on the head with a cudgel, that our visit was a friendly one; then all was again peaceful and quiet. The good man was in the field close by, but soon came home accompanied by his two stalwart sons each "toting" a sack of corn. We found the Andersons—this was the family name—isolated in every sense of the word, and as primitive as heart could wish. The charming simplicity of these good people captivated my crew. We met others along the coast innocent of greed, but of all unselfish men, Anderson the elder was surely the prince.

In purchasing some truck from this good man, we found that change could not be made for the dollar which I tendered in payment. But I protested that I was more than content to let the few odd cents go, having received more garden stuff than I had ever seen offered for a dollar in any part of the world. And indeed I was satisfied. The farmer, however, nothing content, offered me a coon skin or two, but these I didn't want, and there being no other small change about the farm, the matter was dropped, I thought, for good, and I had quite forgotten it, when later in the evening I was electrified by his offering to carry a letter for us which we wished posted, some seven miles away, and call it "square," against the twenty cents of the morning's transaction. The letter went, and in due course of time we got an answer.

I do not say that we stuck strictly to the twenty-cent transaction, but I fear that not enough was paid to fair-dealing Anderson. However all were at last satisfied and warming into conversation, a log fire was improvised and social chat went round.

These good people could hardly understand how it was, as I explained, that the Brazilians had freed the slaves and had no war, Mr. Anderson often exclaiming, "Well, well, I d'clar. Freed the niggers, and had no wah. Mister," said he, turning to me after a long pause, "mister, d'ye know the South were foolish? They had a wah, and they had to free the niggers, too."

"Oh, yes, mister, I was thar! Over thar beyond them oaks was my house."

"Yes, mister, I fought, too, and fought hard, but it warn't no use."

Like many a hard fighter, Anderson, too, was a pious man, living in a state of resignation to be envied. His years of experience on the new island farm had been hard and trying in the extreme. My own misfortunes passed into shade as the harder luck of the Andersons came before my mind, and the resolution which I had made to buy a farm was now shaken and finally dissolved into doubts of the wisdom of such a course. On this farm they had first "started in to raise pork," but found that it "didn't pay, for the pigs got wild and had to be gathered with the dogs," and by the time they were "gathered and then toted, salt would hardly cure them, and they most generally tainted." The enterprise was therefore abandoned, for that of tilling the soil, and a crop was put in, but "the few pigs which the dogs had not gathered came in at night and rooted out all the taters." It then appeared that a fence should be built. "Accordingly," said he, "I and the boys made one which kept out the stock, but, sir, the rats could get in! They took every tater out of the ground! From all that I put in, and my principal work was thar, I didn't see a sprout." How it happened that the rats had left the crop the year before for their relations—the pigs—was what seemed most to bother the farmer's mind. Nevertheless, "there was corn in Egypt yet;" and at the family circle about the board that night a smile of hope played on the good farmer's face, as in deep sincerity he asked that for what they had they might be made truly thankful. We learned a lesson of patience from this family, and were glad that the wind had carried us thither.

Said the farmer, "And you came all the way from Brazil in that boat! Wife, she won't go to Georgetown in the batto that I built because it rares too much. And they freed the niggers and had no wah! Well, well, I d'clar!"

Better folks we may never see than the farmers of South Santee. Bidding them good-bye next morning at early dawn we sailed before a light land wind which, however, soon petered out.

The S. S. *Planter* then coming along took us in tow for Georgetown, where she was bound. We had not the pleasure, however, of visiting the beloved old city; for having some half dozen cocoanuts on board, the remainder of small stores of the voyage, a vigilant

117

officer stopped us at the quarantine ground. Fruit not being admitted into South Carolina until after the first of November, and although it was now late in the afternoon of the first, we had to ride
quarantine that night, with a promise, however, of *pratique* next
morning. But there was no steamer going up the river the next day.
The *Planter* coming down though supplied us with some small provisions, such as not procurable at the Santee farm. Then putting to
sea we beat along slowly against wind and current.

We began now to experience, as might be expected, autumn gales
of considerable violence, the heaviest of which overtaking us at
Frying-pan Shoal, drove us back to leeward of Cape Fear for shelter.
South Port and Wilmington being then so near we determined to
visit both places. Two weeks at these ports refreshed the crew and
made all hands willing for sea again.

Sailing thence through Corn-cake Inlet we cut off Cape Fear and
the Frying-pan Shoals, being of mind to make for the inlets along
the Carolina coast and to get into the inland waters as soon as practicable.

It was our good fortune to fall in with an old and able pilot at
Corn-cake Inlet, one Capt. Bloodgood, who led the way through
the channel in his schooner, the *Packet*, a Carolina pitch and cotton droger of forty tons register, which was manned solely by the
captain and his two sons, one twelve and the other ten years old.
It was in the crew that I became most interested, and not the
schooner. Bloodgood gave the order when the tide served for us to
put to sea. "Come, children," said he, "let's try it." Then we all tried
it together, the *Packet* leading the way. The shaky west wind that
filled our sails as we skimmed along the beach with the breakers
close aboard, carried us but a few leagues when it flew suddenly
round to nor' east and began to pipe.

The gale increasing rapidly inclined me to bear up for New River
Inlet, then close under our lee; with a treacherous bar lying in
front, which to cross safely, would require great care.

But the gale was threatening, and the harbor inside, we could see,
was smooth, then, too, cried my people: "Any port in a storm." I
decided prompt: put the helm up and squared away. Flying thence,
before it, the tempest-tossed canoe came sweeping in from sea over
the rollers in a delightfully thrilling way. One breaker only coming
over us, and even that did no harm more than to give us all the

climax soaking of the voyage. This was the last sea that broke over the canoe on the memorable voyage.

The harbor inside the bar of New River was good. Adding much to our comfort too, was fish and game in abundance.

The *Packet*, which had parted from us made her destined port some three leagues farther on. The last we saw of the children, they were at the main sheets hauling aft, and their father was at the helm, and all were flying through the mist like fearless sailors.

After meeting Carolina seamen, to say nothing of the few still in existence further north, I challenge the story of Greek supremacy.

The little town of South Port was made up almost entirely of pilots possessing, I am sure, every quality of the sailor and the gentleman.

Moored snug in the inlet, it was pleasant to listen to the roar of the breakers on the bar, but not so cheerful was the thought of facing the high waves seaward, therefore the plan suggested itself of sufficiently deepening a ditch that led through the marshes from New River to Bogue Sound; to let us through, thence we could sail inland the rest of the voyage without obstruction or hindrance of any kind. To this end we set about contrivances to heave the canoe over the shoals, and borrowed a shovel from a friendly schooner captain to deepen the ditch which we thought would be necessary to do in order to ford her along that way. However, the prevailing nor'east gales had so raised the water in the west end of the sound as to fill all the creeks and ditches to overflowing. I hesitated then no longer but heading for the ditch through the marshes on a high tide, before a brave west wind took the chances of getting through by hook or by crook or by shovel and spade if required.

The "Coast Pilot," in speaking of this place, says there is never more than a foot of water there, and even that much is rarely found. The *Liberdade* essayed the ditch, drawing two feet and four inches, thus showing the further good fortune or luck which followed perseverance, as it usually does, though sometimes, maybe, it is bad luck! Perhaps I am not lucid on this, which at best must remain a disputed point.

I was getting lost in the maze of sloughs and creeks, which as soon as I entered seemed to lead in every direction but the right one. Hailing a hunter near by, however, I was soon put straight and reassured of success. The most astonished man, though, in North

Carolina, was this same hunter when asked if he knew the ditch that led through where I wished to go.

"Why, stranger," said he, "my gran'ther digged that ditch."

I jumped, I leaped! at thought of what a pilot this man would be.

"Well, stranger," said he, in reply to my query, "stranger, if any man kin take y' thro' that ditch, why, I kin;" adding doubtfully, however, "I have not hearn tell befo' of a vessel from Brazil sailing through these parts; but then you mout get through, and again ye moutent. Well, it's jist here; you mout and you moutent."

A bargain was quickly made, and my pilot came aboard, armed with a long gun, which as we sailed along proved a terror to ducks. The entrance to the ditch, then close by, was made with a flowing sheet, and I soon found that my pilot knew his business. Rush-swamps and corn-fields we left to port and to starboard, and were at times out of sight among brakes that brushed crackling along the sides of the canoe, as she swept briskly through the narrows, passing them all, with many a close hug, though, on all sides. At a point well on in the crooked channel my pilot threw up his hat, and shouted, with all his might:

"Yer trouble is over! Swan to gosh if it ain't! And ye come all the way from Brazil, and come through gran'ther's ditch! Well, I d'clar!"

From this I concluded that we had cleared all the doubtful places, and so it turned out. Before sundown my pilot was looking for the change of a five-dollar-piece; and we of the *Liberdade* sat before a pot-pie, at twilight, the like of which on the whole voyage had not been tasted, from sea fowl laid about by our pilot while sailing through the meadows and marshes. And the pilot himself, returning while the pot-pie was yet steaming hot, declared it "ahead of coon."

A pleasant sail was this through the ditch that gran'ther dug. At the camp fire that night, where we hauled up by a fishing station, thirty stalwart men talked over the adventures of their lives. My pilot, the best speaker, kept the camp in roars. As for myself, always fond of mirth, I got up from the fire sore from laughing. Their curious adventures with coons and 'gators recounted had been considerable.

Many startling stories were told. But frequently reverting to this voyage of the *Liberdade*, they declared with one voice that "it was the greatest thing since the wah." I took this as a kind of complimentary hospitality. "When she struck on a sand reef," said the pilot, "why, the captain he jumped right overboard and the son he jumped right over, too, to tote her over, and the captain's wife she holp."

By daylight next morning we sailed from this camp pleasant, and on the following day, November 28, at noon, arrived at Beaufort.

Mayor Bell of that city and many of his town folk met us at the wharf, and gave me as well as my sea-tossed crew a welcome to their shores, such as to make us feel that the country was partly ours.

"Welcome, welcome home," said the good mayor; "we have read of your adventures, and watched your progress as reported from time to time, with deep interest and sympathy."

So we began to learn now that prayers on shore had gone up for the little canoe at sea. This was indeed America and home, for which we had longed while thousands of miles across the ocean.

From Beaufort to Norfolk and thence to Washington was pleasant inland sailing, with prevailing fair winds and smooth sea. Christmas was spent on the Chesapeake—a fine, enjoyable day it was! with not a white-cap ripple on the bay. Ducks swimming ahead of the canoe as she moved quietly along were loath to take wing in so light a breeze, but flapping away, half paddling, half swimming, as we came toward them, they managed to keep a long gun-shot off; but having laid in at the last port a turkey of no mean proportions, which we made shift to roast in the "caboose" aboard, we could look at a duck without wishing its destruction. With this turkey and a bountiful plum duff, we made out a dinner even on the *Liberdade*.

Of the many Christmas days that come crowding in my recollections now; days spent on the sea and in foreign lands, as falls to the lot of sailors—which was the merriest it would be hard to say. Of this, however, I am certain, that the one on board the *Liberdade* on the Chesapeake was not the least happy among them all.

The day following Christmas found us on the Potomac, enjoying the same fine weather and abundant good cheer of the day before. Fair winds carried us through all the reaches of the river, and the same prosperity which attended our little bark in the beginning of the voyage through tempestuous weather followed her to the end of the journey, which terminated in mild days and pleasant sunshine.

On the 27th of December, 1888, a south wind bore us into harbor at Washington, D. C., where we moored for the winter, furled our sails and coiled up the ropes, after a voyage of joys and sorrows;

crowned with pleasures, however, which lessened the pain of past regrets.

Having moored the *Liberdade* and weather-bitted her cables, it remains only to be said that after bringing us safely through the dangers of a tropical voyage, clearing reefs, shoals, breakers, and all storms without a serious accident of any kind, we learned to love the little canoe as well as anything could be loved that is made by hands.

To say that we had not a moment of ill-health on the voyage would not tell the whole story.

My wife, brave enough to face the worst storms, as women are sometimes known to do on sea and on land, enjoyed not only the best of health, but had gained a richer complexion.

Victor, at the end of the voyage, found that he had grown an inch and had not been frightened out of his boots.

Little Garfield—well he had grown some, too, and continued to be a pretty good boy and had managed to hold his grip through many ups and downs. He it was who stood by the bow line to make fast as quick as the *Liberdade* came to the pier at the end of the voyage.

And I, last, as it should be, lost a few pounds' weight, but like the rest landed in perfect health; taking it altogether, therefore, only pleasant recollections of the voyage remain with us who made it.

With all its vicissitudes I still love a life on the broad, free ocean, never regretting the choice of my profession.

However, the time has come to debark from the *Liberdade*, now breasted to the pier where I leave her for a time; for my people are landed safe in port.

DISPOSAL OF THE "LIBERDADE"

About the middle of April the *Liberdade* cast loose her moorings from the dock at Washington, and spreading sail before a brave west wind, bent her course along down the Potomac with the same facility as experienced in December coming up before a wind from the South; then shaping her course for New York via Baltimore and

Voyage of the "Liberdade"

Philadelphia through inland passages, the voyage was turned into a pleasure excursion. Animation of spring clothed the landscape on all sides in its greatest beauty; and our northern forest the voyagers found upon their return was not less charming than "tropic shade" of foreign climes. And the robin sang even a sweeter trill than ever before heard by the crew, for they listened to it now in the country that they loved.

From New York the *Liberdade* sailed for Boston via New London, New Bedford, Martha's Vineyard, Newport, and Taunton, at which— latter place—she hauled out, and the crew, thence to the Bay State Capital, enjoyed the novelty of a "sail over land."

Then the *Liberdade* moored snug in Boston and her crew spent the winter again among friends. They met here during this time, the man who advised the captain at Buenos Ayres to pitch the *Aquidneck's* cargo of hay into the sea; for not taking the advice—witness, alas! the captain's plight!

Finally, upon return of spring the *Liberdade* was refitted on a voyage retracing her course to Washington, where, following safe arrival, she will end her days in the Smithsonian Institution; a haven of honor that many will be glad to know she has won.

The Loss of the "Aquidneck"

The correspondence below between Slocum and the President, and Slocum and officers of the Department of State, is now published for the first time. It explains what the captain would not, could not, put into his book concerning the last voyage of the *Aquidneck*. His claim for damages suffered in 1887 was against the government of Dom Pedro, overthrown in 1889. Thereafter it became a matter of years before the Department of State could obtain an official report of the incident from the Brazilian government. Meanwhile, by writing and publishing *Voyage of the Liberdade* in 1889 and 1890, Slocum found a new and ingenious way of presenting his case. He cast it into the court of public opinion and also approached individuals in the Department of State on a personal basis. He sent a copy to William F. Wharton, an assistant secretary, and, one surmises, to other officials as well.

Filed under 31 Oct. 1887

To His Excellency
  Grover Cleaveland
    President of the United States

Sir
  I have the honor to address you in reference to a matter, not merely of private interest, but of general interest to shipping as well, in as much as we all claime a right to faire treatement—
  On the 14th day of December last the American bark Aquidneck under my charge, was cleared from Rosario Santa Fé in due form,

125

and with propper documents from the Brazilian Consul at that port to admit us to quarintine at the Bay of Ilha Grand, the quarintine station of Brazil, where ships at the time we sailed and fore some time previous to this, on account of cholera at the port we sailed from—were directed to go to discharge their cargoes, in quarantine.

We sailed in good faith, and in due course arived at the Bay of Ilha Grande and there anchored on the 8th of Jan. 1887 within musket-shot of the Guard-ship.

Our national flag was set, also the quarantine flag,* but no visit came to us that day although the visit boat passed neare us going to and from other ships.

On the morning of the 9th of Jan. the captain of a neighboring ship in quarantine advised me to "try inside" the line of red keggs, which generally indicate the line in So. American ports beyond which we shall *not* come before the doctors visit has passed us, notably so at Rio de Jainearo, where a red buoy is the limit.

There was no pilot neither was there any signal of instructions from the guard-ship, a courtesy shewn to ships on our second arival there— We shifted anchorage however to a berth inshore and came to at 7 AM, no one forbiding us doing so—

We lay there, Sir, with our flags set and sails loose to attract attention till late that afternoon, when a launch came alongsid, with an officer of the port, who ordered us to get underweigh and leave the port at once, and not enter any port in Brazil. The order had come that morning the officer said:—"to admit no more ships from the River Plate

I begged for fresh provision to be sent to us before we put to sea, but was ordered to leave the port at once, or the guard-ship would fire into us.

Having my wife and children on board I would not subject them to the shock of open fire The order came sir after we had already been more than twenty six hours in the port or bay and had sailed about, looking for a visit

My Bill of Health was the same as that of other ships then discharging cargo at Ilha Grand, I certainly stated that cholera did exhist at Rosario, stating how many deaths the day before and how many new cases there wer on the day it was given

Sir, the British Bark Stadacona had the same kind of a Bill of Health and was admitted to quarantine.

We had no sickness onboard and we broke no law. We paid the

* The quarantine, or Q, flag is known as The Yellow Jack.

legal fee for these documents which should have admitted us but were turned away.

The nature of our cargo (hay) necescitated our return to Rosario from whence we came.

The loss to me in consequence of this unjust measure, has been very great.

It is no stretch of fact to say that this will at last pull down the good old flag from the mast of the bark that I have been proud of, under this color, that I have sailed under twenty six years

The mast that carries the flag, I feare must go by the board and my bark be sold for a graceless hulk, unless indeed our country deem it just that such a case be indemnified.

For this I have prayed to our worthy minister at Rio de Jainearo, setting forth particulars, and also protested before the U.S. Consul at that port.

Not having reply to my suplication I know not how else to act, so I come, Sir, with my case to the first man in all the land

I have sustained a ruinous loss through no fault of mine which bids to throw me out of my home afloat

      I am Sir—your obedent serv.

            Joshua Slocum

                Owner of the "Aquidneck"

Address—Capt. J. Slocum

      c/o J. F. Whitney & Co.

      15 State Street, New York, N. Y.

                      2nd Assistant Secretary

                      Nov 4 1887

Copy to U.S. Leg. at Rio, directing Min. to investigate and, if undue discrimination against our vessels appear, to ask an explanation—[The Govt. of Brazil may have a good defense to allege, but it is not *our* business to find it out. Let Brazil explain.]

Act accordingly, but don't give the writer room to suppose that we accept his statements and undertake to press his claim without due substantiation of a sound case.

                      AAA *

* Alvey Augustus Adee (1842-1924) was appointed Second Assistant Secretary of State in 1886, in which post he remained for 36 years.

The Loss of the "Aquidneck"

Department of State,
Washington 10 November 1887

Capt. J. Slocum
  Care of J. F. Whitney & Co.
    15 State St., New York

Sir:

Your letter of recent date to the President, has been referred to this Department.

Our Minister at Rio will be directed to investigate the circumstances under which the bark "Aquidneck" was ordered out of the port of Ilha Grande, Brazil, in January last, and if any discrimination appear, will ask for an explanation in the premises.

I am, Sir, your obedient servant,
T. F. Bayard

No. 74

Department of State
Washington, Nov 10, 1887

Thos. J. Jarvis, Esq.

Sir,

I transmit a copy of a letter from Captain J. Slocum, representing that in January last, his bark the "Aquidneck," an American vessel, was ordered out of the port of Ilha Grande, Brazil, under circumstances which lead him to believe his vessel was discriminated against by the authorities;—suffering thereby very considerable loss.

You will please investigate the matter and if any undue discrimination appears to have been made, you will ask an explanation.

I am, etc.
T. F. Bayard

Enclosure: Mr. Slocum to the President, Recd. Oct. 31, 1887.

No. 76

Department of State
Washington, December 27, 1887

Thos. J. Jarvis, Esq.
Sir,

Referring to Instruction No. 74 of the 10th ultimo, relative to the American bark "Aquidneck" and the circumstances under which it was ordered out of the port of Ilha Grande, Brazil, in January, 1887, I now transmit a copy of a letter from Capt. G. E. Pettis of the British bark "Stadacona" and call your attention to the statements which he makes on behalf of Capt. Slocum, Master of the American bark named.

I am, etc.

G. L. Rives,
Acting Secretary

Enclosure: Capt. Pettis to Mr. Bayard,
October 25, 1887

Montevideo, October 25, 1887

To the Right Honorable Thomas F. Bayard
  Secretary of State Washington D.C.

Honorable Sir,

At the request of Captain Slocum American Barque "Aquidneck," I have taken the liberty of writing to you.

The facts I wish to place before you are as follows:—In the latter part of November 1886, I loaded my vessel British Barque "Stadacona" at Rosario, de Santa Fé, Argentine Republic, with a cargo of hay in bales for Rio de Janeiro. At this time there were a number of American and Nova Scotian vessels loading at Ports in the Rio de la Plata for Ports in the Brazils. The American Barque "Aquidneck" was one of these unfortunates. Previous to my sailing from Rosario there was an outbreak of Cholera in several of the River Plate Ports, and I with all other vessels then in these Ports were obliged to leave with a foul bill of health.

The "Stadacona" arrived at Rio on the 4th of December, but was not allowed to enter that Port, and was ordered to the new quarantine station, Ihla Grande, at which place the "Stadacona" arrived on the 6th day of December. Here I was informed that I would not be allowed to enter any of the Brazilian Ports, but would be allowed to discharge in the quarantine harbour, a ship from Rio being sent for that purpose. During the thirty days I remained at this Lazareto I was treated most courteously by officers of the Guard ship and Lazareto. All my signals were promptly answered by the guardship and all reasonable requests granted. On the 7th

January I was ballasted and ready for sea, at about 2:30 p.m. of this day the American Barque "Aquidneck" arrived from Rosario, cargo and bill of health the same as my vessel and brought up in the Roads (Ihla Grande) in the place set aside for that purpose and marked by a line of buoys.

In re of this cordon, I am positive it was placed there for the purpose of keeping all vessels from these infected Ports as much isolated as possible, and I had during my stay there, seen the guard ship signal all vessels attempting to cross this line to anchor instantly. I also enquired of one of the officers of the guard ship, why this line of buoys were laid down, and he informed me that it was for the above named purpose.

Captain Slocum informed me that the quarantine authorities would neither allow him to communicate with his consignee or to lay in the Roads and he was obliged to put to sea at once.

Captain Slocum takes exception to the treatment extended to the American flag and seems to think that his government should see that his ship should be allowed the same privileges as vessels under the British flag. Trusting that you may be able to help Captain Slocum in this matter, I am honorable Sir

Yours most respectfully

G. E. Pettis

British Bk Stadacona

Mr. Everett:—

I directed this letter of Capt. Pettis to be sent to the Consul Gen. at Rio.

I now find that there has been previous correspondence with the *Minister* on the same subject. You will therefore send copy (which has been already prepared) by the Cons. Bureau) to Mr. Jarvis, referring to instruction of Nov. 10—

GWE

24 Dec 1887

The Loss of the "Aquidneck"

(Received by Department of State, Mar. 24, 1888)

No. 121   Legation of the United States
                 Petropolis, February 15, 1888

Mr. Thomas J. Jarvis to Mr. Thomas F. Bayard

SUBJECT:

Preliminary report on Captain Slocum's claim against Brazil, for damages for discrimination in enforcing quarantine regulations.

Synopsis:

Reciting unofficial presentation of claim to Brazilian Government; its failure to reply; Captain Slocum's complaint to the Department, advised by Mr. Jarvis; and the Department's instructions. Mr. Jarvis asks the Imperial Government for certain information on which to base a judgment.

To the Honorable
Thomas F. Bayard
Secretary of State
Washington, D.C.

Sir:

In acknowledging the receipt of your Nos. 74 & 76, dated, respectively, November 10 & December 27, 1887, in reference to the American bark Aquidneck, I beg leave to submit the following preliminary report:

In June, 1887, Captain Slocum made to me substantially the same statement as that contained in his complaint to you. This statement was subsequently reduced to writing, at my request, and handed to me by his agent in Rio. I told him that I would bring the matter to the attention of the Imperial Government, but that I could not press it without instructions from the Department. I held this view of my duty on account not only of my general instructions, but also of the delicate and doubtful questions involved in matters of quarantine.

In his statement to me, Captain Slocum claimed $10,000, damages; but I did not formally present this claim to the Minister for Foreign Affairs. I simply stated the case in an unofficial note, and expressed the hope and belief that the Imperial Government would give it due attention.

The Loss of the "Aquidneck"

Soon after, Captain Slocum unfortunately killed one of his men, and seriously wounded another, in one of the Southern ports of Brazil. He was tried, and acquitted on the pleas of self-defence. I think his case was reported to the Department by C. R. McCall, Acting Consul General.

The Imperial Government having failed to answer my note, I advised Captain Slocum, through his agent, after his release, to make his complaint to the Department of State, if he wished to prosecute his claim.

Since receiving your instructions, contained in your No. 74, I have formally asked the Minister for Foreign Affairs for certain information, specifically set forth in my note. Should I obtain it, I may then be able to judge whether the charge of discrimination is well founded.

I send this preliminary report, as I do not know when I can make a more extended one. I shall not fail to give the case close attention

I have the honor to be

Your obedient servant

Thos. J. Jarvis

"Aquidneck"

Paranagua Brazil 24th Mar 1888

The Honorable F. Bayard
Secretary of State
Washington D.C.

I have the honor to come, this time, to correct an error, that I made when writing to the President about the harsh treatment we got at Ilha Grand.

My troubled brain made me say that on the 8th of Jan. we arived and on the 9th were turned away whereas I should have said 7th and 8th which I find correct, on refering to my journal and protest; these were not at hand when I wrote.

My letter to our Minister however carries correct dates.

The only excuse I have for a mistake so much against myself is that I was led, perhaps, by an over anxious mind.

We have sailed on a sea of troubles! dated from Ilha Grand—

132

which could not have occured, had we been treated there as the British Bk. Statacona and other hay laden vessels with documents the same as mine, were treated—

The nature of my profession causing often, one adversity to follow one, has made no exception for me; the rehersal of which, but few on shore could meet with full credit— Forgetting my sorrows, I must say here that the prompt and kind attention to the contents of my former poor letter make it seem still worth something to be a subject, even abroad.

Yours very respectfully
Joshua Slocum

No. 52

Consulate of the United States
Pernambuco September 10th, 1888

Honorable George L. Rives
  Assistant Secretary of State
    Washington, D.C.

Sir,

I have the honor to inform the Department that a Mr. Joshua Slocum late master of the American Barque "Aquidneck" of Baltimore which vessel was lost in the vicinity of Paranaguá, Coast of Brazil in the latter part of last year, has built a boat at the latter named port in which he intends to return to the United States; said boat is called the Liberdade, and is about five tons. This so called cutter arrived at Rio de Janeiro on June 26th, received from the Brazilian Minister of Marine guaranteeing none [?] payment of dues in all Brazilian ports, after touching at all principal ports, arrived at Pernambuco on Monday August 27th. His crew is composed of Mr. Slocum's wife and his two sons. Left this port on Tuesday September 4th.

I have the honor to be, Sir

Your obedient Servant
H. Christian Borstel
Consul

The Loss of the "Aquidneck"

Norfolk Va. 12 Dec 1888 *

To the Honorable
Thos F. Bayard
State Department
Washington D.C.

Sir

I have the honor to address you once more on the matter concerning the bark "Aquidneck"—

Before leaving Rio de Janeiro in the present command I wrote our worthy Minister a short history of what befell us after the illegal turning away of the Aquidneck from Ilha Grande which in brief is a chapter of disasters—

Being turned away with cargo in, necessitated my return to the port where that cargo belonged This act so involved me that all my subsequent actions or movements were the force of this circumstance

First I was obliged to waite many months and finally finished the voyage at Rio with the same cargo in—

I had then to secure the first freight offering advance enough to pay the debts of the broken Ilha Grand voyage; this led me south again, instead of north and home—

In the meane time a band of pirates from Argentine prisons had been turned loose (on account of the cholera) and shipped on my vessel as sailors. It was well known at Rosario where they shipped that I owned the vessel

Earley on this second voyage I was set upon by these pirates at my cabin door!

The result of the attack is on record, I believe, at the Department

I had then to vindicate myself before a just tribunal, how well is also on reccord; but what it cost me of money and nerve is known, so fare, only to me!

Thence with a good crew of sons of Brazil we proceeded to finish the voyage; with this crew I sailed from Montevideo, but before cleareing the Plate they went down with black small-pox one, two, and then three, I bore up for a port of refuge and sailed to three ports before I could get succor for my perishing crew! even at Flores Island the quarantine station and lazaretto of Uruguay they were afraid, and bade me go to the next port for

---

* The letter appears to have been written from the *Liberdade,* a few days before the end of the journey in Washington.

aid—this I was loth to try as I had left to work the bark only the carpenter, and my son a lad of 18, and the cook. These might fall as the others had done and leave us all in fact like a drifting pest house

It was however a sorry choice We burried our dead one morning and signaled the Brit Telegraph tender then passing to give due notice of our state, and we then hove on the windlass, to the groanes of dying men, no one sang "Rheubin Ranzo"; oh it was dismal, but we got the anchor; and got away from the most inhospitable place and cowardly people that I had even fallen in with; and was finally relieved of my poor fellows those of them that had not already been taken from their own sufferings

With a new crew I finally sailed once more but at the next place my vessel stranded and became a total loss!

I believe Sir, that in making restitutions it is right to consider the many losses falling on me none of which could have taken place had I been treated as others were at Ilha Grande

I believe too, Sir, that the representatives of so kind and sympathysing a nation as I know the Brazilian people to be will readily consider these losses in my claim.

I have the honor to be Sir

Your humble servant

Joshua Slocum
late owner of the "Aquidneck"

Department of State
Washington, Dec. 20, 1888

Data in the claim of Joshua Slocum against the Brazilian Government for ten thousand dollars, for the illegal refusal by the Brazilian quarantine authorities to admit his vessel, the "Aquidneck," to the port of Ilha Grande, the quarantine port of Rio de Janeiro, in the month of January, 1887.

＊ ＊ ＊

J. Slocum to Dept. Oct. 31, 1887

The American bark "Aquidneck" of Baltimore, Md., U.S.A. owned and commanded by Joshua Slocum sailed from the port of Rosario de Santa Fé, Argentine Republic, in the early part of

The Loss of the "Aquidneck"

December, 1886. She was provided with papers from the Brazilian consul at Rosario, which would permit her to enter the harbor of Ilha Grande, and there discharge her cargo of baled hay into a vessel which would be sent from Rio Janeiro for the purpose of receiving it. Ilha Grande is a small island about 68 miles S. by W. of Rio Janeiro, and was the quarantine of that city. At this time the cholera was raging in the towns of the Argentine, and was particularly bad at Rosario. The Brazilian authorities would not permit any vessels from the La Plata ports to enter Brazilian ports, but compelled them to transfer their cargoes at Ilha Grande.

G. E. Pettis to Dept. Oct. 25, 1887

The bill of health issued to the "Aquidneck" was what is known as a "foul" bill of health, and was of the same general character of those issued to other vessels sailing from Rosario at that time.

J. Slocum to Dept. Oct. 31, 1887
Mar. 24, 1888

The "Aquidneck" arrived at Ilha Grande on January 7, 1887, with all her crew in good health. A portion of the harbor was marked off by a line of red kegs, used as buoys, and no vessels were allowed within this line until they had been visited by the health officer and received permission.

Capt. Slocum anchored outside this line, and "within musket shot of the guardship." He endeavored to get a visit from the quarantine officers but without success, though they passed his vessel repeatedly on their way to others. The "Aquidneck" remained thus anchored all day and night of Jan. 7. Early on the morning of Jan. 8, at the suggestion of the captain of a neighboring vessel, Capt. Slocum shifted his anchorage to a place inside the line of red buoys. Here he remained from 7 A.M. until late in the afternoon, with flag flying and sails loose, endeavoring to get a visit.

Late in the afternoon, an officer of the port came alongside in a launch, who ordered Capt. Slocum to get under way and leave the port at once, and not to enter any other port in Brazil. He said that an order had come that morning to admit no more ships from the river La Plata. Capt. Slocum begged that fresh provisions should be sent to him before he put to sea. This request was refused and he was told that if he did not leave at once, his vessel would be fired on by the guardship. The "Aquidneck" was, therefore, got under way and returned to Rosario.

The Loss of the "Aquidneck"

When the order to leave was given, the "Aquidneck" had been in the harbor more than thirty six hours.

G. E. Pettis to Dept. Oct. 25, 1887

The British bark "Stadacona" Capt. G. E. Pettis left Rosario in November, 1886, and arrived at Ilha Grande on Dec. 6th 1886, and was in the harbor when the "Aquidneck" arrived. The papers of the "Stadacona" were the same as those of the "Aquidneck."

J. Slocum to Dept. Oct. 12, 1888
Consul at Rio 113, 116 & 128 Aug. to Nov. '87

Capt. Slocum afterwards sailed again from Rosario, went to Rio Janeiro, then to Paranaguá where he was arrested for the killing of one of his crew and the wounding of another. He was acquitted by the unanimous vote of the jury, and went to Montevideo.

J. Slocum Dec. 12, 1888

On leaving the latter place small-pox broke out among his crew and their sufferings were terrible, as they were not allowed to land anywhere for a long time.

Consul at Pernambuco No. 52 Sept. 10, '88

He finally got assistance, shipped a new crew, sailed again and was stranded at Paranaguá. He asserts that all these trials and losses are the result of his being turned away from Ilha Grande.

Mr. Jarvis 121. Feb. 15 '88

In June 1887, Capt. Slocum made a statement of his case to Mr. Jarvis, U. S. Minister to Brazil. He was told that the Minister could not formally present the case without instructions from the Department of State.

The case was not formally presented, but was stated by Mr. Jarvis to the Brazilian Minister of Foreign Affairs in an unofficial note, expressing the hope and belief that the Brazilian Government would give it due attention.

This note of Mr. Jarvis' was not answered and it does not appear that any further action has been taken.

Respectfully submitted

John P. Haswill

The Loss of the "Aquidneck"

Department of State
Washington. Dec. 26 /88

Joshua Slocum, Esq.
  Norfolk, Va.

Sir:
I have to acknowledge the receipt of your letter of the 12th instant in reference to the expulsion of the American bark "Aquidneck" from the port of Ilha Grande, Brazil, in 1887.

The case has been again called to the attention of the United States Legation at Rio.

I am Sir your obedient servant

G. L. Rives
Assistant Secretary

No. 127

Department of State
Washington, December 26, 1888

H. C. Armstrong, Esq.

Sir,
  Referring to Instruction No. 74 of 10th November 1887, to Mr. Jarvis, in relation to the expulsion of the American bark "Aquidneck" in January 1887, from the port of Ilha Grande, Brazil, I have to inquire what answer has been made to the Minister's presentation of the case.

I am, etc.

T. F. Bayard

Department of State
Washington, Jan. 9, 1889

Capt. Joshua Slocum,
  Norfolk, Virginia

Sir:
Referring to your oral inquiry at the Department today, in relation to the case of the "Aquidneck" and to your statement that you had failed to receive from the Department any reply to your letter of the 12th of December last dated at Norfolk, Virginia, I have to

138

enclose herewith for your information, a copy of a reply addressed to you on the 26th ultimo, informing you that the case had again been called to the attention of the United States Legation at Rio. I am Sir, your obedient servant.

> G. L. Rives
> Assistant Secretary

Enclosure as above

UNITED STATES SENATE

Washington, D.C. Jan. 18th, 1889

Hon. Thos. F. Bayard
  Secty. of State
    Washington, D.C.

My dear Sir:
  I beg to hand you herewith a commn. to me from Joshua Slocum who claims to be the master of the American Bark "Aquidneck" registered at Balti., Md.

  Capt. Slocum claims that great injustice has been done him by the Brazilian authorities to which he desires me to ask you to give your attention. I know nothing whatever of the case except what I gather from the statements contained in his commn. enclosed herewith.

  I beg that you will take such action in the matter as may be proper.

> Yrs. truly,
>
> A. P. Gorman

Washington D.C. Jan 17th 1889

The Hon. A. P. Gorman
  U.S. Senator
    Washington D.C.

Sir:
  I have the honor to bring to your kind notice the case of the Am. Bk. Aquidneck, owned by Joshua Slocum and Regstd. at Baltimore.

The Loss of the "Aquidneck"

Jan. 8th 1887 this vessel was expelled from the port of Ilha Grand, the quarantine station of Brazil, after having made the voyage from Rosario Santa Fé with documents, all in order, from the Brazilian Consul at Rosario to alow her to discharge her cargo (hay in bales) in quarantine at Ilha Grand

She sailed from Rosario 17th Dec 1886

Arrived at Ilha Grande 7th Jan 1887 with all well on board—had no visit that day altho she had anchored soon after noon.

On the 8th about 4 p.m. officers of the port came alongside in a steam launch received my letter for the Custom House, mustered the crew, saw that we were all well, then ordered us to leave the port at once, or if we did not the Guard Ship would fire into us.

Several vessels were then in Ilha Grand which had left the same port that we were from, having the same kind of cargo in (hay) and with the *same kind* of a *Bill* of *Health*—"foul" on account of cholera which was then in the Argentine, and *for that reason* we were sent to Ilha Grand.

We wandered about then for many months trying to get rid of the cargo so as to engage in some trade to make a living. After going from port to port with this cargo, we were at last admitted to Ilha Grand on the 8th of May 1887; thence to Rio de Janeiro, with the same cargo alway onboard—

My protest against the harsh arbitrary treatment of the Brazilian officers was duly filed at the Consulate General at Rio

I wrote to Hon Minister Thos J. Jarvis explaining the case as I understood it—that the decree to close Ilha Grand as well as all other port in Brazil against vessel from Argentine ports—had been *made after* I had *arived* at Ilha Grand (so the officer told me when ordering us away) and I protested again, and protest now—that we had no sickness onboard and that we broke no law!

Our worthy Minister was instructed to ask of the Brazilian Authorities "what vessels had arrived at Ilha Grand? where from and when? and when had the port been closed?

These questions rightly answered would substantiate my case.

But they are not answered simple as they are. Notwithstanding that they were repeatedly asked by a Minister of the U.S.

At Rio I felt satisfied that our minister would investigate the matter I was told by Mr. Jarvis to call on our Secretary of State, on my arrival here I did so only to learn that Mr. Bayard knew nothing of the case, this was unfortunate because the Hon Assist Secretary tells me flatly that I am romancing (well the chapter of

140

disasters reads like romance) and that nothing has been heard from the Legation, in the matter

I need not say here that the Hon Minister was here in person a short time ago and is now in the United States

A lesser statesman than Mr Jarvis might however succeed in getting the answers to the few pertinent questions asked now nearely two years ago; which would show that there had been a "discrimination," if indeed it were necessary at all to establish the fact of *discrimination* (?)

This vessel with documents all in order and with no sickness onboard—and under the American Flag, was illegally expelled from Ilha Grand

Through this heavy losses have fallen on me, the owner of the Aquidneck some of which have been communicated to the Hon the Secretary of State

My first loss was I estimate small any expert will say = $10,000

Since that my vessel is lost on the coast near Rio while trying to gain money to pay the debts of the broken voyage to Ilha Grand

I have the honor to beg Sir, that my Senator from Baltimore will look into the merits of my case and tell me as I hope all other Senators will before long that I have the protection of that flag under which I have sailed for more than a quarter of a century— My vessel was regestered at Baltimore—I had no home in any section more than home on my ship.

I have the honor sir
Your obedient servant

Joshua Slocum

Department of State
Washington, Jan. 24, /89

The Hon. A. P. Gorman
Senate

Sir:

I have the honour to acknowledge the receipt of your letter of 18th instant, and the letter of the Master of the American bark "Aquidneck" which it enclosed; and to say that a copy of the same has been sent to our Legation at Rio, with a reference to former correspondences.

I have the honour to be, Sir,

Your obedient Servant

T. F. Bayard

No. 136

Department of State

Washington, January 24, 1889

H. C. Armstrong, Esq.

Sir,

In further reference to the case of the expulsion of the American bark "Aquidneck" in January 1887, from the port of Ilha Grande—concerning which you were addressed on the 26th Ultimo,—I transmit a copy of a letter from Senator Gorman and the communication of Capt. Slocum, which accompanies the same.

I am, etc.

T. F. Bayard

Enclosure: Mr. Gorman to Mr. Bayard, Jan. 18, 1889.

No. 174

Legation of the United States.

Rio de Janeiro Feb. 18—1889

Mr. Armstrong to the Secy. of State
    SUBJECT: American Bk. "Aquidneck"

SYNOPSIS

Stating that no reply had been made by the Brazilian Government on the matter of expulsion from Ilha Grande of Am. Bk. Aquidneck.
Attention of Foreign Office called to the matter.

Hon. Thos. F. Bayard
    Secy of State

Sir:

Replying to Departments No 127, I beg to say that the Brazilian Government has made no reply to the note of Mr. Jarvis dated

The Loss of the "Aquidneck"

Janry. 31, 1888 with regard to the expulsion from Ilha Grande of the American Bark "Aquidneck." I have this day addressed a note to the Foreign Office calling attention to the matter and will as soon as reply is made advise the Department promptly.

I have the honor to be

> Your Obdt. Sert.
> H. Clay Armstrong
> Chargé d'affaires ad interim

No. 180

Legation of the United States
Rio de Janeiro, April 26, 1889

Mr. Armstrong, Chargé
To the Secretary of State

SUBJECT: American Bk. "Aquidneck"

SYNOPSIS

Transmitting a translation of a note received from the Brazilian Foreign Office relating to the expulsion of the Am. Bk. "Aquidneck" from the port at Ilha Grande.

Hon. T. F. Bayard
Secretary of State
Washington, D.C.

Sir:

Referring to the Department's Dispatch No. 136 in relation to the case of the expulsion of the Am. Bk. "Aquidneck" from the port of Ilha Grande. I have the honor to enclose herewith translation of note received from the Brazilian Foreign Office some days ago but which, for the reasons stated in my No. 179, I have not been able to report until now.

As soon as any further information is obtained in the matter I will report it promptly to the Department.

I have the honor to be Sir

> Yr. Ob't. Servt.
> H. Clay Armstrong
> Chargé d' affaires ad interim

Enclosures: Translation of note from Brazilian Foreign Office

143

The Loss of the "Aquidneck"

Translation   2d Section.—No. 3—Rio de Janeiro, Department of Foreign Affairs, March 26, 1889

I have received the note of the 21st inst. in which Mr. H. Clay Armstrong, Chargé d' Affaires, *ad interim,* of the United States of America, reminds me, by order of his Government, of the claim of the captain of the bark Aquidneck.—I regret very much that this Department has not yet been able to give a definite answer in regard to this claim. The information furnished by the Department of the Empire not being complete, I myself requested last December that what was wanting should be supplied.—This has not yet been done, and I now write again to that Department.—I have the honor to renew to Mr. Armstrong the assurance of my very distinguished consideration.—To Mr. H. Clay Armstrong.—(Signed) Rodrigo A. da Silva

New York March 11th 1890

To the Hon
   James G. Blaine
      Secretary of State
         Washington D.C.

Sir:
   I have the honor to beg the Department to examine the case of the Aquidneck presented some time ago.
   My only protection is the government of my country.
   I am very respectfully
                          Your Servant
                                Joshua Slocum
                                late owner of the "Aquidneck"

Address Capt. J. Slocum
69 Saratoga Street
E. Boston Mass

The Loss of the "Aquidneck"

Department of State,
Washington, April 7, 1890.

Captain Joshua Slocum,
69 Saratoga St., E. Boston, Mass.

Sir:

I have received your letter of the 11th ultimo, relating to the case of the bark Aquidneck against the Government of Brazil. On March 26, 1889, the Brazilian Minister of Foreign Affairs addressed a note to our chargé d'affaires ad interim, stating that his Department had not received sufficient information from the Department of the Empire, to enable him to reply to the Legation's note presenting the claim. The unsettled condition of political affairs ending in a change of the form of government has naturally further delayed due investigation of the matter. The attention of our Legation will, however, be again called to the case.

I am, Sir, your obedient servant.

William F. Wharton
Assistant Secretary

Department of State
Washington, Nov. 15, '90

Captain Joshua Slocum
c/o J. D. Merritt & Company
925 Pennsylvania Ave.
Washington, D.C.

Sir:

I enclose for your information copies of certain papers relating to the case of the Bark "Aquidneck" against the Government of Brazil, which were transmitted to this Department by our charge at Rio de Janeiro in his No. 131, of September 22, last.

I am Sir, Your obedient Servant

William F. Wharton
Assistant Secretary

Enclosures as above

The Loss of the "Aquidneck"

No. 131.   Legation of the United States
                                Rio de Janeiro, Sept. 22nd, 1890

Mr. Lee
To the Hon. Secretary of State

SUBJECT:

Claim of Bark "Aquidneck"

Synopsis:

Reply of Foreign Office
Copies & Translations of Enclosures accompanying the same.

Hon. James G. Blaine,
  Secretary of State

Sir:—

In reply to Department's Dispatch No. 5, in reference to the claim of the captain of the Bark *"Aquidneck"*—I have the honor to enclose to the Department the following documents:—

No. 1. A copy of my note to the Foreign office.

No. 2. A copy of reply from the Minister for Foreign Affairs with translation.

No. 3. Copy of Instructions given to Health Board on Nov. 3, 1886 & translation of same.

No. 4. Copy of Instructions given to Health Board on Nov. 13, 1886 with translation.

No. 5. Ditto ditto on Nov. 13th   "   "

No. 6. Ditto   "   "   "   11th   "   "

No. 7. Copy and translation of table of vessels that entered the Port of Ilha Grande, also of those that were refused entrance in that Port, during the month of January 1887.

I have the honor, Sir, to be,
                    Your obedient Servant
                                J. Fenner Lee

Copy

                                Legation of the United States
                                Rio de Janeiro, August 21st, 1890

I have the honor to call your attention to the note from the Foreign office of March 26th 1889, relative to the claims of the captain of the Bark *"Aquidneck."*

The Loss of the "Aquidneck"

I am instructed by my Government to request that the reply promised by the Government of Brazil relative to that claim may be made at as early a date as is convenient.

Availing myself of this occasion to renew the assurance of my high regard,

I have the honor, Sir, to be,

Your obedient Servant
(signed)   J. Fenner Lee

His Excellency
Quintino Bocayuva
Minister & Secretary for Foreign Affairs

Translation

Rio de Janeiro, 9th Sept. 1890

Department of Foreign Affairs

I have received the note which Mr. J. Fenner Lee, Chargé d'Affaires of the United States of America, was pleased to send me on the 21st of last month, and I was glad to be reminded by it of the claim of the Captain of the Bark "Aquidneck," which from unforeseen reasons has not yet been definitely decided.

By examining the respective documents, I see from Mr. Jarvis' letter of the 14th of June 1887 that the said Captain brought the following complaints against the authorities of the Quarantine Hospital at Ilha Grande.

1st, that his vessel, loaded with hay, was cleared, on the 14th of December 1886, by the Brazilian Consul at Rozario de Santa Fé, for Ilha Grande, he left there on the 17th of December and arrived at the Island on the 7th of January, 1887;—that no health officer made the sanitary visit till the evening of the 8th, 26 hours after his arrival a little more or less, when a health officer keeping off at a speaking distance, ordered him to leave at once.

2nd, that he asked leave to telegraph to the American Consul and also to obtain from the Island some provisions, but that both these requests were refused with the threat that he would be fired on unless he left.

The captain likewise observed that, having been cleared by the Brazilian Consul for the port designated by the competent authorities and having arrived there he thought himself entitled to go into quarantine the same as other vessels and therefore not being allowed to do so to receive an indemnity.

The Loss of the "Aquidneck"

From the reports by telegraph which the Department of Empire then received daily from the Director of the Sanitary Service of the Quarantine Hospital it has been verified that the Bark "Aquidneck" arrived on the night of the 7th, and that he was ordered to leave the next day before 5 o'clock P.M.

As the sanitary regulations in vigor do not allow sanitary visits to be made after sun set, the Director could only communicate with the said vessel on the next day.

If there was any delay, which would not be surprizing at a time of so much excitement, in no case could it have been for twenty six hours.

The Department of Empire declare positively that never had any captain been denied what the claimant declares he could not obtain; that many vessels, anchored in the Port of the Quarantine Hospital, frequently sent telegrams and obtained provisions and stores, and that the captain of the Aquidneck is the only one who makes such a complaint.

In no case, observed the Department and with reason, could the statement of the claimant, without any show of proof whatever, prevail with the Government over the formal denial made by the Director of the Hospital who could have no motive whatever for making this single exception to the prejudice of the Bark "Aquidneck," to the rule invariably followed.

The complaints to which I have just replied with the information furnished by the Department of Empire, the only competent one, even if they were based on fact would not have the importance the claimant attached to them & I am sure Mr. Lee will recognize this fact.

Furthermore I beg leave to make the following observations.

The great rapidity with which the cholera morbus (?) was spreading throughout the Argentine Republic obliged the Brazilian Government to take, besides general measures of protection, special means of prevention which were suggested from time to time. Thus, the Consul General at Buenos Aires having asked for instructions at a date which must have coincided with the passage of the Bark "Aquidneck" through that port, whether a cargo of alfafa would be admitted at the Quarantine Station at Ilha Grande, he was instructed by a telegram, dated 21st Dec. that it was better to stop the shipment of all kinds of forage to the ports of Brazil until further orders should be sent, thus removing the necessity of admitting anything that might tend to propagate the epidemic in the sea ports of Brazil.

The Loss of the "Aquidneck"

It was in virtue of this resolution that the sanitary authority of the Quarantine Hospital intimated to the Bark Aquidneck to leave & he only did his duty.

The Bark, according to the allegation of the claimant, left Rozario on the 7th [*sic*] of December, 1886, & the prohibition relative to forage was sent out on the 21st, that is, fourteen days afterwards.

On that circumstance, as well as on the clearance granted by the Consul, the claimant bases his right to demand damages.

The Consul cleared the vessel for Ilha Grande because that was the port of destination; & he made no objection to the cargo, because he did not yet know of the prohibition.

This official also did his full duty.

The Government, on whom the gravest responsibility fell, could not admit any dangerous cargo, when its attention was once called to the fact.

Between the date of clearing the "Aquidneck" and that of the telegram mentioned it was found there would be danger in admitting forage.

The Government, therefore, prohibited it and thus it did its duty, because it could not possibly hesitate between a loss to commerce and the possible loss of thousands of lives.

It is true one must avoid loss to commerce by giving notice of any prohibitive resolution, but this cannot be done in every case.

The public health has the preference over mercantile profits & as each State has the right to admit or not certain merchandise into its ports, the Brazilian Government does not consider itself obliged to give any indemnity when it prohibits the entry of merchandise for just motives.

The claimant presents as an argument the circumstance of other ships having been admitted to quarantine, but his arguments are erroneous.

During the month of January, 1887, only four vessels were admitted to quarantine in the port of Ilha Grande coming from Montevideo & Trieste & eight were refused, five in ballast from Rozario, Concordia and from Montevideo, one from the port of La Plata, loaded with corn, one from Montevideo with dried beef and one from Rozario with alfafa, this was the Bark "Aquidneck."

This appears from a table, a copy of which, in conformity with the desire of Mr. Jarvis, I enclose to Mr. Fenner Lee, together with copies of the orders relative to this subject.

This table shows that there was no difference of treatment and that the number of vessels refused was double that of those admitted & not one of these came from an Argentine port.

I believe I have shown that the claim in question has no foundation whatever & I entertain the hope that Mr. Lee will think so likewise.

I take the present occasion to give myself the honor of reiterating to Mr. J. Fenner Lee the assurance of my high regard.

Q. Bocayuva

69 Saratoga St., East Boston, Mass.
Dec. 31, 1890

To the Honorable the Secretary of State,
  Washington, D.C.

Sir:

I am troubled to have used a wrong expression in my letter of the 15th inst. relating to the case of the "Aquidneck."

I beg Sir to amend that letter by the positive assertion: I was *ordered* out *and* threatened with fire in case I did not go at once.

I remain, Sir,

Your humble servant,

Joshua Slocum

Department of State
Washington, Jan. 21, 1891

Captain Joshua Slocum
69 Saratoga St.
East Boston, Mass.

Sir:

The Department has received your letter of the 31st ultimo concerning the case of the bark "Aquidneck."

In reply I have to say that the matter will receive the attention of the Department.

I am, Sir, your obedient servant.

William F. Wharton
Assistant Secy.

The Loss of the "Aquidneck"

Capt. J. Slocum,
  69 Saratoga St.,
    E. Boston, Mass.

New York, Nov. 27th, 1893

The Honorable
  The Secretary of State
    Washington, D.C.

Sir:—

I beg leave to call to your attention the matter concerning the American bark Aquidneck, myself the owner, expelled from the port of Ilha Grande, Brazil, Jan. 18th, [*sic*] 1887. My protest dated U.S. Consulate General, Rio de Janeiro, May 31st, 1887.

I was legally obliged to make the voyage to Ilha Grande, as per Charter Party, Bills of Lading and Bill of Health itself from the Brazilian Consul.

The port of Ilha Grande was closed after my bark sailed from Rosario. I had no knowledge of the decree until I had been actually at Ilha Grande 26 hours, a little more or less.

In a communication from the Brazilian Authorities to the Department of State based on the report of their naval officers, it is asserted that the Aquidneck did not arrive at 2 P.M. of the 7th of January as stated in my protest.

The said document comments on my want of proof of what I have said.

Sir, I hope at last to satisfy the Department of State where I seek protection, that my cause is a just one.

I have the clear evidence now of two unimpeachable witnesses as honorable and upright as any that ever trod deck, within uniform or without it, to wit, Capt. George E. Pettis of the bark Statacona, whose letter in my behalf is already at the Department, and Captain Wm. Foulker, of the "Carpincho" who observed and noted my arrival at Ilha Grande.

Captain Foulker's letter will be forthcoming in a few days.

The Captain will write from Hantsport, Nova Scotia.

The Honorable Secretary of State will I am sure, consider my embarrassment in procuring formal evidence at Ilha Grande where I was allowed no privileges at all, and was finally ordered away before the muzzle of a canon.

I rely on the statements of Captains Pettis and Foulker to indicate to the Secretary of State where the discrepancy of statements rest and where the forgetfulness of the true facts may be placed.

Sir, I am with great respect,

Your servant,

Joshua Slocum

Department of State,
Washington, December 9, 1893

Capt. J. Slocum
  69 Saratoga Street
    E. Boston, Mass.

Sir:—

I have received your letter of the 27th ultimo concerning your complaint against the Brazilian authorities on account of their refusal to permit the American bark "Aquidneck" of which you were master, to enter the port of Ilha Grande, in January, 1887. The letter of Capt. Wm. Folkes, to which you refer, has also come to hand.

From an examination of previous correspondence in reference to this case, on file in this Department, it appears that in October 1887 you requested the intervention of this government on the following state of facts:

Your vessel, with a cargo of hay on board, on December 14, 1886, cleared from Rosario, Argentine, for the port of Ilha Grande, Brazil, the necessary documents having been procured from the Brazilian Consul at Rosario; that on January 8, 1887, you arrived off Ilha Grande, where you anchored some distance from the shore; that on the following morning your vessel was visited by an officer of the port, who ordered you to leave at once and not enter any port of Brazil, at the same time informing you that an order to that effect had been received that morning. You were accordingly obliged to return to Rosario, which subjected you to considerable loss.

The matter was duly called to the attention of the Brazilian Government and an investigation requested. From the reply of the Brazilian Government, a copy of which was furnished you some three years ago, it appeared that at the time of your voyage, cholera existed in Rosario, and other places in Argentine; that while the Consul at Rosario did grant the necessary clearance papers to the bark "Aquidneck" on Dec. 14th yet, owing to the rapid spread of the epidemic, on December 21st before the vessel had arrived at Ilha Grande, an order was issued prohibiting the admission into Brazilian ports of any vessel with a cargo of forage coming from Argentine ports; that it was in consequence of such order that the authorities of Ilha Grande refused to admit the "Aquidneck."

The Brazilian Government denied any liability for damages occasioned by its action, holding that the preservation of the public health was of greater importance than commercial profits.

It is believed that this Government would in a similar case, adopt the same measures.

This Department therefore, does not feel warranted in taking any further action.

[*Signature missing in National Archives records*]

The Homicide Aboard the "Aquidneck"

Were it not for the existence of the following consular dispatches, heretofore unpublished, an uncomfortable mystery would continue to surround the homicide on board the *Aquidneck*. "There are few who will care to hear more about a subject so abhorrent to all, and I care less to write about it," Slocum said in *Voyage of the Liberdade*. However, if there ever was any point in leaving the matter so up in the air, certainly at this distance in time there no longer is.

No. 113

UNITED STATES CONSULATE GENERAL
Rio de Janeiro, Brazil

Aug. 16, 1887

Chas. R. McCall, Acting Consul General

To the Department of State

SUBJECT: Homicide aboard the American bark Aquidneck, in the port of Antonina.

Abstract of Contents,

The Municipal Judge of Antonina communicates the imprisonment of Joshua Slocum, Master of said bark, charged with killing one and wounding another of his crew. Telegrams received from Police Delegate at Antonina on the subject. The wounded man, Jas. Aiken, in hospital at Paranaguá. Detailed information solicited from said Municipal Judge and from the Judge of Law at Antonina.

The Homicide Aboard the "Aquidneck"

Hon. Jas. D. Porter,
  Ass't. Sec'y of State
    Washington

Sir:

I have the honor to inform the Department that I received to-day a communication (translation of which is herewith enclosed) from the Municipal Judge at Antonina, Province of Paraná, stating that Joshua Slocum, Master of the bark Aquidneck, of Baltimore, was in prison in that city charged with killing one and wounding another of his crew. From telegrams received at this office (before my arrival here) from the Delegate of Police of said city, it appears that the occurrence took place on or about the 24th ult. aboard the Aquidneck then anchored in the port of Antonina; and that an enquiry was held by the Police Delegate and the documents in the case remitted by him to the Municipal Judge. This officer, as stated above, decided to hold the accused for trial. The last telegram from the Police Delegate states: "In the preliminary examination the Master declared that he acted in self-defense; the witnesses did not testify contrary to this alleged justification."

The name of the man who was killed is not given with certainty. That of the wounded man is not James Ecken, as given in the Municipal Judge's communication, but James Aiken. This I learn from a letter just received from the wounded man, and from which I conclude also that he is now in hospital at Paranaguá, a city not far South of Antonina. Aiken gives no particulars of the affair, but merely writes to ask that he be "forwarded to Rio de Janeiro."

The Aquidneck, as is shown by the record-books of this Consulate, arrived at Rio de Janeiro on May 11 last, from Rosario, laden with hay, and sailed on June 1 in ballast, for Paranaguá. She was built in 1865 at Mystic, Conn., has a net tonnage of 325 66/100; and Joshua Slocum, the Master, is given as sole owner. The Mate is Victor Slocum, who, I am informed, is a relative of the Master.

Further information than the above I am not able at present to submit to the Department. I have answered the communication of the Municipal Judge, asking that he cause to be furnished me a statement of the facts in the case, a summary of the evidence and the declaration of the accused; inquiring as to the date when the trial would take place, and requesting other pertinent information. I have also written to the *Juiz de Direito* (Judge of Law) of Antonina (whose duty it will be to preside at the trial), requesting to be notified of the date of the same, and, when it shall have been held, of the result; begging, as the official representative of the country of which the accused is a citizen, that he be brought to judgment as speedily as possible and that, as I was assured would be done, the case be disposed of as strict and impartial justice requires.

I have considered it my duty to apprise the Department, so far as possible, of the facts connected with this unfortunate occurrence; and I beg to say that further information will be forwarded when received.

I have the honor to be, Sir,

Very respectfully,

Your Obedient Servant

Chas. R. McCall

Acting Consul General

Enclosure:

Translation of communication from João Passos, Municipal Judge of Antonina, to the U.S. Consul General in Brazil.

Translation.

Municipal Court of Antonina

August 10, 1887

I have the honor to communicate to you that in conformity with the Order of Oct 5, 1833, the North American citizen Joshua Slocum, captain of the American bark Aquidneck, has been imprisoned in this city by order of this Court, being indicted as answerable to the penalties of Art. 193 and the same Article combined with Art. 34, of the Criminal Code for death and wounds practiced on the persons of Thomas and James Eckens, of the crew of said bark.

I avail myself of the opportunity to express to you my sentiments of high esteem and consideration

(Signed)   João Passos,

Municipal Judge

To the Consul General
of the United States
in Brazil

The Homicide Aboard the "Aquidneck"

No. 116

UNITED STATES CONSULATE GENERAL
Rio de Janeiro, Brazil

Sept. 5, 1887

Chas. R. McCall, Acting Consul General
  to the Department of State

SUBJECT: Homicide aboard the Bark "Aquidneck," in the port of Antonina.

ABSTRACT OF CONTENTS,

Information received from the judicial authorities at Antonina of the trial, acquittal and release of Joshua Slocum, Master of said Bark.

Hon. Jas. E. Porter
  Ass't. Sec'y of State,
    Washington

Sir:
  Referring to my No. 113, of 16th ult., I have the honor to apprise the Department that, in response to my enquiries, the judicial authorities at Antonina have informed me that Capt. Slocum, of the "Aquidneck," was brought to trial on the 23d ult. and, the evidence showing that he acted in self-defense, was acquitted and immediately put at liberty.

  It is learned further that the seaman James Aiken, although very severely wounded, is recovering and that the name of the man who was killed was Thomas Maloney.

  I have the honor to be, Sir,
              Very respectfully,
              Your Obedient Servant
                        Chas. R. McCall
                        Acting Consul General

The Homicide Aboard the "Aquidneck"

No. 53

Department of State
Washington, September 17, 1887

Charles R. McCall, Esq.
Acting Consul of the United States
Rio de Janeiro

Sir:

I have to acknowledge the receipt of your dispatch No. 113 dated the 16th ultimo in reference to the homicide on board the American bark "Aquidneck" alleged to have been committed by Joshua Slocum, master of the said vessel.

Your action thus far, as reported, appears to have been discreet and proper, and is approved.

The Department awaits further and more specific information before directing any particular course or policy to be pursued.

I am, Sir

Your obedient servant

Alvin A. Adee
Acting Secretary

No. 128

CONSULATE GENERAL, U. S. A.
Rio de Janeiro

Nov. 18, 1887

Mr. Armstrong
To the DEPARTMENT OF STATE

SUBJECT:

Trial of Joshua Slocum, Master of Bk. "Aquidneck" of Baltimore

ABSTRACT OF CONTENTS

Enclosures—
1. Translation of letter of Municipal Judge
2. Translation of the testimony of Capt. Slocum in the trial, etc.

The Homicide Aboard the "Aquidneck"

Honorable James D. Porter
  Assistant Secretary of State
    Washington, D.C.

Sir:

I have the honor to enclose herewith, Translation of a letter rec'd. by me, from the Judge of the Court before which Joshua Slocum, Master of Bk. "Aquidneck" of Baltimore was tried for the killing of Thomas Maloney and wounding James Aiken (the latter as I am informed has about recovered) American seamen, and also at the time of this unhappy occurrence, were part of the crew of the said vessel. I also send translation of the testimony of Capt. Slocum in said trial. As will be seen, defendants, in the Courts here, are required to testify, as other witnesses, subjected to cross-examination, etc., and great importance is attached to this testimony. Another feature, that seems a little strange to us is, that the *verdict* is made by a *majority* of *the Jury* and when, as was the fact in this case, the verdict is *unanimous,* the case is regarded a very clear one. I have made every inquiry into this unfortunate affair that the remoteness of the scene of its occurrence and place of trial would permit; and from all I have been able to learn, the verdict is in my opinion a righteous one. The authorities, as will be seen, have been very courteous in the matter, complying cheerfully with every request made; for which I have tendered greatful [sic] acknowledgements to the Municipal Judge.

I have the honor to be, Sir,

> Your Obet. Sevt.
>
> > H. Clay Armstrong
> > Consul General

MUNICIPAL COURT OF ANTONINA

Sept. 16th, 1887

Most Excellent Sir:—

I have the honor to acknowledge having received Your Excellency's communication dated Aug. 18. In conformity with your request, I proceed to give you a brief account extracted from the judicial records of the trial of Joshua Slocum. On July 23, at 11 o'clock p.m., when Capt. Slocum was asleep in his room, his wife, who had not been able to sleep, heard the sound of steps of some one coming towards them and the noise caused by the lowering of a boat. She awoke her husband who, proceeding to investigate the matter, went to the door opening on the deck where he met the sailor, James Aiken. Being attacked by the latter, he fired at him with a carbine which he carried, causing the wounds described in the inquest. Afterwards the Irish sailor Thomas * made his appearance, defying the captain and threatening him with a knife. The captain ordered him to go forward, but he refused to obey and attacked the captain who, firing again, killed him. The captain immediately related what had occurred to the police which, taking the steps the case required, caused an inquest to be held, discovering not only what has already been stated, but also that the captain had received several wounds. The citizen, Robert Burnett, being appointed interpreter, an investigation was made, there being nothing, however, very important in the evidence given which was very favorable to the captain who, it was stated, was kind to his subordinates. The evidence of one of the witnesses attracted especially the attention of this court. Antonio Felippe de Miranda, a wealthy merchant of this city, stated that he had been told by Thomas Thomas, carpenter of the bark Aquidneck, that two of the sailors wished to kill the captain. This was said in that merchant's commercial establishment, but Thomas Thomas afterwards denied having said it. The evidence of the witnesses does not explain the cause of the mutiny. The only cause alleged, that is, the refusal of the captain to give the men money to buy matches and tobacco is so inadequate as to be unworthy of serious consideration. Indicted by this court, as I have already had the honor to inform Your Excellency, the captain was tried on the 23d ult. and unanimously acquitted, the jury recognising that he had acted in self-defense. In virtue of this decision he was immediately released. The most important document in the case is that detailing the examination of the captain, in which Dr. David Pacheco acted as interpreter. I therefore send you a copy of this document in which you will find more particulars.

Supposing that I have thus complied with your request, I avail myself of the opportunity to renew to Your Excellency the protestations of my very high esteem and consideration.

May God Guard You.

Signed, João Passos
Municipal Judge

* Thomas Maloney.

The Homicide Aboard the "Aquidneck"

TRANSLATION

Examination of the prisoner Joshua Slocum.

The oath being administered to the twelve jurymen, the judge through an interpreter proceeded to question the prisoner who, under neither material nor moral constraint, freely answered as follows:

Being questioned as to his name, birth, place, age, civil state, and residence, he replied that his name was Joshua Slocum, that he was forty-three years of age, that he was a married man, and that he resided on board the vessel which he commanded.

On being asked how long he had resided on the vessel "Aquidneck" he answered that for about three years and three months, which sailed under the American flag, and of which he was captain and owner. On being asked what were his means of livelihood and his profession, he replied that his profession was that of a seaman and that he followed it by commanding the aforesaid "Aquidneck." On being asked whether he knew how to read and write, he replied that he did. On being asked whether he was aware of the nature of the accusation against him and whether he needed any explanation on this point, he answered that he knew and that consequently he required no explanation. On being questioned as to his whereabouts when, as was alleged, the crime was committed, he replied that he was on the deck of the "Aquidneck" near the door of the cabin. On being asked whether he was acquainted with the witnesses and whether he had anything to allege against their testimony, he answered that he was acquainted with them and that against the witnesses John Shears and Andrew Dubois he wished to say that they had combined with Thomas and James Aiken to raise a meeting on board for the purpose of killing him and his wife. On being asked whether he attributed the accusation against him to any private cause, he replied that he did not. On being asked whether he had any proofs to present in order to justify himself or demonstrate his innocence, he answered by narrating what had taken place on board the Aquidneck resulting in the wounding of the two sailors Thomas * and James Aiken and in the death of one of them. The narration was to the following effect: At half past ten o'clock at night in the cabin of the vessel he was awakened by his wife, who informed him that

* This should be *Thomas Maloney*, such being the name of the man who was killed.

161

some one was whispering and moving quietly on the deck near the cabin. Perceiving this, he took his carbine and went out of the cabin for the purpose of ascertaining who it was that was walking in that way in a part of the ship in which the entrance of the sailors at that hour was prohibited. When he reached the deck, he saw nothing at first, as the night was very dark. But in a little while, his eyes having become accustomed to the darkness, he perceived James at the door opposite that through which he had come out (and which was aft) and heard him calling to him (whom he supposed to be in the cabin) telling him not to be a coward but to come out and send them forward if he dared. He then ordered James to go forward, but the latter, disobeying the order in a mutinous manner, said, "Oh! you are there, are you?" and rushed at him. The captain, however, kept him off with the barrel of the carbine, but James rushed at him again and seized him by the throat, throwing him on his knees. In this position, aware of the character of his assailant who in Rio de Janeiro had assaulted a ship captain, he fired at him with the gun he had in his hands. He further declared that during his struggle with James he saw Thomas near him but that after firing he lost sight of him and did not see him again until he went forward to take the necessary steps in regard to what had occurred. Then in the narrow passage between the cabin and the gunwale he met Thomas who threatened and insulted him saying, "I have this for you" alluding to something in his hand which the captain supposed to be a weapon. Hearing a sound resembling the click of a revolver and knowing the bad reputation of Thomas who, by his own confession, had been in prison for two years in Buenos Ayres for attempting to kill a man with a view to robbing him, the captain, on seeing him raise his arm, again fired in self-defense, the carbine he carried, before Thomas could use the weapon with which he seemed to be armed. On being asked what was the effect of the shots, he had fired, he answered that Thomas * was killed on the spot and that James * was wounded, being afterwards sent on shore where he could have medical attendance. On being asked what weapons were found in the possession of James and Thomas, he answered that he did not examine James at the time when he was wounded, but that he had seen a kevel in his hand and that afterwards a sailor's knife was found to be in his possession. As to Thomas, he also had a kevel in his hand when he was wounded, besides a small

* Thomas Maloney and James.

knife open at an angle of 45 degrees. On being asked whether he had said in the police office or in the municipal court that Thomas, when he was shot, had fallen with a kevel in his hand, he answered that he had not said this or that it had been found in his hand after his death, but that it had been found out of its proper place and near the spot where Thomas had fallen. This is what he had said to the police delegate when on the day following these events the latter had gone on board the Aquidneck. He had then shown this officer the two kevels which were found out of their places and which had evidently been in the possession of Thomas and James on the previous night. On being asked whether he had anything more to say, he answered that he wished to declare that if he had killed Thomas and wounded James it was in self-defense and in defense of his wife and children. On being asked whether he had any relatives on board besides his wife, he replied that he had two children, one of whom between 16 and 17 years of age, acted as mate of the vessel, the other being six years of age. On being asked whether during the struggle with James and Thomas any other sailors had approached, he replied that the struggle had already terminated with the death of Thomas and wounding of James when his son and some other sailors came to the spot. On being asked why he supposed that Thomas and James had plotted with other sailors who were witnesses in this trial, to kill him and his family, he said that it is the invariable usage on board vessels of all nations to prohibit sailors from going aft where the captain's quarters are situated, after a certain hour at night, unless they are expressly called for some purpose; yet James and Thomas had gone there without his permission or that of his son, the mate, and had done so in the manner described, which clearly shows what was their intention. On being asked whether James and Thomas had asked him for money to buy tobacco or any other article on the evening or night of July 23rd, he answered that neither of them had done so on that evening or night and that permission was never given a sailor to go on shore, on any pretext whatever, late at night. On being asked whether he owed wages to the sailors James and Thomas, he replied that both of them had contracted to receive their wages at the termination of the voyage which was not concluded at this port, and that he had advanced them a much larger sum than was customary in such cases. To James he had given more than a month's wages for the purpose of buying clothes, but that the money had been spent for alcoholic liquors. He said further that when Thomas was wounded by the second shot he

163

fired, Dubois and John Shears had come to the spot fully dressed, whereas his son was in his sleeping apparel. It was, moreover, worthy of note that Thomas, when he was killed, had only stockings on his feet. As the prisoner had nothing more to say, this examination was concluded, and, with the assistance of the interpreter, was read to him by me, the undersigned clerk, in order that he might point out any errors or omissions. This being done, the judge countersigned all the sheets of this document and signed it together with the prisoner and the interpreter, to all of which I bear witness—I, Antonio da Costa Ramos Flores, Clerk of jury have written it.

(signed)   Francisco da Cunha Beltrão

"   David Pacheco

"   Joshua Slocum

A true copy

(signed)   Antonio da Costa Ramos Flores

Voyage of the "Destroyer" from New York to Brazil

Foreword

Voyage of the Destroyer is Slocum's footnote to history, personal and otherwise. When on 9 December 1893 the Department of State wrote him it could do nothing further about his "complaint against the Brazilian authorities," the captain was already on his way to Bahia. He had put to sea two days earlier as "navigator in command" of a warship being towed to that country. The vessel had been purchased by the Brazilian government to help suppress a revolt begun at Rio de Janeiro two months before. At that time Admiral Custodio de Mello, on the armored cruiser *Aquidaban,* had seized command of naval forces and demanded the resignation of the President, General Floriano Peixoto.

Peixoto had replied by buying abroad whatever warships his agents could find. In the United States they had acquired the 130-foot iron gunboat *Destroyer,* an invention of the designer of the *Monitor,* John Ericsson. The Swedish-born engineer's "destroyer system," as he called it, a submarine torpedo and means of launching it incorporated into a boat, was the prototype of the later torpedo-boat destroyer. However, a long period of peace had kept him from trying it out. When he died in 1889, the contraption was still untested, and even its seaworthiness uncertain.

Though Slocum could not obtain a merchant command, he was, according to a newspaper report, "highly recommended" to Peixoto's men. It was only four years since he had sailed up in a rather unusual craft. He felt confident he could make the trip down in a larger and even more curious one. Certainly he was willing to undertake the job. Not only was he pleased to be asked, but he needed the money.

167

Furthermore, having been thwarted six years in the matter of his claim for the *Aquidneck,* he welcomed the chance to break through official channels and go to work on his own.

"Frankly it was with a thrill of delight that I joined the service of Brazil to lend a hand to the legal government of a people in whose country I had spent happy days," he wrote in his introduction to *Voyage of the Destroyer.* But actually it was the unhappy ones which provided the greater impetus; and quite near the end of the "story, or the 'yarn' you may call it," he wrote: "Confidentially: I was burning to get a rake at Mello and his *Aquideban.* He it was who in that ship expelled my bark, the *Aquidneck* from Ilha Grand some years ago. . . . I was burning to let him know and palpably feel that this time I had in dynamite instead of hay."

Slocum and de Mello, however, did not meet; the *Destroyer* did not see action. "After being towed under and over a large portion of two oceans," the *Destroyer* made Bahia 13 February 1894 and was handed over to Brazilian sailors. But the new crew, indifferent or inept, very soon sank her in the harbor and with her Slocum's prospects of pay. According to one maritime historian, he had been promised $20,000. What is certain is that he did not receive a dime. The war, as far as Slocum was concerned, was over. Instead of one "complaint" against Brazil he now had two.

In March, Slocum went north by steamer to the sloop in Fairhaven. Once again he found in writing an outlet for his frustration. The raw materials of disappointment and hardship he reshaped and processed into New England style humor. Though it is a somewhat sardonic story he tells, he begins with a Whitmanesque sentence: "From the quiet cabin of my home on the *Spray,* the reminiscence of a war." His characteristic charm breaks through in asides: in a backward glance to an incident of childhood; in a sidelong one at his present condition living alone on the *Spray,* nighttimes sitting among his books or at work on his writing, by daylight turning to "sailorizing" on his "light and airy craft." In a funny way it is in this *Voyage* that Slocum is most clearly seen as the last of the race of New England ship-captain writers. Though he still was to do his grandest sailing, nevertheless, as the gunboat steams in—however uncertainly—sail fades out, and with it, one realizes, not only masters but sailor-poets as well.

Slocum published *Voyage of the Destroyer* in 1894. The Boston papers were delighted with the book, and especially with the more offensive parts, which appealed to the rising and popular imperialist mood of the day. One of the *Destroyer's* crew, however, was not much amused. In a piece in the *Boston Sun*, 3 August 1894, a British soldier of fortune, Lieutenant Carlos A. Rivers, claimed that Slocum defamed him by writing that he, Rivers, was beaten in a scuffle with the *Destroyer's* cook, Big Alec of Salem, a character who could have come straight out of Melville. Thereupon an enterprising reporter decided to carry the news of Rivers' displeasure to the captain. Slocum was sitting on the edge of Long Wharf, the *Spray* alongside, and disentangling a fish line when the reporter came up. Had he heard that Rivers had challenged him to a duel? Concerning which question the newsman reported the following:

The captain exhibited no emotion, but philosophically remarked:
"There are my wife's feelings to be thought of. I have always been of the opinion that duelists should consult their wives. My wife is very set against notoriety. I am sure she would not wish to have it said that I, after sailing the seas, was slain by the man who wanted to fight a cook. It would be too stupid, 'don'cherknow,' " wound up the Captain, quoting an alleged expression from Lieut. Rivers's vocabulary. . . .
"Do you think the Lieutenant is on your track?" asked the reporter.
"I wouldn't be surprised. He is rapacious, and a fire eater. When he comes for me I shall wrap myself up in the American flag and dare him to do his worst. . . ."
Pressed with more questions, Capt. Slocum declined positively to name the place, time and weapons for a duel.
"My wife," he concluded, "would be disturbed to be left a widow. I am going right out of Boston on a voyage. It is better that I catch fish than fight him. Just say that I am a man with a big fist. Do anything to discourage a duel. Good day. . . ."

Slocum sent a copy of *Voyage of the Destroyer* "as a Christmas present and no more" to his friend Samuel Pierpont Langley, secretary of the Smithsonian Institution. Later, he was pleasantly surprised to hear that Langley had placed it in the "Museum Library." Though it took up less Smithsonian space than the *Liberdade* canoe, in the long run its luck was no better. It cannot be found.

Slocum also sent a copy to the *Century* magazine, but the editors showed no interest. Five years later, however, when the *Century* was publishing *Sailing Alone, McClure's* magazine inquired about the *Voyage of the Destroyer*. Slocum's hard-working *Century* editor, Clarence C. Buel, was pained when he heard that *McClure's* proposed to run an abridged version in March 1900. He wrote the captain, and then from 184 Princeton Street, East Boston, 4 November 1899, came the explanation.

> About the Destroyer matter: You may think it strange that I did not submit to Century anything worth printing at all (?) perhaps you do not know that it was submitted when it was quite new. It has lain pretty nearely as it is now for three or four years. . . . I think I know why I am asked for it
>
> You can depend upon this old spruce knot from the North to do the squar thing when ther is anything to do: This sort of timber never swells and I guess I hold pretty fairly on even keel—I try to. . . .

Of the three known copies of *Voyage of the Destroyer*, two have additions and corrections in Slocum's hand. The first is the copy he presented 8 August 1894 to the Commonwealth State Library, where it may still be seen, in the State House in Boston. The other was given "compts of the author" to a Boston man, Commodore John A. Stetson. Sold and resold several times, it now is owned by the present writer. A copy inscribed for M. S. Brown, United States consul at Sydney when Slocum called there in the *Spray* in October 1896, was subsequently acquired by the captain's son, Victor, but some time after the latter's death in 1949 it went to a dealer.

The captain's marginalia in the first two copies mentioned are presented as notes to the text which follows.

Voyage of the "Destroyer" from New York to Brazil

INTRODUCTION

From the quiet cabin of my home on the *Spray,* the reminiscence of a war.

Frankly it was with a thrill of delight that I joined the service of Brazil to lend a hand to the legal government of a people in whose country I had spent happy days; and where moreover I found lasting friends who will join me now in a grin over peacock sailors playing man-o'-war.

Brazil has indeed sailors of her own, but to find them one must go down to the *barcassa* and the *jangada* where the born son of Neptune lives. In his unassuming and lowly condition, a true child of the sea.

To these friends let me tell now, who have come from the war, the story of the voyage of the famous *Destroyer:* the first ship of the strong right arm of future Brazil.

VOYAGE OF THE "DESTROYER"

To sail the *Destroyer* from New York to Brazil in the northern winter months was not promising of great ease or comfort—but what of that! I, for one, undertook the contract of the novel adventure myself, with its boding hardships and risks which soon were met face to face. Twelve brave fellows—better sailors I shall never see—casting their lot with me in the voyage were willing also to accept whatever fate might have in store for them, hoping,—always, for the best. Curiously enough the fatalistic number of the crew (thirteen) was not thought of before sailing. Every one was looking for good omen. Some of the older sailors made a search for rats, but not even the sign of a mouse could be found. Still no one backed out—times were hard ashore!

A young man to fight the ship, in case of being "attacked by pirates" on the coast of Brazil, came from a recent class of Naval Cadets of Annapolis. With sufficient confidence in his theory, this young man came early, bringing plans of * the fight along with him, if there should be any, for he was bound to begin right.

Also a nobleman, who came principally as Count, engaged himself to be with us. The position of "specialist" was spoken of as his, but that was by the way. The Count was a † good judge of an hotel.

There came, too, I should not forget it, a young officer of the Brit-

* of *changed to* for.
† brand-new sailor *inserted.*

172

ish Royal * Marine Artillery, who became in time a feature of the crew. This young man had accumulated handsome gold bands for his caps, which he frequently lost in the sea, upon the voyage,—caps and all. The sword, which by merit he had won, was of enormous size. This sword and a heavy Colt's revolver, which he wore night and day, gave my young officer, I must say—for a little man—a formidable appearance. The prodigious sword, I recall, "won by valor at the Soudan," and "presented by Her Gracious Majesty, the Queen," had the American eagle stamped upon its blade. This was the famous sword, which buckled on over a dashing red coat, secured for him the position of third gunner's mate to the Count, Mr. W——, a gentleman of influence procuring him the place upon first sight of this rig and the cut of his sails, for it must be borne in mind that we are to make a strong warlike appearance when we come to Brazil, if not before.†

Of all these awe inspiring weapons, my old sailors made due note. Well, this young man came also, but taking passage along with the fighting Captain and the Count on the steamer that towed us he was always three hundred fathoms ahead, except in the ports we touched on the voyage, and again came together to recount deeds of valor and trophies won; my sailors always standing in awe of sword or gun; being, too, always touched at the sight of the unmistakable bird spreading its wings over the Queen's gift.

My own position on the ship: of "navigator in command," was hardly less important than those above mentioned. Being a man of a peaceful turn of mind, however, no fighting was expected of me, except in the battle with the elements, which should begin at Sandy Hook. So on the 7th of December, 1893, after devious adventures in the getting ready, we sailed for Brazil, in tow of the *Santuit,* of Boston, and began our fight early in the voyage.

The most noteworthy of the adventures spoken of in "the getting ready" was the destruction of a stout projecting pier, which apparently stood in the *Destroyer's* way, on leaving the Erie basin. It was plain to be seen then that she could do the work well for which she was designed and named: A destroyer not of piers however. But,

*British Royal *crossed out.*

† *Sentence added:* Not having met the enemy & Sir Charles still thirsting for blood chalanged the writer Slocum to dual but coming to ask his wife about it—wives should be consulted in duels—that lady said no!

shades of Ericsson,—ship or pier! She could evidently knock them *all* down!

I was not in command at the time: *better* than that, the fighting captain was— But didn't the splinters fly! I thought of the poor "pirates" on the coast of Brazil and pitied them if, by their misguiding star, they should fall athwart the *Destroyer,* in her fighting mood.*

It was six in the morning when we tripped anchor from Robins' reef, stowed all and proceeded down the bay.

The clear breath of heaven came free to every sailor on board and a voice that I knew hailed: "The ship is all your own." We were free unshackled from the land.

The *Destroyer* towed smoothly and steadily enough; and gliding along by the channel buoys she marked a fair rate of speed.

Off Sandy Hook, and clear of the shoals, the tow was stopped, that we might readjust the thimble in the towline, a sharp point having pressed against the rope threatened to cut it off. This thing, though small in itself, was the beginning of a series of mishaps that came soon enough. My sailors on the beak of the bow with tackle, crowbar and sledge-hammer fixed up the defective thimble, as far as a job of the kind could be remedied. The sailors wondering what longshoremen would do, if they hadn't old tars to finish their work at sea! I mention these things now for the guidance of sailors hereafter.†

The propellor at this point was disconnected, it having been decided to use steam only for the pumps and the whistle. A code of signals was arranged between the two vessels: Rockets and lights for the night: the Universal Code of Flags for the day, and the steam whistle for day or night, making a complete arrangement in all. Nothing was left undone by the agents in New York, looking to the safety of the ship and the completion of the voyage. Having been many years out of commission she got a great overhauling—on paper.

Her lockers bespoke in that department, the highest class of a seaworthy condition.

Long after when we were all under water and could get no fire to burn, one of the stokers, cloyed of good things, damned his fate that

* At this point the "fighting captain, a good man, was transferet to the Santuit where he would be found wen the heavy fighting began

† I have since learned that the thimble was designed by a very learned man Its defects should not therefor be charged to the poor artesan who made it—J.S.

he should ever have to breakfast on cold roast turkey and cold chicken. I shall come upon this low wretch again on the voyage.

The crazy thimble being repaired, all seemed well and the *Destroyer* was again headed on her course.

The wind was from West to Nor'west, blowing a moderate breeze. The sea was smooth. The ship making good headway, skirted the coast with the land close aboard as far South as Winter Quarter Shoal; whence taking her departure she headed boldly away for the Gulf Stream.

At 6 A.M., Dec. 8th, the light on the shoal was visible a-beam.

The latitude at noon was 37° 03′ N.

Longitude at noon was 75° 05′ W.

Distance run in 28 hours 220 miles.

The wind has veered to the N.N.E. The sea is not so smooth as it was. The ship behaves well, however, all things considered, though occasionally now she rolls down low in the water and takes short cuts clean through the waves. Steam is up, it has been kept up since we left New York.

The steam pumps are at work—the vessel is making water. A calamity has overtaken us. The ship's top seams are opening and one of the new sponsons, the starboard one, is already waterlogged.

All hands are pumping and bailing to keep the ship afloat, but the water gains steadily, and by midnight, it is washing the fires and putting them out. Steam *must* be kept up, else we go down.

The sea is rough! What can we do?

Rounds of fat pork are heaped upon the struggling fires. Hard bread smeared with fish oil is hurled into the furnace by the barrel, and all available light stuff, as well, that will burn on the top of dead coals, such as tables and chairs, is thrown on the fire. There is no longer any draft, the rising water has cut the draft off. But the pork, and the bread and oil, and our furniture after a while—a long while it seems—makes a joyful fire that sends steam flying into the tubes and pipes to lend us its giant strength. Danger signals of rockets and blue-lights have been shown through the night.

The *Santuit* responded promptly to all of our signals, and handled the *Destroyer* with great care, on her part, in the rough sea. The storm continued through the 9th. But with energy taxed to the utmost, we gain mastery over the sea, and the water in the hold is so reduced by daylight, that coals may burn again on the grates. A number of holes and leaks have been found through which the water has been streaming all night. We caulk some of them with cotton waste, and plug others with pine wood.

We signal the tug boat to go ahead, that we are "all right." We are out of the first danger!

A stout canvas bag is made now, one that will hold a barrel of water. A derrick at the hatch is also rigged for a hoisting purchase. Hardly is this done, when sorely needed. All night long, (Saturday), this bag is hoisted and emptied by eight pairs of strong arms. The rest of the people on board are driving the steam pumps, and repairing defective valves and making new ones, all as fast as they can. The cook, throughout the storm, prepares warm coffee for all hands. There are no idlers around these days of storm and toil. The steam pumps after a while are working again all right; then a long pull and a strong pull at the big canvas bucket along with the pump for a matter of four hours more, without a rest, and the ship has free bilges once more.

December 10th, 11th, 12th and 13th * are days like those just gone, and ones to come of incessant care, anxiety and toil. The sea runs more regularly, though, as we proceed southward, nearing the regions of the trade winds, which is at least some respite. And although destined to disappointment when we shall actually meet them, the all expected fine weather of the "trades" stands before all on board as a beacon of hope. No energy is spared to "reach the trades."

The water in the hold is kept down from one to three feet. Occasionally a rolling suck is gained, which in our joy of it, we call free bilge. Great quantities of water goes over the ship. She washes heavily, still, going often under the seas, like a great duck, fond of diving. Everything is wet. There is not a dry place in the entire ship! We are most literally sailing under the sea.

The *Destroyer* comes out of the storm today (13th), decked from the top of smokestack to bottom of the lifelines in Saragossa weeds or flowers. All along the man-ropes fore and aft, are hanging in clusters, these flowers of the sea: a rare and beautiful sight!

The good Swede, Ericsson, whom we all know, conceived the *Destroyer*, a ship to turn navies topsy turvy. This, the first one of

* *Changed to:* December 10th, 11th and 12th.

the kind, was intended for harbor defense and to remain on the coast at home. It was a Yankee, so I believe, who guessed that she could be taken to another hemisphere: and here we are well on the way with her, already "across the Gulf," the great bugbear of the voyage. All of her seagoing qualities are tested, we know what they are. The *Destroyer* laughs at the storm, but her sailors cry "shame, shame" on some folk now snug ashore. The solvent sea leaves nothing undone in its work, and Neptune abhors a skim. Putty and paint put in the seams I don't know when, or by whom, washes out like clay, and poor clay at that.

December 13th * comes in with storm and cross sea.

We suffer!

The fires are threatened by water again up to the bars. Pumping and bailing goes on together again all night. The tug upon our signal slows down and heads to the sea, that we may again free the ship of water and plug up more leaks, which we search for now as keenly as one would look for precious gems.

Later in the day, the sea goes down somewhat. The tropical storm was short. Coal and water, under great difficulties, were procured from the *Santuit* to-day. Also some carbolic acid is procured, with which to wash a dangerous wound. Assistant Engineer Hamilton, an oldish man, becoming exhausted in the storm last night, fell backwards down the engine room hatch, receiving a fearful gash clean across his bald pate which had to be herring-boned together. The wound was dressed, and Hamilton, made easy, was stowed away till further comforts could be given.

One Thomas Brennan, the stoker, who complained of roast turkey in the storm, mentioned before, showing frequent signs of mutiny, refused to mind the fires, as directed by Hamilton, his watch officer, before the accident. Brennan kicked Hamilton, when no one was by to interfere, then jumping upon the old man, bit him on the face like a wild beast. My sailors are exceptionally good seamen; up to the standard of manliness in many ways. If the sea could be rid of all such brutes as this Brennan, good sailors would be happy. His case will be attended to later on.

December 14th, the ship is heading for Mona Passage, no great distance away.

* *Changed to:* December 14th.

Voyage of the "Destroyer"

The trade winds are very strong and a heavy cross sea is encountered as we near the Windward Capes of Tahita. Twenty miles N.W. of Mona Passage, the rudder is disabled. We can put it but two spokes to port, and but half of its proper angle to starboard. With this much, however, she is kept fairly in the wake of the tow-boat; both ships steering excellently well.

December 15th, early in the forenoon, the *Destroyer* has entered and is passing through Mona Passage. In the afternoon, she hauled to under the lee of the S.W. point of Porto Rico, to receive more coal and water from our supply ship, the *Santuit*. Thence proceeding instantly to sea, she headed direct for Martinique. Now, if the trade winds were strong outside, they are fierce in the Caribbean Sea. The waves are sharp and fierce in here, where times out of mind, we have all seen it so smooth.

Wet to the bone before, our *hope* is dampened now! body and soul is soaked in the sea! But there's no help for it, we all know—for nearly all on board are sailors—and if the *Destroyer* won't go over the seas, go under them she may. All hands will pump her out and hold on, for go to Brazil she shall; nearly all have decided on that, so far as human skill can decide. To encourage this sentiment, and see that the tow-line is always well fast and secure is largely the duty of the "navigating officer" of the good ship *Destroyer*.

A pump brake more often than the sextant is in his hand, and instead of taking lunar and stellar observations in the higher art of nautical astronomy, he has to acknowledge that the more important part in this case, is of searching out leaks and repairing the defects. To work a lunar distance is one thing, but to free a leaky ship and keep her so in a gale of wind, is quite another thing—it is well at times to have a knowledge of all these fine sciences and arts.

This night, the sea is rough and dangerous. The storm is wild and bad. The port sponson, as well as the starboard one is now waterlogged. He was a clever man who designed those sponsons and saw them constructed in such a manner that both of them didn't fill up together.

The crew have all they can do to keep the ship afloat to-night. The water puts our fires out. All we can do, we can't keep the water down; all hands bailing for life.

The main hull of the *Destroyer* is already a foot under water, and going on down. The crew have not seen the thing as I have looked upon it to-night, all they have seen is hard work and salt water. Not like driven cattle, do they work either, but as stout, loyal men. The owner of the *Destroyer,* seeing that she would not insure, will reward these men handsomely (?) for their excessive exertions in keeping her afloat at all. She could not be insured for the voyage; nor would any company insure a life on board.

Well, I left her going down, a foot under water. Believe me, the *Destroyer,* to-night, was just about ready to make her last dive under the sea, to go down deeper than ever before. The tank that we lived in on deck, was all that buoyed her up; the base of this, too, was well submerged when "Big Alec" of Salem said, "Captain, steam in the man is going down, too; we can't keep up much longer." But the storm was breaking away, and the first streaks of dawn appeared to cheer every soul aboard. With a wild yell the men flew to their work, with redoubled energy and wrought like demons.

This saved the *Destroyer,* and probably our own lives, too, for it is doubtful if a small boat could have lived in the storm, for it was still raging high.

The *Santuit* has seen our signals of distress, and is standing by as near as it is prudent to come in the gale. Twice in the night, I was washed from the wheel, and I usually hold a pretty good grip. Dizziness, from a constant pelting sea made me reel sometimes for a moment. To clear my senses and make sure that the voyage was a fact, and that the iron tank on which we were driving through the waves had in reality a bottom to it somewhere under the sea, was all that I could do and reason out.

The storm goes down by daylight, as suddenly as it came up in the night. And we get in under the lee of a small island for shelter and rest—Ye Gods—a rest!

It was the Island of Caja de Muerties, adjacent to Puerto Rico, which gave us this comfort. Here we cast anchor at 9 A.M. and lay till 8 P.M. of the same day, (December 16th,) when propitious appearances in the heavens, we sailed again on the, now, somewhat irksome voyage. But "the Windward Islands will soon be gained," we all said, and "to the south of them, the trades we *know,* will be fine." And so the expedition went on, heading now for Martinique.

At Caja de Muerties, the *Santuit's* crew lent a liberal hand to straighten things up on board after the hard pumping and bailing.

Voyage of the "Destroyer"

Colonel Burt, himself, on the *Santuit,* in command of the expedition gave ample signs of his appreciation of the merits of a good crew. The ship had free bilges before she cast anchor at the island.

There is but little to say of the rest of the voyage through the Caribbean Sea. The ship is taking a circuitous route, the sooner to gain the lee of the islands. Proceeding under low speed, and changing her course from time to time, to accommodate the ship to the run of the sea, she goes hopefully on.

December 18th, the best steam pump is broken beyond the possibility of repair on board. Nothing, except new, will take the place of the broken parts. But happily enough, the sea has gone down and we suffer but little now from leakage. The kind influence of the islands is with us this time in our need, and we'll soon be in smoother water still. So the ship goes now full speed ahead, with no rough sea to hinder.

December 19th, at daylight in the morning, the islands of Guadaloupe Maria Galante—(God preserve the name), and Dominique, are all in sight. The sea is smooth and the trades regular. The *Destroyer* is heading direct for Martinique, she raises the island soon, and at 4 P.M. of this day, came to anchor at port St. Pierre— in a leaky condition!

Here at St. Pierre, we met the *America,* as was anticipated. The stoker, Brennan, the kicker and biter, was transferred to that ship, where his mutinous conduct could be conveniently restrained in a "brig," which she rated. I own, here, that I was ugly enough to ask it as a favor: that instead of roast turkey and chicken, he should have bread and water, for a day or two, with not too much bread in it.

Poor old Hamilton was still in a very sore condition. He, too, was transferred to the *America,* where there was a good hospital in which to lay up and a very excellent doctor to mend his broken head.

One of the America's engineers took Hamilton's place on the *Destroyer.* And Sir Charles, the hero of the Soudan, coming from the *Santuit,* before we leave Martinique, makes our number again thirteen.

Why is Sturgis towing always the ship of the thirteen crew? We have no use now for number thirteen, the ship's work being better * than it was and why did he cast anchor first at the Island of Caja

* *Changed to:* lighter.

de Muerties? A cold thrill runs through me now, as I ask the question concerning that king of two-boat men and his compact engineer, Mr. Brown, whom we all thought would be hard to kill, even in war.

"Yellow Jack," alas! will answer my question in Rio.

I glance at the page of my manuscript just filled with the thoughts as they came without other shape, and I see that it bears the number thirteen, which was written there before I had thought at all of what I would say.

A small matter, sometimes, sets the greatest of you all to thinking; this "thirteen" comes back to me now, like an echo from over the sea. But it's all right! I suppose I am entranced with emotion. I must put up my nervous pen, else I'll be sentimental here in the small, still hours on the *Spray*.

At daylight this morning, to resume my small task and finish the story, or the "yarn" you may call it, I open a book for the word Noronha. Staring me in the face, is a letter to "Capt. Sturges, S.S. *Santuit*," which I wrote and did not send, here among the pages concerning Fernando de Noronha.

The atmosphere of the whole voyage is around me still. So I turn the matter away for the day to resume other work on my sloop, the *Spray*—some sailorizing on my light and airy craft—I may finish the voyage to-night.

Evening on the *Spray*, brings me back to the days on the *Destroyer:* The old year was escorted out and the new year ushered in at Fort de France Bay, by my sailors in a glorification ashore becoming the importance of the timely occasion. William, one of the smartest of the crew, came aboard from the hospital, some days later, minus a piece of his liver, which quiet John, the fireman, snipped off with a jack-knife in an argument over a bottle.

Now, John, you wouldn't think to see him, the drudge at work, would say bah to a goose. But on a New Year it was different. There was no arrest made.

A policeman brought aboard a sheath-knife that was found at the scene of the fray, merely with the request that "when the crew went ashore again they would leave their knives behind." This reasonable suggestion was strictly respected.

All of our stores were resorted at the Island, dried and repacked. Moving to Fort de France Bay, December 21st, repairs were made there till January 5th, 1894, on which date the *Destroyer* again sailed, at early daylight.

Our condition at sea we find is better than it was. The *Destroyer* goes with some degree of safety now, benefited, to be sure, by her late repairs. The trade winds are still blowing very strong, and although towing in the teeth of the wind, the ship is kept free and handled in all respects without the wear and tear on a man's soul that was suffered in the early part of the voyage. But that, now, is neither here nor there. The procession has passed!

Mr. Mondonca, minister from Brazil, assured us sailors before leaving New York that all the sea south of the "Gulf" would be "like a lake"—We found it so! But what lake, I'll never tell!

Our company of thirteen, I have said, was made good at Martinique. One of the number now is Sir Charles, the "hero of Soudan." Sir Charles is not only in the expedition, but is one of us on the *Destroyer*, to pass the Rubicon in her, now that she has crossed the Gulf. Previous to this his sailing had always been in large ships, therefore he could not, for a long time, be reconcile' to the poetical motion of the *Destroyer* of lesser dimensions.

Sir Charles was, however, a stern disciplinarian.

Numberless were the duels he would have fought on the *Santuit*. But for the want of gentlemanly principles, no one accepted his challenges—not even the nigger cook, to whom he gave choice of weapons. This sanguinary spirit spurting from the third gunner's mate on the voyage, what will be the state of the *Destroyer's* decks? I ask myself, when the gunner himself appears and the fighting captain takes charge.

But the cook, seizing the frying-pan in his black fist, against all the rules of dueling, don't cher know, chased Sir Charles around the deck. That wasn't all; the nigger having gained on Sir Charles sufficiently to reach him, he thought, let fly the blooming pan, but hit something hard. Instead of Sir Charles's head, the steam winch caught the blow, and of course the pan broke into a thousand pieces. It was a bad blow for Sir Charles all the same. Capt. Sturges hearing of the mishap—he was bound to hear of it—it was the *Santuit's* slap-jack pan that was broken, and hearing of Sir Charles's thirst for blood, called him to the bridge for an interview, which could be heard all over the harbor, to the effect that "any more such work on the *San-*

182

tuit, sir, and I'll make shark bait of your d—d * carcass, d'ye hear?
Now, go forward." †

Sir Charles h'went!

Colonel B——, with a twinkle of humor, transferred Sir Charles
then to the *Destroyer*—"to stand by the captain."

Now the crew of the *Destroyer* having had, I may say, a pretty
salt time of it, were ready and willing for anything fresh. The hero
of "many bases" dropped into the vacancy like one born for the place.

But what a fighter he was, to be sure! A duel on the *Destroyer*
bless you, came to a focus in no time. No one up to the present had
thought of personal combat—hadn't found time to even think of a
quarrel. But now ten paces were marked off on the *Destroyer's* deck,
and had not Sir Charles's friend and countryman, Wildgoose, the
engineer, extracted all the bullets from the revolvers, some one on
board might have been hurt! I know it is a sin for me to grin over
the reminiscence of an enthusiast heading for war; but one may
be chief mourner at a funeral itself and be obliged to laugh.

The chap was a good rifle shot, there was no doubt about that.
He was known to have emptied a magazine of bullets into the body
of a dead shark one day at the anchorage. It was a very large monster, but Mr. Brown, the *Santuit's* engineer, had already shot the
brute through the head, killing him instantly. Nevertheless, our
third gunner's mate blazed away, putting every shot that he fired
near one centre close abaft the fin by a method of quick action with
the trigger and lever which he called "pumping." "If this shark
were only Mello!" I thought. This feat led, naturally, to a rehearsal
of exploits at the Soudan, which we had not heard of before. Oh,
no; It was the "Bedouin scouts that came for us one morning, swinging in on their tall war camels, and I just took aim with my rapid
firing gun and pumped the riders out of their saddles, one, two,
three, just like that, Sir." This, in fact, was told confidentially to me
with a coolness to indicate that it was nothing to "pump" a man.

For the admonition of sailors and sea bathers, generally, I say,
put no faith in the yarn about harmless sharks. They are always
liable to be about coral reefs and around ships—and they are always
hungry.

The shark about which I was telling; one of the largest that I

* "d's" *crossed out.*
† forward *changed to* for-rard.

ever saw, in the place, too, where even some natives declared there were none, came near making a dinner off one of our crew. Mr. Kuhn, one of the engineers, was in bathing. I had just advised him to come aboard: that if "John Shark" should chance to sample him sticking plaster would never make him whole again. But, "Oh, there is no sharks," he said, and the American Consul, who was aboard, said there were none in the bay. When up comes this monster, with a bound through the water, right before us; as much as to say, "What do you think of me then, if there are no sharks?" and he struck a bee line for Mr. Kuhn, who, fortunately, was near the ship. It was going to be a close shave, however. The shark, as he darted forward for his would-be victim, lashed the sea with his tail like a pleased tiger.

Then Mr. Brown, the cool engineer of the *Santuit*, snatching his rifle with haste, took aim, holding the range till the monster, rising to make a grand lunge and clean sweep, fired. The ball passing through the shark's head, decided the moment. The brute shot past his mark, with closed jaws and lay lifeless on the water, a target, as I said, for the gunner's mate, who "pumped" the carcass so full of lead that it sank before it could be secured—any way it went down.

Mr. Kuhn proved himself to be a pretty fast swimmer, when he finally concluded to take my advice and come aboard, and being reminded of it by a twenty foot shark close upon his heels. Being an athletic young man, it didn't take him long to get in over the side, without the aid even of a step-ladder.

Mr. Kuhn, I may say in a word, landed on deck like a flying-fish in a gale of wind, and not a moment too soon. It was a day for sharks. Three more of the same species as the one just slain, not less, I should say, than 18 feet long each, now appeared not far from the vessel. They were apparently fighting over a greasy board some ten inches broad by four or five feet long, which had been thrown over from the galley. Pretty soon the board disappeared and didn't show up again. A butter firkin was then thrown over. It drifted about 100 yards away, when it was seized in the huge open jaws of a hungry white shark and went the way of the board. Never a splinter of either came again to the surface of the water.

Whether the board was swallowed whole, or first sawed or ground into smaller lumber, nobody knows. It is only fair to state, however, that it was a soft pine board. The firkin is no matter. The likes of that, or a deck-bucket or two, it is well known, is mere dessert to a shark, if he is a big one.

There was no need of further cautioning the crew to keep out of the water. After the above occurrence one could hardly persuade the *cook*, otherwise a brave man, to draw a bucket of it over the side; and some of the older hands, never yet daunted by even sea-serpent or whale, abstained from water now more than ever before. The monsters, I confess, gave us all a turn.

Jan. 18th the *Destroyer* arrived at Fernando de Noronha where all hands were busied, for the day, taking in coals and water again from the *Santuit*. A very heavy surf on prevented all communication with the shore except by signals and afterwards by dispatches that were brought to us out through the breakers by convicts of the place, in one-man canoes which they skillfully managed. The occupants having no wish, apparently, to end the term of their conviction, which they told us ranged yet ten years ahead of them. Ten years of their lives had already been put in on the windward side of the island. They rejoiced now on the lee side where for the first half of their penal term they might not come, so I was told.

I observed a multitude of people, convicts and guards, on the shore, making efforts to launch a great raft (the governor's "barge" I suppose) which they did not entirely succeed in floating. The heavy breakers on the shore defied all their strength and skill, tossing the cumbersome raft back to land as often as it dipped in the sea. But the nimble canoes—mere cockle shells—came out and went in all right.

Fifty convicts had landed on the island the day before our arrival (President Peixoto's political prisoners). There were, I dare say, senators and congressmen in the busy crowd of workers to-day trying to launch the raft which, like their own thwarted schemes, poor fellows, they could not float. For sinning politicians, even, life on the island met the ends of justice, considering ten years of it on the rugged side, under the constant roar of breakers.

It was about 8 A.M., when the *Destroyer* arrived at Fernando de Noronha. At 7 P.M. of the same day, she sailed with orders for Pernambuco, where she arrived without further incident of note, Jan. 20th 9 A.M. Later in the morning, a pilot with harbor tug brought her into the inner harbor, where she was moored to the

Receife, which finishes the worst part of the hardest voyage that I ever made, without any exception at all.

My voyage home from Brazil in the canoe *Liberdade,* with my family for crew and companions, some years ago, although a much longer voyage was not of the same irksome nature.

Let no one run down the *Liberdade* of sailing fame. Her voyage, to me, was poetry, herself a poem. Such however was not expected of the terrifying *Destroyer* even from the beginning, and no one was disappointed but all were delighted to find her at last in port.

At Pernambuco, we fell in with the loyal fleet of the Brazilian Navy. Passing under the lee of the *Nictheroy,* the crew of that noble ship gave the *Destroyer* three rousing cheers. My old friend, Captain Baker, was on deck, as usual. The *America* and several other small ships were in the inner harbor. And what? my old friend, the *Falcon,* one of New Bedford's most worthy whaleships, which I last saw dismantled and aground at Fairhaven, and out of service: As like as two serving mallets, it is the old *Falcon* or Noah's Ark. Again, how mistaken: It is Admiral Goncalves' flagship, the *Paranahyba,* sure! I see cannon bristling from her sides, and gold-braided officers all about. Yes, it is the Admiral's ship.

My nautical skill is again brought into service at Pernambuco. What a thing it is to be "Navigating Officer in command." Together with the engineers, I am again mending and repairing, for which purpose the ship is grounded on the bank near the Arsenal. A few rivets about the bows having been sheared, consequent upon towing in the heavy seaway, was this time the cause of the leak. One tide sufficed for all the time necessary to repair below the waterline. When about to haul her off the following tide, a boat came from the Arsenal with orders to remain a day longer on the bank, that the work might be regularly inspected. It being a day of *festa,* the ship, even in war time, had to wait over.

On the following day duly appointed officers came, and the work that the engineers and I did in about an hour's time, was in the course of two days "regularly inspected," then, of course, it kept the water out.

I should explain that Sunday is not so much thought of by our Brazilian friends, but all of the fast days are religiously kept, and every thing they can lay their hands upon as well, over there.

The next thing in order was to fire the submarine gun.

Voyage of the "Destroyer"

A thousand pities it was that the gun itself was not in order. The Count and "specialist" wrote, from his hotel, a polite note to Admiral Duarte, begging the Admiral to witness the coming exploit with the *cannon*. There were several other Admirals about, but for special reasons Duarte had the Count's sympathy, so he invited him to come to the show. The note was written in the politest of French, but the Admiral didn't come—and tell it not to the Marines—the gun didn't go off! Worse than that, the *Destroyer* that was by this time tight and comfortable, had now to be put on the bank again, in order to unload the projectile from the cannon, since it wouldn't discharge by fire. This so strained the ship—a swell setting in that rolled her heavily against the bank, that she became leaky again. Though not a severe leak it was still discouraging. The only trouble about the whole affair with the gun was that the *powder got wet*.

But it was now hurrah for the war, boys, get a cargo of powder in and be off, ship and cargo was supposed to go against the arch rebel, Mello, who would have been "Liberator" of Brazil, but for the other man. Peixoto was bound to be "Liberator" himself. There was no time now to be lost! But wait! I'll tell all about that, too, pretty soon.

The *Destroyer* is carrying powder now for the whole fleet, which burnt all they had saluting the admiral on the way to Bahia in his old ark.

These ships preceded us by a few days; ostensibly, in haste, for Rio, but Mello not being ready to leave just then, the "attack" was postponed. It being untimely, however, to come back for more powder, it was shipped along to them on the *Destroyer*. The dear old craft had in already gun-cotton and dynamite enough to make a noise, but Goncalves wanted more thunder of his own old-fashioned sort, so we filled her chock-a-block with the stuff to make it. The submarine cannon was all stowed over with barrels of powder and was not get-atable at all the rest of the voyage to Bahia. In fact powder was all about. Three barrels of it found stowage in the Captain's room. The fourth one we couldn't get in. It was stowed back of the galley. That it didn't all blow up is how I am here to-day—thinking of my sins.

Well, in due course the stuff was all delivered in good order to the various ships in Bahia, for which the *Destroyer* was heartily maligned by all the Naval Officers, except the Minister of Marine,

187

whom I judged to be with the legal government. Goncalves, the Admiral, was himself so enraged that he "romped" my "trata" at once. It was a portion of this same cargo of powder, which, forwarded on to Rio soon afterwards, was laid in the mine to blow up the *Aquideban*—and was fired after the great battleship got by and comfortably out of the way of it.

When I began the "voyage," I had no thought of writing a history of the whole war. Unconsciously I am drawn a distance beyond my first intent by the facts afloat of great achievements.

Horrors of war! how, when a lad, I shuddered at your name. I was in my ninth year, hired out on a farm when the thrilling news came to our township of a probable religious war. The four little churches bounding our small world, had always been in a light warfare, but *now* the *Catholics* were coming.

My employer, the good farmer, I shall never forget, armed his farm hands and his family with pitchforks, scythes, reaping hooks and the like—to do or die! There was great excitement. My own weapon was a hatchet, but that is no matter. The enemy came upon us, as it were, before we got our courage "screwed up to the sticking point." The rumpus began in the hen house, adjoining the kitchen: a heavy roost fell, and the de-il was to pay among the chickens. "The enemy! the enemy!! was the cry; the Pope's men have come sure enough!!! Where upon my employer, with laudable discretion, flinging open his doors, made haste to welcome the invaders. "Gentlemen," he cried, "come in, I have always been of opinion with you. Come in, gentlemen, and make yourselves at home in my house." When lo! it appeared there wasn't a man of any kind to come in. An old warrior cock, with bedraggled feathers, strutted in, however, and said "tooka-rio-rooa," or something to that effect, and the dear little chickens were all put back to roost—all except a few which next day went into the soup, and the war was finished.

But that, so far as I know, had nothing to do with this cruel war in Brazil. Nor can I say that history, in this case, repeats itself. The association is with me in the chain of my own thoughts and feelings. In those days, when I followed the peaceful pursuit of the plough, or rather a harrow it was, which towed by the old gray mare, that I navigated over the fields, already ploughed, and followed at three dollars a month. I say I shuddered then at the thoughts of war. But now I find myself deliberately putting my hand to documents which in those days nothing could have induced me to sign. At this time of life, after being towed under and over a large portion of two oceans, I sign articles of war! And notwithstanding my well-known peaceful disposition, I am expected to fight—in gold braid—to say nothing of the halibut-knife as long as my arm to dangle about the heels of my number elevens.

I observed on board of the Admiral's ship several young officers towing their swords well behind on the deck, thus obviating the danger, to the wearer, of being tripped up by the wicked blade. In the face of all the well known dangers I join the navy. Confidentially: I was burning to get a rake at Mello and his *Aquideban*. He it was, who in that ship expelled my bark, the *Aquidneck*, from Ilha Grand some years ago, under the cowardly pretext that we might have sickness on board. But that story has been told. I was burning to let him know and palpably feel that this time I had in dynamite instead of hay. It would have been, maybe, too great a joke.

The motives of war: two men strive to be "liberators" of Brazil, another is ambitious to give her "a new republic"—charging brokerage for the same—others again are ready to fight for mere lucre. My own frailty I have already confessed.

I had by me still the very best of the good crew, which had followed the fortunes of the *Destroyer* all the way from New York. The Yarrow torpedo boat *Moxoto*, perfect in her construction and in perfect order, was added to our expedition. We were ready now to sail against anything afloat; but had yet to meet and pass, if we might, the fleet of the black bean eaters under Goncalves; not open foes, but lukewarm friends of greater danger, which, as I have said, preceded us to Bahia, burning their powder on the way, saluting the Admiral.

February 9th, 1894, the *Destroyer* sailed for Bahia, accompanied by the *Moxoto*, the handy torpedo boat.

On the 13th she arrived at the destination. Everything was funeral quietness at Bahia. The doughty Goncalves I saw often, passing to and fro, always to the music of a band. A captain of my grade, and foreigner at that, don't get any music in Brazil. All else was quiet and serene. The occasional pop of a champagne cork, at the "Paris" on the hill, might have been heard, but that was all,

except again the sunset gun. The rising sun had to take care of itself.
The average Brazilian Naval man is an amphibious being, spending
his time about equally between hotel and harbor, and is never dangerous.

I was astonished at the quietness of Bahia, there was not even target practice. Indeed the further we got away from stirring New
York, the less it looked like war in Brazil. There was to be torpedo
practice one day. A Howell torpedo was launched, but boomerang
like it returned hitting the ship from which it was hurled. The only
thing lacking to have made it a howling success was the dynamite,
which these remarkable warriors forgot to put in. On the following
day Goncalves, being in a bad humor, seized our ships and then
under the pretext of making ready to move the world, nullified the
great Ericsson cannon, which alone would have settled the business
of the revolt. He rendered it as useless as the "busted" gun at Bunker
Hill. Appearances were, now, that Goncalves would do himself all
that should be done. And that, to be sure, is not saying much—to
which he made a fair beginning.

Goncalves and his officers, I grieve to say, reviled the *Destroyer*,
not only, I was told, for bringing the powder so quickly upon their
heels, cutting thus into their quiet in port and hastening them on
to the front, but for still greater reasons as well. As it proved, however, there was no danger in meeting the enemy, nor any cause of
alarm. Goncalves, it is well known, was fitted out with peaceful,
harmless people in his ships; Mello's outfit was the same. Both sides
as harmless as jay birds! Why should they kill each other? That the
Destroyer, then, most formidable ship of all, must in some way be
disposed of, went without saying. When first she came to Bahia
though, and it was reported that this was the long hoped "money
ship" to follow the fleet—and pay the bills—the large iron "tank" in
which the crew lived fitting in size their expectations of the chest
out of which they would all get rich. Many * visitors came to see her
and called her a very handsome ship, saying many pretty things concerning "her lines," etc. But when to their great disappointment,
instead of bank notes teeming forth, they beheld sea-begrimmed
tars tumbling out of the "tank," and worse still barrels of gunpowder being hoisted out, they said, "*Nao maes,*" we give it up! Their

* *Changed to:* rich: many.

disappointment indeed was considerable, and * her fine lines could no longer be seen.

It was proposed by Goncalves and his officers, to dig a hole in the bank, somewhere, and put the *Destroyer* in it under the mean pretext of putting a patch over the old leak spoken of at Pernambuco—a small matter. The meaning of this was practically the condemnation of the ship.

Robinson Crusoe in the fiction was not in a worse fix than this in which Admiral Goncalves would have himself appear. Starting too from this very Bahia, Crusoe in the course of his wonderful adventures, we all know, found himself obliged to dig his ship out to the sea, else let her rot in land. Exactly opposite, was the dilemma of our modern hero. The *Destroyer*, Goncalves said, should be dug into the *land*, else she would sink at sea.

Nothing of the kind! Why not bring the vessel into the small basin already at hand, I suggested, ground her on the smooth bottom and make the repairs. "Oh, no! Oh, no! That couldn't be done," echoed a chorus of voices from officers, all in a plot.

But his Excellency, Mr. Netto, Minister of Marine, friend of the legal Government, seeing my earnestness and good faith, when I told him that I stood only on the order said, "Bring her in." In she came!

The ship was now all the Admiral's. He had romped my contract, made by the Commander of the forces at Pernambuco, with the advice of the Inspector of the Marine; which was to go against the rebel fleet, and sink them all, if we could find them—big and little— for a handsome sum of gold, considering the danger, for each one that we should destroy—I would have commenced on the small ones, to be sure.

I began to think of the little farm, which so many years ago I promised myself. I say now, I could † almost hear the potatoes growing—but not quite. As the question of docking in the basin, approved of by the Minister, was a matter of small warfare between he and his officers, who one and all wished to have the hole dug, and to put her in it, I exerted myself to please His Excellency on the Government side. I had great success that day. The leak was

* and *crossed out.*
† *Changed to:* I say I could now.

found and repaired before I slept that night, and before daylight the *Destroyer* rode at her anchor again in the bay, as tight as a cup. So in the morning, when the officers of the Arsenal came down to the Basin to inspect the work, the vessel wasn't there. Mr. Netto took my hand very * warmly whenever after this I chanced to meet him alone. I could readily perceive the Minister's position to be a delicate one indeed.

The *Destroyer* was mended and afloat, and barring some slight repairs needed to her machinery, was in far better condition than she was when leaving New York. Had the voyage extended around the globe, a ship to be proud of would have been the ultimate result. To have sailed her first to the land of boiler-makers wouldn't have been amiss.

Goncalves, however, had one more open chance. He would have made a dozen chances to consummate his plan. It was with great interest that I watched the progress of the whole business, and noted the methods employed to the end that the *Destroyer* herself should be destroyed. The great pneumatic gun on the other ship I heard nothing about. That I believe was fixed and made harmless early in the "preparations." The Ericsson *"cannon"* was the gun to be dreaded now. At New York detectives were put on to keep folk away from the Ericsson gun; but here at Bahia it was impossible to get anybody to go near it. A plan was studied to somehow put it out of the way. "Should that once double on us like the Howell torpedo," they said, "it would be worse than the yellow fever around here," and "we must get it out of the way." So on the 28th Feb., 1894, having discharged the sailors and having filled their places with bean-eaters from the fields and the mountains, and having found a captain unfamiliar with the ways of a ship, (a thing by the way not so hard to find) Goncalves sent the ship to sea, he did, with this outfit on board. She was gone only 24 hours, however, and returned with all hands ahoy! flat on deck, seasick and afraid. The Captain—it would be impolite to call sick—lost his appetite and prayed to be thrown overside early in this memorable adventure, which will live in record side by side with the history of the war. The *Destroyer* had proved too much for the greenhorns—they couldn't lose her.

* very *crossed out.*

Voyage of the "Destroyer"

There was, however, one man, a soldier, on board who would have run the engineer through for deserting his post. This man (the soldier) was afterwards thrown in jail, I heard, and, for aught I know, was shot. The Captain, even in his own misery, saved the engineer's life. He said, "Let us each die a natural death. Let us all die friends on deck, since there is no one to help us into the sea, and let us have no more war." Goncalves thought he knew what he was about, when he put that crew on board, but he did not count on the latent strength of the *Destroyer*. On leaving, she at once collided with the stout steamer that towed her from and back into Bahia, and still was not wrecked, in fact, she was but slightly damaged. She was towed with a short steel hawser and no one was at the helm to guide her in the going or in the coming, for there wasn't a soul on board that could steer. She sheered wildly over the ocean. The hawser would have incontinently carried away the bows of a less substantial vessel, but the *Destroyer* of many storms withstood the hard usage.

The day was calm or nearly so, and the sea was smooth; else indeed the ship would have been foundered—with all of those young souls on board! I watched her from the top of the hill going. From the same place the next evening I was rejoiced to see her safely return.

Her best pump was landed before she went out. I saw it at the Arsenal under a tree; her anchors, however, they left on board. She was not pumped from the time she sailed 'till she arrived back into port for reasons already stated. The ballast which would have trimmed the vessel well, was also taken ashore at the same time and same place, with the pump, and was never brought back on board. So the *Destroyer* went by the head, for the want of balance, which caused her to sheer worse than ever. But for all that the other steamship failed to sink her. So the *Destroyer* came back.

And so after triumphantly breasting the winter waves of the North Atlantic Ocean, the *Destroyer* changed her crew, to give up the fight in a summer sea.

I wish I were able to give a better account of the warriors that I met in Brazil, and especially of the sailors(?) who shipped on the *Destroyer*, in lieu of the men who sailed her from New York. But this true account, not always flattering, I know, will be endorsed by every honest Brazilian of whichever side, and will, I am sure, greatly assist the future historian. My own position in the voyage forbids me to say more.

Concerning the last days of my worthy old ship, there is little more to say. The upland navigators at the Arsenal at Bahia, having observed the New York crew put the *Destroyer* in the basin and out again with dispatch, undertook, like some tropical quadrupeds, to do the "trick" themselves. Whether from pure cussedness or not this time, I can't say, but they stove a great hole in her bottom, having grounded her on a rock, "accidentally," they said.

Alas! for all our hardships and perils! The latest account that I heard said that the *Destroyer* lay undone in the basin. The tide ebbing and flowing through her broken hull—a rendezvous for eels and crawfish—and now those high and dry sailors say they had a "narrow escape."

The torpedo boat, *Moxoto,* must not be forgotten. My pen blushes to record it.* A crockery-ware clerk was put in command of her, and she was sent on a trial trip among the ships in the bay. Now to the poor clerk and his earthen-ware crew, all this was strange and dangerous, but they cut up high jinks and made things hum in the bay. Everybody was on his guard for awhile, for they had steam up and couldn't stop her—they didn't know how. The Captain hailed a foreign steamer and shouted to the engineer that he would pay 20 mil reis to be stopped. But the engineer couldn't get aboard—he couldn't catch her. She could steam 18 knots and was now at full speed.

The Vice-Admiral's brig, an old craft of many summers at Bahia, came in for the first ram in the collisions that followed. But the *Moxoto,* not hitting her fair, came off second best in the battle. Then away, always at full speed, she made for brig No. 2 not far away, aground on her own beef bones, and gave her a blow in the quarter that brought the crew, officers and all, on deck in a hurry. Being aground, the danger of a collision had not been thought of. The shock, they at first supposed, came † from an earthquake, but that's no matter. It wasn't, and as nothing less could move them to action, they all went below again, like good, loyal warriors where they should do the least harm—if they should do anything at all— and be most out of danger. There were no bullets flying about, to

* *Changed to:* record it: a.
† came *changed to* was.

be sure, but the sun was dangerously hot at Bahia. It was, in fact, all the fire there was, to speak of, in the whole war.

Early in March, the rebel navy weakened, if I may use the term in their case, and the *Aquideban,* after burning much powder to no effect, proceeded from Rio harbor unmolested to sea; leaving open waters for my old friend Goncalves to take up in turn, which he did, and went on with the business of burning powder in greater salutes than ever. The revolt began in Rio, somewhere in September, 1893, the date don't matter much. The funny war so far as the navy was concerned finished of itself in March, 1894. No historian can ever say more.

They may tell of hot firing and hot fires but it was by the heat of the sun, and by that child of filth, yellow fever, that most lives were lost. In this way, I said, some of the members of our own expedition were taken. Were it not indeed for these darker shades, I could now look back with unalloyed pleasure over the voyage of the *Destroyer;* the voyage of past hardships, now so pleasant to bear. The voyage which gave to the crew, and myself, withal, no end of fun.*

* Calling on a high oficial in the Brazilian Navy some time after to see about a balance of wages still due me from Destroyer that officer said: "so far as we are concerned captain we will give you the ship and if you care to accept the terms I will send an officer to show you where she is—I knew well enough where she was at that very moment J. S.

FINIS.

Sailing Alone Around the World

Foreword

Sailing Alone Around the World is at bottom a record of a man and a boat. It is a beguiling tale of wanderings and escapes, of pressing forward or being blown off course. As nature writing, it reveals an extreme and affecting knowledge of the sea. The testimony of one who faced a far-flung loneliness, it is loved by those who accept man's natural aloneness. Also a narrative of personal realization, it speaks to whoever counts on himself. As a reflection of serene, simple living, it is both actuality and glorification. By and large the voyage Slocum made was a rather vehement form of self-expression; the voyage he wrote about was a kind of art and sublimation. And if *Sailing Alone*, written when the foray was over, portrays the literary captain, the letters that survive, written in the heat of the struggle, depict the historical one. Though closely related, the two are not identical. The reality of life is one thing; the reality of words, another.

"I was born in the breezes, and I had studied the sea as perhaps few men have studied it, neglecting all else," Slocum wrote. For all that, at age fifty-one, he was, in the world's eyes, defeated. As a master, he had failed; he could not get another ship. Nor was he a successful author, nor even, at that point, a functioning family man. He owned almost nothing except the home-made *Spray*. In such a plight, many a man, understandably, might have lost interest. But Captain Slocum, instead of coiling up his ropes, got ready to put to sea. If sailing could no longer serve a practical purpose, it could still provide a perfect illusion of purpose. Command of a vessel, duty

199

to the ship, the necessity for making decisions, for keeping a sharp lookout, for arriving at one's destination, leave no room for doubt as to why one is living. So the captain began fitting out. And almost the first thing he called for was books. In a letter from 69 Saratoga Street, East Boston, to his publisher friend, Eugene Hardy, general manager of Roberts Brothers, undated but very early 1895, he wrote:

> Dear Mr. Hardy: If you could let me have the books you so kindly spoke of the other day, when I was at your office, it would be a great help to me I am sure for I shall have some time to read and shall require all that I can get in that direction for recreation. Mr. Wagnalls (old acquaintance) of the house of Funk and Wagnalls told me the other day that he would also put me up some. I may be able to pay for all this kindness at some future time but not now.
>
> A "shop-worn" book would be as good for me as any: so far as the outside goes. . . .

On 9 January Slocum wrote Hardy again. "The handsome pkg . . . for the Spray library is greatly appreciated. . . . I am completely fascinated with the new books. . . . A thousand thanks."

The captain's library now included Darwin's *The Descent of Man* and *The Expression of the Emotions in Man and Animals*, Newcomb's *Popular Astronomy*, Todd's *Total Eclipses of the Sun*, Bates's *The Naturalist on the Amazons*, a book which perhaps inspired Slocum's last voyage, Macaulay's *History of England*, Trevelyan's *Life of Macaulay*, Washington Irving's *Life of Columbus*, Boswell's *Johnson*, *Don Quixote*, *Life on the Mississippi*, one or more titles by Robert Louis Stevenson, a set of Shakespeare, and in "the poet's corner," as he called it, works of Lamb, Moore, Burns, Tennyson, and Longfellow.

Slocum prepared not only to read but to write. To his responsibilities as captain, cook, and crew he planned adding those of correspondent. He sought commitments from newspapers for a series of travel letters for which Roberts Brothers was to act as agent. Sounding like a professional journalist, he wrote Hardy, in the undated letter above, "My Syndicade is filling up: This morning I got the great Mr. Watterson: The Louisville Courier Journal." But Slocum, eternally optimistic, had misunderstood the *Courier-Jour-*

nal's reply. What one of their editors had, in fact, written was: "I can not contract with you for the whole of your series of letters. . . . I shall be glad if consistent with your arrangements to have you submit the letters to us, we to pay for what is used."

Newspapermen going down to the dock on the East Boston side of the harbor found the captain in cheerful mood as he made his final preparations. How would he handle the boat, he was asked, and how would he get any rest. "She is very easily managed, even in a breeze," he replied. He also said that he had a "steering gear" which would act automatically once the boat was laid on her course, and thereby enable him to rest. As to sleep, there had been many a time in his merchant captain's career when he had gone two or three days without. Slocum had confidence in his exceptional ability to resist fatigue.

The captain told reporters he would sail alone unless his wife changed her mind about staying ashore. But he must have known very well that Hettie wasn't going. He had asked her, and she had replied: "Joshua, I've had a v'yage." He said he thought this would be his last trip, that he hoped to make enough money from it to buy a farm upon his return and settle down with his wife and children. On the verge of departure, he found the cliché of the sailor and wanderer useful.

"To Go Round the World," the *Boston Globe* announced. "Capt. Slocum Starts from East Boston Alone in his 40-Foot Spray." In a last-minute decision Slocum changed the *Spray's* hailing port from Fairhaven to Boston, but he still did not know what his course was to be.

"Where I shall next be heard from I cannot tell," he told a reporter. "I shall make right out to the southward. . . ."

"Courage still good?"

"Just as good as ever," was the hearty reply, as the captain cleared away everything forward and prepared to hoist the jib.

"Good luck to you then. . . ."

"Aye, aye" was the cheery response, and the captain sprang aft to the wheel. As the whistles were sounding noon, he sailed away. . . .

The dramatic exit notwithstanding, Slocum sailed, not southward, but eastward, and only as far as Gloucester, twenty miles across Massachusetts Bay, where he wanted to procure some fishermen's stores—but where also he might, in truth, again "weigh the voyage, and my feelings, and all that."

That Slocum stayed two weeks in Gloucester disappointed the "syndicate." The papers wanted action and speed, but the captain left when he felt ready. And still, he did not turn south but continued eastward, ineluctably drawn to the land of his birth which he had not seen since the day, when a boy of sixteen, he left home to go to sea. As he neared Brier Island, he asked the way of a fisherman at anchor and in reply was given the wrong directions. After sailing "through the worst tide-race in the Bay of Fundy," he arrived at the old familiar village where he at once examined the seams of the *Spray;* and then he wrote this letter to Roberts Brothers.

The Spray
Westport N. S.
May 13th/95

Messrs Roberts Brothers

Dear Sirs: I wrote you from Bristol Me, the other day, and sailed immediately in this direction.

Fetched Westport Friday night. Experienced no difficulties in getting along alone; an no inconveniences I like the novelty of being "alone" even better than I anticipated. I find that I friends, even here, at Westport—"The Island of Plenty"

Will you please give me some hint of how much the first of my experiences was disliked if the worst is known?

I find no want of interest where I come to keep alive all there is in it.

I will as I get along, I think, make it interesting anyhow I shall try— But I have been put to my wit-end to get started right

Do please be patient with me and you will find in the end that I shall try to be fully square

Yours truly
Josh Slocum

Will be here a few days

Almost a month had passed since the captain left Boston, and here he was, only as far as Nova Scotia. Certainly from the newspaper point of view, the trip was not going right. On 21 May, still in

Westport, Slocum wrote again, this time addressing Eugene Hardy. His spelling, worse than usual, reflected an agitated state of mind. Apparently his first reports had not been wholly believed.

> *Dear Mr. Hardy:* All very well for Mr. R to say that; but Mr. H knows how it is himself!
>
> I am in a grand good place to repair my vessel and do it cheaply. Giving her a great going over!
>
> Will sail on the next full tides (full moon)
>
> I think Pernambuco will be my first land-fall, leaving this Thence touching the principal ports on S. A. coast on through Magellan Straits where I hope to be in November. So many courses to be taken after that. I can onlly then go as sircum-stances and my feelings dictate
>
> My mind is deffinately fixed on one thing and that is to go round. Go with care and judgement and speak of what I see
>
> There s' not a reporter here to twist one, that I know of It is a haven of rest, but I shall do my work and sail as quickly as possible
>
> I guess it would bother my friends to proove that things don't happen on this voyoage just as I relate them
>
> Thanking you Sir for your kind note
>
> Very Sincerely Yours
>
> Josh Slocum

Another month passed, and the captain, still in Nova Scotia, had merely edged eastward. From Yarmouth, 20 June 1895, he sent Roberts Brothers a two-part letter: first, an explanation of the delay, and second, his plan for getting on with the voyage. He would not go south after all but east, the English way of going around. The "whale story" which the papers would not publish appears in Chapter II of *Sailing Alone*.

> *Messrs Roberts Brothers*
> *Boston*
>
> *Dear Sirs* I arrived here yesterday with the Spray all in good order after having caulked her all over and recruited myself. I had an attack of malaria at Gloucester, from working at the Sloop on the beach there in a sickning ooze. So I had to leave there with the work unfinish, and bide my time. That explaines my slow movements.

Foreword

The whale story was as real to me, when I wrote it, as anything that ever happened; perhaps the wory over a small leak that I found going on worried me and put me into a night-mare

But if I slept at all that windy night and had a dream at all it was not beyond the space of time of three Seas passing and while I was having even less than "forty winks"

What the papers do not care to publish I would not, upon second sober thought, wish to see in print over my name

After all deliberations and careful study of rout and the seasons, I think my best way is via the Suez Canal; down the Read Sea and along the Coasts of India, in the winter months, calling at Aden and at Ceylon and Singapore taking the S. W. Monsoon next summer up the China Sea. Calling at Hong Kong and other treaty ports in China thence to Japan and on to California

From California I believe I shall cross the Isthmus of Panama The freight agent of the Panama road wrote me that I could not get over the isthmus—we'll see! I'll have a car load of curios beside when I come to that point

My health is excellent now. I experience no inconvenience in working the sloop alone and have not lost a moment so far when sailing. My courage is better than it was and I am now at the edge of slipping off place.

I shall call at Fayal. The season is just right now to go without the wory from typhoons and monsoons. So I go east instead of west and roll around with the world. . . .

All the money I have been able to raise so far I have put into the Spray and into various absolute necessaries for the voyage

I think I shall begin now to knock things togather in better shape and follow a desided course—

I shall wait here for American mail. Sailing the first fair wind after that

Very Sincerely Yours

Joshua Slocum

Before he left Yarmouth, Slocum took in butter, potatoes, and water and bought the shop-worn tin alarm clock, his only timepiece throughout the voyage. Finally, on 2 July, he let go, as he said, his hold on America. The "boisterous Atlantic" lay ahead. He wrote later that during those first days out "a feeling of awe crept over me. My memory worked with startling power. The ominous, the insignificant, the great, the small, the wonderful, the commonplace—all appeared . . . I heard all the voices of the past laughing, crying. . . ."

From his cabin the ex-merchant captain called out orders, then went forward and obeyed them himself. He sang work songs of the merchant service as he had known it—"Reuben Ranzo," "Johnny Boker," and "We'll Pay Darby Doyle for his Boots." He had not accepted the age of steam, the impersonal, the non-singing age. But the sound of his own voice made him lonely, too, except "when the gale was high," and there was "much work to do."

Slocum sailed thus eighteen days. When next heard from, he had reached the Azores. Three months had passed since he sailed from Boston, and all now went well—except for the worry of getting his copy in.

"Spray," Horta Fayal
23rd July '95

Dear Mr. Hardy: I have been trying to scribble a few lines for the newspapers but find it almost impossible to do or to think The Spray is constantly crowded with these good Islanders

But I do hope the editor will make out something of what I send along. I will send in some other letter more details of the voyage.

The only surprise to me has been the contented state of my mind and my perfectly good health. Hope my friends are as well.

I sail for Gibraltar tomorrow. This is the way to go round the globe: roll with it! . . .

Very Sincerly

Joshua Slocum

When he came to Gibraltar, however, he found British naval officers thought it was not the way, at least not for one man alone. It was they who told him there were pirates in the Mediterranean and convinced him his course was unwise. At this point he might have continued eastward by sailing around Africa; however, he decided against it, perhaps to avoid running the easting down—that very long passage from the Cape of Good Hope to Australia which sailing men have always considered the most taxing of seafaring experiences. Slocum had crossed the Atlantic for nothing.

Foreword

Leaving the Rock, he steered the *Spray* westward, more or less following Magellan's route to South America. It took him forty days to reach Pernambuco (Recife), and there he landed 5 October. "Did I tire of the voyage in all that time? Not a bit of it! I was never in better trim in all my life, and was eager for the more perilous experience of rounding the Horn," he wrote in *Sailing Alone*.

But he wrote Eugene Hardy something else. Evidently the *Boston Sun* bought no travel letters. The manager of the *Boston Globe*, Charles Henry Taylor, was not buying at the anticipated price. Completely disregarding punctuation, only three days after making his second Atlantic crossing, the captain sent off this letter.

> The Spray   Pernambuco
> Oct 8th 95

*Dear Mr. Hardy:—*I recd. your kind note I am not surprised that a letter of mine turned out bad, but Mr T— agread on $20 per col for the availables not as a litterary production—the high price—but to encourage the enterprise as I understood it and the editor of the Sunday Sun said "all right I'll go you $20" that was all the contract mad[e]. the latter gentleman promise to give me a note to that afect but seems to have forgotten it Mr Taylor, however, is doing what I expected to pay for: in manifolding editing etc—no small job $5 per col or even less according to number of papers would be all right. Mr T— made the figures, not I.

The original list I have still. But please say nothing about it. I am sorry. Would like at least to help my little boy.

The Sun printed trash of mine freely enough on more than one ocasion when it came for nothing. And I suspect that a case of murder or rape would find space for all the particulars, in all of the papers.

But I can't go to war with them!

I shall get through! I lived awful hard coming down. But dont say anything about it

I could have better the condition but I wouldn't call for fruit or vegetables at the islands. I was eager to get forward I had plenty hard bread coffee & tea and butter

I send one more letter I dare not look it over If it is not interesting, I can not be interesting stirred up from the bottom of my soul

It was the voyage I thought and not me. No sailor has ever done what have done. I thank you sincerely for giving my son the money.

Very truly

Josh Slocum

I will report to you before sailing from here

Before he put to sea again, Slocum shortened the main boom inboard four feet, to make the mainsail a little less cumbersome. This was the first of a number of changes he made in the *Spray's* rig in the course of going around. Leaving Pernambuco 24 October, he came next to Rio de Janeiro, having sailed 1,200 miles in twelve days. He called at once for his mail, and the word he received from Charles Henry Taylor, Jr., seems to have been the "syndicate's" coup de grace.

What is surprising is not that the journalistic venture collapsed but that it survived as long as it did. Slocum, though now seven months out of Boston, had only begun to circle the globe. Whereas journalists like Nellie Bly who sped around the world in seventy-two days to beat the record of the fictive Phileas Fogg were right for the newspapers of the 1890's, Slocum, who eventually took more than three years, was wrong. Hard enough for a man to sail by himself, and never mind writing newspaper pieces, particularly when he really knows nothing about it. The *Boston Globe,* his best customer, published only three letters, and very unevenly written they were. From Rio, 11 November 1895, Slocum for the last time wrote Hardy on newspaper business, jabbing at his adversary, and all in all sounding jaunty and his own man again.

> *Dear Mr. Hardy:* The Spray arrived here 5th, 12 days from Pernambuco A good run considering the stormy head winds which she encontered to a very unusual degree
>
> The Spray will refit and proceed South in a few days. The weather will be growing better ahead for the next two months.
>
> If I find anything of interest to speak of before I tumble into the Antarctic will write; but not to weary the papers nor to wory my best friends
>
> I shall always like to write to Messrs Roberts or to yourself if you care to hear from me as I get along
>
> I havn't, since the last news from Boston, felt like trying to

207

write for a paper I thought there was something in young C—
Taylor but I find he is only a rich mans son after all

I will not give your house any more surprises of the money
order kind. It was kind to advance the $20. I appreciate that
and the books, which I sold as I went along, and by them kept
afloat. I am doing better now and will be doing still better as I
go along Treasure Island is ahead!

I may arrive at Australia some day! You will surely want to
hear from the Spray at the great Southern Continent where our
own language is spoken.

Will you please write me C/o U. S. Consulate Montevideo,
Uruguay, if there is anything to report? I have been more than
paid for *three Liberdade books* which I would like very much
to have sent to the enclosed addresses—if you will on the chances
of getting your pay from me later on

I will sell the balance of the edition by and by on satisfactory
terms I think. . . .

I am in the very best of health and living in great hope

I remaine Yours truly

Joshua Slocum

His self-confidence restored, Slocum got on with business. First,
he called on government officials to inquire again about wages due
in the matter of the "beloved *Destroyer.*" And after that he made
preparations for sailing in waters that were unfamiliar, perhaps unknown to him. He stepped a jiggermast on the *Spray,* thereby con-
verting her rig from sloop to yawl, and making her more convenient
for single-handed sailing.*

On 28 November, he set forth from Rio. He had not gone far,
however, when a mishap occurred: the *Spray* went aground. Using
his dory, Slocum tried to kedge her off, but the dory upset and he
nearly drowned. Remember that he could not swim. "Three times
I had been under water . . . and I was just saying 'Now I lay me,'
when I was seized by a determination to try yet once more, so that
no one of the prophets of evil I had left behind me could say, 'I
told you so.' Whatever the danger may have been . . . I can truly
say that the moment was the most serene of my life."

* In name, however, she remained the sloop *Spray.* In 1903, *Sailing Alone*
was edited and abridged for school use by Edward R. Shaw as "A Geographical
Reader Describing Captain Slocum's Voyage Alone Around the World." Published by Scribner's, its title was *Around the World in the Sloop Spray.*

With help, the *Spray* was soon refloated, and the captain went on his way to Montevideo. There he met an old friend, a Captain Howard of Cape Cod, and together they made a side trip. They sailed in the *Spray* up the Plata River, where, eleven years before, the *Aquidneck* had anchored and where the young boy, B. Aymar, had hoisted the family signal of distress. "I had not been in Buenos Aires for a number of years," Slocum wrote in *Sailing Alone*. That is all. Never a word concerning Virginia and all that had happened there. But probably the true purpose of the excursion was to go to the place where Virginia lay buried. One assumes as much from what Slocum wrote about coming away in Chapter VII. "At the last anchorage on the monotonous and muddy river, weak as it may seem, I gave way to my feelings." Perhaps he knew he would not see that grave again.

Early in February 1896, the *Spray* reached and rounded Cape Virgins, the eastern entrance to the Strait of Magellan. It was the most favorable time of year, but she immediately encountered fierce currents and sudden squalls. "I reefed the sloop's sails," Slocum wrote, "and sitting in the cabin to rest my eyes, I was so strongly impressed with what in all nature I might expect that as I dozed the very air I breathed seemed to warn me of danger. My senses heard '*Spray* ahoy!' shouted in warning. I sprang to the deck wondering who could be there that knew the *Spray* so well as to call out her name passing in the dark; for it was now the blackest of nights all around, except away in the southwest where rose the old familiar white arch, the terror of Cape Horn, rapidly pushed up by a southwest gale. I had only a moment to douse sail and lash all solid when it struck. . . . For thirty hours it kept on blowing hard. . . ."

Days of beating against wind storms and currents followed as Slocum pushed westward. He anchored and weighed anchor many times till at last the western entrance was in sight. "Here I felt the throb of the great ocean that lay before me," he wrote. "I knew now I had put a world behind me, and that I was opening out another world ahead." But hardly had the *Spray* plunged into the Pacific when the wind hauled northwest and blew a very hard gale. It was the kind of wind which four hundred years before had driven Drake south to discover Cape Horn. Slocum could not hold his westward course. The *Spray*, her sails blown to ribbons, ran before the wind.

Under bare poles she headed southeast as though she would round the Horn and carry her captain back into the Atlantic. The waves "rose and fell and bellowed their never-ending story of the sea; but the Hand that held these held also the *Spray*." If Slocum lived by miracles, he did not count on them. He tried to hold the *Spray,* too, paying out sea ropes to steady his craft and break the combers astern.

On the fourth day of the gale the captain believed he was nearing the point of Cape Horn. Through a rift in the clouds he saw a mountain which he took to be the Cape. That decided him to go to the Falkland Islands to refit. He headed east. Actually, however, he was still a hundred miles north of the Cape, and instead of rounding it was fetching in toward the Cockburn Channel, one of the many arms of the Strait. "Night closed in before the sloop reached land, leaving her feeling the way in the pitchy darkness," one reads in *Sailing Alone.* "I saw breakers ahead before long. At this I wore ship and stood offshore, but was immediately startled by the tremendous roaring of breakers again ahead and on the lee bow. This puzzled me for there should have been no broken water where I supposed myself to be. . . . In this way, among dangers, I spent the rest of the night. Hail and sleet in the fierce squalls cut my flesh till the blood trickled over my face, but what of that? It was daylight, and the sloop was in the midst of the Milky Way of the sea . . . and it was the white breakers of a huge sea over sunken rocks which had threatened to engulf her through the night. It was Fury Island I had sighted and steered for . . . God knows how my vessel escaped."

In order to make his way into the Strait again, Slocum now had to sail around the wildest part of Tierra del Fuego. While refitting as he went along, and mending his mainsail, he had to keep a sharp lookout, too. The waters were narrow, he was never far from shore; and aborigines lurked all around. By this time it was known that the *Spray* had a one-man watch. Larger vessels than the sloop had been plundered and their crews never heard from again in that extremely primitive archipelago. When finally he was able to re-enter near Cape Froward, a point he had passed weeks before, Slocum had been carried halfway back to the Atlantic.

Once again the captain turned the *Spray's* prow westward, and for a second time sailed the second half of the Strait. On 13 April he made the Pacific. "Hurray for the *Spray!*" he shouted and sailed away on a northwest course. Ocean to ocean, almost four hundred miles without the detour, had taken more than two months.

Many passages have been made through the Strait of Magellan, but as W. S. Barclay, the English geographer, pointed out, three will be remembered. The first is that of the discoverer; the second, Francis Drake's. The third is Joshua Slocum's. Perhaps his is the most remarkable of all. Alone he navigated and sailed. At the western entrance he survived a Cape Horn equinoctial gale. He passed an entire night cruising and tacking in one of the worst death traps of the Seven Seas. Finding his own way to re-enter the Strait, he sailed west again, thus skirting the most perilous triangle a mariner can imagine. Single-handers who came after Slocum did not attempt the Strait of Magellan but went through the Panama Canal, which was opened a few years later, in 1915.

Shaking out a reef now and setting the whole jib, Slocum pressed on hopefully toward Juan Fernández, or Robinson Crusoe's island, as he called it. Some sixty years earlier, young Richard Dana of Harvard, serving as a sailor on the brig *Pilgrim,* had rounded the Horn and come to the same historic dot in the ocean. ". . . at daylight," he wrote, "we saw the Island of Juan Fernández directly ahead, rising like a deep blue cloud out of the sea. We were then probably nearly seventy miles from it. . . . I shall never forget the peculiar sensation which I experienced on finding myself once more surrounded by land, feeling the night breeze coming from off shore and hearing the frogs and crickets."

After navigating all alone in the smaller and less lofty *Spray,* the aging master mariner wrote: "The blue hills of Juan Fernández, high among the clouds, could be seen about thirty miles off. A thousand emotions thrilled me when I saw the island, and I bowed my head to the deck. We may mock the Oriental salaam, but for my part I could find no other way of expressing myself."

If Slocum's response to the island was distinctively his own, so was his encounter with the islanders. With a courtly air he welcomed them aboard and served them coffee and doughnuts. "They were so benighted," he later told a Massachusetts man, "they'd never seen a doughnut in their lives."

Slocum took his time at Juan Fernández. There was nothing to hurry for, and, besides, he never was in a hurry. He visited the retreat of Alexander Selkirk, the prototype of Robinson Crusoe. Some connection between his actual self and the fictional character seems to have taken his fancy, perhaps the fact that each built his own complete and personal world.

On 5 May 1896 Slocum sailed from Juan Fernández. He picked up the trade winds, and the *Spray* flew before them, toward the west and Samoa, where the captain wished to pay his respects to Fanny Stevenson, widow of an author he admired. Seventy-three days and nights he sailed alone—the longest leg of the journey. He made little of it in his book. "My time was all taken up those days—not by standing at the helm. . . . I did better than that; for I sat and read my books, mended my clothes, or cooked my meals and ate them in peace. . . . I made companionship with what there was around me, sometimes with the universe and sometimes with my own insignificant self; but my books were always my friends, let fail all else."

There was, after all, much to be thankful for. "I awoke, sometimes, to find the sun already shining into my cabin. I heard water rushing by, with only a thin plank between me and the depths, and I said, 'How is this?' But it was all right; it was my ship on her course . . . sailing at full speed. I knew that no human hand was at the helm; I knew that all was well with the hands' forward, and that there was no mutiny on board," wrote the one-time commander of the *Northern Light* and, later, owner and master of the *Aquidneck.*

Slocum made Samoa in mid-July, and Fanny Stevenson welcomed him warmly. She was a woman after his heart, one who had accompanied her husband on his voyages. Samoa was a "summer-land," wholly delightful, yet the captain stayed only a month. He still had miles to go and a life to live with sea and sky, the winds and currents, and the friendly, ingratiating sloop. Before he set sail again, he gave Malietoa, the king, a message from Adam Wagnalls, who had missionary interests. From Toloa, a Samoan lady, he received a bottle of cocoanut oil for his hair, a gift which, the bald-headed captain wrote, "another man might have regarded as coming late."

Once again he was off, this time for forty-two days, "mostly of storms and gales." It was October 1896 when, "in the teeth of a gale of wind," he flew into Newcastle, New South Wales, a year and a half out of Boston and halfway around the world. By now the voyage was becoming known; indeed, word of the captain's coming had traveled

Virginia Slocum.
Age about 33.

Joshua Slocum.
Age about 39.

Three photographs courtesy of B. Aymar Slocum

From a painting of the *Northern Light*. ". . . in the eighties—she was the finest American sailing-vessel afloat," wrote her one-time commander and part-owner.

Captain Slocum and the Gilbert Islanders. Captions by B. Aymar Slocum.

Captain Slocum and the crew of the *Liberdade*— Hettie, Garfield, and Victor.

From Voyage of the Liberdade, *1894*

The *Liberdade* at the end of the voyage.

The bark *Aquidneck* leaving the harbor of Rio de Janiero. Drawn by Charles D. Peirce in 1868 or 1869, when the artist was a young apprentice in the United States Navy, sixteen years before Slocum's purchase of the vessel.

we have'nt been but two days. out when the duff it do'nt seem to differ It has'nt the richness of raisins and sickness. and so we ups and we murmuries

VOYAGE

OF

THE LIBERDADE

BY

CAPTAIN JOSHUA SLOCUM

Joshua Slocum

BOSTON
ROBERTS BROTHERS
1894

Boston Dec 29th, 1902

VOYAGE OF THE DESTROYER

THE DESTROYER AT PERNAMBUCO.

≫≫ FROM ≫≫

NEW YORK TO BRAZIL.

Courtesy of Catherine Woodruff

From Victor Slocum's copy.

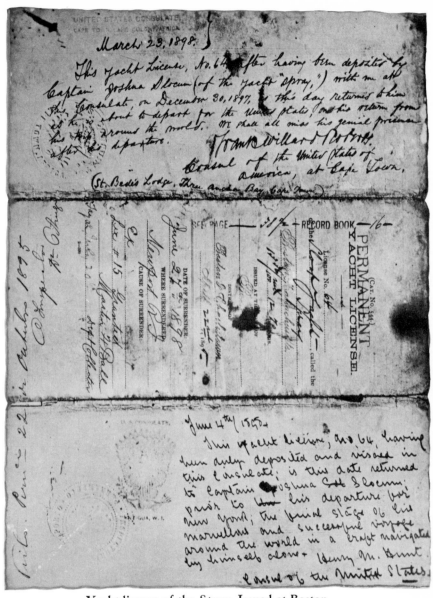

Yacht license of the *Spray*. Issued at Boston,
22 April 1895. Surrendered at Newport, Rhode
Island, 27 June 1898.

Slocum and Hettie on the *Spray*
at Martha's Vineyard in 1902.

Photograph by Clifton Johnson.
Courtesy of Anna M. Johnson.

From Sailing Alone Around the World, *1900*
The *Spray* in Australian waters.

Courtesy of Vincent Gilpin

Hauled out at Miami, Florida, 1908.

In the cabin of the *Spray*

Courtesy of
B. Aymar Slocum

On the *Spray* in home
waters, 1902.

*Photograph by
Clifton Johnson*

With sightseers, Vineyard Haven,
Massachusetts, around 1905.

Courtesy of Charles W. Russell

Courtesy of B. Aymar Slocum

Alone on the voyage around, somewhere in South America, 1895.

In South American waters, 1895.

Courtesy of B. Aymar Slocum

In the Strait of Magellan.

The *Spray* at Shell Cove, Sydney Harbor, 1896.

Captain Slocum's Lectures.

ROUND THE WORLD

INCIDENTS AND EVENTS

WHILE

CIRCUMNAVIGATING THE GLOBE ALONE

IN THE

Yacht "SPRAY."

Illustrated by Lantern Views.

. . . . *PRESS COMMENTS.* . . . .

"The Captain is an excellent reconteur ; he kept a crowded house in a state of highest amusement."—THE OWL (Cape Town). *Doctor Gill Astronomer Royal Chairman*

"At the Bree Street Congregational Church . . . a most interesting account of his voyage in his self-built boat . . . most entertaining . . . beautiful limelight views." —STANDARD AND DIGGERS' NEWS. *Burgamaster Chairman*

"A pleasant style and much natural humor, which took immensely with the audience."—DIAMOND FIELDS' ADVERTISER.

"The placard rarely exhibited in Cape Town "House Full" had to be put up early in the evening . . . a large attendance of ladies. In humorous vein the Captain traced his lonely voyage through all the climes he had visited ; frequent applause rewarding his powers of description."—THE CAPE ARGUS.

"The Captain's graphic and humorous style held the absorbed attention of his listeners throughout."—THE CAPE TIMES.

Head to do something for expenses of the voyage, Other captains might draw bottomary bonds but I lectured the Spray around the world J. S.

The Captain's dodger.

the Azores.) "Mate," he roared to his chief officer
—"mate, come here and listen to the Yankee's
yarn. Haul down the flag, mate, haul down the
flag!" In the best of humor, after all, the *Java*
surrendered to the *Spray*.

The acute pain of solitude experienced at first
never returned. I had penetrated a mystery, and,
by the way, I had sailed through a fog. I had met
Neptune in his wrath, but he found that I had not
treated him with contempt, and so he suffered me
to go on and explore.

In the log for July 18 there is this entry: "Fine
weather, wind south-southwest. Porpoises gamboling all about. The S. S. *Olympia* passed at
11:30 A. M., long. W. 34° 50'."

"It lacks now three minutes of the half-hour,"
shouted the captain, as he gave me the longitude
and the time. I admired the businesslike air of the
Olympia; but I have the feeling still that the captain was just a little too precise in his reckoning.
That may be all well enough, however, where th~~~~
is plenty of ~~~~

British

I absolve the editor
or proof reader or both
for the slip on page 31.
as I hope to be forgiven myself of many sins
Clearly I should have
said *British* S. S. in
the text
J. Slocum

Captain to Editor.

From the illustrations by Thomas Fogarty and George Varian to
Sailing Alone Around the World, 1900.

"A Brush with Fuegians."

Slocum along the Potomac, 1907.

Courtesy of Winfield Scott Clime

The Captain at
Washington, D. C., 1907.

Photograph by
Percy E. Budlong.
Courtesy of A. L. Budlong.

Martha's Vineyard: The *Spray* bound out.

faster than he had. A tremendous reception resulted—and a surprising one, too.

A ghost from Slocum's merchant career suddenly came to life. It was Henry A. Slater, the man whom Slocum shipped in 1883 at Port Elizabeth, South Africa, as an officer on the *Northern Light,* and whom he later imprisoned on board. In the intervening years Slater had emigrated to Sydney. When he heard that his one-time skipper was coming, he began a hot campaign against him, making incriminating speeches and telling the papers his version of events thirteen years before. The papers gave Slater plenty of space and also sent reporters to Newcastle for Slocum's side of the story. Despite Slater's threats of violence, Slocum sailed down to Sydney as planned. "I came to in a snug cove near Manly for the night," he wrote later, "the Sydney harbor police-boat giving me a pluck into anchorage while they gathered data from an old scrap-book of mine, which seemed to interest them. . . . They made a shrewd guess that I could give them some useful information, and they were the first to meet me. Some one said they came to arrest me, and—well, let it go at that." But Slocum was not arrested. Instead, he promptly took the offensive and had Slater brought into Water Police Court, where the magistrate ordered him to keep the peace.

And so the sailorly, small-world affair blew over. Slocum did not even see fit to mention it later, in the book. Within a month he was following his usual pattern of life in port, receiving for the *Spray* and himself all manner of invitations and callers. From Manly, a suburb of Sydney, 11 November, he sent his regrets. "I was not able to avail myself of the honor to attend the Balmain Annual Regatta Prince of Wales Birthday. The friend whom I had engaged to care for the Spray could not come and circumstances were such that I could not bring the beloved old craft along."

Like many a solitary traveler, Slocum made friends along the way. Any man who shows unrelenting purpose attracts admirers and supporters. The unusual voyage appealed to all sorts of people; many wanted to help. In Sydney he mentioned he needed new sails, and almost at once a new suit of sails appeared at his cabin door, a gift from Mark Foy, the Australian department store head. "Time flew fast those days," he wrote. For six months and more he chasséd from port to port in Australian and Tasmanian waters. In Tasmania he first gave lectures in public halls about the voyage. In some ports the *Spray*, as a show, was such a success that to handle the crowds and answer the questions became a real chore. "I never worked so hard in my life," Slocum told a caller years later. "I would be dog-tired at night and drop right down."

It was late June 1897 when the captain left Australia and the Coral Sea behind and sailed for the Indian Ocean. He was on his way home.

The palm-covered Cocos Islands lie six hundred miles southwest of Java. Unless he could hold his course precisely, Slocum would overshoot them. However, he made them dead ahead. "My reckoning was up," he wrote, "and springing aloft, I saw from half-way up the mast cocoa-nut trees standing out of the water ahead. I expected to see this; still, it thrilled me as an electric shock might have done. I slid down the mast, trembling under the strangest sensations; and not able to resist the impulse, I sat on deck and gave way to my emotions. To folks in a parlor on shore this may seem weak indeed, but I am telling the story of a voyage alone."

Slocum still had the urge to write, even though the travel letters had been a failure. Usually true to his own experience, he would once again do the thing he had done before. He would write a book. One might almost say he began it with a letter to Joseph Benson Gilder.

Gilder, younger brother of Richard Watson Gilder, was an editor of *The Critic*, a literary magazine and review of the day. In 1890, when Gilder was thirty-two, he wrote a warm and perceptive review of *Voyage of the Liberdade*. He seems to have been the first man of letters to see in Slocum a literary potential. Now seven years later and from halfway across the globe Slocum sent some paragraphs which later, in more polished form, went into *Sailing Alone*. The lady he spoke of as "in your city born" was, of course, Virginia.

> The Spray tied to a palm-tree at
> Keeling-Cocos Islands
> Aug 20th 1897

Dear Mr. Gilder:—Perhaps you did not expect to get a letter from this little kingdom in the sea; but one never knows what may happen and the risks one runs—on the land

Keeling Cocos is a strange little world owned by the first

settlers, a family of Scotch of the name of Cluenis-Ross Many things here are the reverse of other lands and the women, to use a homely phrase, rule the roost. It comes hard on the men. It would do the soul of the wretched Fuegan woman good to see the Keeling "lord and master" up a cocoanut tree I am looking over these things as I sail along. The heart of a missionary is all on fire to reconstruct the religion of this people If ever one sets foot on this peaceful land, I hope he will not be of the soul-destroying sort that spoiled my early days—

The conversation with yourself, once, often comes to mind, about our thoughts at sea. While I may not think cleare I am certainly clearer at sea than in a busy city and the thing most on my mind, that is, the business in hand, the reckoning, as I sailed along has been better kept than ever before on any ship of mine soever well officered. Was it from being even more alone in my case.

Looking over the journals of all the old voyagers I see none, working the old fashioned methods, so nearly correct as the Spray has been in making her land-falls—seven times now in succession. I never did better when I had even the best of chronometers and officers to assist—now will you tell me where it comes in? my "chro" is a one-dollar tin clock! And of course is almost no time piece at all—I have to boil her often to keep her at it, from noon to noon,* through the months.

Some thinking man will help me out on this else I will never be able to explain how it is done— The one thing most certain about my sea reckonings: They are not kept with any slavish application at all and I have been right every time and seemed *to know* that I was right; Even a lunar observation (so fare have

---

* On shipboard the day begins at noon. The noon sight, a very ancient element of navigation and still considered a principal observation of the day's work at sea, is a simple and convenient means of determining the parallel of latitude. Exact time is useful but not essential. In fact, latitude can be determined without exact time as long as one is skilled in the use of the sextant. By running down the latitude of the desired landfall, a master can bring his ship to port even though he may have no accurate way of determining longitude.

Observation of the moon, day or night, may provide the navigator with a line of position. By observing the changing position of the moon among the fixed stars, he may obtain an approximation of Greenwich time.

Dead reckoning, a corruption of the term "deduced reckoning," is based on knowledge of the speed of the vessel, which, in a sailing vessel, is determined by the taffrail log, a device consisting of a dial attached by a cable to a propeller towed from the stern of the ship. Continuous plotting of course and distance then gives the dead reckoning. W. M. T.

taken only one on the voyage) taken, of course, alone, was practically correct, I found, a few hours later, when I made the land.

There was not a difference of five miles between Lunar obvs dead reckoning and the true position of the vessel asuming the longitude of the Marqueses to be correct. I was then 43 days out and had not lost 6 hours rest But the vessel had sailed at her top speed all that time or nearly all the time that the wind blew hard

Your N. Y. ladies I see are going in for yachting

Why not study navigation too? A lady, in your city born, used to stand on deck with me and take good "sights" and work them, too, as correctly as any one could do

My plan, to be useful, will be to sail a "college ship" around the world!

How I would like to teach young people in the science of Nautical Astronomy

A fine sailing ship would be my choice & she should be a flyer making steamboat time without the bustle of steam and all its discomforts

I smile at some of the comments made on my present insignificent little "outing" Some think I am exploring the resourses of a man under great disadvantages, They are most all very kind in their comments but most all wrong as to the real object of my voyage which to tell the truth I did not think would interest our people; so I merely remarked before shoving off that I was going alone

What I sailed for I have got, and more, I found things I did not dream of meeting with I hoist them all in—have worked harder in port than at sea—I have now a valuable cargo— Sail tomorrow homeward.

Do you think our people will care for a story of the voyage around?

Sincerely yours

Joshua Slocum

Joseph B. Gilder
Spray will call at Capttown S A.

Although Slocum could write at length to friends, he does not seem to have had much to say to his family. Two days after he left Cocos Keeling, he was reported in a New Bedford paper: "Probably Lost. Family of Capt. Josiah [*sic*] Slocum Relinquishes All Hope. . . . Believed That He was Drowned During a Heavy Storm." But heedless of what the papers were saying, Slocum crossed the Indian Ocean and in due course made South Africa. Very much alive and on letterheads of the Royal Hotel, Durban, Natal, he wrote "Messers Roberts Brothers," 9 December 1897, telling of his meeting with the explorer Sir Henry M. Stanley.

Dear Sirs:—I mailed papers to yourselves from ports on the way also from this place, reporting the Spray

By this mail I send you P.O. Order for £5—about the amt, with interest, I hope, that you paid my son Victor, some time ago ($20)

My ambition is to pay all my little debts before I reach home. I see no reason, now, why I shall not be able to do so

I had quite a long pull to get at what I am about now—I shall have reason to remember some of my old friends

I met Stanley, here, the other day. I was at the time a guest of Colonel Saunderson's M. P. Stanley is M. P. you remember. It is said he can do more by keeping quiet than any man alive

He wanted to know what I would do without compartments if the Spray should strike a rock? "Must keep her off the rocks!" "If a sword-fish should run her through? What then?" "That *would* boom my show" Stanley must have been bored for he gave a smile that would make a worried editor yell with envy—

We all had coffee then and Irish stories. Stanley however gave a recipe which I think he said was American; perhaps it is old—I don't know: to keep intoxicating fumes down if one must drink: "take first a wine-glass of oil" that, of course, rises over the liquor— One of the party was an old sea captain and told the worst story, so the Colonel declared that was ever heard and appealing to me asked if ever I heard "so bad a yarn?" It was a bad story, even for a sea captain and I admitted that I never heard worse except some that I myself had told   Stanley smiled again that angelic smile born of practice and of long years of observation—

The best told story of the evening was accorded me! You may see that we had a wretched time! However the Col said it was all right, and thereupon invited me to put up at Saunderson Castle and make that my home when I come to Ireland. which certainly I shall do

With kind regards

Yours as always

Joshua Slocum

217

Foreword

Slocum spent his third Christmas out, storm-tossed off the pitch of the Cape of Good Hope. When the gale abated, he put into Capetown and there took a three months' leave of the *Spray,* touring the gold fields and diamond mines and traveling around the country by rail. It was March 1898 when, for the third time, he faced the Atlantic. Two months later, while skirting the coast of Brazil, the *Spray* "crossed the track, homeward bound, that she had made . . . on the voyage out. . . ." Though still in the South Atlantic and some 4,000 miles from home, Slocum had encircled the world.

Once more the captain was in familiar currents, making two hundred miles a day. He was already north of the Equator when he saw "rising astern as if poked up out of the sea, and then rapidly appearing on the horizon, like a citadel, the *Oregon.*" Laid down in 1891, the battleship *Oregon* displaced 10,000 tons, had a speed of 16 knots, and was a thousand times the size of the *Spray.* Commanded by Captain Charles E. Clark, she was prepared to engage the Spanish Fleet. Instead she encountered the *Spray.* Slocum did not know his country was at war with Spain. "Are there any men-of-war about?" Captain Clark signaled Captain Slocum. "No," Captain Slocum signaled in reply, and added that he had not been looking for any. His final signal to Captain Clark was, "Let us keep together for mutual protection," but this, in Slocum's words, the commander of the *Oregon* "did not seem to regard as necessary."

In June the *Spray* "was booming joyously along for home . . . when of a sudden she struck the horse latitudes, and her sail flapped limp. . . ." For eight days Slocum lay becalmed. The sea was so smooth that evening after evening he read on deck by the light of a candle. Under such circumstances, a less self-sufficient man might have been swallowed up in the solitude of waiting. But the captain knew "a philosophical turn of thought now was not amiss, else one's patience would have given out almost at the harbor entrance."

The final calm of the voyage preceded one of the final storms. On 20 June, a gale was blowing "accompanied by cross-seas that tumbled about and shook things up with great confusion." The *Spray's* jibstay broke at the masthead, and jib and all fell into the water. But the captain and nautical wizard somehow rescued his gear, and then, with no one at the wheel to steady the vessel, he climbed the swaying mast and made the repairs.

As Slocum neared the Long Island coast a cabin boy on board a sloop a couple of miles to windward spotted the yawl-rigged *Spray*. "We saw her start sheets and head in an easterly direction," he wrote long after. "Of course we did not recognize the *Spray* at that time, but later we realized that the little yawl we saw must have been the *Spray* from the fact that she carried not the customary gaff-headed sail but a balanced or 'standing' lug on the jigger. This sail was so rare in the United States—in fact, is so now—that the vessels carrying it can be numbered on the fingers of one hand."

So Slocum steered for Newport. The weather was fine now, but one more danger lay ahead. Newport harbor was mined. However, the *Spray*, hugging the rocks to avoid friend and foe, slipped by. At 1 A.M., 27 June 1898, she was safe inside, and the captain let go the anchor.

Almost immediately, Richard Watson Gilder, editor of the *Century* magazine, alerted by his brother, Joseph, sent a telegram. On his own printed letterhead, sporting a picture of the *Spray*, Slocum replied.

> Yacht "Spray," Newport
> 30th June 1898

Mr. Editor, Century Magazine:—

Your telegram: Magazine material I answered this a.m.

I have a fund of matter tobesure; but have not myself, had experience in writing magazine articles—I have very desided literary tastes and could enter into such parts as I am able to do with a great deal of energy

I have made a voyage such as, even, the emperor of Germany could not do and first building his own ship

It has been, to me, like reading a book and more interesting as I turned the pages over I know what it all means and I know what *men* have said about it. When my countrymen come to know about it and have time to think it over they will not be shamed of the Spray

It would be out of place to make ado of it especially at this time; The story will keep. No one short of bone and muscle and pine knots will lower the record. . . .

The next day Slocum acknowledged a letter from Richard Gilder and added: "There were indeed features of my trip striking enough to interest anybody. It would take the pen of a poet to tell some of the voyage— That of course is beyond me. . . . I claim only to be one of the poorest of American sailors and having nothing else to do, made a voyage. . . ."

The correspondence with *Century* editors marked the beginning of one of the happiest phases of Slocum's later years. It must have been an extraordinary manuscript that confronted them. There was a fine naturalness in the way Slocum used words. His metaphors were sensuous and often poetic, his verbs filled with vigor and movement. But his spelling and punctuation, and doubtless some of his constructions, were atrocious. *Century* editors helped him refine and cut. Sometimes they made him explain himself. Slocum refers to all this as "a touch of the pen."

Always happy in company with literary men, Slocum hit it off especially well with assistant editor Clarence C. Buel. A long correspondence between them began, on Slocum's side, with this note.

57 W Eagle St E Boston
Jan 30th 1899

Dear Mr Buel:—
    This is to report the Spray: My "type-writer" and I are working along around Cape Horn now and will soon have some work ready to submit. Meanwhile the "show" goes on

Very truly yours
Joshua Slocum

Slocum began his book in East Boston, where he was doubling up with relatives. He finished it in the cabin of the *Spray* at Erie Drydocks Basin, Brooklyn. Mabel Wagnalls encouraged him along the way, and when, the next year, the book appeared, he wrote in her copy that it was she "who first read the manuscript of the Voyage." In early summer he made delivery, then sailed for Martha's Vineyard to await the first batches of proof. Presently he was seeing his words in print. From Cottage City, 23 July 1899, he wrote Robert U. Johnson, one of the *Century* editors:

    . . . I myself, upon reading my M. S., in cooler blood, wondered how I could have made some of the points so obscure
    Some I made clearer Will you please send the proofs of the second article. . . . I will be here for some days— It is a charming place. . . .

I am delighted with every touch of the editors pen My reading has been sound and my judgement should be good—I know a good thing when I see it!

A few days later, on 28 July, he wrote Johnson again:

. . . I have a copy of the M S and will do as you wish in boiling down from Rodriquez as far as I may be able

Mr. Johnson I daresay has slaughtered, judiciously and liberally, up to that point

I will be not farther away than Nantucket, for the next two weeks. . . .

I am most anxious to see a clear story appear in both Magazine and book with no superfloss matter. . . .

I think I may be able to give the matter for the book many a touch which shall, when all will have been done, make it not the worst marine story in the world

But I find I must come to anchor and make a business of it if I hope to revise intelligently at all. . . .

And again from Cottage City, 4 August, Slocum wrote Buel:

. . . I am glad that my poor M S fell into good hands; In the Century it will appear far different to the ten fathoms of autograph which I first submitted to Mr. Buel—how patient Century Editors have been!

I appreciate every touch of the pen given to my poor story Mr. Johnson knows that I value also his exceedingly nice way of paying an old sailor a high compliment. Altogather, and best of all, I see my ship coming in under full sail freighted to the load-line.

Fair wind to the Century and may the weather clew of your own mainsail be kept hauled up. . . .

But a summer resort in the season, the captain found, was not the place for productive effort. From Woods Hole, 12 August, he wrote Johnson: "In order to get onto the work of revising . . . I sailed from Cottage City altogather. . . . About three quarters of the matter is greatly improved by the going over. . . . I can do the work better away where it is quiet. . . . To answer some questions . . . I had to refer to my logbook. . . ." And two days later,

221

from Fairhaven: "I find it rather difficult to condense the variety of experiences while sailing free over the smooth sea from Good Hope. It was all ripple ripple. However the editor will know how to slaughter my pet so as to keep the matter down to at least five installments. . . ."

It will be recalled that the first part of what Slocum called the "Spray story" appeared in the *Century* for September 1899. When, in November, the third installment came out, he was delighted to see himself cheek by jowl with Mark Twain. While the serialization continued, he made revisions for the forthcoming book. Published in March 1900, it included the supplementary piece, "Lines and Sail-Plan of the *Spray*," which Slocum prepared in response to demand from yachtsmen and small boat builders. In an undated letter to Buel written late in 1899 he spoke of doing some "measuring aloft." On 1 December he wrote: "The Spray is to be hauled out Sat at Capt Robins yard Bridgeport—Capt Robins is prepareing a model of her—Mr Mower is engaged to draw the line—I am looking, carefully, over the whole of it and will tumble it in very soon." This was followed by a letter dated "Wednesday a m."

> *Dear Mr. Buel:*
> I daresay you wonder what has come of Spray model etc but your heart will soften when you see the very exact model I leave with tonight—scale one inch to the foot— It is a poem!
> It is the certified work of a professional or master moddeler and I blead over it myself besides—
> I take it first to the Rudder designers to transfer the lines onto paper
> Have experienced some drawbacks but will get into port yet
> Very truly yours
> Joshua Slocum

Characteristically, however, Slocum did not reveal enough really to satisfy the sailormen. They have been curious ever since. The published small-scale plans of the *Spray* have been measured, enlarged, analyzed, and studied. Duplicates have been built with mathematical precision, and some, with the duplicators, disappeared at sea.

The fact is that vessels of the vintage of the *Spray* were not, in the modern sense of the word, designed. They were shaped and fashioned by the hand and eye of the builder, and the instinct and experience of men who had been to sea. The features of a wood vessel which characterize her performance are infinitely variable. A wind-driven ship is a marvel of life, and a man like Slocum simply in harmony with it.

But of course the strains of the long sea-voyaging finally told on the *Spray* as well as her consort. The sea which liberates also becomes, with the passing of time, a force for disintegration. Ten years more eroded Slocum's disciplines and wore out the stuff the *Spray* was made of. No slightest trace of her ever was found to hint at the place or cause of her finish. No one can say how her captain died, with what words on his lips or thoughts or regrets. Instead, one conjectures.

Vincent Gilpin, the yachtsman who saw the *Spray* in the years of her decline, suggested that "by the time she got to Miami in 1908, her sails and rigging would have been renewed more than once, and would have always had weak spots. This alone . . . might have caused her loss. . . ."

T. McKean Downs, M.D., observed from careful reading of *Sailing Alone* that when Slocum first rebuilt the sloop his inexpensive and local materials clearly included green timber; and though a boat built of well-seasoned wood may have a long life, one built of green may have quite a short one—especially a boat which spends much time in warm climates, as, obviously, Slocum's did. Downs guessed that the *Spray* broke up, fell apart like the one hoss shay.

But Joshua Slocum, wherever he last went sailing, is not forgotten by the world he sailed around. Nor is it likely that he will be so long as men read books.

Sailing Alone Around the World

TO THE ONE WHO SAID:
"The *Spray* Will Come Back."

Chapter 1

In the fair land of Nova Scotia, a maritime province, there is a ridge called North Mountain, overlooking the Bay of Fundy on one side and the fertile Annapolis valley on the other. On the northern slope of the range grows the hardy spruce-tree, well adapted for ship-timbers, of which many vessels of all classes have been built. The people of this coast, hardy, robust, and strong, are disposed to compete in the world's commerce, and it is nothing against the master mariner if the birthplace mentioned on his certificate be Nova Scotia. I was born in a cold spot, on coldest North Mountain, on a cold February 20, though I am a citizen of the United States— a naturalized Yankee, if it may be said that Nova Scotians are not Yankees in the truest sense of the word. On both sides my family were sailors; and if any Slocum should be found not seafaring, he will show at least an inclination to whittle models of boats and contemplate voyages. My father was the sort of man who, if wrecked on a desolate island, would find his way home, if he had a jack-knife and could find a tree. He was a good judge of a boat, but the old clay farm which some calamity made his was an anchor to him.

He was not afraid of a capful of wind, and he never took a back seat at a camp-meeting or a good, old-fashioned revival.

As for myself, the wonderful sea charmed me from the first. At the age of eight I had already been afloat along with other boys on the bay, with chances greatly in favor of being drowned. When a lad I filled the important post of cook on a fishing-schooner; but I was not long in the galley, for the crew mutinied at the appearance of my first duff, and "chucked me out" before I had a chance to shine as a culinary artist. The next step toward the goal of happiness found me before the mast in a full-rigged ship bound on a foreign voyage. Thus I came "over the bows," and not in through the cabin windows, to the command of a ship.

My best command was that of the magnificent ship *Northern Light*, of which I was part-owner. I had a right to be proud of her, for at that time—in the eighties—she was the finest American sailing-vessel afloat. Afterward I owned and sailed the *Aquidneck*, a little bark which of all man's handiwork seemed to me the nearest to perfection of beauty, and which in speed, when the wind blew, asked no favors of steamers. I had been nearly twenty years a shipmaster when I quit her deck on the coast of Brazil, where she was wrecked. My home voyage to New York with my family was made in the canoe *Liberdade*, without accident.

My voyages were all foreign. I sailed as freighter and trader principally to China, Australia, and Japan, and among the Spice Islands. Mine was not the sort of life to make one long to coil up one's ropes on land, the customs and ways of which I had finally almost forgotten. And so when times for freighters got bad, as at last they did, and I tried to quit the sea, what was there for an old sailor to do? I was born in the breezes, and I had studied the sea as perhaps few men have studied it, neglecting all else. Next in attractiveness, after seafaring, came ship-building. I longed to be master in both professions, and in a small way, in time, I accomplished my desire. From the decks of stout ships in the worst gales I had made calculations as to the size and sort of ship safest for all weather and all seas. Thus the voyage which I am now to narrate was a natural outcome not only of my love of adventure, but of my lifelong experience.

One midwinter day of 1892, in Boston, where I had been cast up from old ocean, so to speak, a year or two before, I was cogitat-

ing whether I should apply for a command, and again eat my
bread and butter on the sea, or go to work at the shipyard, when
I met an old acquaintance, a whaling-captain, who said: "Come to
Fairhaven and I'll give you a ship. But," he added, "she wants some
repairs." The captain's terms, when fully explained, were more than
satisfactory to me. They included all the assistance I would require
to fit the craft for sea. I was only too glad to accept, for I had already found that I could not obtain work in the shipyard without
first paying fifty dollars to a society, and as for a ship to command
—there were not enough ships to go round. Nearly all our tall vessels had been cut down for coal-barges, and were being igno-
miniously towed by the nose from port to port, while many worthy
captains addressed themselves to Sailors' Snug Harbor.

The next day I landed at Fairhaven, opposite New Bedford, and
found that my friend had something of a joke on me. For seven years
the joke had been on him. The "ship" proved to be a very antiquated
sloop called the *Spray*, which the neighbors declared had been built
in the year 1. She was affectionately propped up in a field, some
distance from salt water, and was covered with canvas. The people
of Fairhaven, I hardly need say, are thrifty and observant. For seven
years they had asked, "I wonder what Captain Eben Pierce is going
to do with the old *Spray?*" The day I appeared there was a buzz
at the gossip exchange: at last some one had come and was actually
at work on the old *Spray*. "Breaking her up, I s'pose?" "No; going
to rebuild her." Great was the amazement. "Will it pay?" was the
question which for a year or more I answered by declaring that I
would make it pay.

My ax felled a stout oak-tree near by for a keel, and Farmer
Howard, for a small sum of money, hauled in this and enough timbers for the frame of the new vessel. I rigged a steam-box and a
pot for a boiler. The timbers for ribs, being straight saplings, were
dressed and steamed till supple, and then bent over a log, where they
were secured till set. Something tangible appeared every day to
show for my labor, and the neighbors made the work sociable.
It was a great day in the *Spray* shipyard when her new stem was
set up and fastened to the new keel. Whaling-captains came from
far to survey it. With one voice they pronounced it "A1," and in
their opinion "fit to smash ice." The oldest captain shook my hand
warmly when the breast-hooks were put in, declaring that he could

see no reason why the *Spray* should not "cut in bow-head" yet off the coast of Greenland. The much-esteemed stem-piece was from the butt of the smartest kind of a pasture oak. It afterward split a coral patch in two at the Keeling Islands, and did not receive a blemish. Better timber for a ship than pasture white oak never grew. The breast-hooks, as well as all the ribs, were of this wood, and were steamed and bent into shape as required. It was hard upon March when I began work in earnest; the weather was cold; still, there were plenty of inspectors to back me with advice. When a whaling-captain hove in sight I just rested on my adz awhile and "gammed" with him.

New Bedford, the home of whaling-captains, is connected with Fairhaven by a bridge, and the walking is good. They never "worked along up" to the shipyard too often for me. It was the charming tales about arctic whaling that inspired me to put a double set of breast-hooks in the *Spray,* that she might shunt ice.

The seasons came quickly while I worked. Hardly were the ribs of the sloop up before apple-trees were in bloom. Then the daisies and the cherries came soon after. Close by the place where the old *Spray* had now dissolved rested the ashes of John Cook, a revered Pilgrim father. So the new *Spray* rose from hallowed ground. From the deck of the new craft I could put out my hand and pick cherries that grew over the little grave. The planks for the new vessel, which I soon came to put on, were of Georgia pine an inch and a half thick. The operation of putting them on was tedious, but, when on, the calking was easy. The outward edges stood slightly open to receive the calking, but the inner edges were so close that I could not see daylight between them. All the butts were fastened by through bolts, with screw-nuts tightening them to the timbers, so that there would be no complaint from them. Many bolts with screw-nuts were used in other parts of the construction, in all about a thousand. It was my purpose to make my vessel stout and strong.

Now, it is a law in Lloyd's that the *Jane* repaired all out of the old until she is entirely new is still the *Jane.* The *Spray* changed her being so gradually that it was hard to say at what point the old died or the new took birth, and it was no matter. The bulwarks I built up of white-oak stanchions fourteen inches high, and covered with seven-eighth-inch white pine. These stanchions, mortised through a two-inch covering-board, I calked with thin cedar wedges. They have remained perfectly tight ever since. The deck I made of one-and-a-half-inch by three-inch white pine spiked to beams, six by six inches, of yellow or Georgia pine, placed three feet apart. The deck-inclosures were one over the aperture of the main hatch, six feet by six, for a cooking-galley, and a trunk farther aft, about ten feet by twelve, for a cabin. Both of these rose about three feet above the deck, and were sunk sufficiently into the hold to afford head-room. In the spaces along the sides of the cabin, under the deck, I arranged a berth to sleep in, and shelves for small storage, not forgetting a place for the medicine-chest. In the midship hold, that is, the space between cabin and galley, under the deck, was room for provision of water, salt beef, etc., ample for many months.

The hull of my vessel being now put together as strongly as wood and iron could make her, and the various rooms partitioned off, I set about "calking ship." Grave fears were entertained by some that at this point I should fail. I myself gave some thought to the advisability of a "professional calker." The very first blow I struck on the cotton with the calking-iron, which I thought was right, many others thought wrong. "It'll crawl!" cried a man from Marion, passing with a basket of clams on his back. "It'll crawl!" cried another from West Island, when he saw me driving cotton into the seams. Bruno simply wagged his tail. Even Mr. Ben J——, a noted authority on whaling-ships, whose mind, however, was said to totter, asked rather confidently if I did not think "it would crawl." "How fast will it crawl?" cried my old captain friend, who had been towed by many a lively sperm-whale. "Tell us how fast," cried he, "that we may get into port in time." However, I drove a thread of oakum on top of the cotton, as from the first I had intended to do. And Bruno again wagged his tail. The cotton never "crawled." When the calking was finished, two coats of copper paint were slapped on the bottom, two of white lead on the topsides and bulwarks. The rudder was then shipped and painted, and on the following day the *Spray* was launched. As she rode at her ancient, rust-eaten anchor, she sat on the water like a swan.

The *Spray's* dimensions were, when finished, thirty-six feet nine inches long, over all, fourteen feet two inches wide, and four feet two inches deep in the hold, her tonnage being nine tons net and twelve and seventy-one hundredths tons gross.

Then the mast, a smart New Hampshire spruce, was fitted, and likewise all the small appurtenances necessary for a short cruise. Sails were bent, and away she flew with my friend Captain Pierce and me, across Buzzard's Bay on a trial-trip—all right. The only thing that now worried my friends along the beach was, "Will she pay?" The cost of my new vessel was $553.62 for materials, and thirteen months of my own labor. I was several months more than that at Fairhaven, for I got work now and then on an occasional whale-ship fitting farther down the harbor, and that kept me the overtime.

Chapter 2

I spent a season in my new craft fishing on the coast, only to find that I had not the cunning properly to bait a hook. But at last the time arrived to weigh anchor and get to sea in earnest. I had resolved on a voyage around the world, and as the wind on the morning of April 24, 1895, was fair, at noon I weighed anchor, set sail, and filled away from Boston, where the *Spray* had been moored snugly all winter. The twelve-o'clock whistles were blowing just as the sloop shot ahead under full sail. A short board was made up the harbor on the port tack, then coming about she stood seaward, with her boom well off to port, and swung past the ferries with lively heels. A photographer on the outer pier at East Boston got a picture of her as she swept by, her flag at the peak throwing its folds clear. A thrilling pulse beat high in me. My step was light on deck in the crisp air. I felt that there could be no turning back, and that I was engaging in an adventure the meaning of which I thoroughly understood. I had taken little advice from any one, for I had a right to my own opinions in matters pertaining to the sea. That the best of sailors might do worse than even I alone was borne in upon me not a league from Boston docks, where a great steamship, fully manned, officered, and piloted, lay stranded and broken. This was the *Venetian*. She was broken completely in two over a ledge. So in the first hour of my lone voyage I had proof that the *Spray* could at least do better than this full-handed steamship, for I was already farther on my voyage than she. "Take warning, *Spray*, and have a care," I uttered aloud to my bark, passing fairylike silently down the bay.

The wind freshened, and the *Spray* rounded Deer Island light, going at the rate of seven knots. Passing it, she squared away direct for Gloucester, where she was to procure some fishermen's stores. Waves dancing joyously across Massachusetts Bay met the sloop coming out, to dash themselves instantly into myriads of sparkling gems that hung about her breast at every surge. The day was perfect, the sunlight clear and strong. Every particle of water thrown into the air became a gem, and the *Spray*, making good her name as she dashed ahead, snatched necklace after necklace from the sea, and as often threw them away. We have all seen miniature rainbows about a ship's prow, but the *Spray* flung out a bow of her own that day, such as I had never seen before. Her good angel had embarked on the voyage; I so read it in the sea.

Bold Nahant was soon abeam, then Marblehead was put astern. Other vessels were outward bound, but none of them passed the *Spray* flying along on her course. I heard the clanking of the dismal bell on Norman's Woe as we went by; and the reef where the schooner *Hesperus* struck I passed close aboard. The "bones" of a wreck tossed up lay bleaching on the shore abreast. The wind still freshening, I settled the throat of the mainsail to ease the sloop's helm, for I could hardly hold her before it with the whole mainsail set. A schooner ahead of me lowered all sail and ran into port under bare poles, the wind being fair. As the *Spray* brushed by the stranger, I saw that some of his sails were gone, and much broken canvas hung in his rigging, from the effects of a squall.

I made for the cove, a lovely branch of Gloucester's fine harbor, again to look the *Spray* over and again to weigh the voyage, and my feelings, and all that. The bay was feather-white as my little vessel tore in, smothered in foam. It was my first experience of coming into port alone, with a craft of any size, and in among shipping. Old fishermen ran down to the wharf for which the *Spray* was heading, apparently intent upon braining herself there. I hardly know how a calamity was averted, but with my heart in my mouth, almost, I let go the wheel, stepped quickly forward, and downed the jib. The sloop naturally rounded in the wind, and just ranging ahead, laid her cheek against a mooring-pile at the windward corner of the wharf, so quietly, after all, that she would not have broken an egg. Very leisurely I passed a rope around the post, and she was moored. Then a cheer went up from the little crowd on the wharf. "You couldn't 'a' done it better," cried an old skipper, "if you weighed a ton!" Now, my weight was rather less than the fifteenth part of a ton, but I said nothing, only putting on a look of careless indifference to say for me, "Oh, that's nothing"; for some of the ablest sailors in the world were looking at me, and my wish was not to appear green, for I had a mind to stay in Gloucester several days. Had I uttered a word it surely would have betrayed me, for I was still quite nervous and short of breath.

I remained in Gloucester about two weeks, fitting out with the various articles for the voyage most readily obtained there. The owners of the wharf where I lay, and of many fishing vessels, put on board dry cod galore, also a barrel of oil to calm the waves. They were old skippers themselves, and took a great interest in the voyage. They also made the *Spray* a present of a "fisherman's own" lantern, which I found would throw a light a great distance round. Indeed, a ship that would run another down having such a good light aboard would be capable of running into a light-ship. A gaff, a pugh, and a dip-net, all of which an old fisherman declared I could not sail without, were also put aboard. Then, too, from across the cove came a case of copper paint, a famous antifouling article, which stood me in good stead long after. I slapped two coats of this paint on the bottom of the *Spray* while she lay a tide or so on the hard beach.

For a boat to take along, I made shift to cut a castaway dory in two athwartships, boarding up the end where it was cut. This half-dory I could hoist in and out by the nose easily enough, by hooking the throat-halyards into a strop fitted for the purpose. A whole dory would be heavy and awkward to handle alone. Manifestly there was not room on deck for more than the half of a boat, which, after all, was better than no boat at all, and was large enough for one man. I perceived, moreover, that the newly arranged craft would answer for a washing-machine when placed athwartships, and also for a bath-tub. Indeed, for the former office my razeed dory gained such a reputation on the voyage that my washerwoman at Samoa would not take no for an answer. She could see with one eye that it was a new invention which beat any Yankee notion ever brought by missionaries to the islands, and she had to have it.

The want of a chronometer for the voyage was all that now worried me. In our newfangled notions of navigation it is supposed that a mariner cannot find his way without one; and I had myself drifted into this way of thinking. My old chronometer, a good one, had been long in disuse. It would cost fifteen dollars to clean and rate it. Fifteen dollars! For sufficient reasons I left that timepiece at home, where the Dutchman left his anchor. I had the great lantern, and a lady in Boston sent me the price of a large two-burner cabin lamp, which lighted the cabin at night, and by some small contriving served for a stove through the day.

Being thus refitted I was once more ready for sea, and on May 7 again made sail. With little room in which to turn, the *Spray*, in gathering headway, scratched the paint off an old, fine-weather craft in the fairway, being puttied and painted for a summer voyage. "Who'll pay for that?" growled the painters. "I will," said I. "With the main-sheet," echoed the captain of the *Bluebird*, close by, which was his way of saying that I was off. There was nothing to pay for above five cents' worth of paint, maybe, but such a din was raised between the old "hooker" and the *Bluebird*, which now took up my case, that the first cause of it was forgotten altogether. Anyhow, no bill was sent after me.

The weather was mild on the day of my departure from Gloucester. On the point ahead, as the *Spray* stood out of the cove, was a lively picture, for the front of a tall factory was a flutter of handkerchiefs and caps. Pretty faces peered out of the windows from the top to the bottom of the building, all smiling *bon voyage*. Some hailed me to know where away and why alone. Why? When I made as if to stand in, a hundred pairs of arms reached out, and said come, but the shore was dangerous! The sloop worked out of the bay against a light southwest wind, and about noon squared away off Eastern Point, receiving at the same time a hearty salute—the last of many kindnesses to her at Gloucester. The wind freshened off the point, and skipping along smoothly, the *Spray* was soon off Thatcher's Island lights. Thence shaping her course east, by compass, to go north of Cashes Ledge and the Amen Rocks, I sat and considered the matter all over again, and asked myself once more whether it were best to sail beyond the ledge and rocks at all. I had only said that I would sail round the world in the *Spray*, "dangers of the sea excepted," but I must have said it very much in earnest.

The "charter-party" with myself seemed to bind me, and so I sailed on. Toward night I hauled the sloop to the wind, and baiting a hook, sounded for bottom-fish, in thirty fathoms of water, on the edge of Cashes Ledge. With fair success I hauled till dark, landing on deck three cod and two haddocks, one hake, and, best of all, a small halibut, all plump and spry. This, I thought, would be the place to take in a good stock of provisions above what I already had; so I put out a sea-anchor that would hold her head to windward. The current being southwest, against the wind, I felt quite sure I would find the *Spray* still on the bank or near it in the morning. Then "stradding" the cable and putting my great lantern in the rigging, I lay down, for the first time at sea alone, not to sleep, but to doze and to dream.

I had read somewhere of a fishing-schooner hooking her anchor into a whale, and being towed a long way and at great speed. This was exactly what happened to the *Spray*—in my dream! I could not shake it off entirely when I awoke and found that it was the wind blowing and the heavy sea now running that had disturbed my short rest. A scud was flying across the moon. A storm was brewing; indeed, it was already stormy. I reefed the sails, then hauled in my sea-anchor, and setting what canvas the sloop could carry, headed her away for Monhegan light, which she made before daylight on the morning of the 8th. The wind being free, I ran on into Round Pond harbor, which is a little port east from Pemaquid. Here I rested a day, while the wind rattled among the pine-trees on shore. But the following day was fine enough, and I put to sea, first writing up my log from Cape Ann, not omitting a full account of my adventure with the whale.

The *Spray*, heading east, stretched along the coast among many islands and over a tranquil sea. At evening of this day, May 10, she came up with a considerable island, which I shall always think of as the Island of Frogs, for the *Spray* was charmed by a million voices. From the Island of Frogs we made for the Island of Birds, called Gannet Island, and sometimes Gannet Rock, whereon is a bright, intermittent light, which flashed fitfully across the *Spray's* deck as she coasted along under its light and shade. Thence shaping a course for Briar's Island, I came among vessels the following afternoon on the western fishing-grounds, and after speaking a fisherman at anchor, who gave me a wrong course, the *Spray* sailed directly over the southwest ledge through the worst tide-race in the Bay of Fundy, and got into Westport harbor in Nova Scotia, where I had spent eight years of my life as a lad.

The fisherman may have said "east-southeast," the course I was steering when I hailed him; but I thought he said "east-northeast," and I accordingly changed it to that. Before he made up his mind to answer me at all, he improved the occasion of his own curiosity to know where I was from, and if I was alone, and if I didn't have "no dorg nor no cat." It was the first time in all my life at sea that I had heard a hail for information answered by a question. I think the chap belonged to the Foreign Islands. There was one thing I was sure of, and that was that he did not belong to Briar's Island, because he dodged a sea that slopped over the rail, and stopping to brush the water from his face, lost a fine cod which he was about to ship. My islander would not have done that. It is known that a Briar Islander, fish or no fish on his hook, never flinches from a sea. He just tends to his lines and hauls or "saws." Nay, have I not seen my old friend Deacon W. D——, a good man of the island, while listening to a sermon in the little church on the hill, reach out his hand over the door of his pew and "jig" imaginary squid in the aisle, to the intense delight of the young people, who did not realize that to catch good fish one must have good bait, the thing most on the deacon's mind.

I was delighted to reach Westport. Any port at all would have been delightful after the terrible thrashing I got in the fierce sou'west rip, and to find myself among old schoolmates now was charming. It was the 13th of the month, and 13 is my lucky number—a fact registered long before Dr. Nansen sailed in search of the north pole with his crew of thirteen. Perhaps he had heard of my success in taking a most extraordinary ship successfully to Brazil with that number of crew. The very stones on Briar's Island I was glad to see again, and I knew them all. The little shop round the corner, which for thirty-five years I had not seen, was the same, except that it looked a deal smaller. It wore the same shingles—I was sure of it; for did not I know the roof where we boys, night after night, hunted for the skin of a black cat, to be taken on a dark night, to make a plaster for a poor lame man? Lowry the tailor lived there when boys were boys. In his day he was fond of the gun. He always carried his powder loose in the tail pocket of his coat. He usually had in his mouth a short dudeen; but in an evil moment he put the dudeen, lighted, in the pocket among the powder. Mr. Lowry was an eccentric man.

At Briar's Island I overhauled the *Spray* once more and tried her seams, but found that even the test of the sou'west rip had started nothing. Bad weather and much head wind prevailing outside, I was in no hurry to round Cape Sable. I made a short excursion with some friends to St. Mary's Bay, an old cruising-ground, and back to the island. Then I sailed, putting into Yarmouth the following day on account of fog and head wind. I spent some days pleasantly enough in Yarmouth, took in some butter for the voyage, also a barrel of potatoes, filled six barrels of water, and stowed all under deck. At Yarmouth, too, I got my famous tin clock, the only timepiece I carried on the whole voyage. The price of it was a dollar and a half, but on account of the face being smashed the merchant let me have it for a dollar.

Chapter 3

I now stowed all my goods securely, for the boisterous Atlantic was before me, and I sent the topmast down, knowing that the *Spray* would be the wholesomer with it on deck. Then I gave the lanyards a pull and hitched them afresh, and saw that the gammon was secure, also that the boat was lashed, for even in summer one may meet with bad weather in the crossing.

In fact, many weeks of bad weather had prevailed. On July 1, however, after a rude gale, the wind came out nor'west and clear, propitious for a good run. On the following day, the head sea having gone down, I sailed from Yarmouth, and let go my last hold on America. The log of my first day on the Atlantic in the *Spray* reads briefly: "9:30 A.M. sailed from Yarmouth. 4:30 P.M. passed Cape Sable; distance, three cables from the land. The sloop making eight knots. Fresh breeze N. W." Before the sun went down I was taking my supper of strawberries and tea in smooth water under the lee of the east-coast land, along which the *Spray* was now leisurely skirting.

At noon on July 3 Ironbound Island was abeam. The *Spray* was again at her best. A large schooner came out of Liverpool, Nova Scotia, this morning, steering eastward. The *Spray* put her hull down astern in five hours. At 6:45 P.M. I was in close under Chebucto Head light, near Halifax Harbor. I set my flag and squared away, taking my departure from George's Island before dark to sail east of Sable Island. There are many beacon lights along the coast. Sambro, the Rock of Lamentations, carries a noble light, which, however, the liner *Atlantic*, on the night of her terrible disaster, did not see. I watched light after light sink astern as I sailed into the unbounded sea, till Sambro, the last of them all, was below the horizon. The *Spray* was then alone, and sailing on, she held her course. July 4, at 6 A.M., I put in double reefs, and at 8:30 A.M. turned out all reefs. At 9:40 P.M. I raised the sheen only of the light on the west end of Sable Island, which may also be called the Island of Tragedies. The fog, which till this moment had held off, now lowered over the sea like a pall. I was in a world of fog, shut off from the universe. I did not see any more of the light. By the lead, which I cast often, I found that a little after midnight I was passing the east point of the island, and should soon be clear of dangers of land and shoals. The wind was holding free, though it was from the foggy point, south-southwest. It is said that within a few years Sable Island has been reduced from forty miles in length to twenty, and that of three lighthouses built on it since 1880, two have been washed away and the third will soon be engulfed.

On the evening of July 5 the *Spray*, after having steered all day over a lumpy sea, took it into her head to go without the helmsman's aid. I had been steering southeast by south, but the wind hauling forward a bit, she dropped into a smooth lane, heading southeast, and making about eight knots, her very best work. I crowded on sail to cross the track of the liners without loss of time, and to reach as soon as possible the friendly Gulf Stream. The fog lifting before night, I was afforded a look at the sun just as it was touching the sea. I watched it go down and out of sight. Then I turned my face eastward, and there, apparently at the very end of the bowsprit, was the smiling full moon rising out of the sea. Neptune himself coming over the bows could not have startled me more. "Good evening, sir," I cried; "I'm glad to see you." Many a long talk since then I have had with the man in the moon; he had my confidence on the voyage.

About midnight the fog shut down again denser than ever before. One could almost "stand on it." It continued so for a number of days, the wind increasing to a gale. The waves rose high, but I had a good ship. Still, in the dismal fog I felt myself drifting into loneliness, an insect on a straw in the midst of the elements. I lashed the helm, and my vessel held her course, and while she sailed I slept.

During these days a feeling of awe crept over me. My memory worked with startling power. The ominous, the insignificant, the great, the small, the wonderful, the commonplace—all appeared before my mental vision in magical succession. Pages of my history were recalled which had been so long forgotten that they seemed to belong to a previous existence. I heard all the voices of the past laughing, crying, telling what I had heard them tell in many corners of the earth.

The loneliness of my state wore off when the gale was high and I found much work to do. When fine weather returned, then came the sense of solitude, which I could not shake off. I used my voice often, at first giving some order about the affairs of a ship, for I had been told that from disuse I should lose my speech. At the meridian altitude of the sun I called aloud, "Eight bells," after the custom on a ship at sea. Again from my cabin I cried to an imaginary man at the helm, "How does she head, there?" and again, "Is she on her course?" But getting no reply, I was reminded the more palpably of my condition. My voice sounded hollow on the empty air, and I dropped the practice. However, it was not long before the thought came to me that when I was a lad I used to sing; why not try that now, where it would disturb no one? My musical talent had never bred envy in others, but out on the Atlantic, to realize what it meant, you should have heard me sing. You should have seen the porpoises leap when I pitched my voice for the waves and the sea and all that was in it. Old turtles, with large eyes, poked their heads up out of the sea as I sang "Johnny Boker," and "We'll Pay Darby Doyl for his Boots," and the like. But the porpoises were, on the whole, vastly more appreciative than the turtles; they jumped a deal higher. One day when I was humming a favorite chant, I think it was "Babylon's a-Fallin',", a porpoise jumped higher than the bowsprit. Had the *Spray* been going a little faster she would have scooped him in. The sea-birds sailed around rather shy.

July 10, eight days at sea, the *Spray* was twelve hundred miles east of Cape Sable. One hundred and fifty miles a day for so small a vessel must be considered good sailing. It was the greatest run the *Spray* ever made before or since in so few days. On the evening of July 14, in better humor than ever before, all hands cried, "Sail ho!" The sail was a barkantine, three points on the weather bow, hull down. Then came the night. My ship was sailing along now without attention to the helm. The wind was south; she was heading east. Her sails were trimmed like the sails of the nautilus. They drew steadily all night. I went frequently on deck, but found all well. A merry breeze kept on from the south. Early in the morning of the 15th the *Spray* was close aboard the stranger, which proved to be *La Vaguisa* of Vigo, twenty-three days from Philadelphia, bound for Vigo. A lookout from his masthead had spied the *Spray* the evening before. The captain, when I came near enough, threw a line to me and sent a bottle of wine across slung by the neck, and very good wine it was. He also sent his card, which bore the name of Juan Gantes. I think he was a good man, as Spaniards go. But when I asked him to report me "all well" (the *Spray* passing him in a lively manner), he hauled his shoulders much above his head; and when his mate, who knew of my expedition, told him that I was alone, he crossed himself and made for his cabin. I did not see him again. By sundown he was as far astern as he had been ahead the evening before.

There was now less and less monotony. On July 16 the wind was northwest and clear, the sea smooth, and a large bark, hull down, came in sight on the lee bow, and at 2:30 P.M. I spoke the stranger. She was the bark *Java* of Glasgow, from Peru for Queenstown for orders. Her old captain was bearish, but I met a bear once in Alaska that looked pleasanter. At least, the bear seemed pleased to meet me, but this grizzly old man! Well, I suppose my hail disturbed his siesta, and my little sloop passing his great ship had somewhat the effect on him that a red rag has upon a bull. I had the advantage over heavy ships, by long odds, in the light winds of this and the two previous days. The wind was light; his ship was heavy and foul, making poor headway, while the *Spray*, with a great mainsail bellying even to light winds, was just skipping along as nimbly as one could wish. "How long has it been calm about here?" roared the captain of the *Java*, as I came within hail of him. "Dunno, cap'n," I shouted back as loud as I could bawl. "I haven't been here long." At this the mate on the forecastle wore a broad grin. "I left Cape Sable fourteen days ago," I added. (I was now well across toward the Azores.) "Mate," he roared to his chief officer—"mate, come here and listen to the Yankee's yarn. Haul down the flag, mate, haul down the flag!" In the best of humor, after all, the *Java* surrendered to the *Spray*.

The acute pain of solitude experienced at first never returned. I had penetrated a mystery, and, by the way, I had sailed through a fog. I had met Neptune in his wrath, but he found that I had not treated him with contempt, and so he suffered me to go on and explore.

In the log for July 18 there is this entry: "Fine weather, wind south-southwest. Porpoises gamboling all about. The S.S. *Olympia* passed at 11:30 A.M., long. W. 34° 50'."

"It lacks now three minutes of the half-hour," shouted the captain, as he gave me the longitude and the time. I admired the business-like air of the *Olympia*; but I have the feeling still that the captain was just a little too precise in his reckoning. That may be all well enough, however, where there is plenty of sea-room. But over-confidence, I believe, was the cause of the disaster to the liner *Atlantic*, and many more like her. The captain knew too well where he was. There were no porpoises at all skipping along with the *Olympia!* Porpoises always prefer sailing-ships. The captain was a young man, I observed, and had before him, I hope, a good record.

Land ho! On the morning of July 19 a mystic dome like a mountain of silver stood alone in the sea ahead. Although the land was completely hidden by the white, glistening haze that shone in the sun like polished silver, I felt quite sure that it was Flores Island. At half-past four P.M. it was abeam. The haze in the meantime had disappeared. Flores is one hundred and seventy-four miles from Fayal, and although it is a high island, it remained many years undiscovered after the principal group of the islands had been colonized.

Early on the morning of July 20 I saw Pico looming above the clouds on the starboard bow. Lower lands burst forth as the sun burned away the morning fog, and island after island came into view. As I approached nearer, cultivated fields appeared, "and oh, how green the corn!" Only those who have seen the Azores from the deck of a vessel realize the beauty of the mid-ocean picture.

At 4:30 P.M. I cast anchor at Fayal, exactly eighteen days from Cape Sable. The American consul, in a smart boat, came alongside before the *Spray* reached the breakwater, and a young naval officer, who feared for the safety of my vessel, boarded, and offered his services as pilot. The youngster, I have no good reason to doubt, could have handled a man-of-war, but the *Spray* was too small for the amount of uniform he wore. However, after fouling all the craft in port and sinking a lighter, she was moored without much damage to herself. This wonderful pilot expected a "gratification," I understood, but whether for the reason that his government, and not I, would have to pay the cost of raising the lighter, or because he did not sink the *Spray*, I could never make out. But I forgive him.

It was the season for fruit when I arrived at the Azores, and there was soon more of all kinds of it put on board than I knew what to do with. Islanders are always the kindest people in the world, and I met none anywhere kinder than the good hearts of this place. The people of the Azores are not a very rich community. The burden of taxes is heavy, with scant privileges in return, the air they breathe being about the only thing that is not taxed. The mother-country does not even allow them a port of entry for a foreign mail service. A packet passing never so close with mails for Horta must deliver them first in Lisbon, ostensibly to be fumigated, but really for the tariff from the packet. My own letters posted at Horta reached the United States six days behind my letter from Gibraltar, mailed thirteen days later.

The day after my arrival at Horta was the feast of a great saint. Boats loaded with people came from other islands to celebrate at Horta, the capital, or Jerusalem, of the Azores. The deck of the *Spray* was crowded from morning till night with men, women, and children. On the day after the feast a kind-hearted native harnessed a team and drove me a day over the beautiful roads all about Fayal, "because," said he, in broken English, "when I was in America and couldn't speak a word of English, I found it hard till I met some one who seemed to have time to listen to my story, and I promised my good saint then that if ever a stranger came to my country I would try to make him happy." Unfortunately, this gentleman brought

241

along an interpreter, that I might "learn more of the country." The fellow was nearly the death of me, talking of ships and voyages, and of the boats he had steered, the last thing in the world I wished to hear. He had sailed out of New Bedford, so he said, for "that Joe Wing they call 'John.' " My friend and host found hardly a chance to edge in a word. Before we parted my host dined me with a cheer that would have gladdened the heart of a prince, but he was quite alone in his house. "My wife and children all rest there," said he, pointing to the churchyard across the way. "I moved to this house from far off," he added, "to be near the spot, where I pray every morning."

I remained four days at Fayal, and that was two days more than I had intended to stay. It was the kindness of the islanders and their touching simplicity which detained me. A damsel, as innocent as an angel, came alongside one day, and said she would embark on the *Spray* if I would land her at Lisbon. She could cook flying-fish, she thought, but her forte was dressing *bacalhao*. Her brother Antonio, who served as interpreter, hinted that, anyhow, he would like to make the trip. Antonio's heart went out to one John Wilson, and he was ready to sail for America by way of the two capes to meet his friend. "Do you know John Wilson of Boston?" he cried. "I knew a John Wilson," I said, "but not of Boston." "He had one daughter and one son," said Antonio, by way of identifying his friend. If this reaches the right John Wilson, I am told to say that "Antonio of Pico remembers him."

Chapter 4

I set sail from Horta early on July 24. The southwest wind at the time was light, but squalls came up with the sun, and I was glad enough to get reefs in my sails before I had gone a mile. I had hardly set the mainsail, double-reefed, when a squall of wind down the mountains struck the sloop with such violence that I thought her mast would go. However, a quick helm brought her to the wind. As it was, one of the weather lanyards was carried away and the other was stranded. My tin basin, caught up by the wind, went flying across a French school-ship to leeward. It was more or less squally all day, sailing along under high land; but rounding close under a bluff, I found an opportunity to mend the lanyards broken in the squall. No sooner had I lowered my sails when a four-oared boat shot out from some gully in the rocks, with a customs officer on board, who thought he had come upon a smuggler. I had some difficulty in making him comprehend the true case. However, one of his crew, a sailorly chap, who understood how matters were, while we palavered jumped on board and rove off the new lanyards I had already prepared, and with a friendly hand helped me "set up the rigging." This incident gave the turn in my favor. My story was then clear to all. I have found this the way of the world. Let one be without a friend, and see what will happen!

Passing the island of Pico, after the rigging was mended, the *Spray* stretched across to leeward of the island of St. Michael's, which she was up with early on the morning of July 26, the wind blowing hard. Later in the day she passed the Prince of Monaco's fine steam-yacht bound to Fayal, where, on a previous voyage, the prince had slipped his cables to "escape a reception" which the padres of the island wished to give him. Why he so dreaded the "ovation" I could not make out. At Horta they did not know. Since reaching the islands I had lived most luxuriously on fresh bread, butter, vegetables, and fruits of all kinds. Plums seemed the most plentiful on the *Spray,* and these I ate without stint. I had also a Pico white cheese that General Manning, the American consul-general, had given me, which I supposed was to be eaten, and of this I partook with the plums. Alas! by night-time I was doubled up with cramps. The wind, which was already a smart breeze, was increasing somewhat, with a heavy sky to the sou'west. Reefs had been turned out, and I must turn them in again somehow. Between cramps I got the mainsail down, hauled out the earings as best I could, and tied away point by point, in the double reef. There being sea-room, I should, in strict prudence, have made all snug and gone down at once to my cabin. I am a careful man at sea, but this night, in the coming storm, I swayed up my sails, which, reefed though they were, were still too much in such heavy weather; and I saw to it that the sheets were securely belayed. In a word, I should have laid to, but did not. I gave her the double-reefed mainsail and whole jib instead, and set her on her course.

Then I went below, and threw myself upon the cabin floor in great pain. How long I lay there I could not tell, for I became delirious. When I came to, as I thought, from my swoon, I realized that the sloop was plunging into a heavy sea, and looking out of the companionway, to my amazement I saw a tall man at the helm. His rigid hand, grasping the spokes of the wheel, held them as in a vise. One may imagine my astonishment. His rig was that of a foreign sailor, and the large red cap he wore was cockbilled over his left ear, and all was set off with shaggy black whiskers. He would have been taken for a pirate in any part of the world. While I gazed upon his threatening aspect I forgot the storm, and wondered if he had come to cut my throat. This he seemed to divine. "Señor," said he, doffing his cap, "I have come to do you no harm." And a smile, the faintest in the world, but still a smile, played on his face, which seemed not unkind when he spoke. "I have come to do you no harm. I have sailed free," he said, "but was never worse than a *contrabandista*. I am one of Columbus's crew," he continued. "I am the pilot of the *Pinta* come to aid you. Lie quiet, señor captain," he added, "and I will guide your ship to-night. You have a *calentura*, but you will be all right to-morrow." I thought what a very devil he was to carry sail. Again, as if he read my mind, he exclaimed: "Yonder is the *Pinta* ahead; we must overtake her. Give her sail; give her sail! *Vale, vale, muy vale!*" Biting off a large quid of black twist, he said: "You did wrong, captain, to mix cheese with plums. White cheese is never safe unless you know whence it comes. *Quien sabe,* it may have been from *leche de Capra* and becoming capricious———"

"Avast, there!" I cried. "I have no mind for moralizing."

I made shift to spread a mattress and lie on that instead of the hard floor, my eyes all the while fastened on my strange guest, who, remarking again that I would have "only pains and calentura," chuckled as he chanted a wild song:

High are the waves, fierce, gleaming,
  High is the tempest roar!
High the sea-bird screaming!
  High the Azore!

I suppose I was now on the mend, for I was peevish, and complained: "I detest your jingle. Your Azore should be at roost, and would have been were it a respectable bird!" I begged he would tie a rope-yarn on the rest of the song, if there was any more of it. I was still in agony. Great seas were boarding the *Spray*, but in my fevered brain I thought they were boats falling on deck, that careless draymen were throwing from wagons on the pier to which I imagined the *Spray* was now moored, and without fenders to breast her off. "You'll smash your boats!" I called out again and again, as the seas crashed on the cabin over my head. "You'll smash your boats, but you can't hurt the *Spray*. She is strong!" I cried.

I found, when my pains and calentura had gone, that the deck, now as white as a shark's tooth from seas washing over it, had been swept of everything movable. To my astonishment, I saw now at broad day that the *Spray* was still heading as I had left her, and was going like a race-horse. Columbus himself could not have held her more exactly on her course. The sloop had made ninety miles in the night through a rough sea. I felt grateful to the old pilot, but I marveled some that he had not taken in the jib. The gale was moderating, and by noon the sun was shining. A meridian altitude and the distance on the patent log, which I always kept towing, told me that she had made a true course throughout the twenty-four hours. I was getting much better now, but was very weak, and did not turn out reefs that day or the night following, although the wind fell light; but I just put my wet clothes out in the sun when it was shining, and lying down there myself, fell asleep. Then who should visit me again but my old friend of the night before, this time, of course, in a dream. "You did well last night to take my advice," said he, "and if you would, I should like to be with you often on the voyage, for the love of adventure alone." Finishing what he had to say, he again doffed his cap and disappeared as mysteriously as he came, returning, I suppose, to the phantom *Pinta*. I awoke much refreshed, and with the feeling that I had been in the presence of a friend and a seaman of vast experience. I gathered up my clothes, which by this time were dry, then, by inspiration, I threw overboard all the plums in the vessel.

July 28 was exceptionally fine. The wind from the northwest was light and the air balmy. I overhauled my wardrobe, and bent on a white shirt against nearing some coasting-packet with genteel folk on board. I also did some washing to get the salt out of my clothes. After it all I was hungry, so I made a fire and very cautiously stewed a dish of pears and set them carefully aside till I had made a pot of delicious coffee, for both of which I could afford sugar and cream. But the crowning dish of all was a fish-hash, and there was enough of it for two. I was in good health again, and my appetite was simply ravenous. While I was dining I had a large onion over the double lamp stewing for a luncheon later in the day. High living to-day!

In the afternoon the *Spray* came upon a large turtle asleep on the sea. He awoke with my harpoon through his neck, if he awoke at all. I had much difficulty in landing him on deck, which I finally accomplished by hooking the throat-halyards to one of his flippers, for he was about as heavy as my boat. I saw more turtles, and I rigged a burton ready with which to hoist them in; for I was obliged to lower the mainsail whenever the halyards were used for such purposes, and it was no small matter to hoist the large sail again. But the turtle-steak was good. I found no fault with the cook, and it was the rule of the voyage that the cook found no fault with me. There was never a ship's crew so well agreed. The bill of fare that evening was turtle-steak, tea and toast, fried potatoes, stewed onions; with dessert of stewed pears and cream.

Sometime in the afternoon I passed a barrel-buoy adrift, floating light on the water. It was painted red, and rigged with a signal-staff about six feet high. A sudden change in the weather coming on, I got no more turtle or fish of any sort before reaching port. July 31 a gale sprang up suddenly from the north, with heavy seas, and I shortened sail. The *Spray* made only fifty-one miles on her course that day. August 1 the gale continued, with heavy seas. Through the night the sloop was reaching, under close-reefed mainsail and bobbed jib. At 3 P.M. the jib was washed off the bowsprit and blown to rags and ribbons. I bent the "jumbo" on a stay at the night-heads. As for the jib, let it go; I saved pieces of it, and, after all, I was in want of pot-rags.

On August 3 the gale broke, and I saw many signs of land. Bad weather having made itself felt in the galley, I was minded to try my hand at a loaf of bread, and so rigging a pot of fire on deck by which to bake it, a loaf soon became an accomplished fact. One great feature about ship's cooking is that one's appetite on the sea is always good—a fact that I realized when I cooked for the crew of fishermen in the before-mentioned boyhood days. Dinner being over, I sat for hours reading the life of Columbus, and as the day wore on I watched the birds all flying in one direction, and said, "Land lies there."

Early the next morning, August 4, I discovered Spain. I saw fires on shore, and knew that the country was inhabited. The *Spray* continued on her course till well in with the land, which was that about Trafalgar. Then keeping away a point, she passed through the Strait of Gibraltar, where she cast anchor at 3 P.M. of the same day, less than twenty-nine days from Cape Sable. At the finish of this preliminary trip I found myself in excellent health, not overworked or cramped, but as well as ever in my life, though I was as thin as a reef-point.

Two Italian barks, which had been close alongside at daylight, I saw long after I had anchored, passing up the African side of the strait. The *Spray* had sailed them both hull down before she reached Tarifa. So far as I know, the *Spray* beat everything going across the Atlantic except the steamers.

All was well, but I had forgotten to bring a bill of health from Horta, and so when the fierce old port doctor came to inspect there was a row. That, however, was the very thing needed. If you want to get on well with a true Britisher you must first have a deuce of a row with him. I knew that well enough, and so I fired away, shot for shot, as best I could. "Well, yes," the doctor admitted at last, "your crew are healthy enough, no doubt, but who knows the diseases of your last port?"—a reasonable enough remark. "We ought to put you in the fort, sir!" he blustered; "but never mind. Free pratique, sir! Shove off, cockswain!" And that was the last I saw of the port doctor.

But on the following morning a steam-launch, much longer than the *Spray*, came alongside,—or as much of her as could get alongside,—with compliments from the senior naval officer, Admiral Bruce, saying there was a berth for the *Spray* at the arsenal. This was around at the new mole. I had anchored at the old mole, among the native craft, where it was rough and uncomfortable. Of course I was glad to shift, and did so as soon as possible, thinking of the great company the *Spray* would be in among battle-ships such as the *Collingwood*, *Balfleur*, and *Cormorant*, which were at that time stationed there, and on board all of which I was entertained, later, most royally.

" 'Put it thar!' as the Americans say," was the salute I got from Admiral Bruce, when I called at the admiralty to thank him for his

247

courtesy of the berth, and for the use of the steam-launch which towed me into dock. "About the berth, it is all right if it suits, and we'll tow you out when you are ready to go. But, say, what repairs do you want? Ahoy the *Hebe*, can you spare your sailmaker? The *Spray* wants a new jib. Construction and repair, there! will you see to the *Spray*? Say, old man, you must have knocked the devil out of her coming over alone in twenty-nine days! But we'll make it smooth for you here!" Not even her Majesty's ship the *Collingwood* was better looked after than the *Spray* at Gibraltar.

Later in the day came the hail: "*Spray* ahoy! Mrs. Bruce would like to come on board and shake hands with the *Spray*. Will it be convenient to-day?" "Very!" I joyfully shouted. On the following day Sir F. Carrington, at the time governor of Gibraltar, with other high officers of the garrison, and all the commanders of the battle-ships, came on board and signed their names in the *Spray's* log-book. Again there was a hail, "*Spray* ahoy!" "Hello!" "Commander Reynolds's compliments. You are invited on board H.M.S. *Collingwood*, 'at home' at 4:30 P.M. Not later than 5:30 P.M." I had already hinted at the limited amount of my wardrobe, and that I could never succeed as a dude. "You are expected, sir, in a stovepipe hat and a claw-hammer coat!" "Then I can't come." "Dash it! come in what you have on; that is what we mean." "Aye, aye, sir!" The *Collingwood's* cheer was good, and had I worn a silk hat as high as the moon I could not have had a better time or been made more at home. An Englishman, even on his great battle-ship, unbends when the stranger passes his gangway, and when he says "at home" he means it.

That one should like Gibraltar would go without saying. How could one help loving so hospitable a place? Vegetables twice a week and milk every morning came from the palatial grounds of the admiralty. "*Spray* ahoy!" would hail the admiral. "*Spray* ahoy!" "Hello!" "To-morrow is your vegetable day, sir." "Aye, aye, sir!"

I rambled much about the old city, and a gunner piloted me through the galleries of the rock as far as a stranger is permitted to go. There is no excavation in the world, for military purposes, at all approaching these of Gibraltar in conception or execution. Viewing the stupendous works, it became hard to realize that one was within the Gibraltar of his little old Morse geography.

Before sailing I was invited on a picnic with the governor, the officers of the garrison, and the commanders of the war-ships at the station; and a royal affair it was. Torpedo-boat No. 91, going twenty-two knots, carried our party to the Morocco shore and back. The day was perfect—too fine, in fact, for comfort on shore, and so no one landed at Morocco. No. 91 trembled like an aspen-leaf as she raced through the sea at top speed. Sublieutenant Boucher, apparently a mere lad, was in command, and handled his ship with the skill of an older sailor. On the following day I lunched with General Carrington, the governor, at Line Wall House, which was once the Franciscan convent. In this interesting edifice are preserved relics of the fourteen sieges which Gibraltar has seen. On the next day I supped with the admiral at his residence, the palace, which was once the convent of the Mercenaries. At each place, and all about, I felt the friendly grasp of a manly hand, that lent me vital strength to pass the coming long days at sea. I must confess that the perfect discipline, order, and cheerfulness at Gibraltar were only a second wonder in the great stronghold. The vast amount of business going forward caused no more excitement than the quiet sailing of a well-appointed ship in a smooth sea. No one spoke above his natural voice, save a boatswain's mate now and then. The Hon. Horatio J. Sprague, the venerable United States consul at Gibraltar, honored the *Spray* with a visit on Sunday, August 24, and was much pleased to find that our British cousins had been so kind to her.

Chapter 5

Monday, August 25, the *Spray* sailed from Gibraltar, well repaid for whatever deviation she had made from a direct course to reach the place. A tug belonging to her Majesty towed the sloop into the steady breeze clear of the mount, where her sails caught a volant wind, which carried her once more to the Atlantic, where it rose rapidly to a furious gale. My plan was, in going down this coast, to haul offshore, well clear of the land, which hereabouts is the home of pirates; but I had hardly accomplished this when I perceived a felucca making out of the nearest port, and finally following in the wake of the *Spray*. Now, my course to Gibraltar had been taken with a view to proceed up the Mediterranean Sea, through the Suez Canal, down the Red Sea, and east about, instead of a western route, which I finally adopted. By officers of vast experience in navigating these seas, I was influenced to make the change. Longshore pirates on both coasts being numerous, I could not afford to make light of the advice. But here I was, after all, evidently in the midst of pirates and thieves! I changed my course; the felucca did the same, both vessels sailing very fast, but the distance growing less and less between us. The *Spray* was doing nobly; she was even more than at her best; but, in spite of all I could do, she would broach now and then. She was carrying too much sail for safety. I must reef or be dismasted and lose all, pirate or no pirate. I must reef, even if I had to grapple with him for my life.

I was not long in reefing the mainsail and sweating it up—probably not more than fifteen minutes; but the felucca had in the meantime so shortened the distance between us that I now saw the tuft of hair on the heads of the crew,—by which, it is said, Mohammed will pull the villains up into heaven,—and they were coming on like the wind. From what I could clearly make out now, I felt them to be the sons of generations of pirates, and I saw by their movements that they were now preparing to strike a blow. The exultation on their faces, however, was changed in an instant to a look of fear and rage. Their craft, with too much sail on, broached to on the crest of a great wave. This one great sea changed the aspect of affairs suddenly as the flash of a gun. Three minutes later the same wave overtook the *Spray* and shook her in every timber. At the same moment the sheet-strop parted, and away went the main-boom, broken short at the rigging. Impulsively I sprang to the jib-halyards and down-haul, and instantly downed the jib. The head-sail being off, and the helm put hard down, the sloop came in the wind with a bound. While shivering there, but a moment though it was, I got the mainsail down and secured inboard, broken boom and all. How I got the boom in before the sail was torn I hardly know; but not a stitch of it was broken. The mainsail being secured, I hoisted away the jib, and, without looking round, stepped quickly to the cabin and snatched down my loaded rifle and cartridges at hand; for I made mental calculations that the pirate would by this time have recovered his course and be close aboard, and that when I saw him it would be better for me to be looking at him along the barrel of a gun. The piece was at my shoulder when I peered into the mist, but there was no pirate within a mile. The wave and squall that carried away my boom dismasted the felucca outright. I perceived his thieving crew, some dozen or more of them, struggling to recover their rigging from the sea. Allah blacken their faces!

I sailed comfortably on under the jib and forestaysail, which I now set. I fished the boom and furled the sail snug for the night; then hauled the sloop's head two points offshore to allow for the set of current and heavy rollers toward the land. This gave me the wind three points on the starboard quarter and a steady pull in the head-sails. By the time I had things in this order it was dark, and a flying-fish had already fallen on deck. I took him below for my supper, but found myself too tired to cook, or even to eat a thing already prepared. I do not remember to have been more tired before or since in all my life than I was at the finish of that day. Too fatigued to sleep, I rolled about with the motion of the vessel till near midnight, when I made shift to dress my fish and prepare a dish of tea. I fully realized now, if I had not before, that the voyage ahead would call for exertions ardent and lasting. On August 27 nothing could be seen of the Moor, or his country either, except two peaks, away in the east through the clear atmosphere of morning. Soon after the sun rose even these were obscured by haze, much to my satisfaction.

The wind, for a few days following my escape from the pirates, blew a steady but moderate gale, and the sea, though agitated into long rollers, was not uncomfortably rough or dangerous, and while sitting in my cabin I could hardly realize that any sea was running at all, so easy was the long, swinging motion of the sloop over the waves. All distracting uneasiness and excitement being now over, I was once more alone with myself in the realization that I was on the mighty sea and in the hands of the elements. But I was happy, and was becoming more and more interested in the voyage.

Columbus, in the *Santa Maria*, sailing these seas more than four hundred years before, was not so happy as I, nor so sure of success in what he had undertaken. His first troubles at sea had already begun. His crew had managed, by foul play or otherwise, to break the ship's rudder while running before probably just such a gale as the *Spray* had passed through; and there was dissension on the *Santa Maria*, something that was unknown on the *Spray*.

251

After three days of squalls and shifting winds I threw myself down to rest and sleep, while, with helm lashed, the sloop sailed steadily on her course.

September 1, in the early morning, land-clouds rising ahead told of the Canary Islands not far away. A change in the weather came next day: storm-clouds stretched their arms across the sky; from the east, to all appearances, might come a fierce harmattan, or from the south might come the fierce hurricane. Every point of the compass threatened a wild storm. My attention was turned to reefing sails, and no time was to be lost over it, either, for the sea in a moment was confusion itself, and I was glad to head the sloop three points or more away from her true course that she might ride safely over the waves. I was now scudding her for the channel between Africa and the island of Fuerteventura, the easternmost of the Canary Islands, for which I was on the lookout. At 2 P.M., the weather becoming suddenly fine, the island stood in view, already abeam to starboard, and not more than seven miles off. Fuerteventura is twenty-seven hundred feet high, and in fine weather is visible many leagues away.

The wind freshened in the night, and the *Spray* had a fine run through the channel. By daylight, September 3, she was twenty-five miles clear of all the islands, when a calm ensued, which was the precursor of another gale of wind that soon came on, bringing with it dust from the African shore. It howled dismally while it lasted, and though it was not the season of the harmattan, the sea in the course of an hour was discolored with a reddish-brown dust. The air remained thick with flying dust all the afternoon, but the wind, veering northwest at night, swept it back to land, and afforded the *Spray* once more a clear sky. Her mast now bent under a strong, steady pressure, and her bellying sail swept the sea as she rolled scuppers under, courtesying to the waves. These rolling waves thrilled me as they tossed my ship, passing quickly under her keel. This was grand sailing.

September 4, the wind, still fresh, blew from the north-northeast, and the sea surged along with the sloop. About noon a steamship, a bullock-droger, from the river Plate hove in sight, steering northeast, and making bad weather of it. I signaled her, but got no answer. She was plunging into the head sea and rolling in a most astonishing manner, and from the way she yawed one might have said that a wild steer was at the helm.

On the morning of September 6 I found three flying-fish on deck, and a fourth one down the fore-scuttle as close as possible to the frying-pan. It was the best haul yet, and afforded me a sumptuous breakfast and dinner.

The *Spray* had now settled down to the trade-winds and to the business of her voyage. Later in the day another droger hove in sight, rolling as badly as her predecessor. I threw out no flag to this one, but got the worst of it for passing under her lee. She was, indeed, a stale one! And the poor cattle, how they bellowed! The time was when ships passing one another at sea backed their topsails and had a "gam," and on parting fired guns; but those good old days have gone. People have hardly time nowadays to speak even on the broad ocean, where news is news, and as for a salute of guns, they cannot afford the powder. There are no poetry-enshrined freighters on the sea now; it is a prosy life when we have no time to bid one another good morning.

My ship, running now in the full swing of the trades, left me days to myself for rest and recuperation. I employed the time in reading and writing, or in whatever I found to do about the rigging and the sails to keep them all in order. The cooking was always done quickly, and was a small matter, as the bill of fare consisted mostly of flying-fish, hot biscuits and butter, potatoes, coffee and cream—dishes readily prepared.

On September 10 the *Spray* passed the island of St. Antonio, the northwesternmost of the Cape Verdes, close aboard. The landfall was wonderfully true, considering that no observations for longitude had been made. The wind, northeast, as the sloop drew by the island, was very squally, but I reefed her sails snug, and steered broad from the highland of blustering St. Antonio. Then leaving the Cape Verde Islands out of sight astern, I found myself once more sailing a lonely sea and in a solitude supreme all around. When I slept I dreamed that I was alone. This feeling never left me; but, sleeping or waking, I seemed always to know the position of the sloop, and I saw my vessel moving across the chart, which became a picture before me.

One night while I sat in the cabin under this spell, the profound stillness all about was broken by human voices alongside! I sprang instantly to the deck, startled beyond my power to tell. Passing close

253

under lee, like an apparition, was a white bark under full sail. The sailors on board of her were hauling on ropes to brace the yards, which just cleared the sloop's mast as she swept by. No one hailed from the white-winged flier, but I heard some one on board say that he saw lights on the sloop, and that he made her out to be a fisherman. I sat long on the starlit deck that night, thinking of ships, and watching the constellations on their voyage.

On the following day, September 13, a large four-masted ship passed some distance to windward, heading north.

The sloop was now rapidly drawing toward the region of doldrums, and the force of the trade-winds was lessening. I could see by the ripples that a counter-current had set in. This I estimated to be about sixteen miles a day. In the heart of the counter-stream the rate was more than that setting eastward.

September 14 a lofty three-masted ship, heading north, was seen from the masthead. Neither this ship nor the one seen yesterday was within signal distance, yet it was good even to see them. On the following day heavy rain-clouds rose in the south, obscuring the sun; this was ominous of doldrums. On the 16th the *Spray* entered this gloomy region, to battle with squalls and to be harassed by fitful calms; for this is the state of the elements between the northeast and the southeast trades, where each wind, struggling in turn for mastery, expends its force whirling about in all directions. Making this still more trying to one's nerve and patience, the sea was tossed into confused cross-lumps and fretted by eddying currents. As if something more were needed to complete a sailor's discomfort in this state, the rain poured down in torrents day and night. The *Spray* struggled and tossed for ten days, making only three hundred miles on her course in all that time. I didn't say anything!

On September 23 the fine schooner *Nantasket* of Boston, from Bear River, for the river Plate, lumber-laden, and just through the doldrums, came up with the *Spray*, and her captain passing a few words, she sailed on. Being much fouled on the bottom by shell-fish, she drew along with her fishes which had been following the *Spray*, which was less provided with that sort of food. Fishes will always follow a foul ship. A barnacle-grown log adrift has the same attraction for deep-sea fishes. One of this little school of deserters was a dolphin that had followed the *Spray* about a thousand miles, and had been content to eat scraps of food thrown overboard from my table; for, having been wounded, it could not dart through the sea to prey on other fishes. I had become accustomed to seeing the dolphin, which I knew by its scars, and missed it whenever it took occasional excursions away from the sloop. One day, after it had been off some hours, it returned in company with three yellowtails, a sort of cousin to the dolphin. This little school kept together, except when in danger and when foraging about the sea. Their lives were often threatened by hungry sharks that came round the vessel, and more than once they had narrow escapes. Their mode of escape interested me greatly, and I passed hours watching them. They would dart away, each in a different direction, so that the wolf of the sea, the shark, pursuing one, would be led away from the others; then after a while they would all return and rendezvous under one side or the other of the sloop. Twice their pursuers were diverted by a tin pan, which I towed astern of the sloop, and which was mistaken for a bright fish; and while turning, in the peculiar way that sharks have when about to devour their prey, I shot them through the head.

Their precarious life seemed to concern the yellowtails very little, if at all. All living beings, without doubt, are afraid of death. Nevertheless, some of the species I saw huddle together as though they knew they were created for the larger fishes, and wished to give the least possible trouble to their captors. I have seen, on the other hand, whales swimming in a circle around a school of herrings, and with mighty exertion "bunching" them together in a whirlpool set in motion by their flukes, and when the small fry were all whirled nicely together, one or the other of the leviathans, lunging through the center with open jaws, take in a boat-load or so at a single mouthful. Off the Cape of Good Hope I saw schools of sardines or other small fish being treated in this way by great numbers of cavally-fish. There was not the slightest chance of escape for the sardines, while the cavally circled round and round, feeding from the edge of the mass. It was interesting to note how rapidly the small fry disappeared; and though it was repeated before my eyes over and over, I could hardly perceive the capture of a single sardine, so dexterously was it done.

Along the equatorial limit of the southeast trade-winds the air was heavily charged with electricity, and there was much thunder and lightning. It was hereabout I remembered that, a few years before, the American ship *Alert* was destroyed by lightning. Her people, by wonderful good fortune, were rescued on the same day and brought to Pernambuco, where I then met them.

On September 25, in the latitude of 5° N., longitude 26° 30' W., I spoke the ship *North Star* of London. The great ship was out forty-eight days from Norfolk, Virginia, and was bound for Rio, where we met again about two months later. The *Spray* was now thirty days from Gibraltar.

The *Spray's* next companion of the voyage was a swordfish, that swam alongside, showing its tall fin out of the water, till I made a stir for my harpoon, when it hauled its black flag down and disappeared. September 30, at half-past eleven in the morning, the *Spray* crossed the equator in longitude 29° 30' W. At noon she was two miles south of the line. The southeast trade-winds, met, rather light, in about 4° N., gave her sails now a stiff full sending her handsomely over the sea toward the coast of Brazil, where on October 5, just north of Olinda Point, without further incident, she made the land, casting anchor in Pernambuco harbor about noon: forty days from Gibraltar, and all well on board. Did I tire of the voyage in all that time? Not a bit of it! I was never in better trim in all my life, and was eager for the more perilous experience of rounding the Horn.

It was not at all strange in a life common to sailors that, having already crossed the Atlantic twice and being now half-way from Boston to the Horn, I should find myself still among friends. My determination to sail westward from Gibraltar not only enabled me to escape the pirates of the Red Sea, but, in bringing me to Pernambuco, landed me on familiar shores. I had made many voyages to this and other ports in Brazil. In 1893 I was employed as master to take the famous Ericsson ship *Destroyer* from New York to Brazil to go against the rebel Mello and his party. The *Destroyer*, by the way, carried a submarine cannon of enormous length.

In the same expedition went the *Nictheroy*, the ship purchased by the United States government during the Spanish war and renamed the *Buffalo*. The *Destroyer* was in many ways the better ship of the two, but the Brazilians in their curious war sank her themselves at Bahia. With her sank my hope of recovering wages due me; still, I could but try to recover, for to me it meant a great deal. But now within two years the whirligig of time had brought the Mello party into power, and although it was the legal government which had employed me, the so-called "rebels" felt under less obligation to me than I could have wished.

During these visits to Brazil I had made the acquaintance of Dr. Perera, owner and editor of "El Commercio Jornal," and soon after the *Spray* was safely moored in Upper Topsail Reach, the doctor, who is a very enthusiastic yachtsman, came to pay me a visit and to carry me up the waterway of the lagoon to his country residence. The approach to his mansion by the waterside was guarded by his armada, a fleet of boats including a Chinese sampan, a Norwegian pram, and a Cape Ann dory, the last of which he obtained from the *Destroyer*. The doctor dined me often on good Brazilian fare, that I might, as he said, "salle gordo" for the voyage; but he found that even on the best I fattened slowly.

Fruits and vegetables and all other provisions necessary for the voyage having been taken in, on the 23d of October I unmoored and made ready for sea. Here I encountered one of the unforgiving Mello faction in the person of the collector of customs, who charged the *Spray* tonnage dues when she cleared, notwithstanding that she sailed with a yacht license and should have been exempt from port charges. Our consul reminded the collector of this and of the fact— without much diplomacy, I thought—that it was I who brought the *Destroyer* to Brazil. "Oh, yes," said the bland collector; "we remember it very well," for it was now in a small way his turn.

Mr. Lungrin, a merchant, to help me out of the trifling difficulty, offered to freight the *Spray* with a cargo of gunpowder for Bahia, which would have put me in funds; and when the insurance companies refused to take the risk on cargo shipped on a vessel manned by a crew of only one, he offered to ship it without insurance, taking all the risk himself. This was perhaps paying me a greater compliment than I deserved. The reason why I did not accept the business was that in so doing I found that I should vitiate my yacht license and run into more expense for harbor dues around the world than the freight would amount to. Instead of all this, another old merchant friend came to my assistance, advancing the cash direct.

While at Pernambuco I shortened the boom, which had been broken when off the coast of Morocco, by removing the broken piece, which took about four feet off the inboard end; I also refitted the jaws. On October 24, 1895, a fine day even as days go in Brazil, the *Spray* sailed, having had abundant good cheer. Making about one hundred miles a day along the coast, I arrived at Rio de Janeiro November 5, without any event worth mentioning, and about noon cast anchor near Villaganon, to await the official port visit. On the following day I bestirred myself to meet the highest lord of the admiralty and the ministers, to inquire concerning the matter of wages due me from the beloved *Destroyer*. The high official I met said: "Captain, so far as we are concerned, you may have the ship, and if you care to accept her we will send an officer to show you where she is." I knew well enough where she was at that moment. The top of her smoke-stack being awash in Bahia, it was more than likely that she rested on the bottom there. I thanked the kind officer, but declined his offer.

The *Spray*, with a number of old shipmasters on board, sailed about the harbor of Rio the day before she put to sea. As I had decided to give the *Spray* a yawl rig for the tempestuous waters of Patagonia, I here placed on the stern a semicircular brace to support a jigger mast. These old captains inspected the *Spray's* rigging, and each one contributed something to her outfit. Captain Jones, who had acted as my interpreter at Rio, gave her an anchor, and one of the steamers gave her a cable to match it. She never dragged Jones's anchor once on the voyage, and the cable not only stood the strain on a lee shore, but when towed off Cape Horn helped break combing seas astern that threatened to board her.

Chapter 6

On November 28 the *Spray* sailed from Rio de Janeiro, and first of all ran into a gale of wind, which tore up things generally along the coast, doing considerable damage to shipping. It was well for her, perhaps, that she was clear of the land. Coasting along on this part of the voyage, I observed that while some of the small vessels I fell in with were able to outsail the *Spray* by day, they fell astern of her by night. To the *Spray* day and night were the same; to the others clearly there was a difference. On one of the very fine days experienced after leaving Rio, the steamship *South Wales* spoke the

Spray and unsolicited gave the longitude by chronometer as 48° W., "as near as I can make it," the captain said. The *Spray*, with her tin clock, had exactly the same reckoning. I was feeling at ease in my primitive method of navigation, but it startled me not a little to find my position by account verified by the ship's chronometer.

On December 5 a barkantine hove in sight, and for several days the two vessels sailed along the coast together. Right here a current was experienced setting north, making it necessary to hug the shore, with which the *Spray* became rather familiar. Here I confess a weakness: I hugged the shore entirely too close. In a word, at daybreak on the morning of December 11 the *Spray* ran hard and fast on the beach. This was annoying; but I soon found that the sloop was in no great danger. The false appearance of the sand-hills under a bright moon had deceived me, and I lamented now that I had trusted to appearances at all. The sea, though moderately smooth, still carried a swell which broke with some force on the shore. I managed to launch my small dory from the deck, and ran out a kedge-anchor and warp; but it was too late to kedge the sloop off, for the tide was falling and she had already sewed a foot. Then I went about "laying out" the larger anchor, which was no easy matter, for my only life-boat, the frail dory, when the anchor and cable were in it, was swamped at once in the surf, the load being too great for her. Then I cut the cable and made two loads of it instead of one. The anchor, with forty fathoms bent and already buoyed, I now took and succeeded in getting through the surf; but my dory was leaking fast, and by the time I had rowed far enough to drop the anchor she was full to the gunwale and sinking. There was not a moment to spare, and I saw clearly that if I failed now all might be lost. I sprang from the oars to my feet, and lifting the anchor above my head, threw it clear just as she was turning over. I grasped her gunwale and held on as she turned bottom up, for I suddenly remembered that I could not swim. Then I tried to right her, but with too much eagerness, for she rolled clean over, and left me as before, clinging to her gunwale, while my body was still in the water. Giving a moment to cool reflection, I found that although the wind was blowing moderately toward the land, the current was carrying me to sea, and that something would have to be done. Three times I had been under water, in trying to right the dory, and I was just saying, "Now I lay me," when I was seized by a determination to try yet once more, so that no one of the prophets of evil I had left behind me could say, "I told you so." Whatever the danger may have been, much or little, I can truly say that the moment was the most serene of my life.

After righting the dory for the fourth time, I finally succeeded by the utmost care in keeping her upright while I hauled myself into her and with one of the oars, which I had recovered, paddled to the shore, somewhat the worse for wear and pretty full of salt water. The position of my vessel, now high and dry, gave me anxiety. To get her afloat again was all I thought of or cared for. I had little difficulty in carrying the second part of my cable out and securing it to the first, which I had taken the precaution to buoy before I put it into the boat. To bring the end back to the sloop was a smaller matter still, and I believe I chuckled above my sorrows when I found that in all the haphazard my judgment or my good genius had faithfully stood by me. The cable reached from the anchor in deep water to the sloop's windlass by just enough to secure a turn and no more. The anchor had been dropped at the right distance from the vessel. To heave all taut now and wait for the coming tide was all I could do.

I had already done enough work to tire a stouter man, and was only too glad to throw myself on the sand above the tide and rest; for the sun was already up, and pouring a generous warmth over the land. While my state could have been worse, I was on the wild coast of a foreign country, and not entirely secure in my property, as I soon found out. I had not been long on the shore when I heard the patter, patter of a horse's feet approaching along the hard beach, which ceased as it came abreast of the sand-ridge where I lay sheltered from the wind. Looking up cautiously, I saw mounted on a nag probably the most astonished boy on the whole coast. He had found a sloop! "It must be mine," he thought, "for am I not the first to see it on the beach?" Sure enough, there it was all high and dry and painted white. He trotted his horse around it, and finding no owner, hitched the nag to the sloop's bobstay and hauled as though he would take her home; but of course she was too heavy for one horse to move. With my skiff, however, it was different; this he hauled some distance, and concealed behind a dune in a bunch of tall grass. He had made up his mind, I dare say, to bring more horses and drag his bigger prize away, anyhow, and was starting off for the settlement a mile or so away for the reinforcement when I discovered myself to him, at which he seemed displeased and disappointed. "Buenos dias, muchacho," I said. He grunted a reply, and eyed me keenly from head to foot. Then bursting into a volley of questions,—more than six Yankees could ask,—he wanted to know, first, where my ship was from, and how many days she had been coming. Then he asked what I was doing here ashore so early in the morning. "Your questions are easily answered," I replied; "my ship is from the moon, it has taken her a month to come, and she is here for a cargo of boys." But the intimation of this enterprise, had I not been on the alert, might have cost me dearly; for while I spoke this child of the campo coiled his lariat ready to throw, and instead of being himself carried to the moon, he was apparently thinking of towing me home by the neck, astern of his wild cayuse, over the fields of Uruguay.

The exact spot where I was stranded was at the Castillo Chicos, about seven miles south of the dividing-line of Uruguay and Brazil, and of course the natives there speak Spanish. To reconcile my early visitor, I told him that I had on my ship biscuits, and that I wished to trade them for butter and milk. On hearing this a broad grin lighted up his face, and showed that he was greatly interested, and that even in Uruguay a ship's biscuit will cheer the heart of a boy and make him your bosom friend. The lad almost flew home, and returned quickly with butter, milk, and eggs. I was, after all, in a land of plenty. With the boy came others, old and young, from neighboring ranches, among them a German settler, who was of great assistance to me in many ways.

A coast-guard from Fort Teresa, a few miles away, also came, "to protect your property from the natives of the plains," he said. I took occasion to tell him, however, that if he would look after the people of his own village, I would take care of those from the plains, pointing, as I spoke, to the nondescript "merchant" who had already stolen my revolver and several small articles from my cabin, which by a bold front I had recovered. The chap was not a native Uruguayan. Here, as in many other places that I visited, the natives themselves were not the ones discreditable to the country.

Early in the day a despatch came from the port captain of Montevideo, commanding the coastguards to render the *Spray* every assistance. This, however, was not necessary, for a guard was already on the alert, and making all the ado that would become the wreck of a steamer with a thousand emigrants aboard. The same messenger brought word from the port captain that he would despatch a steam-tug to tow the *Spray* to Montevideo. The officer was as good as his word; a powerful tug arrived on the following day; but, to make a long story short, with the help of the German and one soldier and one Italian, called "Angel of Milan," I had already floated the sloop and was sailing for port with the boom off before a fair wind. The adventure cost the *Spray* no small amount of pounding on the hard sand; she lost her shoe and part of her false keel, and received other damage, which, however, was readily mended afterward in dock.

On the following day I anchored at Maldonado. The British consul, his daughter, and another young lady came on board, bringing with them a basket of fresh eggs, strawberries, bottles of milk, and a great loaf of sweet bread. This was a good landfall, and better cheer than I had found at Maldonado once upon a time when I entered the port with a stricken crew in my bark, the *Aquidneck*.

In the waters of Maldonado Bay a variety of fishes abound, and fur-seals in their season haul out on the island abreast the bay to breed. Currents on this coast are greatly affected by the prevailing winds, and a tidal wave higher than that ordinarily produced by the moon is sent up the whole shore of Uruguay before a southwest gale, or lowered by a northeaster, as may happen. One of these waves having just receded before the northeast wind which brought the *Spray* in left the tide now at low ebb, with oyster-rocks laid bare for some distance along the shore. Other shellfish of good flavor were also plentiful, though small in size. I gathered a mess of oysters and mussels here, while a native with hook and line, and with mussels for bait, fished from a point of detached rocks for bream, landing several good-sized ones.

The fisherman's nephew, a lad about seven years old, deserves mention as the tallest blasphemer, for a short boy, that I met on the voyage. He called his old uncle all the vile names under the sun for not helping him across the gully. While he swore roundly in all the moods and tenses of the Spanish language, his uncle fished on, now and then congratulating his hopeful nephew on his accomplishment. At the end of his rich vocabulary the urchin sauntered off into the fields, and shortly returned with a bunch of flowers, and with all smiles handed them to me with the innocence of an angel. I remembered having seen the same flower on the banks of the river farther up, some years before. I asked the young pirate why he had brought them to me. Said he, "I don't know; I only wished to do so." Whatever the influence was that put so amiable a wish in this wild pampa boy, it must be far-reaching, thought I, and potent, seas over.

Shortly after, the *Spray* sailed for Montevideo, where she arrived on the following day and was greeted by steam-whistles till I felt embarrassed and wished that I had arrived unobserved. The voyage so far alone may have seemed to the Uruguayans a feat worthy of some recognition; but there was so much of it yet ahead, and of such an arduous nature, that any demonstration at this point seemed, somehow, like boasting prematurely.

The *Spray* had barely come to anchor at Montevideo when the agents of the Royal Mail Steamship Company, Messrs. Humphreys & Co., sent word that they would dock and repair her free of expense and give me twenty pounds sterling, which they did to the letter, and more besides. The calkers at Montevideo paid very careful attention to the work of making the sloop tight. Carpenters mended the keel and also the life-boat (the dory), painting it till I hardly knew it from a butterfly.

Christmas of 1895 found the *Spray* refitted even to a wonderful makeshift stove which was contrived from a large iron drum of some sort punched full of holes to give it a draft; the pipe reached straight up through the top of the forecastle. Now, this was not a stove by mere courtesy. It was always hungry, even for green wood; and in cold, wet days off the coast of Tierra del Fuego it stood me in good stead. Its one door swung on copper hinges, which one of the yard apprentices, with laudable pride, polished till the whole thing blushed like the brass binnacle of a P. & O. steamer.

The *Spray* was now ready for sea. Instead of proceeding at once on her voyage, however, she made an excursion up the river, sailing December 29. An old friend of mine, Captain Howard of Cape Cod and of River Plate fame, took the trip in her to Buenos Aires, where she arrived early on the following day, with a gale of wind and a current so much in her favor that she outdid herself. I was glad to have a sailor of Howard's experience on board to witness her performance of sailing with no living being at the helm. Howard sat near the binnacle and watched the compass while the sloop held her course so steadily that one would have declared that the card was nailed fast. Not a quarter of a point did she deviate from her course. My old friend had owned and sailed a pilot-sloop on the river for many years, but this feat took the wind out of his sails at last, and he cried, "I'll be stranded on Chico Bank if ever I saw the like of it!" Perhaps he had never given his sloop a chance to show what she could do. The point I make for the *Spray* here, above all other points, is that she sailed in shoal water and in a strong current, with other difficult and unusual conditions. Captain Howard took all this into account.

In all the years away from his native home Howard had not forgotten the art of making fish chowders; and to prove this he brought along some fine rockfish and prepared a mess fit for kings. When the savory chowder was done, chocking the pot securely between two boxes on the cabin floor, so that it could not roll over, we helped ourselves and swapped yarns over it while the *Spray* made her own way through the darkness on the river. Howard told me stories about the Fuegian cannibals as she reeled along, and I told him about the pilot of the *Pinta* steering my vessel through the storm off the coast of the Azores, and that I looked for him at the helm in a gale such as this. I do not charge Howard with superstition,—we are none of us superstitious,—but when I spoke about his returning to Montevideo on the *Spray* he shook his head and took a steam-packet instead.

I had not been in Buenos Aires for a number of years. The place where I had once landed from packets, in a cart, was now built up with magnificent docks. Vast fortunes had been spent in remodeling the harbor; London bankers could tell you that. The port captain, after assigning the *Spray* a safe berth, with his compliments, sent me word to call on him for anything I might want while in port, and I felt quite sure that his friendship was sincere. The sloop was well cared for at Buenos Aires; her dockage and tonnage dues were all free, and the yachting fraternity of the city welcomed her with a good will. In town I found things not so greatly changed as about the docks, and I soon felt myself more at home.

From Montevideo I had forwarded a letter from Sir Edward Hairby to the owner of the "Standard," Mr. Mulhall, and in reply to it was assured of a warm welcome to the warmest heart, I think, outside of Ireland. Mr. Mulhall, with a prancing team, came down to the docks as soon as the *Spray* was berthed, and would have me go to his house at once, where a room was waiting. And it was New Year's day, 1896. The course of the *Spray* had been followed in the columns of the "Standard."

Mr. Mulhall kindly drove me to see many improvements about the city, and we went in search of some of the old landmarks. The man who sold "lemonade" on the plaza when first I visited this wonderful city I found selling lemonade still at two cents a glass; he had made a fortune by it. His stock in trade was a wash-tub and a neighboring hydrant, a moderate supply of brown sugar, and about six lemons that floated on the sweetened water. The water from time to time was renewed from the friendly pump, but the lemon "went on forever," and all at two cents a glass.

But we looked in vain for the man who once sold whisky and coffins in Buenos Aires; the march of civilization had crushed him —memory only clung to his name. Enterprising man that he was, I fain would have looked him up. I remember the tiers of whisky-barrels, ranged on end, on one side of the store, while on the other side, and divided by a thin partition, were the coffins in the same order, of all sizes and in great numbers. The unique arrangement seemed in order, for as a cask was emptied a coffin might be filled. Besides cheap whisky and many other liquors, he sold "cider," which he manufactured from damaged Malaga raisins. Within the scope of his enterprise was also the sale of mineral waters, not entirely blameless of the germs of disease. This man surely catered to all the tastes, wants, and conditions of his customers.

Farther along in the city, however, survived the good man who wrote on the side of his store, where thoughtful men might read and learn: "This wicked world will be destroyed by a comet! The owner of this store is therefore bound to sell out at any price and avoid the catastrophe." My friend Mr. Mulhall drove me round to view the fearful comet with streaming tail pictured large on the trembling merchant's walls.

I unshipped the sloop's mast at Buenos Aires and shortened it by seven feet. I reduced the length of the bowsprit by about five feet, and even then I found it reaching far enough from home; and more than once, when on the end of it reefing the jib, I regretted that I had not shortened it another foot.

Chapter 7

On January 26, 1896, the *Spray*, being refitted and well provisioned in every way, sailed from Buenos Aires. There was little wind at the start; the surface of the great river was like a silver disk, and I was glad of a tow from a harbor tug to clear the port entrance. But a gale came up soon after, and caused an ugly sea, and instead of being all silver, as before, the river was now all mud. The Plate is a treacherous place for storms. One sailing there should always be on the alert for squalls. I cast anchor before dark in the best lee I could find near the land, but was tossed miserably all night, heartsore of choppy seas. On the following morning I got the sloop under way, and with reefed sails worked her down the river against a head wind. Standing in that night to the place where pilot Howard joined me for the up-river sail, I took a departure, shaping my course to clear Point Indio on the one hand, and the English Bank on the other.

I had not for many years been south of these regions. I will not say that I expected all fine sailing on the course for Cape Horn direct, but while I worked at the sails and rigging I thought only of onward and forward. It was when I anchored in the lonely places that a feeling of awe crept over me. At the last anchorage on the monotonous and muddy river, weak as it may seem, I gave way to my feelings. I resolved then that I would anchor no more north of the Strait of Magellan.

On the 28th of January the *Spray* was clear of Point Indio, English Bank, and all the other dangers of the River Plate. With a fair wind she then bore away for the Strait of Magellan, under all sail, pressing farther and farther toward the wonderland of the South, till I forgot the blessings of our milder North.

My ship passed in safety Bahia Blanca, also the Gulf of St. Matias and the mighty Gulf of St. George. Hoping that she might go clear of the destructive tide-races, the dread of big craft or little along this coast, I gave all the capes a berth of about fifty miles, for these dangers extend many miles from the land. But where the sloop avoided one danger she encountered another. For, one day, well off the Patagonian coast, while the sloop was reaching under short sail, a tremendous wave, the culmination, it seemed, of many waves, rolled down upon her in a storm, roaring as it came. I had only a moment to get all sail down and myself up on the peak halliards, out of danger, when I saw the mighty crest towering masthead-high above me. The mountain of water submerged my vessel. She shook in every timber and reeled under the weight of the sea, but rose quickly out of it, and rode grandly over the rollers that followed. It may have been a minute that from my hold in the rigging I could see no part of the *Spray's* hull. Perhaps it was even less time than that, but it seemed a long while, for under great excitement one lives fast, and in a few seconds one may think a great deal of one's past life. Not only did the past, with electric speed, flash before me, but I had time while in my hazardous position for resolutions for the future that would take a long time to fulfil. The first one was, I remember, that if the *Spray* came through this danger I would dedicate my best energies to building a larger ship on her lines, which I hope yet to do. Other promises, less easily kept, I should have made under protest. However, the incident, which filled me with fear, was only one more test of the *Spray's* seaworthiness. It reassured me against rude Cape Horn.

From the time the great wave swept over the *Spray* until she reached Cape Virgins nothing occurred to move a pulse and set blood in motion. On the contrary, the weather became fine and the sea smooth and life tranquil. The phenomenon of mirage frequently occurred. An albatross sitting on the water one day loomed up like a large ship; two fur-seals asleep on the surface of the sea appeared like great whales, and a bank of haze I could have sworn was high land. The kaleidoscope then changed, and on the following day I sailed in a world peopled by dwarfs.

On February 11 the *Spray* rounded Cape Virgins and entered the Strait of Magellan. The scene was again real and gloomy; the wind, northeast, and blowing a gale, sent feather-white spume along the coast; such a sea ran as would swamp an ill-appointed ship. As the sloop neared the entrance to the strait I observed that two great tide-races made ahead, one very close to the point of the land and one farther offshore. Between the two, in a sort of channel, through combers, went the *Spray* with close-reefed sails. But a rolling sea followed her a long way in, and a fierce current swept around the cape against her; but this she stemmed, and was soon chirruping under the lee of Cape Virgins and running every minute into smoother water. However, long trailing kelp from sunken rocks waved forebodingly under her keel, and the wreck of a great steamship smashed on the beach abreast gave a gloomy aspect to the scene.

I was not to be let off easy. The Virgins would collect tribute even from the *Spray* passing their promontory. Fitful rain-squalls from the northwest followed the northeast gale. I reefed the sloop's sails, and sitting in the cabin to rest my eyes, I was so strongly impressed with what in all nature I might expect that as I dozed the very air I breathed seemed to warn me of danger. My senses heard "*Spray* ahoy!" shouted in warning. I sprang to the deck, wondering who could be there that knew the *Spray* so well as to call out her name passing in the dark; for it was now the blackest of nights all around, except away in the southwest, where the old familiar white arch, the terror of Cape Horn, rapidly pushed up by a southwest gale. I had only a moment to douse sail and lash all solid when it struck like a shot from a cannon, and for the first half-hour it was something to be remembered by way of a gale. For thirty hours it kept on blowing hard. The sloop could carry no more than a three-reefed mainsail and forestaysail; with these she held on stoutly and was not blown out of the strait. In the height of the squalls in this gale she doused all sail, and this occurred often enough.

After this gale followed only a smart breeze, and the *Spray*, passing through the narrows without mishap, cast anchor at Sandy Point on February 14, 1896.

Sandy Point (Punta Arenas) is a Chilean coaling-station, and boasts about two thousand inhabitants, of mixed nationality, but mostly Chileans. What with sheep-farming, gold-mining, and hunting, the settlers in this dreary land seemed not the worst off in the world. But the natives, Patagonian and Fuegian, on the other hand, were as squalid as contact with unscrupulous traders could make them. A large percentage of the business there was traffic in "firewater." If there was a law against selling the poisonous stuff to the natives, it was not enforced. Fine specimens of the Patagonian race, looking smart in the morning when they came into town, had repented before night of ever having seen a white man, so beastly drunk were they, to say nothing about the peltry of which they had been robbed.

The port at that time was free, but a custom-house was in course of construction, and when it is finished, port and tariff dues are to be collected. A soldier police guarded the place, and a sort of vigilante force besides took down its guns now and then; but as a general thing, to my mind, whenever an execution was made they killed the wrong man. Just previous to my arrival the governor, himself of a jovial turn of mind, had sent a party of young bloods to foray a Fuegian settlement and wipe out what they could of it on account of the recent massacre of a schooner's crew somewhere else. Altogether the place was quite newsy and supported two papers— dailies, I think. The port captain, a Chilean naval officer, advised me to ship hands to fight Indians in the strait farther west, and spoke of my stopping until a gunboat should be going through, which would give me a tow. After canvassing the place, however, I found only one man willing to embark, and he on condition that I should ship another "mon and a doog." But as no one else was willing to come along, and as I drew the line at dogs, I said no more about the matter, but simply loaded my guns. At this point in my dilemma Captain Pedro Samblich, a good Austrian of large experience, coming along, gave me a bag of carpet-tacks, worth more than all the fighting men and dogs of Tierra del Fuego. I protested that I had no use for carpet-tacks on board. Samblich smiled at my want of experience, and maintained stoutly that I would have use for them. "You must use them with discretion," he said; "that is to say, don't step on them yourself." With this remote hint about the use of the tacks I got on all right, and saw the way to maintain clear decks at night without the care of watching.

Samblich was greatly interested in my voyage, and after giving me the tacks he put on board bags of biscuits and a large quantity of smoked venison. He declared that my bread, which was ordinary sea-biscuits and easily broken, was not nutritious as his, which was so hard that I could break it only with a stout blow from a maul. Then he gave me, from his own sloop, a compass which was certainly better than mine, and offered to unbend her mainsail for me if I would accept it. Last of all, this large-hearted man brought out a bottle of Fuegian gold-dust from a place where it had been *cached* and begged me to help myself from it, for use farther along on the voyage. But I felt sure of success without this draft on a friend, and I was right. Samblich's tacks, as it turned out, were of more value than gold.

The port captain finding that I was resolved to go, even alone, since there was no help for it, set up no further objections, but advised me, in case the savages tried to surround me with their canoes, to shoot straight, and begin to do it in time, but to avoid killing them if possible, which I heartily agreed to do. With these simple injunctions the officer gave me my port clearance free of charge, and I sailed on the same day, February 19, 1896. It was not without thoughts of strange and stirring adventure beyond all I had yet encountered that I now sailed into the country and very core of the savage Fuegians.

A fair wind from Sandy Point brought me on the first day to St. Nicholas Bay, where, so I was told, I might expect to meet savages; but seeing no signs of life, I came to anchor in eight fathoms of water, where I lay all night under a high mountain. Here I had my first experience with the terrific squalls, called williwaws, which extended from this point on through the strait to the Pacific. They were compressed gales of wind that Boreas handed down over the hills in chunks. A full-blown williwaw will throw a ship, even without sail on, over on her beam ends; but, like other gales, they cease now and then, if only for a short time.

February 20 was my birthday, and I found myself alone, with hardly so much as a bird in sight, off Cape Froward, the southern-most point of the continent of America. By daylight in the morning I was getting my ship under way for the bout ahead.

The sloop held the wind fair while she ran thirty miles farther on her course, which brought her to Fortescue Bay, and at once among the natives' signal-fires, which blazed up now on all sides. Clouds flew over the mountain from the west all day; at night my good east wind failed, and in its stead a gale from the west soon came on. I gained anchorage at twelve o'clock that night, under the lee of a little island, and then prepared myself a cup of coffee, of which I was sorely in need; for, to tell the truth, hard beating in the heavy squalls and against the current had told on my strength. Finding that the anchor held, I drank my beverage, and named the place Coffee Island. It lies to the south of Charles Island, with only a narrow channel between.

Sailing Alone Around the World

By daylight the next morning the *Spray* was again under way, beating hard; but she came to in a cove in Charles Island, two and a half miles along on her course. Here she remained undisturbed two days, with both anchors down in a bed of kelp. Indeed, she might have remained undisturbed indefinitely had not the wind moderated; for during these two days it blew so hard that no boat could venture out on the strait, and the natives being away to other hunting-grounds, the island anchorage was safe. But at the end of the fierce wind-storm fair weather came; then I got my anchors, and again sailed out upon the strait.

Canoes manned by savages from Fortescue now came in pursuit. The wind falling light, they gained on me rapidly till coming within hail, when they ceased paddling, and a bow-legged savage stood up and called to me, "Yammerschooner! yammerschooner!" which is their begging term. I said, "No!" Now, I was not for letting on that I was alone, and so I stepped into the cabin, and, passing through the hold, came out at the fore-scuttle, changing my clothes as I went along. That made two men. Then the piece of bowsprit which I had sawed off at Buenos Aires, and which I had still on board, I arranged forward on the lookout, dressed as a seaman, attaching a line by which I could pull it into motion. That made three of us, and we didn't want to "yammerschooner"; but for all that the savages came on faster than before. I saw that besides four at the paddles in the canoe nearest to me, there were others in the bottom, and that they were shifting hands often. At eighty yards I fired a shot across the bows of the nearest canoe, at which they all stopped, but only for a moment. Seeing that they persisted in coming nearer, I fired the second shot so close to the chap who wanted to "yammerschooner" that he changed his mind quickly enough and bellowed with fear, "Bueno jo via Isla," and sitting down in his canoe, he rubbed his starboard cat-head for some time. I was thinking of the good port captain's advice when I pulled the trigger, and must have aimed pretty straight; however, a miss was as good as a mile for Mr. "Black Pedro," as he it was, and no other, a leader in several bloody massacres. He made for the island now, and the others followed him. I knew by his Spanish lingo and by his full beard that he was the villain I have named, a renegade mongrel, and the worst murderer in Tierra del Fuego. The authorities had been in search of him for two years. The Fuegians are not bearded.

So much for the first day among the savages. I came to anchor at midnight in Three Island Cove, about twenty miles along from Fortescue Bay. I saw on the opposite side of the strait signal-fires, and heard the barking of dogs, but where I lay it was quite deserted by natives. I have always taken it as a sign that where I found birds sitting about, or seals on the rocks, I should not find savage Indians. Seals are never plentiful in these waters, but in Three Island Cove I saw one on the rocks, and other signs of the absence of savage men.

On the next day the wind was again blowing a gale, and although she was in the lee of the land, the sloop dragged her anchors, so that I had to get her under way and beat farther into the cove, where I came to in a landlocked pool. At another time or place this would have been a rash thing to do, and it was safe now only from the fact that the gale which drove me to shelter would keep the Indians from crossing the strait. Seeing this was the case, I went ashore with gun and ax on an island, where I could not in any event be surprised, and there felled trees and split about a cord of firewood, which loaded my small boat several times.

While I carried the wood, though I was morally sure there were no savages near, I never once went to or from the skiff without my gun. While I had that and a clear field of over eighty yards about me I felt safe.

The trees on the island, very scattering, were a sort of beech and a stunted cedar, both of which made good fuel. Even the green limbs of the beech, which seemed to possess a resinous quality, burned readily in my great drum-stove. I have described my method of wooding up in detail, that the reader who has kindly borne with me so far may see that in this, as in all other particulars of my voyage, I took great care against all kinds of surprises, whether by animals or by the elements. In the Strait of Magellan the greatest vigilance was necessary. In this instance I reasoned that I had all about me the greatest danger of the whole voyage—the treachery of cuning savages, for which I must be particularly on the alert.

The *Spray* sailed from Three Island Cove in the morning after the gale went down, but was glad to return for shelter from another sudden gale. Sailing again on the following day, she fetched Borgia Bay, a few miles on her course, where vessels had anchored from time to time and had nailed boards on the trees ashore with name and date of harboring carved or painted. Nothing else could I see to indicate that civilized man had ever been there. I had taken a survey of the gloomy place with my spy-glass, and was getting my boat out to land and take notes, when the Chilean gunboat *Huemel* came in, and officers, coming on board, advised me to leave the place at once, a thing that required little eloquence to persuade me to do. I accepted the captain's kind offer of a tow to the next anchorage, at the place called Notch Cove, eight miles farther along, where I should be clear of the worst of the Fuegians.

We made anchorage at the cove about dark that night, while the wind came down in fierce williwaws from the mountains. An instance of Magellan weather was afforded when the *Huemel*, a well-appointed gunboat of great power, after attempting on the following day to proceed on her voyage, was obliged by sheer force of the wind to return and take up anchorage again and remain till the gale abated; and lucky she was to get back!

Meeting this vessel was a little godsend. She was commanded and officered by high-class sailors and educated gentlemen. An entertainment that was gotten up on her, impromptu, at the Notch would be hard to beat anywhere. One of her midshipmen sang popular songs in French, German, and Spanish, and one (so he said) in Russian. If the audience did not know the lingo of one song from another, it was no drawback to the merriment.

I was left alone the next day, for then the *Huemel* put out on her voyage, the gale having abated. I spent a day taking in wood and water; by the end of that time the weather was fine. Then I sailed from the desolate place.

There is little more to be said concerning the *Spray's* first passage through the straight that would differ from what I have already recorded. She anchored and weighed many times, and beat many days against the current, with now and then a "slant" for a few miles, till finally she gained anchorage and shelter for the night at Port Tamar, with Cape Pillar in sight to the west. Here I felt the throb of the great ocean that lay before me. I knew now that I had put a world behind me, and that I was opening out another world ahead. I had passed the haunts of savages. Great piles of granite mountains of bleak and lifeless aspect were now astern; on some of them not even a speck of moss had ever grown. There was an unfinished newness all about the land. On the hill back of Port Tamar a

273

small beacon had been thrown up, showing that some man had been there. But how could one tell but that he had died of loneliness and grief? In a bleak land is not the place to enjoy solitude.

Throughout the whole of the strait west of Cape Froward I saw no animals except dogs owned by savages. These I saw often enough, and heard them yelping night and day. Birds were not plentiful. The scream of a wild fowl, which I took for a loon, sometimes startled me with its piercing cry. The steamboat duck, so called because it propels itself over the sea with its wings, and resembles a miniature side-wheel steamer in its motion, was sometimes seen scurrying on out of danger. It never flies, but, hitting the water instead of the air with its wings, it moves faster than a rowboat or a canoe. The few fur-seals I saw were very shy; and of fishes I saw next to none at all. I did not catch one; indeed, I seldom or never put a hook over during the whole voyage. Here in the strait I found great abundance of mussels of an excellent quality. I fared sumptuously on them. There was a sort of swan, smaller than a Muscovy duck, which might have been brought down with the gun, but in the loneliness of life about the dreary country I found myself in no mood to make one life less, except in self-defense.

Chapter 8

It was the 3d of March when the *Spray* sailed from Port Tamar direct for Cape Pillar, with the wind from the northeast, which I fervently hoped might hold till she cleared the land; but there was no such good luck in store. It soon began to rain and thicken in the northwest, boding no good. The *Spray* neared Cape Pillar rapidly, and, nothing loath, plunged into the Pacific Ocean at once, taking her first bath of it in the gathering storm. There was no turning back even had I wished to do so, for the land was now shut out by the darkness of night. The wind freshened, and I took in a third reef. The sea was confused and treacherous. In such a time as this the old fisherman prayed, "Remember, Lord, my ship is small and thy sea is so wide!" I saw now only the gleaming crests of the waves.

They showed white teeth while the sloop balanced over them. "Everything for an offing," I cried, and to this end I carried on all the sail she would bear. She ran all night with a free sheet, but on the morning of March 4 the wind shifted to southwest, then back suddenly to northwest, and blew with terrific force. The *Spray*, stripped of her sails, then bore off under bare poles. No ship in the world could have stood up against so violent a gale. Knowing that this storm might continue for many days, and that it would be impossible to work back to the westward along the coast outside of Tierra del Fuego, there seemed nothing to do but to keep on and go east about, after all. Anyhow, for my present safety the only course lay in keeping her before the wind. And so she drove southeast, as though about to round the Horn, while the waves rose and fell and bellowed their never-ending story of the sea; but the Hand that held these held also the *Spray*. She was running now with a reefed forestaysail, the sheets flat amidship. I paid out two long ropes to steady her course and to break combing seas astern, and I lashed the helm amidship. In this trim she ran before it, shipping never a sea. Even while the storm raged at its worst, my ship was wholesome and noble. My mind as to her seaworthiness was put at ease for aye.

When all had been done that I could do for the safety of the vessel, I got to the fore-scuttle, between seas, and prepared a pot of coffee over a wood fire, and made a good Irish stew. Then, as before and afterward on the *Spray*, I insisted on warm meals. In the tide-race off Cape Pillar, however, where the sea was marvelously high, uneven, and crooked, my appetite was slim, and for a time I postponed cooking. (Confidentially, I was seasick!)

The first day of the storm gave the *Spray* her actual test in the worst sea that Cape Horn or its wild regions could afford, and in no part of the world could a rougher sea be found than at this particular point, namely, off Cape Pillar, the grim sentinel of the Horn.

Farther offshore, while the sea was majestic, there was less apprehension of danger. There the *Spray* rode, now like a bird on the crest of a wave, and now like a waif deep down in the hollow between seas; and so she drove on. Whole days passed, counted as other days, but with always a thrill—yes, of delight.

On the fourth day of the gale, rapidly nearing the pitch of Cape Horn, I inspected my chart and pricked off the course and distance to Port Stanley, in the Falkland Islands, where I might find my way and refit, when I saw through a rift in the clouds a high mountain, about seven leagues away on the port beam. The fierce edge of the gale by this time had blown off, and I had already bent a square-sail on the boom in place of the mainsail, which was torn to rags. I hauled in the trailing ropes, hoisted this awkward sail reefed, the forestaysail being already set, and under this sail brought her at once on the wind heading for the land, which appeared as an island in the sea. So it turned out to be, though not the one I had supposed.

I was exultant over the prospect of once more entering the Strait of Magellan and beating through again into the Pacific, for it was more than rough on the outside coast of Tierra del Fuego. It was indeed a mountainous sea. When the sloop was in the fiercest squalls, with only the reefed forestaysail set, even that small sail shook her from keelson to truck when it shivered by the leech. Had I harbored the shadow of a doubt for her safety, it would have been that she might spring a leak in the garboard at the heel of the mast; but she never called me once to the pump. Under pressure of the smallest sail I could set she made for the land like a race-horse, and steering her over the crests of the waves so that she might not trip was nice work. I stood at the helm now and made the most of it.

Night closed in before the sloop reached the land, leaving her feeling the way in pitchy darkness. I saw breakers ahead before long. At this I wore ship and stood offshore, but was immediately startled by the tremendous roaring of breakers again ahead and on the lee bow. This puzzled me, for there should have been no broken water where I supposed myself to be. I kept off a good bit, then wore round, but finding broken water also there, threw her head again offshore. In this way, among dangers, I spent the rest of the night. Hail and sleet in the fierce squalls cut my flesh till the blood trickled over my face; but what of that? It was daylight, and the sloop was in the midst of the Milky Way of the sea, which is north-west of Cape Horn, and it was the white breakers of a huge sea over sunken rocks which had threatened to engulf her through the night. It was Fury Island I had sighted and steered for, and what a pano-rama was before me now and all around! It was not the time to complain of a broken skin. What could I do but fill away among the breakers and find a channel between them, now that it was day? Since she had escaped the rocks through the night, surely she would

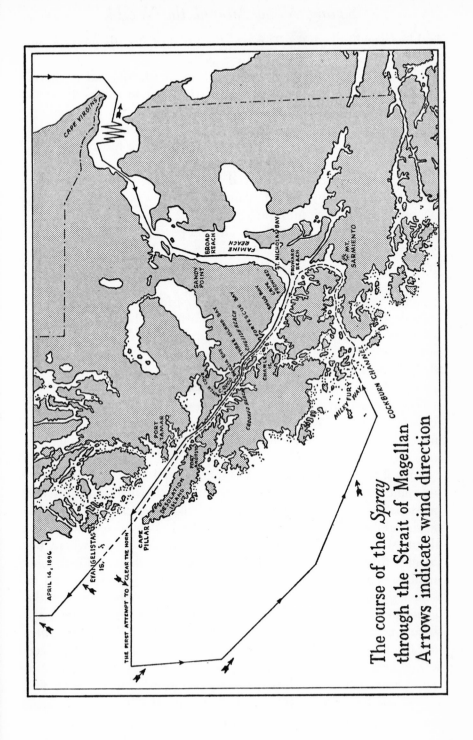

The course of the *Spray*
through the Strait of Magellan
Arrows indicate wind direction

find her way by daylight. This was the greatest sea adventure of my life. God knows how my vessel escaped.

The sloop at last reached inside of small islands that sheltered her in smooth water. Then I climbed the mast to survey the wild scene astern. The great naturalist Darwin looked over this seascape from the deck of the *Beagle,* and wrote in his journal, "Any landsman seeing the Milky Way would have nightmare for a week." He might have added, "or seaman" as well.

The *Spray's* good luck followed fast. I discovered, as she sailed along through a labyrinth of islands, that she was in the Cockburn Channel, which leads into the Strait of Magellan at a point opposite Cape Froward, and that she was already passing Thieves' Bay, suggestively named. And at night, March 8, behold, she was at anchor in a snug cove at the Turn! Every heart-beat on the *Spray* now counted thanks.

Here I pondered on the events of the last few days, and, strangely enough, instead of feeling rested from sitting or lying down, I now began to feel jaded and worn; but a hot meal of venison stew soon put me right, so that I could sleep. As drowsiness came on I sprinkled the deck with tacks, and then I turned in, bearing in mind the advice of my old friend Samblich that I was not to step on them myself. I saw to it that not a few of them stood "business end" up; for when the *Spray* passed Thieves' Bay two canoes had put out and followed in her wake, and there was no disguising the fact any longer that I was alone.

Now, it is well known that one cannot step on a tack without saying something about it. A pretty good Christian will whistle when he steps on the "commercial end" of a carpet-tack; a savage will howl and claw the air, and that was just what happened that night about twelve o'clock, while I was asleep in the cabin, where the savages thought they "had me," sloop and all, but changed their minds when they stepped on deck, for then they thought that I or somebody else had them. I had no need of a dog; they howled like a pack of hounds. I had hardly use for a gun. They jumped pell-mell, some into their canoes and some into the sea, to cool off, I suppose, and there was a deal of free language over it as they went. I fired several guns when I came on deck, to let the rascals know that I was home, and then I turned in again, feeling sure I should not be disturbed any more by people who left in so great a hurry.

The Fuegians, being cruel, are naturally cowards; they regard a rifle with superstitious fear. The only real danger one could see that might come from their quarter would be from allowing them to surround one within bow-shot, or to anchor within range where they might lie in ambush. As for their coming on deck at night, even had I not put tacks about, I could have cleared them off by shots from the cabin and hold. I always kept a quantity of ammunition within reach in the hold and in the cabin and in the forepeak, so that re-treating to any of these places I could "hold the fort" simply by shooting up through the deck.

Perhaps the greatest danger to be apprehended was from the use of fire. Every canoe carries fire; nothing is thought of that, for it is their custom to communicate by smoke-signals. The harmless brand that lies smoldering in the bottom of one of their canoes might be ablaze in one's cabin if he were not on the alert. The port captain of Sandy Point warned me particularly of this danger. Only a short time before they had fired a Chilean gunboat by throwing brands in through the stern windows of the cabin. The *Spray* had no openings in the cabin or deck, except two scuttles, and these were guarded by fastenings which could not be undone without waking me if I were asleep.

On the morning of the 9th, after a refreshing rest and a warm breakfast, and after I had swept the deck of tacks, I got out what spare canvas there was on board, and began to sew the pieces to-gether in the shape of a peak for my square-mainsail, the tarpaulin. The day to all appearances promised fine weather and light winds, but appearances in Tierra del Fuego do not always count. While I was wondering why no trees grew on the slope abreast of the anchor-age, half minded to lay by the sail-making and land with my gun for some game and to inspect a white boulder on the beach, near the brook, a williwaw came down with such terrific force as to carry the *Spray*, with two anchors down, like a feather out of the cove and away into deep water. No wonder trees did not grow on the side of that hill! Great Boreas! a tree would need to be all roots to hold on against such a furious wind.

From the cove to the nearest land to leeward was a long drift, however, and I had ample time to weigh both anchors before the sloop came near any danger, and so no harm came of it. I saw no more savages that day or the next; they probably had some sign by which they knew of the coming williwaws; at least, they were wise in not being afloat even on the second day, for I had no sooner gotten to work at sail-making again, after the anchor was down, than the wind, as on the day before, picked the sloop up and flung her seaward with a vengeance, anchor and all, as before. This fierce wind, usual to the Magellan country, continued on through the day, and swept the sloop by several miles of steep bluffs and precipices overhanging a bold shore of wild and uninviting appearance. I was not sorry to get away from it, though in doing so it was no Elysian shore to which I shaped my course. I kept on sailing in hope, since I had no choice but to go on, heading across for St. Nicholas Bay, where I had cast anchor February 19. It was now the 10th of March! Upon reaching the bay the second time I had circumnavigated the wildest part of desolate Tierra del Fuego. But the *Spray* had not yet arrived at St. Nicholas, and by the merest accident her bones were saved from resting there when she did arrive. The parting of a stay-sail-sheet in a williwaw, when the sea was turbulent and she was plunging into the storm, brought me forward to see instantly a dark cliff ahead and breakers so close under the bows that I felt surely lost, and in my thoughts cried, "Is the hand of fate against me, after all, leading me in the end to this dark spot?" I sprang aft again, unheeding the flapping sail, and threw the wheel over, expecting, as the sloop came down into the hollow of a wave, to feel her timbers smash under me on the rocks. But at the touch of her helm she swung clear of the danger, and in the next moment she was in the lee of the land.

It was the small island in the middle of the bay for which the sloop had been steering, and which she made with such unerring aim as nearly to run it down. Farther along in the bay was the anchorage, which I managed to reach, but before I could get the anchor down another squall caught the sloop and whirled her round like a top and carried her away, altogether to leeward of the bay. Still farther to leeward was a great headland, and I bore off for that. This was retracing my course toward Sandy Point, for the gale was from the southwest.

I had the sloop soon under good control, however, and in a short time rounded to under the lee of a mountain, where the sea was as smooth as a mill-pond, and the sails flapped and hung limp while she carried her way close in. Here I thought I would anchor and rest till morning, the depth being eight fathoms very close to the shore. But it was interesting to see, as I let go the anchor, that it did not reach the bottom before another williwaw struck down from this mountain and carried the sloop off faster than I could pay out cable. Instead of resting, I had to "man the windlass" and heave up the anchor and fifty fathoms of cable hanging up and down in deep water. This was in that part of the strait called Famine Reach. I could have wished it Jericho! On that little crab-windlass I worked the rest of the night, thinking how much easier it was for me when I could say, "Do that thing or the other," than to do it myself. But I hove away on the windlass and sang the old chants that I sang when I was a sailor, from "Blow, Boys, Blow for Californy, O" to "Sweet By and By."

It was daybreak when the anchor was at the hawse. By this time the wind had gone down, and cat's-paws took the place of willi-waws. The sloop was then drifting slowly toward Sandy Point. She came within sight of ships at anchor in the roads, and I was more than half minded to put in for new sails, but the wind coming out from the northeast, which was fair for the other direction, I turned the prow of the *Spray* westward once more for the Pacific, to tra-verse a second time the second half of my first course through the strait.

Chapter 9

I was determined to rely on my own small resources to repair the damages of the great gale which drove me southward toward the Horn, after I had passed from the Strait of Magellan out into the Pacific. So when I had got back into the strait, by way of Cockburn Channel, I did not proceed eastward for help at the Sandy Point settlement, but turning again into the northwestward reach of the strait, set to work with my palm and needle at every opportunity, when at anchor and when sailing. It was slow work; but little by little the squaresail on the boom expanded to the dimensions of a serviceable mainsail with a peak to it and a leech besides. If it was not the best-setting sail afloat, it was at least very strongly made and would stand a hard blow. A ship, meeting the *Spray* long afterward, reported her as wearing a mainsail of some improved design and patent reefer, but that was not the case.

The *Spray* for a few days after the storm enjoyed fine weather, and made fair time through the strait for the distance of twenty miles, which, in these days of many adversities, I called a long run. The weather, I say, was fine for a few days; but it brought little rest. Care for the safety of my vessel, and even for my own life, was in no wise lessened by the absence of heavy weather. Indeed, the peril was even greater, inasmuch as the savages on comparatively fine days ventured forth on their marauding excursions, and in boisterous weather disappeared from sight, their wretched canoes being frail and undeserving the name of craft at all. This being so, I now enjoyed gales of wind as never before, and the *Spray* was never long without them during her struggles about Cape Horn. I became in a measure inured to the life, and began to think that one more trip through the strait, if perchance the sloop should be blown off again, would make me the aggressor, and put the Fuegians entirely on the defensive. This feeling was forcibly borne in on me at Snug Bay, where I anchored at gray morning after passing Cape Froward, to find, when broad day appeared, that two canoes which I had eluded by sailing all night were now entering the same bay stealthily under the shadow of the high headland. They were well manned, and the savages were well armed with spears and bows. At a shot from my rifle across the bows, both turned aside into a small creek out of range. In danger now of being flanked by the savages in the bush close aboard, I was obliged to hoist the sails, which I had barely lowered, and make across to the opposite side of the strait, a distance of six miles. But now I was put to my wit's end as to how I should weigh anchor, for through an accident to the windlass right here I could not budge it. However, I set all sail and filled away, first hauling short by hand. The sloop carried her anchor away, as though it was meant to be always towed in this way underfoot, and with it she towed a ton or more of kelp from a reef in the bay, the wind blowing a wholesale breeze.

Meanwhile I worked till blood started from my fingers, and with one eye over my shoulder for savages, I watched at the same time, and sent a bullet whistling whenever I saw a limb or a twig move;

for I kept a gun always at hand, and an Indian appearing then within range would have been taken as a declaration of war. As it was, however, my own blood was all that was spilt—and from the trifling accident of sometimes breaking the flesh against a cleat or a pin which came in the way when I was in haste. Sea-cuts in my hands from pulling on hard, wet ropes were sometimes painful and often bled freely; but these healed when I finally got away from the strait into fine weather.

After clearing Snug Bay I hauled the sloop to the wind, repaired the windlass, and hove the anchor to the hawse, catted it, and then stretched across to a port of refuge under a high mountain about six miles away, and came to in nine fathoms close under the face of a perpendicular cliff. Here my own voice answered back, and I named the place "Echo Mountain." Seeing dead trees farther along where the shore was broken, I made a landing for fuel, taking, besides my ax, a rifle, which on these days I never left far from hand; but I saw no living thing here, except a small spider, which had nested in a dry log that I boated to the sloop. The conduct of this insect interested me now more than anything else around the wild place. In my cabin it met, oddly enough, a spider of its own size and species that had come all the way from Boston—a very civil little chap, too, but mighty spry. Well, the Fuegian threw up its antennae for a fight; but my little Bostonian downed it at once, then broke its legs, and pulled them off, one by one, so dexterously that in less than three minutes from the time the battle began the Fuegian spider didn't know itself from a fly.

I made haste the following morning to be under way after a night of wakefulness on the weird shore. Before weighing anchor, however, I prepared a cup of warm coffee over a smart wood fire in my great Montevideo stove. In the same fire was cremated the Fuegian spider, slain the day before by the little warrior from Boston, which a Scots lady at Cape Town long after named "Bruce" upon hearing of its prowess at Echo Mountain. The *Spray* now reached away for Coffee Island, which I sighted on my birthday, February 20, 1896.

There she encountered another gale, that brought her in the lee of great Charles Island for shelter. On a bluff point on Charles were signal-fires, and a tribe of savages, mustered here since my first trip through the strait, manned their canoes to put off for the sloop. It was not prudent to come to, the anchorage being within bow-shot of the shore, which was thickly wooded; but I made signs that one canoe might come alongside, while the sloop ranged about under sail in the lee of the land. The others I motioned to keep off, and incidentally laid a smart Martini-Henry rifle in sight, close at hand, on the top of the cabin. In the canoe that came alongside, crying their never-ending begging word "yammerschooner," were two squaws and one Indian, the hardest specimens of humanity I had ever seen in any of my travels. "Yammerschooner" was their plaint when they pushed off from the shore, and "yammerschooner" it was when they got alongside. The squaws beckoned for food, while the Indian, a black-visaged savage, stood sulkily as if he took no interest at all in the matter, but on my turning my back for some biscuits and jerked beef for the squaws, the "buck" sprang on deck and confronted me, saying in Spanish jargon that we had met before. I thought I recognized the tone of his "yammerschooner," and his full beard identified him as the Black Pedro whom, it was true, I had met before. "Where are the rest of the crew?" he asked, as he looked uneasily around, expecting hands, maybe, to come out of the fore-scuttle and deal him his just deserts for many murders. "About three weeks ago," said he, "when you passed up here, I saw three men on board. Where are the other two?" I answered him briefly that the same crew was still on board. "But," said he, "I see you are doing all the work," and with a leer he added, as he glanced at the mainsail, "hombre valiente." I explained that I did all the work in the day, while the rest of the crew slept, so that they would be fresh to watch for Indians at night. I was interested in the subtle cunning of this savage, knowing him, as I did, better perhaps than he was aware. Even had I not been advised before I sailed from Sandy Point, I should have measured him for an arch-villain now. Moreover, one of the squaws, with that spark of kindliness which is somehow found in the breast of even the lowest savage, warned me by a sign to be on my guard, or Black Pedro would do me harm. There was no need of the warning, however, for I was on my guard from the first, and at that moment held a smart revolver in my hand ready for instant service.

"When you sailed through here before," he said, "you fired a shot at me," adding with some warmth that it was "muy malo." I affected not to understand, and said, "You have lived at Sandy Point, have you not?" He answered frankly, "Yes," and appeared delighted to meet one who had come from the dear old place. "At the mission?" I queried. "Why, yes," he replied, stepping forward as if to embrace an old friend. I motioned him back, for I did not share his flattering humor. "And you know Captain Pedro Samblich?" continued I. "Yes," said the villain, who had killed a kinsman of Samblich—"yes, indeed; he is a great friend of mine." "I know it," said I. Samblich had told me to shoot him on sight. Pointing to my rifle on the cabin, he wanted to know how many times it fired. "Cuantos?" said he. When I explained to him that that gun kept right on shooting, his jaw fell, and he spoke of getting away. I did not hinder him from going. I gave the squaws biscuits and beef, and one of them gave me several lumps of tallow in exchange, and I think it worth mentioning that she did not offer me the smallest pieces, but with some extra trouble handed me the largest of all the pieces in the canoe. No Christian could have done more. Before pushing off from the sloop the cunning savage asked for matches, and made as if to reach with the end of his spear the box I was about to give him; but I held it toward him on the muzzle of my rifle, the one that "kept on shooting." The chap picked the box off the gun gingerly enough, to be sure, but he jumped when I said, "Quedao [Look out]," at which the squaws laughed and seemed not at all displeased. Perhaps the wretch had clubbed them that morning for not gathering mussels enough for his breakfast. There was a good understanding among us all.

From Charles Island the *Spray* crossed over to Fortescue Bay, where she anchored and spent a comfortable night under the lee of high land, while the wind howled outside. The bay was deserted now. They were Fortescue Indians whom I had seen at the island, and I felt quite sure they could not follow the *Spray* in the present hard blow. Not to neglect a precaution, however, I sprinkled tacks on deck before I turned in.

On the following day the loneliness of the place was broken by the appearance of a great steamship, making for the anchorage with a lofty bearing. She was no Diego craft. I knew the sheer, the model, and the poise. I threw out my flag, and directly saw the Stars and Stripes flung to the breeze from the great ship.

The wind had then abated, and toward night the savages made their appearance from the island, going direct to the steamer to "yammerschooner." Then they came to the *Spray* to beg more, or to steal all, declaring that they got nothing from the steamer. Black Pedro here came alongside again. My own brother could not have been more delighted to see me, and he begged me to lend him my rifle to shoot a guanaco for me in the morning. I assured the fellow that if I remained there another day I would lend him the gun, but I had no mind to remain. I gave him a cooper's draw-knife and some other small implements which would be of service in canoe-making, and bade him be off.

Under the cover of darkness that night I went to the steamer, which I found to be the *Colombia*, Captain Henderson, from New York, bound for San Francisco. I carried all my guns along with me, in case it should be necessary to fight my way back. In the chief mate of the *Colombia*, Mr. Hannibal, I found an old friend, and he referred affectionately to days in Manila when we were there together, he in the *Southern Cross* and I in the *Northern Light*, both ships as beautiful as their names.

The *Colombia* had an abundance of fresh stores on board. The captain gave his steward some order, and I remember that the guileless young man asked me if I could manage, besides other things, a few cans of milk and a cheese. When I offered my Montevideo gold for the supplies, the captain roared like a lion and told me to put my money up. It was a glorious outfit of provisions of all kinds that I got.

Returning to the *Spray*, where I found all secure, I prepared for an early start in the morning. It was agreed that the steamer should blow her whistle for me if first on the move. I watched the steamer, off and on, through the night for the pleasure alone of seeing her electric lights, a pleasing sight in contrast to the ordinary Fuegian canoe with a brand of fire in it. The sloop was the first under way, but the *Colombia*, soon following, passed, and saluted as she went by. Had the captain given me his steamer, his company would have been no worse off than they were two or three months later. I read afterward, in a late California paper, "The *Colombia* will be a total loss." On her second trip to Panama she was wrecked on the rocks of the California coast.

The *Spray* was then beating against wind and current, as usual in the strait. At this point the tides from the Atlantic and the Pacific meet, and in the strait, as on the outside coast, their meeting makes a commotion of whirlpools and combers that in a gale of wind is dangerous to canoes and other frail craft.

A few miles farther along was a large steamer ashore, bottom up. Passing this place, the sloop ran into a streak of light wind, and then—a most remarkable condition for strait weather—it fell entirely calm. Signal-fires sprang up at once on all sides, and then more than twenty canoes hove in sight, all heading for the *Spray*. As they came within hail, their savage crews cried, "Amigo yammerschooner," "Anclas aqui," "Bueno puerto aqui," and like scraps of Spanish mixed with their own jargon. I had no thought of anchoring in their "good port." I hoisted the sloop's flag and fired a gun, all of which they might construe as a friendly salute or an invitation to come on. They drew up in a semicircle, but kept outside of eighty yards, which in self-defense would have been the death-line.

In their mosquito fleet was a ship's boat stolen probably from a murdered crew. Six savages paddled this rather awkwardly with the blades of oars which had been broken off. Two of the savages standing erect wore sea-boots, and this sustained the suspicion that they had fallen upon some luckless ship's crew, and also added a hint that they had already visited the *Spray's* deck, and would now, if they could, try her again. Their sea-boots, I have no doubt, would have protected their feet and rendered carpet-tacks harmless. Paddling clumsily, they passed down the strait at a distance of a hundred yards from the sloop, in an offhand manner and as if bound to Fortescue Bay. This I judged to be a piece of strategy, and so kept a sharp lookout over a small island which soon came in range between them and the sloop, completely hiding them from view, and toward which the *Spray* was now drifting helplessly with the tide, and with every prospect of going on the rocks, for there was no anchorage, at least, none that my cables would reach. And, sure enough, I soon saw a movement in the grass just on top of the island, which is called Bonet Island and is one hundred and thirty-six feet high. I fired several shots over the place, but saw no other sign of the savages. It was they that had moved the grass, for as the sloop swept past the island, the rebound of the tide carrying her clear, there on the other side was the boat, surely enough exposing their cunning and treachery. A stiff breeze, coming up suddenly, now scattered the canoes while it extricated the sloop from a dangerous position, albeit the wind, though friendly, was still ahead.

The *Spray*, flogging against current and wind, made Borgia Bay on the following afternoon, and cast anchor there for the second time. I would now, if I could, describe the moonlit scene on the strait at midnight after I had cleared the savages and Bonet Island. A heavy cloud-bank that had swept across the sky then cleared away, and the night became suddenly as light as day, or nearly so. A high mountain was mirrored in the channel ahead, and the *Spray* sailing along with her shadow was as two sloops on the sea.

The sloop being moored, I threw out my skiff, and with ax and gun landed at the head of the cove, and filled a barrel of water from a stream. Then, as before, there was no sign of Indians at the place. Finding it quite deserted, I rambled about near the beach for an hour or more. The fine weather seemed, somehow, to add loneliness to the place, and when I came upon a spot where a grave was marked I went no farther. Returning to the head of the cove, I came to a sort of Calvary, it appeared to me, where navigators, carrying their cross, had each set one up as a beacon to others coming after. They had anchored here and gone on, all except the one under the little mound. One of the simple marks, curiously enough, had been left there by the steamship *Colimbia*, sister ship to the *Colombia*, my neighbor of that morning.

I read the names of many other vessels; some of them I copied in my journal, others were illegible. Many of the crosses had decayed and fallen, and many a hand that put them there I had known, many a hand now still. The air of depression was about the place, and I hurried back to the sloop to forget myself again in the voyage.

Early the next morning I stood out from Borgia Bay, and off Cape Quod, where the wind fell light, I moored the sloop by kelp in twenty fathoms of water, and held her there a few hours against a three-knot current. That night I anchored in Langara Cove, a few miles farther along, where on the following day I discovered wreckage and goods washed up from the sea. I worked all day now, salving and boating off a cargo to the sloop. The bulk of the goods was tallow in casks and in lumps from which the casks had broken away; and embedded in the seaweed was a barrel of wine, which I also towed alongside. I hoisted them all in with the throat-halyards, which I took to the windlass. The weight of some of the casks was a little over eight hundred pounds.

There were no Indians about Langara; evidently there had not been any since the great gale which had washed the wreckage on shore. Probably it was the same gale that drove the *Spray* off Cape Horn, from March 3 to 8. Hundreds of tons of kelp had been torn from beds in deep water and rolled up into ridges on the beach. A specimen stalk which I found entire, roots, leaves, and all, measured one hundred and thirty-one feet in length. At this place I filled a barrel of water at night, and on the following day sailed with a fair wind at last.

I had not sailed far, however, when I came abreast of more tallow in a small cove, where I anchored, and boated off as before. It rained and snowed hard all that day, and it was no light work carrying tallow in my arms over the boulders on the beach. But I worked on till the *Spray* was loaded with a full cargo. I was happy then in the prospect of doing a good business farther along on the voyage, for the habits of an old trader would come to the surface. I sailed from the cove about noon, greased from top to toe, while my vessel was tallowed from keelson to truck. My cabin, as well as the hold and deck, was stowed full of tallow, and all were thoroughly smeared.

Chapter 10

Another gale had then sprung up, but the wind was still fair, and I had only twenty-six miles to run for Port Angosto, a dreary enough place, where, however, I would find a safe harbor in which to refit and stow cargo. I carried on sail to make the harbor before dark, and she fairly flew along, all covered with snow, which fell thick and fast, till she looked like a white winter bird. Between the storm-bursts I saw the headland of my port, and was steering for it when a flaw of wind caught the mainsail by the lee, jibed it over, and dear! dear! how nearly was this the cause of disaster; for the sheet parted and the boom unshipped, and it was then close upon night. I worked till the perspiration poured from my body to get things adjusted and in working order before dark, and, above all, to get it done before the sloop drove to leeward of the port of refuge. Even then I did not get the boom shipped in its saddle. I was at the entrance of the harbor before I could get this done, and it was time to haul her to or lose the port; but in that condition, like a bird with a broken wing, she made the haven. The accident which so jeopardized my vessel and cargo came of a defective sheet-rope, one made from sisal, a treacherous fiber which has caused a deal of strong language among sailors.

I did not run the *Spray* into the inner harbor of Port Angosto, but came to inside a bed of kelp under a steep bluff on the port hand going in. It was an exceedingly snug nook, and to make doubly sure of holding on here against all williwaws I moored her with two anchors and secured her, besides, by cables to trees. However, no wind ever reached there except back flaws from the mountains on the opposite side of the harbor. There, as elsewhere in that region, the country was made up of mountains. This was the place where I was to refit and whence I was to sail direct, once more, for Cape Pillar and the Pacific.

I remained at Port Angosto some days, busily employed about the sloop. I stowed the tallow from the deck to the hold, arranged my cabin in better order, and took in a good supply of wood and water. I also mended the sloop's sails and rigging, and fitted a jigger, which changed the rig to a yawl, though I called the boat a sloop just the same, the jigger being merely a temporary affair.

I never forgot, even at the busiest time of my work there, to have my rifle by me ready for instant use; for I was of necessity within range of savages, and I had seen Fuegian canoes at this place when I anchored in the port, farther down the reach, on the first trip through the strait. I think it was on the second day, while I was busily employed about decks, that I heard the swish of something through the air close by my ear, and heard a "zip"-like sound in the water, but saw nothing. Presently, however, I suspected that it was an arrow of some sort, for just then one passing not far from me struck the mainmast, where it stuck fast, vibrating from the shock—a Fuegian autograph. A savage was somewhere near, there could be no doubt about that. I did not know but he might be shooting at me, with a view to getting my sloop and her cargo; and so I threw up my old Martini-Henry, the rifle that kept on shooting, and the first shot uncovered three Fuegians, who scampered from a clump of bushes where they had been concealed, and made over the hills. I fired away a good many cartridges, aiming under their feet to encourage their climbing. My dear old gun woke up the hills, and at every report all three of the savages jumped as if shot; but they kept on, and put Fuego real estate between themselves and the *Spray* as fast as their legs could carry them. I took care then, more than ever before, that all my firearms should be in order and that a supply of ammunition should always be ready at hand. But the savages did not return, and although I put tacks on deck every night, I never discovered that any more visitors came, and I had only to sweep the deck of tacks carefully every morning after.

As the days went by, the season became more favorable for a chance to clear the strait with a fair wind, and so I made up my mind after six attempts, being driven back each time, to be in no further haste to sail. The bad weather on my last return to Port Angosto for shelter brought the Chilean gunboat *Condor* and the Argentine cruiser *Azopardo* into port. As soon as the latter came to anchor, Captain Mascarella, the commander, sent a boat to the *Spray* with the message that he would take me in tow for Sandy Point if I would give up the voyage and return—the thing farthest from my mind. The officers of the *Azopardo* told me that, coming up the strait after the *Spray* on her first passage through, they saw Black Pedro and learned that he had visited me. The *Azopardo*, being a foreign man-of-war, had no right to arrest the Fuegian outlaw, but her captain blamed me for not shooting the rascal when he came to my sloop.

I procured some cordage and other small supplies from these vessels, and the officers of each of them mustered a supply of warm flannels, of which I was most in need. With these additions to my outfit, and with the vessel in good trim, though somewhat deeply laden, I was well prepared for another bout with the Southern, mis-named Pacific, Ocean.

In the first week in April southeast winds, such as appear about Cape Horn in the fall and winter seasons, bringing better weather than that experienced in the summer, began to disturb the upper clouds; a little more patience, and the time would come for sailing with a fair wind.

At Port Angosto I met Professor Dusen of the Swedish scientific expedition to South America and the Pacific Islands. The professor was camped by the side of a brook at the head of the harbor, where there were many varieties of moss, in which he was interested, and where the water was, as his Argentine cook said, "muy rico." The professor had three well-armed Argentines along in his camp to fight savages. They seemed disgusted when I filled water at a small stream near the vessel, slighting their advice to go farther up to the greater brook, where it was "muy rico." But they were all fine fellows, though it was a wonder that they did not all die of rheumatic pains from living on wet ground.

Of all the little haps and mishaps to the *Spray* at Port Angosto, of the many attempts to put to sea, and of each return for shelter, it is not my purpose to speak. Of hindrances there were many to keep her back, but on the thirteenth day of April, and for the seventh and last time, she weighed anchor from that port. Difficulties, however, multiplied all about in so strange a manner that had I been given to superstitious fears I should not have persisted in sailing on a thirteenth day, notwithstanding that a fair wind blew in the offing. Many of the incidents were ludicrous. When I found myself, for instance, disentangling the sloop's mast from the branches of a tree after she had drifted three times around a small island, against my will, it seemed more than one's nerves could bear, and I had to speak about it, so I thought, or die of lockjaw, and I apostrophized the *Spray* as an impatient farmer might his horse or his ox. "Didn't you know," cried I—"didn't you know that you couldn't climb a tree?" But the poor old *Spray* had essayed, and successfully too, nearly everything else in the Strait of Magellan, and my heart softened toward her when I thought of what she had gone through. Moreover, she had discovered an island. On the charts this one that she had sailed around was traced as a point of land. I named it Alan Erric Island, after a worthy literary friend whom I had met in strange by-places, and I put up a sign, "Keep off the grass," which, as discoverer, was within my rights.

Now at last the *Spray* carried me free of Tierra del Fuego. If by a close shave only, still she carried me clear, though her boom actually hit the beacon rocks to leeward as she lugged on sail to clear the point. The thing was done on the 13th of April, 1896. But a close shave and a narrow escape were nothing new to the *Spray*.

The waves doffed their white caps beautifully to her in the strait that day before the southeast wind, the first true winter breeze of the season from that quarter, and here she was out on the first of it, with every prospect of clearing Cape Pillar before it should shift. So it turned out; the wind blew hard, as it always blows about Cape Horn, but she had cleared the great tide-race off Cape Pillar and the Evangelistas, the outermost rocks of all, before the change came. I remained at the helm, humoring my vessel in the cross seas, for it was rough, and I did not dare to let her take a straight course. It was necessary to change her course in the combing seas, to meet them with what skill I could when they rolled up ahead, and to keep off when they came up abeam.

On the following morning, April 14, only the tops of the highest mountains were in sight, and the *Spray*, making good headway on a northwest course, soon sank these out of sight. "Hurrah for the *Spray!*" I shouted to seals, sea-gulls, and penguins; for there were no other living creatures about, and she had weathered all the dangers of Cape Horn. Moreover, she had on her voyage round the Horn salved a cargo of which she had not jettisoned a pound. And why should not one rejoice also in the main chance coming so of itself?

I shook out a reef, and set the whole jib, for, having sea-room, I could square away two points. This brought the sea more on her quarter, and she was the wholesomer under a press of sail. Occasionally an old southwest sea, rolling up, combed athwart her, but did no harm. The wind freshened as the sun rose half-mast or more, and the air, a bit chilly in the morning, softened later in the day; but I gave little thought to such things as these.

One wave, in the evening, larger than others that had threatened all day,—one such as sailors call "fine-weather seas,"—broke over the sloop fore and aft. It washed over me at the helm, the last that swept over the *Spray* off Cape Horn. It seemed to wash away old regrets. All my troubles were now astern; summer was ahead; all the world was again before me. The wind was even literally fair. My "trick" at the wheel was now up, and it was 5 P.M. I had stood at the helm since eleven o'clock the morning before, or thirty hours.

Then was the time to uncover my head, for I sailed alone with God. The vast ocean was again around me, and the horizon was unbroken by land. A few days later the *Spray* was under full sail, and I saw her for the first time with a jigger spread. This was indeed a small incident, but it was the incident following a triumph. The wind was still southwest, but it had moderated, and roaring seas had

293

turned to gossiping waves that rippled and pattered against her sides as she rolled among them, delighted with their story. Rapid changes went on, those days, in things all about while she headed for the tropics. New species of birds came around; albatrosses fell back and became scarcer and scarcer, lighter gulls came in their stead, and pecked for crumbs in the sloop's wake.

On the tenth day from Cape Pillar a shark came along, the first of its kind on this part of the voyage to get into trouble. I harpooned him and took out his ugly jaws. I had not till then felt inclined to take the life of any animal, but when John Shark hove in sight my sympathy flew to the winds. It is a fact that in Magellan I let pass many ducks that would have made a good stew, for I had no mind in the lonesome strait to take the life of any living thing.

From Cape Pillar I steered for Juan Fernandez, and on the 26th of April, fifteen days out, made that historic island right ahead.

The blue hills of Juan Fernandez, high among the clouds, could be seen about thirty miles off. A thousand emotions thrilled me when I saw the island, and I bowed my head to the deck. We may mock the Oriental salaam, but for my part I could find no other way of expressing myself.

The wind being light through the day, the *Spray* did not reach the island till night. With what wind there was to fill her sails she stood close in to shore on the northeast side, where it fell calm and remained so all night. I saw the twinkling of a small light farther along in a cove, and fired a gun, but got no answer, and soon the light disappeared altogether. I heard the sea booming against the cliffs all night, and realized that the ocean swell was still great, although from the deck of my little ship it was apparently small. From the cry of animals in the hills, which sounded fainter and fainter through the night, I judged that a light current was drifting the sloop from the land, though she seemed all night dangerously near the shore, for, the land being very high, appearances were deceptive.

Soon after daylight I saw a boat putting out toward me. As it pulled near, it so happened that I picked up my gun, which was on the deck, meaning only to put it below; but the people in the boat, seeing the piece in my hands, quickly turned and pulled back for shore, which was about four miles distant. There were six rowers in her, and I observed that they pulled with oars in oar-locks, after the manner of trained seamen, and so I knew they belonged to a civilized race; but their opinion of me must have been anything but flattering when they mistook my purpose with the gun and pulled away with all their might. I made them understand by signs, but not without difficulty, that I did not intend to shoot, that I was simply putting the piece in the cabin, and that I wished them to return. When they understood my meaning they came back and were soon on board.

One of the party, whom the rest called "king," spoke English; the others spoke Spanish. They had all heard of the voyage of the *Spray* through the papers of Valparaiso, and were hungry for news concerning it. They told me of a war between Chile and the Argentine, which I had not heard of when I was there. I had just visited both countries, and I told them that according to the latest reports, while I was in Chile, their own island was sunk. (This same report that Juan Fernandez had sunk was current in Australia when I arrived there three months later.)

I had already prepared a pot of coffee and a plate of doughnuts, which, after some words of civility, the islanders stood up to and discussed with a will, after which they took the *Spray* in tow of their boat and made toward the island with her at the rate of a good three knots. The man they called king took the helm, and with whirling it up and down he so rattled the *Spray* that I thought she would never carry herself straight again. The others pulled away lustily with their oars. The king, I soon learned, was king only by courtesy. Having lived longer on the island than any other man in the world,—thirty years,—he was so dubbed. Juan Fernandez was then under the administration of a governor of Swedish nobility, so I was told. I was also told that his daughter could ride the wildest goat on the island. The governor, at the time of my visit, was away at Valparaiso with his family, to place his children at school. The king had been away once for a year or two, and in Rio de Janeiro had married a Brazilian woman who followed his fortunes to the far-off island. He was himself a Portuguese and a native of the Azores. He had sailed in New Bedford whale-ships and had steered a boat. All this I learned, and more too, before we reached the anchorage. The sea-breeze, coming in before long, filled the *Spray's* sails, and the experienced Portuguese mariner piloted her to a safe berth in the bay, where she was moored to a buoy abreast the settlement.

Chapter 11

The *Spray* being secured, the islanders returned to the coffee and doughnuts, and I was more than flattered when they did not slight my buns, as the professor had done in the Strait of Magellan. Between buns and doughnuts there was little difference except in name. Both had been fried in tallow, which was the strong point in both, for there was nothing on the island fatter than a goat, and a goat is but a lean beast, to make the best of it. So with a view to business I hooked my steelyards to the boom at once, ready to weigh out tallow, there being no customs officer to say, "Why do you do so?" and before the sun went down the islanders had learned the art of making buns and doughnuts. I did not charge a high price for what I sold, but the ancient and curious coins I got in payment, some of them from the wreck of a galleon sunk in the bay no one knows when, I sold afterward to antiquarians for more than face-value. In this way I made a reasonable profit. I brought away money of all denominations from the island, and nearly all there was, so far as I could find out.

Juan Fernandez, as a place of call, is a lovely spot. The hills are well wooded, the valleys fertile, and pouring down through many ravines are streams of pure water. There are no serpents on the island, and no wild beasts other than pigs and goats, of which I saw a number, with possibly a dog or two. The people lived without the use of rum or beer of any sort. There was not a police officer or a lawyer among them. The domestic economy of the island was simplicity itself. The fashions of Paris did not affect the inhabitants; each dressed according to his own taste. Although there was no doctor, the people were all healthy, and the children were all beautiful. There were about forty-five souls on the island all told. The adults were mostly from the mainland of South America. One lady there, from Chile, who made a flying-jib for the *Spray,* taking her pay in tallow, would be called a belle at Newport. Blessed island of Juan Fernandez! Why Alexander Selkirk ever left you was more than I could make out.

A large ship which had arrived some time before, on fire, had been stranded at the head of the bay, and as the sea smashed her to pieces on the rocks, after the fire was drowned, the islanders picked up the timbers and utilized them in the construction of houses, which naturally presented a ship-like appearance. The house of the king of Juan Fernandez, Manuel Carroza by name, besides resembling the ark, wore a polished brass knocker on its only door, which was painted green. In front of this gorgeous entrance was a flag-mast all ataunto, and near it a smart whale-boat painted red and blue, the delight of the king's old age.

I of course made a pilgrimage to the old lookout place at the top of the mountain, where Selkirk spent many days peering into the distance for the ship which came at last. From a tablet fixed into the face of the rock I copied these words, inscribed in Arabic capitals:

IN MEMORY

OF

ALEXANDER SELKIRK,

MARINER,

A native of Largo, in the county of Fife, Scotland, who lived on this island in complete solitude for four years and four months. He was landed from the *Cinque Ports* galley, 96 tons, 18 guns, A.D. 1704, and was taken off in the *Duke,* privateer, 12th February, 1709. He died Lieutenant of H.M.S. *Weymouth,* A.D. 1723,[1] aged 47. This tablet is erected near Selkirk's lookout, by Commodore Powell and the officers of H.M.S. *Topaze,* A.D. 1868.

The cave in which Selkirk dwelt while on the island is at the head of the bay now called Robinson Crusoe Bay. It is around a bold headland west of the present anchorage and landing. Ships have anchored there, but it affords a very indifferent berth. Both of these anchorages are exposed to north winds, which, however, do not

---

[1] Mr. J. Cuthbert Hadden, in the "Century Magazine" for July, 1899, shows that the tablet is in error as to the year of Selkirk's death. It should be 1721.

reach home with much violence. The holding-ground being good in the first-named bay to the eastward, the anchorage there may be considered safe, although the undertow at times makes it wild riding.

I visited Robinson Crusoe Bay in a boat, and with some difficulty landed through the surf near the cave, which I entered. I found it dry and inhabitable. It is located in a beautiful nook sheltered by high mountains from all the severe storms that sweep over the island, which are not many; for it lies near the limits of the trade-wind regions, being in latitude 35½° S. The island is about fourteen miles in length, east and west, and eight miles in width; its height is over three thousand feet. Its distance from Chile, to which country it belongs, is about three hundred and forty miles.

Juan Fernandez was once a convict station. A number of caves in which the prisoners were kept, damp, unwholesome dens, are no longer in use, and no more prisoners are sent to the island.

The pleasantest day I spent on the island, if not the pleasantest on my whole voyage, was my last day on shore,—but by no means because it was the last,—when the children of the little community, one and all, went out with me to gather wild fruits for the voyage. We found quinces, peaches, and figs, and the children gathered a basket of each. It takes very little to please children, and these little ones, never hearing a word in their lives except Spanish, made the hills ring with mirth at the sound of words in English. They asked me the names of all manner of things on the island. We came to a wild fig-tree loaded with fruit, of which I gave them the English name. "Figgies, figgies!" they cried, while they picked till their baskets were full. But when I told them that the *cabra* they pointed out was only a goat, they screamed with laughter, and rolled on the grass in wild delight to think that a man had come to their island who would call a cabra a goat.

The first child born on Juan Fernandez, I was told, had become a beautiful woman and was now a mother. Manuel Carroza and the good soul who followed him here from Brazil had laid away their only child, a girl, at the age of seven, in the little churchyard on the point. In the same half-acre were other mounds among the rough lava rocks, some marking the burial-place of native-born children, some the resting-places of seamen from passing ships, landed here to end days of sickness and get into a sailors' heaven.

The greatest drawback I saw in the island was the want of a

school. A class there would necessarily be small, but to some kind soul who loved teaching and quietude life on Juan Fernandez would, for a limited time, be one of delight.

On the morning of May 5, 1896, I sailed from Juan Fernandez, having feasted on many things, but on nothing sweeter than the adventure itself of a visit to the home and to the very cave of Robinson Crusoe. From the island the *Spray* bore away to the north, passing the island of St. Felix before she gained the trade-winds, which seemed slow in reaching their limits.

If the trades were tardy, however, when they did come they came with a bang, and made up for lost time; and the *Spray*, under reefs, sometimes one, sometimes two, flew before a gale for a great many days, with a bone in her mouth, toward the Marquesas, in the west, which she made on the forty-third day out, and still kept on sailing. My time was all taken up those days—not by standing at the helm; no man, I think, could stand or sit and steer a vessel round the world: I did better than that; for I sat and read my books, mended my clothes, or cooked my meals and ate them in peace. I had already found that it was not good to be alone, and so I made companionship with what there was around me, sometimes with the universe and sometimes with my own insignificant self; but my books were always my friends, let fail all else. Nothing could be easier or more restful than my voyage in the trade-winds.

I sailed with a free wind day after day, marking the position of my ship on the chart with considerable precision; but this was done by intuition, I think, more than by slavish calculations. For one whole month my vessel held her course true; I had not, the while, so much as a light in the binnacle. The Southern Cross I saw every night abeam. The sun every morning came up astern; every evening it went down ahead. I wished for no other compass to guide me, for these were true. If I doubted my reckoning after a long time at sea I verified it by reading the clock aloft made by the Great Architect, and it was right.

There was no denying that the comical side of the strange life appeared. I awoke, sometimes, to find the sun already shining into my cabin. I heard water rushing by, with only a thin plank between me and the depths, and I said, "How is this?" But it was all right; it was my ship on her course, sailing as no other ship had ever sailed before in the world. The rushing water along her side told me that she was sailing at full speed. I knew that no human hand was at the helm; I knew that all was well with "the hands" forward, and that there was no mutiny on board.

The phenomena of ocean meteorology were interesting studies even here in the trade-winds. I observed that about every seven days the wind freshened and drew several points farther than usual from the direction of the pole; that is, it went round from east-southeast to south-southeast, while at the same time a heavy swell rolled up from the southwest. All this indicated that gales were going on in the anti-trades. The wind then hauled day after day as it moderated, till it stood again at the normal point, east-southeast. This is more or less the constant state of the winter trades in latitude 12° S., where I "ran down the longitude" for weeks. The sun, we all know, is the creator of the trade-winds and of the wind system over all the earth. But ocean meteorology is, I think, the most fascinating of all. From Juan Fernandez to the Marquesas I experienced six changes of these great palpitations of sea-winds and of the sea itself, the effect of far-off gales. To know the laws that govern the winds, and to know that you know them, will give you an easy mind on your voyage round the world; otherwise you may tremble at the appearance of every cloud. What is true of this in the trade-winds is much more so in the variables, where changes run more to extremes.

To cross the Pacific Ocean, even under the most favorable circumstances, brings you for many days close to nature, and you realize the vastness of the sea. Slowly but surely the mark of my little ship's course on the track-chart reached out on the ocean and across it, while at her utmost speed she marked with her keel still slowly the sea that carried her. On the forty-third day from land,—a long time to be at sea alone,—the sky being beautifully clear and the moon being "in distance" with the sun, I threw up my sextant for sights. I found from the result of three observations, after long wrestling with lunar tables, that her longitude by observation agreed within five miles of that by dead-reckoning.

This was wonderful; both, however, might be in error, but somehow I felt confident that both were nearly true, and that in a few hours more I should see land; and so it happened, for then I made the island of Nukahiva, the southernmost of the Marquesas group, clear-cut and lofty. The verified longitude when abreast was somewhere between the two reckonings; this was extraordinary. All navigators will tell you that from one day to another a ship may lose or gain more than five miles in her sailing-account, and again, in the matter of lunars, even expert lunarians are considered as doing clever work when they average within eight miles of the truth.

I hope I am making it clear that I do not lay claim to cleverness or to slavish calculations in my reckonings. I think I have already stated that I kept my longitude, at least, mostly by intuition. A rotator log always towed astern, but so much has to be allowed for currents and for drift, which the log never shows, that it is only an approximation, after all, to be corrected by one's own judgment from data of a thousand voyages; and even then the master of the ship, if he be wise, cries out for the lead and the lookout.

Unique was my experience in nautical astronomy from the deck of the *Spray*—so much so that I feel justified in briefly telling it here. The first set of sights, just spoken of, put her many hundred miles west of my reckoning by account. I knew that this could not be correct. In about an hour's time I took another set of observations with the utmost care; the mean result of these was about the same as that of the first set. I asked myself why, with my boasted self-dependence, I had not done at least better than this. Then I went in search of a discrepancy in the tables, and I found it. In the tables I found that the column of figures from which I had got an important logarithm was in error. It was a matter I could prove beyond a doubt, and it made the difference as already stated. The tables being corrected, I sailed on with self-reliance unshaken, and with my tin clock fast asleep. The result of these observations naturally tickled my vanity, for I knew that it was something to stand on a great ship's deck and with two assistants take lunar observations approximately near the truth. As one of the poorest of American sailors, I was proud of the little achievement alone on the sloop, even by chance though it may have been.

I was *en rapport* now with my surroundings, and was carried on a vast stream where I felt the buoyancy of His hand who made all the worlds. I realized the mathematical truth of their motions, so well known that astronomers compile tables of their positions through the years and the days, and the minutes of a day, with such precision that one coming along over the sea even five years later may, by their aid, find the standard time of any given meridian on the earth.

To find local time is a simpler matter. The difference between local and standard time is longitude expressed in time—four minutes, we all know, representing one degree. This, briefly, is the principle on which longitude is found independent of chronometers. The work of the lunarian, though seldom practised in these days of chronometers, is beautifully edifying, and there is nothing in the realm of navigation that lifts one's heart up more in adoration.

Chapter 12

To be alone forty-three days would seem a long time, but in reality, even here, winged moments flew lightly by, and instead of my hauling in for Nukahiva, which I could have made as well as not, I kept on for Samoa, where I wished to make my next landing. This occupied twenty-nine days more, making seventy-two days in all. I was not distressed in any way during that time. There was no end of companionship; the very coral reefs kept me company, or gave me no time to feel lonely, which is the same thing, and there were many of them now in my course to Samoa.

First among the incidents of the voyage from Juan Fernandez to Samoa (which were not many) was a narrow escape from collision with a great whale that was absent-mindedly plowing the ocean at night while I was below. The noise from his startled snort and the commotion he made in the sea, as he turned to clear my vessel, brought me on deck in time to catch a wetting from the water he threw up with his flukes. The monster was apparently frightened. He headed quickly for the east; I kept on going west. Soon another whale passed, evidently a companion, following in its wake. I saw no more on this part of the voyage, nor did I wish to.

Hungry sharks came about the vessel often when she neared islands or coral reefs. I own to a satisfaction in shooting them as one would a tiger. Sharks, after all, are the tigers of the sea. Nothing is more dreadful to the mind of a sailor, I think, than a possible encounter with a hungry shark.

A number of birds were always about; occasionally one poised on the mast to look the *Spray* over, wondering, perhaps, at her odd wings, for she now wore her Fuego mainsail, which, like Joseph's coat, was made of many pieces. Ships are less common on the Southern seas than formerly. I saw not one in the many days crossing the Pacific.

My diet on these long passages usually consisted of potatoes and salt cod and biscuits, which I made two or three times a week. I had always plenty of coffee, tea, sugar, and flour. I carried usually a good supply of potatoes, but before reaching Samoa I had a mishap which left me destitute of this highly prized sailors' luxury. Through meeting at Juan Fernandez the Yankee Portuguese named Manuel Carroza, who nearly traded me out of my boots, I ran out of potatoes in mid-ocean, and was wretched thereafter. I prided myself on being something of a trader; but this Portuguese from the Azores by way of New Bedford, who gave me new potatoes for the older ones I had got from the *Colombia*, a bushel or more of the best, left me no ground for boasting. He wanted mine, he said, "for changee the seed." When I got to sea I found that his tubers were rank and unedible, and full of fine yellow streaks of repulsive appearance. I tied the sack up and returned to the few left of my old stock, thinking that maybe when I got right hungry the island potatoes would improve in flavor. Three weeks later I opened the bag again, and out flew millions of winged insects! Manuel's potatoes had all turned to moths. I tied them up quickly and threw all into the sea.

Manuel had a large crop of potatoes on hand, and as a hint to whalemen, who are always eager to buy vegetables, he wished me to report whales off the island of Juan Fernandez, which I have already done, and big ones at that, but they were a long way off.

Taking things by and large, as sailors say, I got on fairly well in the matter of provisions even on the long voyage across the Pacific. I found always some small stores to help the fare of luxuries; what I lacked of fresh meat was made up in fresh fish, at least while in the trade-winds, where flying-fish crossing on the wing at night would hit the sails and fall on deck, sometimes two or three of them, sometimes a dozen. Every morning except when the moon was large I got a bountiful supply by merely picking them up from the lee scuppers. All tinned meats went begging.

On the 16th of July, after considerable care and some skill and hard work, the *Spray* cast anchor at Apia, in the kingdom of Samoa, about noon. My vessel being moored, I spread an awning, and instead of going at once on shore I sat under it till late in the evening, listening with delight to the musical voices of the Samoan men and women.

A canoe coming down the harbor, with three young women in it, rested her paddles abreast the sloop. One of the fair crew, hailing with the naïve salutation, "Talofa lee" ("Love to you, chief"), asked:

"Schoon come Melike?"

"Love to you," I answered, and said, "Yes."

"You man come 'lone?"

Again I answered, "Yes."

"I don't believe that. You had other mans, and you eat 'em."

At this sally the others laughed. "What for you come long way?" they asked.

"To hear you ladies sing," I replied.

"Oh, talofa lee!" they all cried, and sang on. Their voices filled the air with music that rolled across to the grove of tall palms on the other side of the harbor and back. Soon after this six young men came down in the United States consul-general's boat, singing in parts and beating time with their oars. In my interview with them I came off better than with the damsels in the canoe. They bore an invitation from General Churchill for me to come and dine at the consulate. There was a lady's hand in things about the consulate at Samoa. Mrs. Churchill picked the crew for the general's boat, and saw to it that they wore a smart uniform and that they could sing the Samoan boatsong, which in the first week Mrs. Churchill herself could sing like a native girl.

Next morning bright and early Mrs. Robert Louis Stevenson came to the *Spray* and invited me to Vailima the following day. I was of course thrilled when I found myself, after so many days of adventure, face to face with this bright woman, so lately the companion of the author who had delighted me on the voyage. The kindly eyes, that looked me through and through, sparkled when we compared notes of adventure. I marveled at some of her experiences and escapes. She told me that, along with her husband, she had voyaged in all manner of rickety craft among the islands of the Pacific, reflectively adding, "Our tastes were similar."

Following the subject of voyages, she gave me the four beautiful volumes of sailing directories for the Mediterranean, writing on the fly-leaf of the first:

Sailing Alone Around the World

To CAPTAIN SLOCUM. These volumes have been read and re-read many times by my husband, and I am very sure that he would be pleased that they should be passed on to the sort of seafaring man that he liked above all others.

FANNY V. DE G. STEVENSON.

Mrs. Stevenson also gave me a great directory of the Indian Ocean. It was not without a feeling of reverential awe that I received the books so nearly direct from the hand of Tusitala, "who sleeps in the forest." Aolele, the *Spray* will cherish your gift.

The novelist's stepson, Mr. Lloyd Osbourne, walked through the Vailima mansion with me and bade me write my letters at the old desk. I thought it would be presumptuous to do that; it was sufficient for me to enter the hall on the floor of which the "Writer of Tales," according to the Samoan custom, was wont to sit.

Coming through the main street of Apia one day, with my hosts, all bound for the *Spray*, Mrs. Stevenson on horseback, I walking by her side, and Mr. and Mrs. Osbourne close in our wake on bicycles, at a sudden turn in the road we found ourselves mixed with a re-markable native procession, with a somewhat primitive band of music, in front of us, while behind was a festival or a funeral, we could not tell which. Several of the stoutest men carried bales and bundles on poles. Some were evidently bales of tapa-cloth. The burden of one set of poles, heavier than the rest, however, was not so easily made out. My curiosity was whetted to know whether it was a roast pig or something of a gruesome nature, and I inquired about it. "I don't know," said Mrs. Stevenson, "whether this is a wedding or a funeral. Whatever it is, though, captain, our place seems to be at the head of it."

The *Spray* being in the stream, we boarded her from the beach abreast, in the little razeed Gloucester dory, which had been painted a smart green. Our combined weight loaded it gunwale to the water, and I was obliged to steer with great care to avoid swamping. The adventure pleased Mrs. Stevenson greatly, and as we paddled along she sang, "They went to sea in a pea-green boat." I could understand her saying of her husband and herself, "Our tastes were similar."

As I sailed farther from the center of civilization I heard less and less of what would and what would not pay. Mrs. Stevenson, in speaking of my voyage, did not once ask me what I would make out of it. When I came to a Samoan village, the chief did not ask the price of gin, or say, "How much will you pay for roast pig?" but, "Dollar, dollar," said he; "white man know only dollar."

"Never mind dollar. The *tapo* has prepared ava; let us drink and rejoice." The tapo is the virgin hostess of the village; in this instance it was Taloa, daughter of the chief. "Our taro is good; let us eat. On the tree there is fruit. Let the day go by; why should we mourn over that? There are millions of days coming. The breadfruit is yellow in the sun, and from the cloth-tree is Taloa's gown. Our house, which is good, cost but the labor of building it, and there is no lock on the door."

While the days go thus in these Southern islands we at the North are struggling for the bare necessities of life.

For food the islanders have only to put out their hand and take what nature has provided for them; if they plant a banana-tree, their only care afterward is to see that too many trees do not grow. They have great reason to love their country and to fear the white man's yoke, for once harnessed to the plow, their life would no longer be a poem.

The chief of the village of Caini, who was a tall and dignified Tonga man, could be approached only through an interpreter and talking man. It was perfectly natural for him to inquire the object of my visit, and I was sincere when I told him that my reason for casting anchor in Samoa was to see their fine men, and fine women, too. After a considerable pause the chief said: "The captain has come a long way to see so little; but," he added, "the tapo must sit nearer the captain." "Yack," said Taloa, who had so nearly learned to say yes in English, and suiting the action to the word, she hitched a peg nearer, all hands sitting in a circle upon mats. I was no less taken with the chief's eloquence than delighted with the simplicity of all he said. About him there was nothing pompous; he might have been taken for a great scholar or statesman, the least assuming of the men I met on the voyage. As for Taloa, a sort of Queen of the May, and the other tapo girls, well, it is wise to learn as soon as possible the manners and customs of these hospitable people, and meanwhile not to mistake for overfamiliarity that which is intended as honor to a guest. I was fortunate in my travels in the islands, and saw nothing to shake one's faith in native virtue.

To the unconventional mind the punctilious etiquette of Samoa is perhaps a little painful. For instance, I found that in partaking of ava, the social bowl, I was supposed to toss a little of the beverage over my shoulder, or pretend to do so, and say, "Let the gods drink," and then drink it all myself; and the dish, invariably a cocoanut-shell, being empty, I might not pass it politely as we would do, but politely throw it twirling across the mats at the tapo.

My most grievous mistake while at the islands was made on a nag, which, inspired by a bit of good road, must needs break into a smart trot through a village. I was instantly hailed by the chief's deputy, who in an angry voice brought me to a halt. Perceiving that I was in trouble, I made signs for pardon, the safest thing to do, though I did not know what offense I had committed. My interpreter coming up, however, put me right, but not until a long palaver had ensued. The deputy's hail, liberally translated, was: "Ahoy, there, on the frantic steed! Know you not that it is against the law to ride thus through the village of our fathers?" I made what apologies I could, and offered to dismount and, like my servant, lead my nag by the bridle. This, the interpreter told me, would also be a grievous wrong, and so I again begged for pardon. I was summoned to appear before a chief; but my interpreter, being a wit as well as a bit of a rogue, explained that I was myself something of a chief, and should not be detained, being on a most important mission. In my own behalf I could only say that I was a stranger, but, pleading all this, I knew I still deserved to be roasted, at which the chief showed a fine row of teeth and seemed pleased, but allowed me to pass on.

The chief of the Tongas and his family at Caini, returning my visit, brought presents of tapa-cloth and fruits. Taloa, the princess, brought a bottle of cocoanut-oil for my hair, which another man might have regarded as coming late.

It was impossible to entertain on the *Spray* after the royal manner in which I had been received by the chief. His fare had included all that the land could afford, fruits, fowl, fishes, and flesh, a hog having been roasted whole. I set before them boiled salt pork and salt beef, with which I was well supplied, and in the evening took them all to a new amusement in the town, a rocking-horse merry-go-round, which they called a "kee-kee," meaning theater; and in a spirit of justice they pulled off the horses' tails, for the proprietors of the show, two hard-fisted countrymen of mine, I grieve to say, unceremoniously hustled them off for a new set, almost at the first spin. I was not a little proud of my Tonga friends; the chief, finest of them all, carried a portentous club. As for the theater, through the greed of the proprietors it was becoming unpopular, and the representatives of the three great powers, in want of laws which they could enforce, adopted a vigorous foreign policy, taxing it twenty-five per cent. on the gate-money. This was considered a great stroke of legislative reform!

It was the fashion of the native visitors to the *Spray* to come over the bows, where they could reach the head-gear and climb aboard with ease, and on going ashore to jump off the stern and swim away; nothing could have been more delightfully simple. The modest natives wore *lava-lava* bathing-dresses, a native cloth from the bark of the mulberry-tree, and they did no harm to the *Spray*. In summerland Samoa their coming and going was only a merry every-day scene.

One day the head teachers of Papauta College, Miss Schultze and Miss Moore, came on board with their ninety-seven young women students. They were all dressed in white, and each wore a red rose, and of course came in boats or canoes in the cold-climate style. A merrier bevy of girls it would be difficult to find. As soon as they got on deck, by request of one of the teachers, they sang "The Watch on the Rhine," which I had never heard before. "And now," said they all, "let's up anchor and away." But I had no inclination to sail from Samoa so soon. On leaving the *Spray* these accomplished young women each seized a palm-branch or paddle, or whatever else would serve the purpose, and literally paddled her own canoe. Each could have swum as readily, and would have done so, I dare say, had it not been for the holiday muslin.

It was not uncommon at Apia to see a young woman swimming alongside a small canoe with a passenger for the *Spray*. Mr. Trood, an old Eton boy, came in this manner to see me, and he exclaimed, "Was ever king ferried in such state?" Then, suiting his action to the sentiment, he gave the damsel pieces of silver till the natives watching on shore yelled with envy. My own canoe, a small dugout, one day when it had rolled over with me, was seized by a party of fair bathers, and before I could get my breath, almost, was towed around and around the *Spray*, while I sat in the bottom of it, wondering what they would do next. But in this case there were six of them, three on a side, and I could not help myself. One of the sprites, I remember, was a young English lady, who made more sport of it than any of the others.

Chapter 13

At Apia I had the pleasure of meeting Mr. A. Young, the father of the late Queen Margaret, who was Queen of Manua from 1891 to 1895. Her grandfather was an English sailor who married a princess. Mr. Young is now the only survivor of the family, two of his children, the last of them all, having been lost in an island trader which a few months before had sailed, never to return. Mr. Young was a Christian gentleman, and his daughter Margaret was accomplished in graces that would become any lady. It was with pain that I saw in the newspapers a sensational account of her life and death, taken evidently from a paper in the supposed interest of a benevolent society, but without foundation in fact. And the startling head-lines saying, "Queen Margaret of Manua is dead," could hardly be called news in 1898, the queen having then been dead three years.

While hobnobbing, as it were, with royalty, I called on the king himself, the late Malietoa. King Malietoa was a great ruler; he never got less than forty-five dollars a month for the job, as he told me himself, and this amount had lately been raised, so that he could live on the fat of the land and not any longer be called "Tin-of-salmon Malietoa" by graceless beach-combers.

As my interpreter and I entered the front door of the palace, the king's brother, who was viceroy, sneaked in through a taro-patch by the back way, and sat cowering by the door while I told my story to the king. Mr. W—— of New York, a gentleman interested in missionary work, had charged me, when I sailed, to give his remembrance to the king of the Cannibal Islands, other islands of course being meant; but the good King Malietoa, notwithstanding that his people have not eaten a missionary in a hundred years, received the message himself, and seemed greatly pleased to hear so directly from the publishers of the "Missionary Review," and wished me to make his compliments in return. His Majesty then excused himself, while I talked with his daughter, the beautiful Faamu-Sami (a name signifying "To make the sea burn"), and soon reappeared in the full-dress uniform of the German commander-in-chief, Emperor William himself; for, stupidly enough, I had not sent my credentials ahead that the king might be in full regalia to receive me. Calling a few days later to say good-by to Faamu-Sami, I saw King Malietoa for the last time.

Of the landmarks in the pleasant town of Apia, my memory rests first on the little school just back of the London Missionary Society coffee-house and reading-rooms, where Mrs. Bell taught English to about a hundred native children, boys and girls. Brighter children you will not find anywhere.

"Now, children," said Mrs. Bell, when I called one day, "let us show the captain that we know something about the Cape Horn he passed in the *Spray*," at which a lad of nine or ten years stepped nimbly forward and read Basil Hall's fine description of the great cape, and read it well. He afterward copied the essay for me in a clear hand.

Calling to say good-by to my friends at Vailima, I met Mrs. Stevenson in her Panama hat, and went over the estate with her. Men were at work clearing the land, and to one of them she gave an order to cut a couple of bamboo-trees for the *Spray* from a clump she had planted four years before, and which had grown to the height of sixty feet. I used them for spare spars, and the butt of one made a serviceable jib-boom on the homeward voyage. I had then only to take ava with the family and be ready for sea. This ceremony, important among Samoans, was conducted after the native fashion. A Triton horn was sounded to let us know when the beverage was ready, and in response we all clapped hands. The bout being in honor of the *Spray*, it was my turn first, after the custom of the country, to spill a little over my shoulder; but having forgotten the Samoan for "Let the gods drink," I repeated the equivalent in Russian and Chinook, as I remembered a word in each, whereupon Mr. Osbourne pronounced me a confirmed Samoan. Then I said "Tofah!" to my good friends of Samoa, and all wishing the *Spray* *bon voyage,* she stood out of the harbor August 20, 1896, and continued on her course. A sense of loneliness seized upon me as the islands faded astern, and as a remedy for it I crowded on sail for lovely Australia, which was not a strange land to me; but for long days in my dreams Vailima stood before the prow.

The *Spray* had barely cleared the islands when a sudden burst of the trades brought her down to close reefs, and she reeled off one hundred and eighty-four miles the first day, of which I counted forty miles of current in her favor. Finding a rough sea, I swung her off free and sailed north of the Horn Islands, also north of Fiji instead of south, as I had intended, and coasted down the west side of the archipelago. Thence I sailed direct for New South Wales, passing south of New Caledonia, and arrived at Newcastle after a passage of forty-two days, mostly of storms and gales.

One particularly severe gale encountered near New Caledonia foundered the American clipper-ship *Patrician* farther south. Again, nearer the coast of Australia, when, however, I was not aware that the gale was extraordinary, a French mail-steamer from New Caledonia for Sydney, blown considerably out of her course, on her arrival reported it an awful storm, and to inquiring friends said: "Oh, my! we don't know what has become of the little sloop *Spray*. We saw her in the thick of the storm." The *Spray* was all right, lying to like a duck. She was under a goose's wing mainsail, and had had a dry deck while the passengers on the steamer, I heard later, were up to their knees in water in the saloon. When their ship arrived at Sydney they gave the captain a purse of gold for his skill and seamanship in bringing them safe into port. The captain of the *Spray* got nothing of this sort. In this gale I made the land about Seal Rocks, where the steamship *Catherton,* with many lives, was lost a short time before. I was many hours off the rocks, beating back and forth, but weathered them at last.

I arrived at Newcastle in the teeth of a gale of wind. It was a stormy season. The government pilot, Captain Cumming, met me at the harbor bar, and with the assistance of a steamer carried my vessel to a safe berth. Many visitors came on board, the first being the United States consul, Mr. Brown. Nothing was too good for the *Spray* here. All government dues were remitted, and after I had rested a few days a port pilot with a tug carried her to sea again, and she made along the coast toward the harbor of Sydney, where she arrived on the following day, October 10, 1896.

I came to in a snug cove near Manly for the night, the Sydney harbor police-boat giving me a pluck into anchorage while they gathered data from an old scrap-book of mine, which seemed to interest them. Nothing escapes the vigilance of the New South Wales police; their reputation is known the world over. They made a shrewd guess that I could give them some useful information, and they were the first to meet me. Some one said they came to arrest me, and—well, let it go at that.

Summer was approaching, and the harbor of Sydney was blooming with yachts. Some of them came down to the weather-beaten *Spray* and sailed round her at Shelcote, where she took a berth for a few days. At Sydney I was at once among friends. The *Spray* remained at the various watering-places in the great port for several weeks, and was visited by many agreeable people, frequently by officers of H.M.S. *Orlando* and their friends. Captain Fisher, the commander, with a party of young ladies from the city and gentlemen belonging to his ship, came one day to pay me a visit in the midst of a deluge of rain. I never saw it rain harder even in Australia. But they were out for fun, and rain could not dampen their feelings, however hard it poured. But, as ill luck would have it, a young gentleman of another party on board, in the full uniform of a very great yacht club, with brass buttons enough to sink him, stepping quickly to get out of the wet, tumbled holus-bolus, head and heels, into a barrel of water I had been coopering, and being a short man, was soon out of sight, and nearly drowned before he was rescued. It was the nearest to a casualty on the *Spray* in her whole course, so far as I know. The young man having come on board with compliments made the mishap most embarrassing. It had been decided by his club that the *Spray* could not be officially recognized, for the reason that she brought no letters from yacht-clubs in America, and so I say it seemed all the more embarrassing and strange that I should have caught at least one of the members, in a barrel, and, too, when I was not fishing for yachtsmen.

The typical Sydney boat is a handy sloop of great beam and enormous sail-carrying power; but a capsize is not uncommon, for they carry sail like vikings. In Sydney I saw all manner of craft, from the smart steam-launch and sailing-cutter to the smaller sloop and canoe pleasuring on the bay. Everybody owned a boat. If a boy in Australia has not the means to buy him a boat he builds one, and it is usually one not to be ashamed of. The *Spray* shed her Joseph's coat, the Fuego mainsail, in Sydney, and wearing a new suit, the handsome present of Commodore Foy, she was flagship of the Johnstone's Bay Flying Squadron when the circumnavigators of Sydney harbor sailed in their annual regatta. They "recognized" the *Spray* as belonging to "a club of her own," and with more Australian sentiment than fastidiousness gave her credit for her record.

Time flew fast those days in Australia, and it was December 6, 1896, when the *Spray* sailed from Sydney. My intention was now to sail around Cape Leeuwin direct for Mauritius on my way home, and so I coasted along toward Bass Strait in that direction.

There was little to report on this part of the voyage, except changeable winds, "busters," and rough seas. The 12th of December, however, was an exceptional day, with a fine coast wind, northeast. The *Spray* early in the morning passed Twofold Bay and later Cape Bundooro in a smooth sea with land close aboard. The lighthouse on the cape dipped a flag to the *Spray's* flag, and children on the balconies of a cottage near the shore waved handkerchiefs as she passed by. There were only a few people all told on the shore, but the scene was a happy one. I saw festoons of evergreen in token of Christmas, near at hand. I saluted the merrymakers, wishing them a "Merry Christmas," and could hear them say, "I wish you the same."

From Cape Bundooro I passed by Cliff Island in Bass Strait, and exchanged signals with the lightkeepers while the *Spray* worked up under the island. The wind howled that day while the sea broke over their rocky home.

A few days later, December 17, the *Spray* came in close under Wilson's Promontory, again seeking shelter. The keeper of the light at that station, Mr. J. Clark, came on board and gave me directions for Waterloo Bay, about three miles to leeward, for which I bore up at once, finding good anchorage there in a sandy cove protected from all westerly and northerly winds.

Anchored here was the ketch *Secret*, a fisherman, and the *Mary* of Sydney, a steam ferry-boat fitted for whaling. The captain of the *Mary* was a genius, and an Australian genius at that, and smart. His crew, from a sawmill up the coast, had not one of them seen a live whale when they shipped; but they were boatmen after an Australian's own heart, and the captain had told them that to kill a whale was no more than to kill a rabbit. They believed him, and that settled it. As luck would have it, the very first one they saw on their cruise, although an ugly humpback, was a dead whale in no time, Captain Young, the master of the *Mary*, killing the monster at a single thrust of a harpoon. It was taken in tow for Sydney, where they put it on exhibition. Nothing but whales interested the crew of the gallant *Mary*, and they spent most of their time here gathering fuel along shore for a cruise on the grounds off Tasmania. Whenever the word "whale" was mentioned in the hearing of these men their eyes glistened with excitement.

We spent three days in the quiet cove, listening to the wind outside. Meanwhile Captain Young and I explored the shores, visited abandoned miners' pits, and prospected for gold ourselves.

Our vessels, parting company the morning they sailed, stood away like sea-birds each on its own course. The wind for a few days was moderate, and, with unusual luck of fine weather, the *Spray* made Melbourne Heads on the 22d of December, and, taken in tow by the steam-tug *Racer*, was brought into port.

Christmas day was spent at a berth in the river Yarrow, but I lost little time in shifting to St. Kilda, where I spent nearly a month.

The *Spray* paid no port charges in Australia or anywhere else on the voyage, except at Pernambuco, till she poked her nose into the custom-house at Melbourne, where she was charged tonnage dues; in this instance, sixpence a ton on the gross. The collector exacted six shillings and sixpence, taking off nothing for the fraction under thirteen tons, her exact gross being 12.70 tons. I squared the matter by charging people sixpence each for coming on board, and when this business got dull I caught a shark and charged them sixpence each to look at that. The shark was twelve feet six inches in length, and carried a progeny of twenty-six, not one of them less than two feet in length. A slit of a knife let them out in a canoe full of water, which, changed constantly, kept them alive one whole day. In less than an hour from the time I heard of the ugly brute it was on deck and on exhibition, with rather more than the amount of the *Spray's* tonnage dues already collected. Then I hired a good Irishman, Tom Howard by name,—who knew all about sharks, both on the land and in the sea, and could talk about them,—to answer questions and lecture. When I found that I could not keep abreast of the questions I turned the responsibility over to him.

Returning from the bank, where I had been to deposit money early in the day, I found Howard in the midst of a very excited crowd, telling imaginary habits of the fish. It was a good show; the people wished to see it, and it was my wish that they should; but owing to his over-stimulated enthusiasm, I was obliged to let Howard resign. The income from the show and the proceeds of the tallow I had gathered in the Strait of Magellan, the last of which I had disposed of to a German soap-boiler at Samoa, put me in ample funds.

January 24, 1897, found the *Spray* again in tow of the tug *Racer*, leaving Hobson's Bay after a pleasant time in Melbourne and St. Kilda, which had been protracted by a succession of southwest winds that seemed never-ending.

In the summer months, that is, December, January, February, and sometimes March, east winds are prevalent through Bass Strait and round Cape Leeuwin; but owing to a vast amount of ice drifting up from the Antarctic, this was all changed now and emphasized with much bad weather, so much so that I considered it impracticable to pursue the course farther. Therefore, instead of thrashing round cold and stormy Cape Leeuwin, I decided to spend a pleasanter and more profitable time in Tasmania, waiting for the season for favorable winds through Torres Strait, by way of the Great Barrier Reef, the route I finally decided on. To sail this course would be taking advantage of anticyclones, which never fail, and besides it would give me the chance to put foot on the shores of Tasmania, round which I had sailed years before.

I should mention that while I was at Melbourne there occurred one of those extraordinary storms sometimes called "rain of blood," the first of the kind in many years about Australia. The "blood" came from a fine brick-dust matter afloat in the air from the deserts. A rain-storm setting in brought down this dust simply as mud; it fell in such quantities that a bucketful was collected from the sloop's awnings, which were spread at the time. When the wind blew hard and I was obliged to furl awnings, her sails, unprotected on the booms, got mud-stained from clue to earing.

The phenomena of dust-storms, well understood by scientists, are not uncommon on the coast of Africa. Reaching some distance out over the sea, they frequently cover the track of ships, as in the case of the one through which the *Spray* passed in the earlier part of her voyage. Sailors no longer regard them with superstitious fear, but our credulous brothers on the land cry out "Rain of blood!" at the first splash of the awful mud.

The rip off Port Phillip Heads, a wild place, was rough when the *Spray* entered Hobson's Bay from the sea, and was rougher when she stood out. But, with sea-room and under sail, she made good weather immediately after passing it. It was only a few hours' sail to Tasmania across the strait, the wind being fair and blowing hard. I carried the St. Kilda shark along, stuffed with hay, and disposed of it to Professor Porter, the curator of the Victoria Museum of Launceston, which is at the head of the Tamar. For many a long day to come may be seen there the shark of St. Kilda. Alas! the good but mistaken people of St. Kilda, when the illustrated journals with pictures of my shark reached their news-stands, flew into a passion, and swept all papers containing mention of fish into the fire; for St. Kilda was a watering-place—and the idea of a shark *there!* But my show went on.

The *Spray* was berthed on the beach at a small jetty at Launceston while the tide driven in by the gale that brought her up the river was unusually high; and she lay there hard and fast, with not enough water around her at any time after to wet one's feet till she was ready to sail; then, to float her, the ground was dug from under her keel.

In this snug place I left her in charge of three children, while I made journeys among the hills and rested my bones, for the coming voyage, on the moss-covered rocks at the gorge hard by, and among the ferns I found wherever I went. My vessel was well taken care of. I never returned without finding that the decks had been washed and that one of the children, my nearest neighbor's little girl from across the road, was at the gangway attending to visitors, while the others, a brother and sister, sold marine curios such as were in the cargo, on "ship's account." They were a bright, cheerful crew, and people came a long way to hear them tell the story of the voyage, and of the monsters of the deep "the captain had slain." I had only to keep myself away to be a hero of the first water; and it suited me very well to do so and to rusticate in the forests and among the streams.

Chapter 14

February 1, 1897, on returning to my vessel I found waiting for me the letter of sympathy which I subjoin:

A lady sends Mr. Slocum the inclosed five-pound note as a token of her appreciation of his bravery in crossing the wide seas on so small a boat, and all alone, without human sympathy to help when danger threatened. All success to you.

To this day I do not know who wrote it or to whom I am indebted for the generous gift it contained. I could not refuse a thing so kindly meant, but promised myself to pass it on with interest at the first opportunity, and this I did before leaving Australia.

The season of fair weather around the north of Australia being yet a long way off, I sailed to other ports in Tasmania, where it is fine the year round, the first of these being Beauty Point, near which are Beaconsfield and the great Tasmania gold-mine, which I visited in turn. I saw much gray, uninteresting rock being hoisted out of the mine there, and hundreds of stamps crushing it into powder. People told me there was gold in it, and I believed what they said.

I remember Beauty Point for its shady forest and for the road among the tall gum-trees. While there the governor of New South Wales, Lord Hampden, and his family came in on a steam-yacht, sight-seeing. The *Spray*, anchored near the landing-pier, threw her bunting out, of course, and probably a more insignificant craft bearing the Stars and Stripes was never seen in those waters. However, the governor's party seemed to know why it floated there, and all about the *Spray*, and when I heard his Excellency say, "Introduce me to the captain," or "Introduce the captain to me," whichever it was, I found myself at once in the presence of a gentleman and a friend, and one greatly interested in my voyage. If any one of the party was more interested than the governor himself, it was the Honorable Margaret, his daughter. On leaving, Lord and Lady Hampden promised to rendezvous with me on board the *Spray* at the Paris Exposition in 1900. "If we live," they said, and I added, for my part, "Dangers of the seas excepted."

From Beauty Point the *Spray* visited Georgetown, near the mouth of the river Tamar. This little settlement, I believe, marks the place where the first footprints were made by whites in Tasmania, though it never grew to be more than a hamlet.

Considering that I had seen something of the world, and finding people here interested in adventure, I talked the matter over before my first audience in a little hall by the country road. A piano having been brought in from a neighbor's, I was helped out by the severe thumping it got, and by a "Tommy Atkins" song from a strolling comedian. People came from a great distance, and the attendance all told netted the house about three pounds sterling. The owner of the hall, a kind lady from Scotland, would take no rent, and so my lecture from the start was a success.

From this snug little place I made sail for Devonport, a thriving place on the river Mersey, a few hours' sail westward along the coast, and fast becoming the most important port in Tasmania. Large steamers enter there now and carry away great cargoes of farm produce, but the *Spray* was the first vessel to bring the Stars and Stripes to the port, the harbor-master, Captain Murray, told me, and so it is written in the port records. For the great distinction the *Spray* enjoyed many civilities while she rode comfortably at anchor in her port-duster awning that covered her from stem to stern.

From the magistrate's house, "Malunnah," on the point, she was saluted by the Jack both on coming in and on going out, and dear Mrs. Aikenhead, the mistress of Malunnah, supplied the *Spray* with jams and jellies of all sorts, by the case, prepared from the fruits of her own rich garden—enough to last all the way home and to spare. Mrs. Wood, farther up the harbor, put up bottles of raspberry wine for me. At this point, more than ever before, I was in the land of good cheer. Mrs. Powell sent on board chutney prepared "as we prepare it in India." Fish and game were plentiful here, and the voice of the gobbler was heard, and from Pardo, farther up the country, came an enormous cheese; and yet people inquire: "What did you live on? What did you eat?"

I was haunted by the beauty of the landscape all about, of the natural ferneries then disappearing, and of the domed forest-trees on the slopes, and was fortunate in meeting a gentleman intent on preserving in art the beauties of his country. He presented me with many reproductions from his collection of pictures, also many originals, to show to my friends.

By another gentleman I was charged to tell the glories of Tasmania in every land and on every occasion. This was Dr. McCall, M.L.C. The doctor gave me useful hints on lecturing. It was not without misgivings, however, that I filled away on this new course, and I am free to say that it is only by the kindness of sympathetic audiences that my oratorical bark was held on even keel. Soon after my first talk the kind doctor came to me with words of approval. As in many other of my enterprises, I had gone about it at once and without second thought. "Man, man," said he, "great nervousness is only a sign of brain, and the more brain a man has the longer it takes him to get over the affliction; but," he added reflectively, "you will get over it." However, in my own behalf I think it only fair to say that I am not yet entirely cured.

The *Spray* was hauled out on the marine railway at Devonport and examined carefully top and bottom, but was found absolutely free from the destructive teredo, and sound in all respects. To protect her further against the ravage of these insects the bottom was coated once more with copper paint, for she would have to sail through the Coral and Arafura seas before refitting again. Everything was done to fit her for all the known dangers. But it was not without regret that I looked forward to the day of sailing from a country of so many pleasant associations. If there was a moment in my voyage when I could have given it up, it was there and then; but no vacancies for a better post being open, I weighed anchor April 16, 1897, and again put to sea.

The season of summer was then over; winter was rolling up from the south, with fair winds for the north. A foretaste of winter wind sent the *Spray* flying round Cape Howe and as far as Cape Bundooro farther along, which she passed on the following day, retracing her course northward. This was a fine run, and boded good for the long voyage home from the antipodes. My old Christmas friends on Bundooro seemed to be up and moving when I came the second time by their cape, and we exchanged signals again, while the sloop sailed along as before in a smooth sea and close to the shore.

The weather was fine, with clear sky the rest of the passage to

Port Jackson (Sydney), where the *Spray* arrived April 22, 1897, and anchored in Watson's Bay, near the heads, in eight fathoms of water. The harbor from the heads to Parramatta, up the river, was more than ever alive with boats and yachts of every class. It was, indeed, a scene of animation, hardly equaled in any other part of the world.

A few days later the bay was flecked with tempestuous waves, and none but stout ships carried sail. I was in a neighboring hotel then, nursing a neuralgia which I had picked up alongshore, and had only that moment got a glance of just the stern of a large, unmanageable steamship passing the range of my window as she forged in by the point, when the bell-boy burst into my room shouting that the *Spray* had "gone bung." I tumbled out quickly, to learn that "bung" meant that a large steamship had run into her, and that it was the one of which I saw the stern, the other end of her having hit the *Spray*. It turned out, however, that no damage was done beyond the loss of an anchor and chain, which from the shock of the collision had parted at the hawse. I had nothing at all to complain of, though, in the end, for the captain, after he clubbed his ship, took the *Spray* in tow up the harbor, clear of all dangers, and sent her back again, in charge of an officer and three men, to her anchorage in the bay, with a polite note saying he would repair any damages done. But what yawing about she made of it when she came with a stranger at the helm! Her old friend the pilot of the *Pinta* would not have been guilty of such lubberly work. But to my great delight they got her into a berth, and the neuralgia left me then, or was forgotten. The captain of the steamer, like a true seaman, kept his word, and his agent, Mr. Collishaw, handed me on the very next day the price of the lost anchor and chain, with something over for anxiety of mind. I remember that he offered me twelve pounds at once; but my lucky number being thirteen, we made the amount thirteen pounds, which squared all accounts.

I sailed again, May 9, before a strong southwest wind, which sent the *Spray* gallantly on as far as Port Stevens, where it fell calm and then came up ahead; but the weather was fine, and so remained for many days, which was a great change from the state of the weather experienced here some months before.

Having a full set of admiralty sheet-charts of the coast and Barrier Reef, I felt easy in mind. Captain Fisher, R.N., who had steamed through the Barrier passages in H.M.S. *Orlando*, advised me from the first to take this route, and I did not regret coming back to it now.

The wind, for a few days after passing Port Stevens, Seal Rocks, and Cape Hawk, was light and dead ahead; but these points are photographed on my memory from the trial of beating round them some months before when bound the other way. But now, with a good stock of books on board, I fell to reading day and night, leaving this pleasant occupation merely to trim sails or tack, or to lie down and rest, while the *Spray* nibbled at the miles. I tried to compare my state with that of old circumnavigators, who sailed exactly over the route which I took from Cape Verde Islands or farther back to this point and beyond, but there was no comparison so far as I had got. Their hardships and romantic escapes—those of them who escaped death and worse sufferings—did not enter into my experience, sailing all alone around the world. For me is left to tell only of pleasant experiences, till finally my adventures are prosy and tame.

I had just finished reading some of the most interesting of the old voyages in woe-begone ships, and was already near Port Macquarie, on my own cruise, when I made out, May 13, a modern dandy craft in distress, anchored on the coast. Standing in for her, I found that she was the cutter-yacht *Akbar*,[1] which had sailed from Watson's Bay about three days ahead of the *Spray*, and that she had run at once into trouble. No wonder she did so. It was a case of babes in the wood or butterflies at sea. Her owner, on his maiden voyage, was all duck trousers; the captain, distinguished for the enormous yachtsman's cap he wore, was a Murrumbidgee [2] whaler before he took command of the *Akbar;* and the navigating officer, poor fellow, was almost as deaf as a post, and nearly as stiff and immovable as a post in the ground. These three jolly tars comprised the crew. None of them knew more about the sea or about a vessel than a newly born babe knows about another world. They were bound for New Guinea, so they said; perhaps it was as well that three tenderfeet so tender as those never reached that destination.

[1] *Akbar* was not her registered name, which need not be told.
[2] The Murrumbidgee is a small river winding among the mountains of Australia, and would be the last place in which to look for a whale.

The owner, whom I had met before he sailed, wanted to race the poor old *Spray* to Thursday Island en route. I declined the challenge, naturally, on the ground of the unfairness of three young yachtsmen in a clipper against an old sailor all alone in a craft of coarse build; besides that, I would not on any account race in the Coral Sea.

"*Spray* ahoy!" they all hailed now. "What's the weather goin' t' be? Is it a-goin' to blow? And don't you think we'd better go back t' r-r-refit?"

I thought, "If ever you get back, don't refit," but I said: "Give me the end of a rope, and I'll tow you into yon port farther along; and on your lives," I urged, "do not go back round Cape Hawk, for it's winter to the south of it."

They purposed making for Newcastle under jury-sails; for their mainsail had been blown to ribbons, even the jigger had been blown away, and her rigging flew at loose ends. The *Akbar*, in a word, was a wreck.

"Up anchor," I shouted, "up anchor, and let me tow you into Port Macquarie, twelve miles north of this."

"No," cried the owner; "we'll go back to Newcastle. We missed Newcastle on the way coming; we didn't see the light, and it was not thick, either." This he shouted very loud, ostensibly for my hearing, but closer even than necessary, I thought, to the ear of the navigating officer. Again I tried to persuade them to be towed into the port of refuge so near at hand. It would have cost them only the trouble of weighing their anchor and passing me a rope; of this I assured them, but they declined even this, in sheer ignorance of a rational course.

"What is your depth of water?" I asked.

"Don't know; we lost our lead. All the chain is out. We sounded with the anchor."

"Send your dinghy over, and I'll give you a lead."

"We've lost our dinghy, too," they cried.

"God is good, else you would have lost yourselves," and "Farewell" was all I could say.

The trifling service proffered by the *Spray* would have saved their vessel.

"Report us," they cried, as I stood on—"report us with sails blown away, and that we don't care a dash and are not afraid."

"Then there is no hope for you," and again "Farewell."

I promised I would report them, and did so at the first opportunity, and out of humane reasons I do so again. On the following day I spoke the steamship *Sherman,* bound down the coast, and reported the yacht in distress and that it would be an act of humanity to tow her somewhere away from her exposed position on an open coast. That she did not get a tow from the steamer was from no lack of funds to pay the bill; for the owner, lately heir to a few hundred pounds, had the money with him. The proposed voyage to New Guinea was to look that island over with a view to its purchase. It was about eighteen days before I heard of the *Akbar* again, which was on the 31st of May, when I reached Cooktown, on the Endeavor River, where I found this news:

May 31, the yacht *Akbar,* from Sydney for New Guinea, three hands on board, lost at Crescent Head; the crew saved.

So it took them several days to lose the yacht, after all.

After speaking the distressed *Akbar* and the *Sherman,* the voyage for many days was uneventful save in the pleasant incident on May 16 of a chat by signal with the people on South Solitary Island, a dreary stone heap in the ocean just off the coast of New South Wales, in latitude 30° 12′ south.

"What vessel is that?" they asked, as the sloop came abreast of their island. For answer I tried them with the Stars and Stripes at the peak. Down came their signals at once, and up went the British ensign instead, which they dipped heartily. I understood from this that they made out my vessel and knew all about her, for they asked no more questions. They didn't even ask if the "voyage would pay," but they threw out this friendly message, "Wishing you a pleasant voyage," which at that very moment I was having.

May 19 the *Spray,* passing the Tweed River, was signaled from Danger Point, where those on shore seemed most anxious about the state of my health, for they asked if "all hands" were well, to which I could say, "Yes."

On the following day the *Spray* rounded Great Sandy Cape, and, what is a notable event in every voyage, picked up the trade-winds, and these winds followed her now for many thousands of miles, never ceasing to blow from a moderate gale to a mild summer breeze, except at rare intervals.

From the pitch of the cape was a noble light seen twenty-seven miles; passing from this to Lady Elliott Light, which stands on an island as a sentinel at the gateway of the Barrier Reef, the *Spray* was at once in the fairway leading north. Poets have sung of beacon-light and of pharos, but did ever poet behold a great light flash up before his path on a dark night in the midst of a coral sea? If so, he knew the meaning of his song.

The *Spray* had sailed for hours in suspense, evidently stemming a current. Almost mad with doubt, I grasped the helm to throw her head off shore, when blazing out of the sea was the light ahead. "Excalibur!" cried "all hands," and rejoiced, and sailed on. The *Spray* was now in a protected sea and smooth water, the first she had dipped her keel into since leaving Gibraltar, and a change it was from the heaving of the misnamed "Pacific" Ocean.

The Pacific is perhaps, upon the whole, no more boisterous than other oceans, though I feel quite safe in saying that it is not more pacific except in name. It is often wild enough in one part or another. I once knew a writer who, after saying beautiful things about the sea, passed through a Pacific hurricane, and he became a changed man. But where, after all, would be the poetry of the sea were there no wild waves? At last here was the *Spray* in the midst of a sea of coral. The sea itself might be called smooth indeed, but coral rocks are always rough, sharp, and dangerous. I trusted now to the mercies of the Maker of all reefs, keeping a good lookout at the same time for perils on every hand.

Lo! the Barrier Reef and the waters of many colors studded all about with enchanted islands! I behold among them after all many safe harbors, else my vision is astray. On the 24th of May, the sloop, having made one hundred and ten miles a day from Danger Point, now entered Whitsunday Pass, and that night sailed through among the islands. When the sun rose next morning I looked back and regretted having gone by while it was dark, for the scenery far astern was varied and charming.

Chapter 15

On the morning of the 26th Gloucester Island was close aboard, and the *Spray* anchored in the evening at Port Denison, where rests, on a hill, the sweet little town of Bowen, the future watering place and health-resort of Queensland. The country all about here had a healthful appearance.

The harbor was easy of approach, spacious and safe, and afforded excellent holding-ground. It was quiet in Bowen when the *Spray* arrived, and the good people with an hour to throw away on the second evening of her arrival came down to the School of Arts to talk about the voyage, it being the latest event. It was duly advertised in the two little papers, "Boomerang" and "Nully Nully," in the one the day before the affair came off, and in the other the day after, which was all the same to the editor, and, for that matter, it was the same to me.

Besides this, circulars were distributed with a flourish, and the "best bellman" in Australia was employed. But I could have keel-hauled the wretch, bell and all, when he came to the door of the little hotel where my prospective audience and I were dining, and with his clattering bell and fiendish yell made noises that would awake the dead, all over the voyage of the *Spray* from "Boston to Bowen, the two Hubs in the cart-wheels of creation," as the "Boomerang" afterward said.

Mr. Myles, magistrate, harbor-master, land commissioner, gold warden, etc., was chairman, and introduced me, for what reason I never knew, except to embarrass me with a sense of vain ostentation and embitter my life, for Heaven knows I had met every person in town the first hour ashore. I knew them all by name now, and they all knew me. However, Mr. Myles was a good talker. Indeed, I tried to induce him to go on and tell the story while I showed the pictures, but this he refused to do. I may explain that it was a talk illustrated by stereopticon. The views were good, but the lantern, a thirty-shilling affair, was wretched, and had only an oil-lamp in it.

I sailed early the next morning before the papers came out, thinking it best to do so. They each appeared with a favorable column, however, of what they called a lecture, so I learned afterward, and they had a kind word for the bellman besides.

From Port Denison the sloop ran before the constant trade-wind, and made no stop at all, night or day, till she reached Cooktown, on the Endeavor River, where she arrived Monday, May 31, 1897, before a furious blast of wind encountered that day fifty miles down the coast. On this parallel of latitude is the high ridge and backbone of the trade-winds, which about Cooktown amount often to a hard gale.

I had been charged to navigate the route with extra care, and to feel my way over the ground. The skilled officer of the royal navy who advised me to take the Barrier Reef passage wrote me that H.M.S. *Orlando* steamed nights as well as days through it, but that I, under sail, would jeopardize my vessel on coral reefs if I undertook to do so.

Confidentially, it would have been no easy matter finding anchorage every night. The hard work, too, of getting the sloop under way every morning was finished, I had hoped, when she cleared the Strait of Magellan. Besides that, the best of admiralty charts made it possible to keep on sailing night and day. Indeed, with a fair wind, and in the clear weather of that season, the way through the Barrier Reef Channel, in all sincerity, was clearer than a highway in a busy city, and by all odds less dangerous. But to any one contemplating the voyage I would say, beware of reefs day or night, or, remaining on the land, be wary still.

"The *Spray* came flying into port like a bird," said the longshore daily papers of Cooktown the morning after she arrived; "and it seemed strange," they added, "that only one man could be seen on board working the craft." The *Spray* was doing her best, to be sure, for it was near night, and she was in haste to find a perch before dark.

Tacking inside of all the craft in port, I moored her at sunset nearly abreast the Captain Cook monument, and next morning went ashore to feast my eyes on the very stones the great navigator had seen, for I was now on a seaman's consecrated ground. But there seemed a question in Cooktown's mind as to the exact spot where his ship, the *Endeavor,* hove down for repairs on her memorable voyage around the world. Some said it was not at all at the place where the monument now stood. A discussion of the subject was going on one morning where I happened to be, and a young lady present, turning to me as one of some authority in nautical matters, very flatteringly asked my opinion. Well, I could see no reason why Captain Cook, if he made up his mind to repair his ship inland, couldn't have dredged out a channel to the place where the monument now stood, if he had a dredging-machine with him, and afterward fill it up again; for Captain Cook could do 'most anything, and nobody ever said that he hadn't a dredger along. The young lady seemed to lean to my way of thinking, and following up the story of the historical voyage, asked if I had visited the point farther down the harbor where the great circumnavigator was murdered. This took my breath, but a bright school-boy coming along relieved my embarrassment, for, like all boys, seeing that information was wanted, he volunteered to supply it. Said he: "Captain Cook wasn't murdered 'ere at all, ma'am; 'e was killed in Hafrica: a lion et 'im."

Here I was reminded of distressful days gone by. I think it was in 1866 that the old steamship *Soushay,* from Batavia for Sydney, put in at Cooktown for scurvy-grass, as I always thought, and "incidentally" to land mails. On her sick-list was my fevered self; and so I didn't see the place till I came back on the *Spray* thirty-one years later. And now I saw coming into port the physical wrecks of miners from New Guinea, destitute and dying. Many had died on the way and had been buried at sea. He would have been a hardened wretch who could look on and not try to do something for them.

The sympathy of all went out to these sufferers, but the little town was already straitened from a long run on its benevolence. I thought of the matter, of the lady's gift to me at Tasmania, which I had promised myself I would keep only as a loan, but found now, to my embarrassment, that I had invested the money. However, the good Cooktown people wished to hear a story of the sea, and how the crew of the *Spray* fared when illness got aboard of her. Accordingly the little Presbyterian church on the hill was opened for a conversation; everybody talked, and they made a roaring success of it. Judge Chester, the magistrate, was at the head of the gam, and so it was bound to succeed. He it was who annexed the island of New Guinea to Great Britain. "While I was about it," said he, "I annexed the blooming lot of it." There was a ring in the statement pleasant to the ear of an old voyager. However, the Germans made such a row over the judge's mainsail haul that they got a share in the venture.

Well, I was now indebted to the miners of Cooktown for the great privilege of adding a mite to a worthy cause, and to Judge Chester all the town was indebted for a general good time. The matter standing so, I sailed on June 6, 1897, heading away for the north as before.

Arrived at a very inviting anchorage about sundown, the 7th, I came to, for the night, abreast the Claremont light-ship. This was the only time throughout the passage of the Barrier Reef Channel that the *Spray* anchored, except at Port Denison and at Endeavor River. On the very night following this, however (the 8th), I regretted keenly, for an instant, that I had not anchored before dark, as I might have done easily under the lee of a coral reef. It happened in this way. The *Spray* had just passed M Reef light-ship, and left the light dipping astern, when, going at full speed, with sheets off, she hit the M Reef itself on the north end, where I expected to see a beacon.

She swung off quickly on her heel, however, and with one more bound on a swell cut across the shoal point so quickly that I hardly knew how it was done. The beacon wasn't there; at least, I didn't see it. I hadn't time to look for it after she struck, and certainly it didn't much matter then whether I saw it or not.

But this gave her a fine departure for Cape Greenville, the next point ahead. I saw the ugly boulders under the sloop's keel as she flashed over them, and I made a mental note of it that the letter M, for which the reef was named, was the thirteenth one in our alphabet, and that thirteen, as noted years before, was still my lucky number. The natives of Cape Greenville are notoriously bad, and I was advised to give them the go-by. Accordingly, from M Reef I steered outside of the adjacent islands, to be on the safe side. Skipping along now, the *Spray* passed Home Island, off the pitch of the cape, soon after midnight, and squared away on a westerly course. A short time later she fell in with a steamer bound south, groping her way in the dark and making the night dismal with her own black smoke.

From Home Island I made for Sunday Island, and bringing that abeam, shortened sail, not wishing to make Bird Island, farther along, before daylight, the wind being still fresh and the islands being low, with dangers about them. Wednesday, June 9, 1897, at daylight, Bird Island was dead ahead, distant two and a half miles, which I considered near enough. A strong current was pressing the sloop forward. I did not shorten sail too soon in the night! The first and only Australian canoe seen on the voyage was encountered here standing from the mainland, with a rag of sail set, bound for this island.

A long, slim fish that leaped on board in the night was found on deck this morning. I had it for breakfast. The spry chap was no larger around than a herring, which it resembled in every respect, except that it was three times as long; but that was so much the better, for I am rather fond of fresh herring, anyway. A great number of fisher-birds were about this day, which was one of the pleasantest on God's earth. The *Spray*, dancing over the waves, entered Albany Pass as the sun drew low in the west over the hills of Australia.

At 7:30 P.M. the *Spray*, now through the pass, came to anchor in a cove in the mainland, near a pearl-fisherman, called the *Tarawa*, which was at anchor, her captain from the deck of his vessel directing me to a berth. This done, he at once came on board to clasp hands. The *Tarawa* was a Californian, and Captain Jones, her master, was an American.

On the following morning Captain Jones brought on board two pairs of exquisite pearl shells, the most perfect ones I ever saw. They were probably the best he had, for Jones was the heart-yarn of a sailor. He assured me that if I would remain a few hours longer some friends from Somerset, near by, would pay us all a visit, and one of the crew, sorting shells on deck, "guessed" they would. The mate "guessed" so, too. The friends came, as even the second mate and cook had "guessed" they would. They were Mr. Jardine, stockman, famous throughout the land, and his family. Mrs. Jardine was the niece of King Malietoa, and cousin to the beautiful Faamu-Sami ("To make the sea burn"), who visited the *Spray* at Apia. Mr. Jardine was himself a fine specimen of a Scotsman. With his little family about him, he was content to live in this remote place, accumulating the comforts of life.

The fact of the *Tarawa* having been built in America accounted for the crew, boy Jim and all, being such good guessers. Strangely enough, though, Captain Jones himself, the only American aboard, was never heard to guess at all.

After a pleasant chat and good-by to the people of the *Tarawa*, and to Mr. and Mrs. Jardine, I again weighed anchor and stood across for Thursday Island, now in plain view, mid-channel in Torres Strait, where I arrived shortly after noon. Here the *Spray* remained over until June 24. Being the only American representative in port, this tarry was imperative, for on the 22d was the Queen's diamond jubilee. The two days over were, as sailors say, for "coming up."

Meanwhile I spent pleasant days about the island. Mr. Douglas, resident magistrate, invited me on a cruise in his steamer one day among the islands in Torres Strait. This being a scientific expedition in charge of Professor Mason Bailey, botanist, we rambled over Friday and Saturday islands, where I got a glimpse of botany. Miss Bailey, the professor's daughter, accompanied the expedition, and told me of many indigenous plants with long names.

The 22d was the great day on Thursday Island, for then we had not only the jubilee, but a jubilee with a grand corroboree in it, Mr. Douglas having brought some four hundred native warriors and their wives and children across from the mainland to give the celebration the true native touch, for when they do a thing on Thursday Island they do it with a roar. The corroboree was, at any rate, a howling success. It took place at night, and the performers, painted in fantastic colors, danced or leaped about before a blazing fire. Some were rigged and painted like birds and beasts, in which the emu and kangaroo were well represented. One fellow leaped like a frog. Some had the human skeleton painted on their bodies, while they jumped about threateningly, spear in hand, ready to strike down some imaginary enemy. The kangaroo hopped and danced with natural ease and grace, making a fine figure. All kept time to music, vocal and instrumental, the instruments (save the mark!) being bits of wood, which they beat one against the other, and saucer-like bones, held in the palm of the hands, which they knocked together, making a dull sound. It was a show at once amusing, spectacular, and hideous.

The warrior aborigines that I saw in Queensland were for the most part lithe and fairly well built, but they were stamped always with repulsive features, and their women were, if possible, still more ill favored.

I observed that on the day of the jubilee no foreign flag was waving in the public grounds except the Stars and Stripes, which along with the Union Jack guarded the gateway, and floated in many places, from the tiniest to the standard size. Speaking to Mr. Douglas, I ventured a remark on this compliment to my country. "Oh," said he, "this is a family affair, and we do not consider the Stars and Stripes a foreign flag." The *Spray* of course flew her best bunting, and hoisted the Jack as well as her own noble flag as high as she could.

On June 24 the *Spray*, well fitted in every way, sailed for the long voyage ahead, down the Indian Ocean. Mr. Douglas gave her a flag as she was leaving his island. The *Spray* had now passed nearly all the dangers of the Coral Sea and Torres Strait, which, indeed, were not a few; and all ahead from this point was plain sailing and a straight course. The trade-wind was still blowing fresh, and could be safely counted on now down to the coast of Madagascar, if not beyond that, for it was still early in the season.

I had no wish to arrive off the Cape of Good Hope before midsummer, and it was now early winter. I had been off that cape once in July, which was, of course, midwinter there. The stout ship I then commanded encountered only fierce hurricanes, and she bore them ill. I wished for no winter gales now. It was not that I feared them more, being in the *Spray* instead of a large ship, but that I preferred fine weather in any case. It is true that one may encounter heavy gales off the Cape of Good Hope at any season of the year, but in the summer they are less frequent and do not continue so long. And so with time enough before me to admit of a run ashore on the islands en route, I shaped the course now for Keeling Cocos, atoll islands, distant twenty-seven hundred miles. Taking a departure from Booby Island, which the sloop passed early in the day, I decided to sight Timor on the way, an island of high mountains.

Booby Island I had seen before, but only once, however, and that was when in the steamship *Soushay*, on which I was "hove-down" in a fever. When she steamed along this way I was well enough to crawl on deck to look at Booby Island. Had I died for it, I would have seen that island. In those days passing ships landed stores in a cave on the island for shipwrecked and distressed wayfarers. Captain Airy of the *Soushay*, a good man, sent a boat to the cave with his contribution to the general store. The stores were landed in safety, and the boat, returning, brought back from the improvised post-office there a dozen or more letters, most of them left by whale-men, with the request that the first homeward-bound ship would carry them along and see to their mailing, which had been the custom of this strange postal service for many years. Some of the letters brought back by our boat were directed to New Bedford, and some to Fairhaven, Massachusetts.

There is a light to-day on Booby Island, and regular packet communication with the rest of the world, and the beautiful uncertainty of the fate of letters left there is a thing of the past. I made no call at the little island, but standing close in, exchanged signals with the keeper of the light. Sailing on, the sloop was at once in the Arafura Sea, where for days she sailed in water milky white and green and purple. It was my good fortune to enter the sea on the last quarter of the moon, the advantage being that in the dark nights I witnessed the phosphorescent light effect at night in its greatest splendor. The sea, where the sloop disturbed it, seemed all ablaze, so that by its light I could see the smallest articles on deck, and her wake was a path of fire.

On the 25th of June the sloop was already clear of all the shoals and dangers, and was sailing on a smooth sea as steadily as before, but with speed somewhat slackened. I got out the flying-jib made at Juan Fernandez, and set it as a spinnaker from the stoutest bamboo that Mrs. Stevenson had given me at Samoa. The spinnaker pulled like a sodger, and the bamboo holding its own, the *Spray* mended her pace.

Several pigeons flying across to-day from Australia toward the islands bent their course over the *Spray*. Smaller birds were seen flying in the opposite direction. In the part of the Arafura that I came to first, where it was shallow, sea-snakes writhed about on the surface and tumbled over and over in the waves. As the sloop sailed farther on, where the sea became deep, they disappeared. In the ocean, where the water is blue, not one was ever seen.

In the days of serene weather there was not much to do but to read and take rest on the *Spray,* to make up as much as possible for the rough time off Cape Horn, which was not yet forgotten, and to forestall the Cape of Good Hope by a store of ease. My sea journal was now much the same from day to day—something like this of June 26 and 27, for example:

June 26, in the morning, it is a bit squally; later in the day blowing a steady breeze.

On the log at noon is	130	miles
Subtract correction for slip	10	"
	120	"
Add for current	10	"
	130	"

Latitude by observation at noon, 10° 25′ S.
Longitude as per mark on the chart.

There wasn't much brain-work in that log, I'm sure. June 27 makes a better showing, when all is told:

First of all, to-day, was a flying-fish on deck; fried it in butter.
133 miles on the log.
For slip, off, and for current, on, as per guess, about equal—let it go at that.
Latitude by observation at noon, 10° 25′ S.

For several days now the *Spray* sailed west on the parallel of 10° 25′ S., as true as a hair. If she deviated at all from that, through the day or night,—and this may have happened,—she was back, strangely enough, at noon, at the same latitude. But the greatest science was in reckoning the longitude. My tin clock and only time-piece had by this time lost its minute-hand, but after I boiled her she told the hours, and that was near enough on a long stretch.

On the 2d of July the great island of Timor was in view away to the nor'ard. On the following day I saw Dana Island, not far off, and a breeze came up from the land at night, fragrant of the spices or what not of the coast.

On the 11th, with all sail set and with the spinnaker still abroad, Christmas Island, about noon, came into view one point on the starboard bow. Before night it was abeam and distant two and a half miles. The surface of the island appeared evenly rounded from the sea to a considerable height in the center. In outline it was as smooth as a fish, and a long ocean swell, rolling up, broke against the sides, where it lay like a monster asleep, motionless on the sea. It seemed to have the proportions of a whale, and as the sloop sailed along its side to the part where the head would be, there was a nostril, even, which was a blow-hole through a ledge of rock where every wave that dashed threw up a shaft of water, lifelike and real.

It had been a long time since I last saw this island; but I remember my temporary admiration for the captain of the ship I was then in, the *Tanjore,* when he sang out one morning from the quarter-deck, well aft, "Go aloft there, one of ye, with a pair of eyes, and see Christmas Island." Sure enough, there the island was in sight from the royal-yard. Captain M—— had thus made a great hit, and he never got over it. The chief mate, terror of us ordinaries in the ship, walking never to windward of the captain, now took himself very humbly to leeward altogether. When we arrived at Hong-Kong there was a letter in the ship's mail for me. I was in the boat with the captain some hours while he had it. But do you suppose he could hand a letter to a seaman? No, indeed; not even to an ordinary seaman. When we got to the ship he gave it to the first mate; the first mate gave it to the second mate, and he laid it, michingly, on the capstan-head, where I could get it!

Chapter 16

To the Keeling Cocos Islands was now only five hundred and fifty miles; but even in this short run it was necessary to be extremely careful in keeping a true course else I would miss the atoll.

On the 12th, some hundred miles southwest of Christmas Island, I saw anti-trade clouds flying up from the southwest very high over the regular winds, which weakened now for a few days, while a swell heavier than usual set in also from the southwest. A winter gale was going on in the direction of the Cape of Good Hope.

Accordingly, I steered higher to windward, allowing twenty miles a day while this went on, for change of current; and it was not too much, for on that course I made the Keeling Islands right ahead. The first unmistakable sign of the land was a visit one morning from a white tern that fluttered very knowingly about the vessel, and then took itself off westward with a businesslike air in its wing. The tern is called by the islanders the "pilot of Keeling Cocos." Farther on I came among a great number of birds fishing, and fighting over whatever they caught. My reckoning was up, and springing aloft, I saw from half-way up the mast cocoanut-trees standing out of the water ahead. I expected to see this; still, it thrilled me as an electric shock might have done. I slid down the mast, trembling under the strangest sensations; and not able to resist the impulse, I sat on deck and gave way to my emotions. To folks in a parlor on shore this may seem weak indeed, but I am telling the story of a voyage alone.

I didn't touch the helm, for with the current and heave of the sea the sloop found herself at the end of the run absolutely in the fairway of the channel. You couldn't have beaten it in the navy! Then I trimmed her sails by the wind, took the helm, and flogged her up the couple of miles or so abreast the harbor landing, where I cast anchor at 3:30 P.M., July 17, 1897, twenty-three days from Thursday Island. The distance run was twenty-seven hundred miles as the crow flies. This would have been a fair Atlantic voyage. It was a delightful sail! During those twenty-three days I had not spent altogether more than three hours at the helm, including the time occupied in beating into Keeling harbor. I just lashed the helm and let her go; whether the wind was abeam or dead aft, it was all the same: she always sailed on her course. No part of the voyage up to this point, taking it by and large, had been so finished as this.[1]

[1] Mr. Andrew J. Leach, reporting, July 21, 1897, through Governor Kynnersley of Singapore, to Joseph Chamberlain, Colonial Secretary, said concerning the *Iphegenia's* visit to the atoll: "As we left the ocean depths of deepest blue and entered the coral circle, the contrast was most remarkable. The brilliant colors of the waters, transparent to a depth of over thirty feet, now purple, now of the bluest sky-blue, and now green, with the white crests of the waves flashing under a brilliant sun, the encircling . . . palm-clad islands, the gaps between which were to the south undiscernible, the white sand shores and the whiter gaps where breakers appeared, and, lastly, the lagoon itself, seven or eight miles across from north to south, and five to six from

Sailing Alone Around the World

The Keeling Cocos Islands, according to Admiral Fitzroy, R.N., lie between the latitudes of 11° 50′ and 12° 12′ S., and the longitudes of 96° 51′ and 96° 58′ E. They were discovered in 1608-9 by Captain William Keeling, then in the service of the East India Company. The southern group consists of seven or eight islands and islets on the atoll, which is the skeleton of what some day, according to the history of coral reefs, will be a continuous island. North Keeling has no harbor, is seldom visited, and is of no importance. The South Keelings are a strange little world, with a romantic history all their own. They have been visited occasionally by the floating spar of some hurricane-swept ship, or by a tree that has drifted all the way from Australia, or by an ill-starred ship cast away, and finally by man. Even a rock once drifted to Keeling, held fast among the roots of a tree.

After the discovery of the islands by Captain Keeling, their first notable visitor was Captain John Clunis-Ross, who in 1814 touched in the ship *Borneo* on a voyage to India. Captain Ross returned two years later with his wife and family and his mother-in-law, Mrs. Dymoke, and eight sailor-artisans, to take possession of the islands, but found there already one Alexander Hare, who meanwhile had marked the little atoll as a sort of Eden for a seraglio of Malay women which he moved over from the coast of Africa. It was Ross's own brother, oddly enough, who freighted Hare and his crowd of women to the islands, not knowing of Captain John's plans to occupy the little world. And so Hare was there with his outfit, as if he had come to stay.

On his previous visit, however, Ross had nailed the English Jack to a mast on Horsburg Island, one of the group. After two years shreds of it still fluttered in the wind, and his sailors, nothing loath, began at once the invasion of the new kingdom to take possession of it, women and all. The force of forty women, with only one man

---

east to west, presented a sight never to be forgotten. After some little delay, Mr. Sidney Ross, the eldest son of Mr. George Ross, came off to meet us, and soon after, accompanied by the doctor and another officer, we went ashore.

"On reaching the landing-stage, we found, hauled up for cleaning, etc., the *Spray* of Boston, a yawl of 12.70 tons gross, the property of Captain Joshua Slocum. He arrived at the island on the 17th of July, twenty-three days out from Thursday Island. This extraordinary solitary traveler left Boston some two years ago single-handed, crossed to Gibraltar, sailed down to Cape Horn, passed through the Strait of Magellan to the Society Islands, thence to Australia, and through the Torres Strait to Thursday Island."

to command them, was not equal to driving eight sturdy sailors back into the sea.[1]

From this time on Hare had a hard time of it. He and Ross did not get on well as neighbors. The islands were too small and too near for characters so widely different. Hare had "oceans of money," and might have lived well in London; but he had been governor of a wild colony in Borneo, and could not confine himself to the tame life that prosy civilization affords. And so he hung on to the atoll with his forty women, retreating little by little before Ross and his sturdy crew, till at last he found himself and his harem on the little island known to this day as Prison Island, where, like Bluebeard, he confined his wives in a castle. The channel between the islands was narrow, the water was not deep, and the eight Scotch sailors wore long boots. Hare was now dismayed. He tried to compromise with rum and other luxuries, but these things only made matters worse. On the day following the first St. Andrew's celebration on the island, Hare, consumed with rage, and no longer on speaking terms with the captain, dashed off a note to him, saying: "DEAR ROSS: I thought when I sent rum and roast pig to your sailors that they would stay away from my flower-garden." In reply to which the captain, burning with indignation, shouted from the center of the island, where he stood, "Ahoy, there, on Prison Island! You Hare, don't you know that rum and roast pig are not a sailor's heaven?" Hare said afterward that one might have heard the captain's roar across to Java.

The lawless establishment was soon broken up by the women deserting Prison Island and putting themselves under Ross's protection. Hare then went to Batavia, where he met his death.

My first impression upon landing was that the crime of infanticide had not reached the islands of Keeling Cocos. "The children have all come to welcome you," explained Mr. Ross, as they mustered at the jetty by hundreds, of all ages and sizes. The people of this country were all rather shy, but, young or old, they never passed one or saw one passing their door without a salutation. In their musical voices they would say, "Are you walking?" ("Jalan, jalan?") "Will you come along?" one would answer.

[1] In the accounts given in Findlay's "Sailing Directory" of some of the events there is a chronological discrepancy. I follow the accounts gathered from the old captain's grandsons and from records on the spot.

Sailing Alone Around the World

For a long time after I arrived the children regarded the "one-man ship" with suspicion and fear. A native man had been blown away to sea many years before, and they hinted to one another that he might have been changed from black to white, and returned in the sloop. For some time every movement I made was closely watched. They were particularly interested in what I ate. One day, after I had been "boot-topping" the sloop with a composition of coal-tar and other stuff, and while I was taking my dinner, with the luxury of blackberry jam, I heard a commotion, and then a yell and a stampede, as the children ran away yelling: "The captain is eating coal-tar! The captain is eating coal-tar!" But they soon found out that this same "coal-tar" was very good to eat, and that I had brought a quantity of it. One day when I was spreading a sea-biscuit thick with it for a wide-awake youngster, I heard them whisper, "Chut-chut!" meaning that a shark had bitten my hand, which they observed was lame. Thenceforth they regarded me as a hero, and I had not fingers enough for the little bright-eyed tots that wanted to cling to them and follow me about. Before this, when I held out my hand and said, "Come!" they would shy off for the nearest house, and say, "Dingin" ("It's cold"), or "Ujan" ("It's going to rain"). But it was now accepted that I was not the returned spirit of the lost black, and I had plenty of friends about the island, rain or shine.

One day after this, when I tried to haul the sloop and found her fast in the sand, the children all clapped their hands and cried that a *kpeting* (crab) was holding her by the keel; and little Ophelia, ten or twelve years of age, wrote in the *Spray's* log-book:

> A hundred men with might and main
> On the windlass hove, yeo ho!
> The cable only came in twain;
> The ship she would not go;
> For, child, to tell the strangest thing,
> The keel was held by a great kpeting.

This being so or not, it was decided that the Mohammedan priest, Sama the Emim, for a pot of jam, should ask Mohammed to bless the voyage and make the crab let go the sloop's keel, which it did, if it had hold, and she floated on the very next tide.

On the 22d of July arrived H.M.S. *Iphegenia*, with Mr. Justice Andrew J. Leech and court officers on board, on a circuit of inspection among the Straits Settlements, of which Keeling Cocos was a dependency, to hear complaints and try cases by law, if any there were to try. They found the *Spray* hauled ashore and tied to a cocoa-nut-tree. But at the Keeling Islands there had not been a grievance to complain of since the day that Hare migrated, for the Rosses have always treated the islanders as their own family.

If there is a paradise on this earth it is Keeling. There was not a case for a lawyer, but something had to be done, for here were two ships in port, a great man-of-war and the *Spray*. Instead of a lawsuit a dance was got up, and all the officers who could leave their ship came ashore. Everybody on the island came, old and young, and the governor's great hall was filled with people. All that could get on their feet danced, while the babies lay in heaps in the corners of the room, content to look on. My little friend Ophelia danced with the judge. For music two fiddles screeched over and over again the good old tune, "We won't go home till morning." And we did not.

The women at the Keelings do not do all the drudgery, as in many places visited on the voyage. It would cheer the heart of a Fuegian woman to see the Keeling lord of creation up a cocoanut-tree. Be-sides cleverly climbing the trees, the men of Keeling build exquisitely modeled canoes. By far the best workmanship in boat-building I saw on the voyage was here. Many finished mechanics dwelt under the palms at Keeling, and the hum of the band-saw and the ring of the anvil were heard from morning till night. The first Scotch settlers left there the strength of Northern blood and the inheritance of steady habits. No benevolent society has ever done so much for any islanders as the noble Captain Ross, and his sons, who have followed his example of industry and thrift.

Admiral Fitzroy of the *Beagle*, who visited here, where many things are reversed, spoke of "these singular though small islands, where crabs eat cocoanuts, fish eat coral, dogs catch fish, men ride on turtles, and shells are dangerous man-traps," adding that the greater part of the sea-fowl roost on branches, and many rats make their nests in the tops of palm-trees.

My vessel being refitted, I decided to load her with the famous mammoth tridacna shell of Keeling, found in the bayou near by. And right here, within sight of the village, I came near losing "the crew of the *Spray*"—not from putting my foot in a man-trap shell, however, but from carelessly neglecting to look after the details of a trip across the harbor in a boat. I had sailed over oceans; I have since completed a course over them all, and sailed round the whole world without so nearly meeting a fatality as on that trip across a lagoon, where I trusted all to some one else, and he, weak mortal that he was, perhaps trusted all to me. However that may be, I found myself with a thoughtless African negro in a rickety bateau that was fitted with a rotten sail, and this blew away in mid-channel in a squall, that sent us drifting helplessly to sea, where we should have been incontinently lost. With the whole ocean before us to leeward, I was dismayed to see, while we drifted, that there was not a paddle or an oar in the boat! There was an anchor, to be sure, but not enough rope to tie a cat, and we were already in deep water. By great good fortune, however, there was a pole. Plying this as a paddle with the utmost energy, and by the merest accidental flaw in the wind to favor us, the trap of a boat was worked into shoal water, where we could touch bottom and push her ashore. With Africa, the nearest coast to leeward, three thousand miles away, with not so much as a drop of water in the boat, and a lean and hungry negro—well, cast the lot as one might, the crew of the *Spray* in a little while would have been hard to find. It is needless to say that I took no more such chances. The tridacna were afterward procured in a safe boat, thirty of them taking the place of three tons of cement ballast, which I threw overboard to make room and give buoyancy.

On August 22, the kpeting, or whatever else it was that held the sloop in the islands, let go its hold, and she swung out to sea under all sail, heading again for home. Mounting one or two heavy rollers on the fringe of the atoll, she cleared the flashing reefs. Long before dark Keeling Cocos, with its thousand souls, as sinless in their lives as perhaps it is possible for frail mortals to be, was left out of sight, astern. Out of sight, I say, except in my strongest affection.

The sea was rugged, and the *Spray* washed heavily when hauled on the wind, which course I took for the island of Rodriguez, and which brought the sea abeam. The true course for the island was west by south, one quarter south, and the distance was nineteen hundred miles; but I steered considerably to the windward of that to allow for the heave of the sea and other leeward effects. My sloop on this course ran under reefed sails for days together. I naturally tired of the never-ending motion of the sea, and, above all, of the wetting I got whenever I showed myself on deck. Under these heavy weather conditions the *Spray* seemed to lag behind on her course; at least, I attributed to these conditions a discrepancy in the log, which by the fifteenth day out from Keeling amounted to one hundred and fifty miles between the rotator and the mental calculations I had kept of what she should have gone, and so I kept an eye lifting for land. I could see about sundown this day a bunch of clouds that stood in one spot, right ahead, while the other clouds floated on; this was a sign of something. By midnight, as the sloop sailed on, a black object appeared where I had seen the resting clouds. It was still a long way off, but there could be no mistaking this: it was the high island of Rodriguez. I hauled in the patent log, which I was now towing more from habit than from necessity, for I had learned the *Spray* and her ways long before this. If one thing was clearer than another in her voyage, it was that she could be trusted to come out right and in safety, though at the same time I always stood ready to give her the benefit of even the least doubt. The officers who are over-sure, and "know it all like a book," are the ones, I have observed, who wreck the most ships and lose the most lives. The cause of the discrepancy in the log was one often met with, namely, coming in contact with some large fish; two out of the four blades of the rotator were crushed or bent, the work probably of a shark. Being sure of the sloop's position, I lay down to rest and to think, and I felt better for it. By daylight the island was abeam, about three miles away. It wore a hard, weather-beaten appearance there, all alone, far out in the Indian Ocean, like land adrift. The windward side was uninviting, but there was a good port to leeward, and I hauled in now close on the wind for that. A pilot came out to take me into the inner harbor, which was reached through a narrow channel among coral reefs.

It was a curious thing that at all of the islands some reality was insisted on as unreal, while improbabilities were clothed as hard facts; and so it happened here that the good abbé, a few days before, had been telling his people about the coming of Antichrist, and when they saw the *Spray* sail into the harbor, all feather-white before a gale of wind, and run all standing upon the beach, and with only one man aboard, they cried, "May the Lord help us, it is he, and he has come in a boat!" which I say would have been the most improbable way of his coming. Nevertheless, the news went flying through the place. The governor of the island, Mr. Roberts, came down immediately to see what it was all about, for the little town was in a great commotion. One elderly woman, when she heard of my advent, made for her house and locked herself in. When she heard that I was actually coming up the street she barricaded her doors, and did not come out while I was on the island, a period of eight days. Governor Roberts and his family did not share the fears of their people, but came on board at the jetty, where the sloop was berthed, and their example induced others to come also. The governor's young boys took charge of the *Spray's* dinghy at once, and my visit cost his Excellency, besides great hospitality to me, the building of a boat for them like the one belonging to the *Spray.*

My first day at this Land of Promise was to me like a fairy-tale. For many days I had studied the charts and counted the time of my arrival at this spot, as one might his entrance to the Islands of the Blessed, looking upon it as the terminus of the last long run, made irksome by the want of many things with which, from this time on, I could keep well supplied. And behold, here was the sloop, arrived, and made securely fast to a pier in Rodriguez. On the first evening ashore, in the land of napkins and cut glass, I saw before me still the ghosts of hempen towels and of mugs with handles knocked off. Instead of tossing on the sea, however, as I might have been, here was I in a bright hall, surrounded by sparkling wit, and dining with the governor of the island! "Aladdin," I cried, "where is your lamp? My fisherman's lantern, which I got at Gloucester, has shown me better things than your smoky old burner ever revealed."

The second day in port was spent in receiving visitors. Mrs. Roberts and her children came first to "shake hands," they said, "with the *Spray.*" No one was now afraid to come on board except the poor old woman, who still maintained that the *Spray* had Antichrist in the hold, if, indeed, he had not already gone ashore. The governor entertained that evening, and kindly invited the "destroyer of the world" to speak for himself. This he did, elaborating most effusively on the dangers of the sea (which, after the manner of many of our frailest mortals, he would have had smooth had he made it); also by contrivances of light and darkness he exhibited on the wall pictures of the places and countries visited on the voyage (nothing like the countries, however, that he would have made), and of the people seen, savage and other, frequently groaning, "Wicked world! Wicked world!" When this was finished his Excellency the governor, speaking words of thankfulness, distributed pieces of gold.

On the following day I accompanied his Excellency and family on a visit to San Gabriel, which was up the country among the hills. The good abbé of San Gabriel entertained us all royally at the convent, and we remained his guests until the following day. As I was leaving his place, the abbé said, "Captain, I embrace you, and of whatever religion you may be, my wish is that you succeed in making your voyage, and that our Saviour the Christ be always with you!" To this good man's words I could only say, "My dear abbé, had all religionists been so liberal there would have been less bloodshed in the world."

At Rodriguez one may now find every convenience for filling pure and wholesome water in any quantity, Governor Roberts having built a reservoir in the hills, above the village, and laid pipes to the jetty, where, at the time of my visit, there were five and a half feet at high tide. In former years well-water was used, and more or less sickness occurred from it. Beef may be had in any quantity on the island, and at a moderate price. Sweet potatoes were plentiful and cheap; the large sack of them that I bought there for about four shillings kept unusually well. I simply stored them in the sloop's dry hold. Of fruits, pomegranates were most plentiful; for two shillings I obtained a large sack of them, as many as a donkey could pack from the orchard, which, by the way, was planted by nature herself.

Chapter 17

On the 16th of September, after eight restful days at Rodriguez, the mid-ocean land of plenty, I set sail, and on the 19th arrived at Mauritius, anchoring at quarantine about noon. The sloop was towed in later on the same day by the doctor's launch, after he was satisfied that I had mustered all the crew for inspection. Of this he seemed in doubt until he examined the papers, which called for a crew of one all told from port to port, throughout the voyage. Then finding that I had been well enough to come thus far alone, he gave me pratique without further ado. There was still another official visit for the *Spray* to pass farther in the harbor. The governor of Rodriguez, who had most kindly given me, besides a regular mail, private letters of introduction to friends, told me I should meet, first of all, Mr. Jenkins of the postal service, a good man. "How do you do, Mr. Jenkins?" cried I, as his boat swung alongside. "You don't know me," he said. "Why not?" I replied. "From where is the sloop?" "From around the world," I again replied, very solemnly. "And alone?" "Yes; why not?" "And you know me?" "Three thousand years ago," cried I, "when you and I had a warmer job than we have now" (even this was hot). "You were then Jenkinson, but if you have changed your name I don't blame you for that." Mr. Jenkins, forbearing soul, entered into the spirit of the jest, which served the *Spray* a good turn, for on the strength of this tale it got out that if any one should go on board after dark the devil would get him at once. And so I could leave the *Spray* without the fear of her being robbed at night. The cabin, to be sure, was broken into, but it was done in daylight, and the thieves got no more than a box of smoked herrings before "Tom" Ledson, one of the port officials, caught them red-handed, as it were, and sent them to jail. This was discouraging to pilferers, for they feared Ledson more than they feared Satan himself. Even Mamode Hajee Ayoob, who was the day-watchman on board,—till an empty box fell over in the cabin and frightened him out of his wits,—could not be hired to watch nights, or even till the sun went down. "Sahib," he cried, "there is no need of it," and what he said was perfectly true.

At Mauritius, where I drew a long breath, the *Spray* rested her wings, it being the season of fine weather. The hardships of the voyage, if there had been any, were now computed by officers of experience as nine tenths finished, and yet somehow I could not forget that the United States was still a long way off.

The kind people of Mauritius, to make me richer and happier, rigged up the opera-house, which they had named the "Ship *Pantai*." [1] All decks and no bottom was this ship, but she was as stiff as a church. They gave me free use of it while I talked over the *Spray's* adventures. His Honor the mayor introduced me to his Excellency the governor from the poop-deck of the *Pantai*. In this way I was also introduced again to our good consul, General John

[1] Guinea-hen.

P. Campbell, who had already introduced me to his Excellency. I was becoming well acquainted, and was in for it now to sail the voyage over again. How I got through the story I hardly know. It was a hot night, and I could have choked the tailor who made the coat I wore for this occasion. The kind governor saw that I had done my part trying to rig like a man ashore, and he invited me to Government House at Reduit, where I found myself among friends.

It was winter still off stormy Cape of Good Hope, but the storms might whistle there. I determined to see it out in milder Mauritius, visiting Rose Hill, Curipepe, and other places on the island. I spent a day with the elder Mr. Roberts, father of Governor Roberts of Rodriguez, and with his friends the Very Reverend Fathers O'Loughlin and McCarthy. Returning to the *Spray* by way of the great flower conservatory near Moka, the proprietor, having only that morning discovered a new and hardy plant, to my great honor named it "Slocum," which he said Latinized it at once, saving him some trouble on the twist of a word; and the good botanist seemed pleased that I had come. How different things are in different countries! In Boston, Massachusetts, at that time, a gentleman, so I was told, paid thirty thousand dollars to have a flower named after his wife, and it was not a big flower either, while "Slocum," which came without the asking, was bigger than a mangel-wurzel!

I was royally entertained at Moka, as well as at Reduit and other places—once by seven young ladies, to whom I spoke of my inability to return their hospitality except in my own poor way of taking them on a sail in the sloop. "The very thing! The very thing!" they all cried. "Then please name the time," I said, as meek as Moses. "To-morrow!" they all cried. "And, aunty, we may go, mayn't we, and we'll be real good for a whole week afterward, aunty! Say yes, aunty dear!" All this after saying "To-morrow"; for girls in Mauritius are, after all, the same as our girls in America; and their dear aunt said "Me, too" about the same as any really good aunt might say in my own country.

I was then in a quandary, it having recurred to me that on the very "to-morrow" I was to dine with the harbor-master, Captain Wilson. However, I said to myself, "The *Spray* will run out quickly into rough seas; these young ladies will have *mal de mer* and a good time, and I'll get in early enough to be at the dinner, after all." But not a bit of it. We sailed almost out of sight of Mauritius, and they just stood up and laughed at seas tumbling aboard, while I was at the helm making the worst weather of it I could, and spinning yarns to the aunt about sea-serpents and whales. But she, dear lady, when I had finished with stories of monsters, only hinted at a basket of provisions they had brought along, enough to last a week, for I had told them about my wretched steward.

The more the *Spray* tried to make these young ladies seasick, the more they all clapped their hands and said, "How lovely it is!" and "How beautifully she skims over the sea!" and "How beautiful our island appears from the distance!" and they still cried, "Go on!" We were fifteen miles or more at sea before they ceased the eager cry, "Go on!" Then the sloop swung round, I still hoping to be back to Port Louis in time to keep my appointment. The *Spray* reached the island quickly, and flew along the coast fast enough; but I made a mistake in steering along the coast on the way home, for as we came abreast of Tombo Bay it enchanted my crew. "Oh, let's anchor here!" they cried. To this no sailor in the world would have said nay. The sloop came to anchor, ten minutes later, as they wished, and a young man on the cliff abreast, waving his hat, cried, *"Vive la Spray!"* My passengers said, "Aunty, mayn't we have a swim in the surf along the shore?" Just then the harbor-master's launch hove in sight, coming out to meet us; but it was too late to get the sloop into Port Louis that night. The launch was in time, however, to land my fair crew for a swim; but they were determined not to desert the ship. Meanwhile I prepared a roof for the night on deck with the sails, and a Bengali man-servant arranged the evening meal. That night the *Spray* rode in Tombo Bay with her precious freight. Next morning bright and early, even before the stars were gone, I awoke to hear praying on deck.

The port officers' launch reappeared later in the morning, this time with Captain Wilson himself on board, to try his luck in getting the *Spray* into port, for he had heard of our predicament. It was worth something to hear a friend tell afterward how earnestly the good harbor-master of Mauritius said, "I'll find the *Spray* and I'll get her into port." A merry crew he discovered on her. They could hoist sails like old tars, and could trim them, too. They could tell all about the ship's "hoods," and one should have seen them clap a bonnet on the jib. Like the deepest of deep-water sailors, they could heave the lead, and—as I hope to see Mauritius again!—any of them could have put the sloop in stays. No ship ever had a fairer crew.

The voyage was the event of Port Louis; such a thing as young ladies sailing about the harbor, even, was almost unheard of before.

While at Mauritius the *Spray* was tendered the use of the military dock free of charge, and was thoroughly refitted by the port authorities. My sincere gratitude is also due other friends for many things needful for the voyage put on board, including bags of sugar from some of the famous old plantations.

The favorable season now set in, and thus well equipped, on the 26th of October, the *Spray* put to sea. As I sailed before a light wind the island receded slowly, and on the following day I could still see the Puce Mountain near Moka. The *Spray* arrived next day off Galets, Réunion, and a pilot came out and spoke her. I handed him a Mauritius paper and continued on my voyage; for rollers were running heavily at the time, and it was not practicable to make a landing. From Réunion I shaped a course direct for Cape St. Mary, Madagascar.

The sloop was now drawing near the limits of the trade-wind, and the strong breeze that had carried her with free sheets the many thousands of miles from Sandy Cape, Australia, fell lighter each day until October 30, when it was altogether calm, and a motionless sea held her in a hushed world. I furled the sails at evening, sat down on deck, and enjoyed the vast stillness of the night.

October 31 a light east-northeast breeze sprang up, and the sloop passed Cape St. Mary about noon. On the 6th, 7th, 8th, and 9th of November, in the Mozambique Channel, she experienced a hard gale of wind from the southwest. Here the *Spray* suffered as much as she did anywhere, except off Cape Horn. The thunder and lightning preceding this gale were very heavy. From this point until the sloop arrived off the coast of Africa, she encountered a succession of gales of wind, which drove her about in many directions, but on the 17th of November she arrived at Port Natal.

This delightful place is the commercial center of the "Garden Colony," Durban itself, the city, being the continuation of a garden. The signalman from the bluff station reported the *Spray* fifteen miles off. The wind was freshening, and when she was within eight miles he said: "The *Spray* is shortening sail; the mainsail was reefed and set in ten minutes. One man is doing all the work."

This item of news was printed three minutes later in a Durban morning journal, which was handed to me when I arrived in port. I could not verify the time it had taken to reef the sail, for, as I have already said, the minute-hand of my timepiece was gone. I only knew that I reefed as quickly as I could.

The same paper, commenting on the voyage, said: "Judging from the stormy weather which has prevailed off this coast during the past few weeks, the *Spray* must have had a very stormy voyage from Mauritius to Natal." Doubtless the weather would have been called stormy by sailors in any ship, but it caused the *Spray* no more inconvenience than the delay natural to head winds generally.

The question of how I sailed the sloop alone, often asked, is best answered, perhaps, by a Durban newspaper. I would shrink from repeating the editor's words but for the reason that undue estimates have been made of the amount of skill and energy required to sail a sloop of even the *Spray's* small tonnage. I heard a man who called himself a sailor say that "it would require three men to do what it was claimed" that I did alone, and what I found perfectly easy to do over and over again; and I have heard that others made similar nonsensical remarks, adding that I would work myself to death. But here is what the Durban paper said:

As briefly noted yesterday, the *Spray*, with a crew of one man, arrived at this port yesterday afternoon on her cruise round the world. The *Spray* made quite an auspicious entrance to Natal. Her commander sailed his craft right up the channel past the main wharf, and dropped his anchor near the old *Forerunner* in the creek, before any one had a chance to get on board. The *Spray* was naturally an object of great curiosity to the Point people, and her arrival was witnessed by a large crowd. The skilful manner in which Captain Slocum steered his craft about the vessels which were occupying the waterway was a treat to witness.

The *Spray* was not sailing in among greenhorns when she came to Natal. When she arrived off the port the pilot-ship, a fine, able steam-tug, came out to meet her, and led the way in across the bar, for it was blowing a smart gale and was too rough for the sloop to be towed with safety. The trick of going in I learned by watching the steamer; it was simply to keep on the windward side of the channel and take the combers end on.

I found that Durban supported two yacht-clubs, both of them full

348

of enterprise. I met all the members of both clubs, and sailed in the crack yacht *Florence* of the Royal Natal, with Captain Spradbrow and the Right Honorable Harry Escombe, premier of the colony. The yacht's center-board plowed furrows through the mud-banks, which, according to Mr. Escombe, Spradbrow afterward planted with potatoes. The *Florence,* however, won races while she tilled the skipper's land. After our sail on the *Florence* Mr. Escombe offered to sail the *Spray* round the Cape of Good Hope for me, and hinted at his famous cribbage-board to while away the hours. Spradbrow, in retort, warned me of it. Said he, "You would be played out of the sloop before you could round the cape." By others it was not thought probable that the premier of Natal would play cribbage off the Cape of Good Hope to win even the *Spray.*

It was a matter of no small pride to me in South Africa to find that American humor was never at a discount, and one of the best American stories I ever heard was told by the premier. At Hotel Royal one day, dining with Colonel Saunderson, M.P., his son, and Lieutenant Tipping, I met Mr. Stanley. The great explorer was just from Pretoria, and had already as good as flayed President Krüger with his trenchant pen. But that did not signify, for everybody has a whack at Oom Paul, and no one in the world seems to stand the joke better than he, not even the Sultan of Turkey himself. The colonel introduced me to the explorer, and I hauled close to the wind, to go slow, for Mr. Stanley was a nautical man once himself,—on the Nyanza, I think,—and of course my desire was to appear in the best light before a man of his experience. He looked me over carefully, and said, "What an example of patience!" "Patience is all that is required," I ventured to reply. He then asked if my vessel had water-tight compartments. I explained that she was all water-tight and all compartment. "What if she should strike a rock?" he asked. "Compartments would not save her if she should hit the rocks lying along her course," said I; adding, "she must be kept away from the rocks." After a considerable pause Mr. Stanley asked, "What if a swordfish should pierce her hull with its sword?" Of course I had thought of that as one of the dangers of the sea, and also of the chance of being struck by lightning. In the case of the swordfish, I ventured to say that "the first thing would be to secure the sword." The colonel invited me to dine with the party on the following day, that we might go further into this matter, and so I had the pleasure of meeting Mr. Stanley a second time, but got no more hints in navigation from the famous explorer.

It sounds odd to hear scholars and statesmen say the world is flat; but it is a fact that three Boers favored by the opinion of President Krüger prepared a work to support that contention. While I was at Durban they came from Pretoria to obtain data from me, and they seemed annoyed when I told them that they could not prove it by my experience. With the advice to call up some ghost of the dark ages for research, I went ashore, and left these three wise men poring over the *Spray's* track on a chart of the world, which, however, proved nothing to them, for it was on Mercator's projection, and behold, it was "flat." The next morning I met one of the party in a clergyman's garb, carrying a large Bible, not different from the one I had read. He tackled me, saying, "If you respect the Word of God, you must admit that the world is flat." "If the Word of God stands on a flat world—" I began. "What!" cried he, losing himself in a passion, and making as if he would run me through with an assagai. "What!" he shouted in astonishment and rage, while I jumped aside to dodge the imaginary weapon. Had this good but misguided fanatic been armed with a real weapon, the crew of the *Spray* would have died a martyr there and then. The next day, seeing him across the street, I bowed and made curves with my hands. He responded with a level, swimming movement of his hands, meaning "the world is flat." A pamphlet by these Transvaal geographers, made up of arguments from sources high and low to prove their theory, was mailed to me before I sailed from Africa on my last stretch around the globe.

While I feebly portray the ignorance of these learned men, I have great admiration for their physical manhood. Much that I saw first and last of the Transvaal and the Boers was admirable. It is well known that they are the hardest of fighters, and as generous to the fallen as they are brave before the foe. Real stubborn bigotry with them is only found among old fogies, and will die a natural death, and that, too, perhaps long before we ourselves are entirely free from bigotry. Education in the Transvaal is by no means neglected, English as well as Dutch being taught to all that can afford both; but the tariff duty on English school-books is heavy, and from necessity the poorer people stick to the Transvaal Dutch and their flat world, just as in Samoa and other islands a mistaken policy has kept the natives down to Kanaka.

350

I visited many public schools at Durban, and had the pleasure of meeting many bright children.

But all fine things must end, and December 14, 1897, the "crew" of the *Spray*, after having a fine time in Natal, swung the sloop's dinghy in on deck, and sailed with a morning land-wind, which carried her clear of the bar, and again she was "off on her alone," as they say in Australia.

Chapter 18

The Cape of Good Hope was now the most prominent point to pass. From Table Bay I could count on the aid of brisk trades, and then the *Spray* would soon be at home. On the first day out from Durban it fell calm, and I sat thinking about these things and the end of the voyage. The distance to Table Bay, where I intended to call, was about eight hundred miles over what might prove a rough sea. The early Portuguese navigators, endowed with patience, were more than sixty-nine years struggling to round this cape before they got as far as Algoa Bay, and there the crew mutinied. They landed on a small island, now called Santa Cruz, where they devoutly set up the cross, and swore they would cut the captain's throat if he attempted to sail farther. Beyond this they thought was the edge of the world, which they too believed was flat; and fearing that their ship would sail over the brink of it, they compelled Captain Diaz, their commander, to retrace his course, all being only too glad to get home. A year later, we are told, Vasco da Gama sailed successfully round the "Cape of Storms," as the Cape of Good Hope was then called, and discovered Natal on Christmas or Natal day; hence the name. From this point the way to India was easy.

Gales of wind sweeping round the cape even now were frequent enough, one occurring, on an average, every thirty-six hours; but one gale was much the same as another, with no more serious result than to blow the *Spray* along on her course when it was fair, or to blow her back somewhat when it was ahead. On Christmas, 1897, I came to the pitch of the cape. On this day the *Spray* was trying to stand on her head, and she gave me every reason to believe that she would accomplish the feat before night. She began very early in the morning to pitch and toss about in a most unusual manner, and I have to record that, while I was at the end of the bowsprit reefing the jib, she ducked me under water three times for a Christmas box. I got wet and did not like it a bit: never in any other sea was I put under more than once in the same short space of time, say three minutes. A large English steamer passing ran up the signal, "Wishing you a Merry Christmas." I think the captain was a humorist; his own ship was throwing her propeller out of water.

Two days later, the *Spray,* having recovered the distance lost in the gale, passed Cape Agulhas in company with the steamship *Scotsman,* now with a fair wind. The keeper of the light on Agulhas exchanged signals with the *Spray* as she passed, and afterward wrote me at New York congratulations on the completion of the voyage. He seemed to think the incident of two ships of so widely different types passing his cape together worthy of a place on canvas, and he went about having the picture made. So I gathered from his letter. At lonely stations like this hearts grow responsive and sympathetic, and even poetic. This feeling was shown toward the *Spray* along many a rugged coast, and reading many a kind signal thrown out to her gave one a grateful feeling for all the world.

One more gale of wind came down upon the *Spray* from the west after she passed Cape Agulhas, but that one she dodged by getting into Simons Bay. When it moderated she beat around the Cape of Good Hope, where they say the *Flying Dutchman* is still sailing. The voyage then seemed as good as finished; from this time on I knew that all, or nearly all, would be plain sailing.

Here I crossed the dividing-line of weather. To the north it was clear and settled, while south it was humid and squally, with, often enough, as I have said, a treacherous gale. From the recent hard weather the *Spray* ran into a calm under Table Mountain, where she lay quietly till the generous sun rose over the land and drew a breeze in from the sea.

The steam-tug *Alert,* then out looking for ships, came to the *Spray* off the Lion's Rump, and in lieu of a larger ship towed her into port. The sea being smooth, she came to anchor in the bay off the city of Cape Town, where she remained a day, simply to rest clear of the bustle of commerce. The good harbor-master sent his steam-launch to bring the sloop to a berth in dock at once, but I preferred to remain for one day alone, in the quiet of a smooth sea, enjoying the retrospect of the passage of the two great capes. On the following morning the *Spray* sailed into the Alfred Dry-docks, where she remained for about three months in the care of the port authorities, while I traveled the country over from Simons Town to Pretoria, being accorded by the colonial government a free railroad pass over all the land.

The trip to Kimberley, Johannesburg, and Pretoria was a pleasant one. At the last-named place I met Mr. Krüger, the Transvaal president. His Excellency received me cordially enough; but my friend Judge Beyers, the gentleman who presented me, by mentioning that I was on a voyage around the world, unwittingly gave great offense to the venerable statesman, which we both regretted deeply. Mr. Krüger corrected the judge rather sharply, reminding him that the world is flat. "You don't mean *round* the world," said the president; "it is impossible! You mean *in* the world. Impossible!" he said, "impossible!" and not another word did he utter either to the judge or to me. The judge looked at me and I looked at the judge, who should have known his ground, so to speak, and Mr. Krüger glowered at us both. My friend the judge seemed embarrassed, but I was delighted; the incident pleased me more than anything else that could have happened. It was a nugget of information quarried out of Oom Paul, some of whose sayings are famous. Of the English he said, "They took first my coat and then my trousers." He also said, "Dynamite is the corner-stone of the South African Republic." Only unthinking people call President Krüger dull.

Soon after my arrival at the cape, Mr. Krüger's friend Colonel Saunderson,[1] who had arrived from Durban some time before, invited me to Newlands Vineyard, where I met many agreeable people. His Excellency Sir Alfred Milner, the governor, found time to come aboard with a party. The governor, after making a survey of the deck, found a seat on a box in my cabin; Lady Muriel sat on a keg, and Lady Saunderson sat by the skipper at the wheel, while the colonel, with his kodak, away in the dinghy, took snap shots of the sloop and her distinguished visitors. Dr. David Gill, astronomer royal, who was of the party, invited me the next day to the famous Cape

[1] Colonel Saunderson was Mr. Krüger's very best friend, inasmuch as he advised the president to avast mounting guns.

Observatory. An hour with Dr. Gill was an hour among the stars. His discoveries in stellar photography are well known. He showed me the great astronomical clock of the observatory, and I showed him the tin clock on the *Spray*, and we went over the subject of standard time at sea, and how it was found from the deck of the little sloop without the aid of a clock of any kind. Later it was advertised that Dr. Gill would preside at a talk about the voyage of the *Spray:* that alone secured for me a full house. The hall was packed, and many were not able to get in. This success brought me sufficient money for all my needs in port and for the homeward voyage.

After visiting Kimberley and Pretoria, and finding the *Spray* all right in the docks, I returned to Worcester and Wellington, towns famous for colleges and seminaries, passed coming in, still traveling as the guest of the colony. The ladies of all these institutions of learning wished to know how one might sail round the world alone, which I thought augured of sailing-mistresses in the future instead of sailing-masters. It will come to that yet if we men-folk keep on saying we "can't."

On the plains of Africa I passed through hundreds of miles of rich but still barren land, save for scrub-bushes, on which herds of sheep were browsing. The bushes grew about the length of a sheep apart, and they, I thought, were rather long of body; but there was still room for all. My longing for a foothold on land seized upon me here, where so much of it lay waste; but instead of remaining to plant forests and reclaim vegetation, I returned again to the *Spray* at the Alfred Docks, where I found her waiting for me, with everything in order, exactly as I had left her.

I have often been asked how it was that my vessel and all appurtenances were not stolen in the various ports where I left her for days together without a watchman in charge. This is just how it was: The *Spray* seldom fell among thieves. At the Keeling Islands, at Rodriguez, and at many such places, a wisp of cocoanut fiber in the door-latch, to indicate that the owner was away, secured the goods against even a longing glance. But when I came to a great island nearer home, stout locks were needed; the first night in port things which I had always left uncovered disappeared, as if the deck on which they were stowed had been swept by a sea.

A pleasant visit from Admiral Sir Harry Rawson of the Royal Navy and his family brought to an end the *Spray's* social relations with the

Cape of Good Hope. The admiral, then commanding the South African Squadron, and now in command of the great Channel fleet, evinced the greatest interest in the diminutive *Spray* and her behavior off Cape Horn, where he was not an entire stranger. I have to admit that I was delighted with the trend of Admiral Rawson's questions, and that I profited by some of his suggestions, notwithstanding the wide difference in our respective commands.

On March 26, 1898, the *Spray* sailed from South Africa, the land of distances and pure air, where she had spent a pleasant and profitable time. The steam-tug *Tigre* towed her to sea from her wonted berth at the Alfred Docks, giving her a good offing. The light morning breeze, which scantily filled her sails when the tug let go the tow-line, soon died away altogether, and left her riding over a heavy swell, in full view of Table Mountain and the high peaks of the Cape of Good Hope. For a while the grand scenery served to relieve the monotony. One of the old circumnavigators (Sir Francis Drake, I think), when he first saw this magnificent pile, sang, " 'Tis the fairest thing and the grandest cape I've seen in the whole circumference of the earth."

The view was certainly fine, but one has no wish to linger long to look in a calm at anything, and I was glad to note, finally, the short heaving sea, precursor of the wind which followed on the second day. Seals playing about the *Spray* all day, before the breeze came, looked with large eyes when, at evening, she sat no longer like a lazy bird with folded wings. They parted company now, and the *Spray* soon sailed the highest peaks of the mountains out of sight, and the world changed from a mere panoramic view to the light of a homeward-bound voyage. Porpoises and dolphins, and such other fishes as did not mind making a hundred and fifty miles a day, were her companions now for several days. The wind was from the southeast; this suited the *Spray* well, and she ran along steadily at her best speed, while I dipped into the new books given me at the cape, reading day and night. March 30 was for me a fast-day in honor of them. I read on, oblivious of hunger or wind or sea, thinking that all was going well, when suddenly a comber rolled over the stern and slopped saucily into the cabin, wetting the very book I was reading. Evidently it was time to put in a reef, that she might not wallow on her course.

March 31 the fresh southeast wind had come to stay. The *Spray* was running under a single-reefed mainsail, a whole jib, and a flying-jib besides, set on the Vailima bamboo, while I was reading Stevenson's delightful "Inland Voyage." The sloop was again doing her work smoothly, hardly rolling at all, but just leaping along among the white horses, a thousand gamboling porpoises keeping her company on all sides. She was again among her old friends the flying-fish, interesting denizens of the sea. Shooting out of the waves like arrows, and with outstretched wings, they sailed on the wind in graceful curves; then falling till again they touched the crest of the waves to wet their delicate wings and renew the flight. They made merry the livelong day. One of the joyful sights on the ocean of a bright day is the continual flight of these interesting fish.

One could not be lonely in a sea like this. Moreover, the reading of delightful adventures enhanced the scene. I was now in the *Spray* and on the Oise in the *Arethusa* at one and the same time. And so the *Spray* reeled off the miles, showing a good run every day till April 11, which came almost before I knew it. Very early that morning I was awakened by that rare bird, the booby, with its harsh quack, which I recognized at once as a call to go on deck; it was as much as to say, "Skipper, there's land in sight." I tumbled out quickly, and sure enough, away ahead in the dim twilight, about twenty miles off, was St. Helena.

My first impulse was to call out, "Oh, what a speck in the sea!" It is in reality nine miles in length and two thousand eight hundred and twenty-three feet in height. I reached for a bottle of port-wine out of the locker, and took a long pull from it to the health of my invisible helmsman—the pilot of the *Pinta*.

Chapter 19

It was about noon when the *Spray* came to anchor off Jamestown, and "all hands" at once went ashore to pay respects to his Excellency the governor of the island, Sir R. A. Sterndale. His Excellency, when I landed, remarked that it was not often, nowadays, that a circumnavigator came his way, and he cordially welcomed me, and arranged that I should tell about the voyage, first at Garden Hall to the people of Jamestown, and then at Plantation House—the governor's residence, which is in the hills a mile or two back—to his Excellency and the officers of the garrison and their friends. Mr. Poole, our worthy consul, introduced me at the castle, and in the course of his remarks asserted that the sea-serpent was a Yankee.

Most royally was the crew of the *Spray* entertained by the governor. I remained at Plantation House a couple of days, and one of the rooms in the mansion, called the "west room," being haunted, the butler, by command of his Excellency, put me up in that—like a prince. Indeed, to make sure that no mistake had been made, his Excellency came later to see that I was in the right room, and to tell me all about the ghosts he had seen or heard of. He had discovered all but one, and wishing me pleasant dreams, he hoped I might have the honor of a visit from the unknown one of the west room. For the rest of the chilly night I kept the candle burning, and often looked from under the blankets, thinking that maybe I should meet the great Napoleon face to face; but I saw only furniture, and the horseshoe that was nailed over the door opposite my bed.

St. Helena has been an island of tragedies—tragedies that have been lost sight of in wailing over the Corsican. On the second day of my visit the governor took me by carriage-road through the turns over the island. At one point of our journey the road, in winding around spurs and ravines, formed a perfect W within the distance of a few rods. The roads, though tortuous and steep, were fairly good, and I was struck with the amount of labor it must have cost to build them. The air on the heights was cool and bracing. It is said that, since hanging for trivial offenses went out of fashion, no one has died there, except from falling over the cliffs in old age, or from being crushed by stones rolling on them from the steep mountains! Witches at one time were persistent at St. Helena, as with us in America in the days of Cotton Mather. At the present day crime is rare in the island. While I was there, Governor Sterndale, in token of the fact that not one criminal case had come to court within the year, was presented with a pair of white gloves by the officers of justice.

Returning from the governor's house to Jamestown, I drove with Mr. Clark, a countryman of mine, to "Longwood," the home of Napoleon. M. Morilleau, French consular agent in charge, keeps the place respectable and the buildings in good repair. His family at Longwood, consisting of wife and grown daughters, are natives of courtly and refined manners, and spend here days, months, and years of contentment, though they have never seen the world beyond the horizon of St. Helena.

On the 20th of April the *Spray* was again ready for sea. Before going on board I took luncheon with the governor and his family at the castle. Lady Sterndale had sent a large fruit-cake, early in the morning, from Plantation House, to be taken along on the voyage. It was a great high-decker, and I ate sparingly of it, as I thought, but it did not keep as I had hoped it would. I ate the last of it along with my first cup of coffee at Antigua, West Indies, which, after all, was quite a record. The one my own sister made me at the little island in the Bay of Fundy, at the first of the voyage, kept about the same length of time, namely, forty-two days.

After luncheon a royal mail was made up for Ascension, the island next on my way. Then Mr. Poole and his daughter paid the *Spray* a farewell visit, bringing me a basket of fruit. It was late in the evening before the anchor was up, and I bore off for the west, loath to leave my new friends. But fresh winds filled the sloop's sails once more, and I watched the beacon-light at Plantation House, the governor's parting signal for the *Spray*, till the island faded in the darkness astern and became one with the night, and by midnight the light itself had disappeared below the horizon.

When morning came there was no land in sight, but the day went on the same as days before, save for one small incident. Governor Sterndale had given me a bag of coffee in the husk, and Clark, the American, in an evil moment, had put a goat on board, "to butt the sack and hustle the coffee-beans out of the pods." He urged that the animal, besides being useful, would be as companionable as a dog. I soon found that my sailing-companion, this sort of dog with horns, had to be tied up entirely. The mistake I made was that I did not chain him to the mast instead of tying him with grass ropes less securely, and this I learned to my cost. Except for the first day, before the beast got his sea-legs on, I had no peace of mind. After that, actuated by a spirit born, maybe, of his pasturage, this incarnation of evil threatened to devour everything from flying-jib to sterndavits. He was the worst pirate I met on the whole voyage. He began depredations by eating my chart of the West Indies, in the cabin, one day, while I was about my work for'ard, thinking that the critter was securely tied on deck by the pumps. Alas! there was not a rope in the sloop proof against that goat's awful teeth!

It was clear from the very first that I was having no luck with animals on board. There was the tree-crab from the Keeling Islands. No sooner had it got a claw through its prison-box than my sea-jacket, hanging within reach, was torn to ribbons. Encouraged by this success, it smashed the box open and escaped into my cabin, tearing up things generally, and finally threatening my life in the dark. I had hoped to bring the creature home alive, but this did not prove feasible. Next the goat devoured my straw hat, and so when I arrived in port I had nothing to wear ashore on my head. This last unkind stroke decided his fate. On the 27th of April the *Spray* arrived at Ascension, which is garrisoned by a man-of-war crew, and the boatswain of the island came on board. As he stepped out of his boat the mutinous goat climbed into it, and defied boatswain and crew. I hired them to land the wretch at once, which they were only too willing to do, and there he fell into the hands of a most excellent Scotchman, with the chances that he would never get away. I was destined to sail once more into the depths of solitude, but these experiences had no bad effect upon me; on the contrary, a spirit of charity and even benevolence grew stronger in my nature through the meditations of these supreme hours on the sea.

In the loneliness of the dreary country about Cape Horn I found myself in no mood to make one life less in the world, except in self-defense, and as I sailed this trait of the hermit character grew till the mention of killing food-animals was revolting to me. However well I may have enjoyed a chicken stew afterward at Samoa, a new self rebelled at the thought suggested there of carrying chickens to be slain for my table on the voyage, and Mrs. Stevenson, hearing my protest, agreed with me that to kill the companions of my voyage and eat them would be indeed next to murder and cannibalism.

As to pet animals, there was no room for a noble large dog on the *Spray* on so long a voyage, and a small cur was for many years associated in my mind with hydrophobia. I witnessed once the death of a sterling young German from that dreadful disease, and about the same time heard of the death, also by hydrophobia, of the young gentleman who had just written a line of insurance in his company's books for me. I have seen the whole crew of a ship scamper up the rigging to avoid a dog racing about the decks in a fit. It would never do, I thought, for the crew of the *Spray* to take a canine risk, and with these just prejudices indelibly stamped on my mind, I have, I am afraid, answered impatiently too often the query, "Didn't you have a dog?" with, "I and the dog wouldn't have been very long in the same boat, in any sense." A cat would have been a harmless animal, I dare say, but there was nothing for puss to do on board, and she is an unsociable animal at best. True, a rat got into my vessel at the Keeling Cocos Islands, and another at Rodriguez, along with a centiped stowed away in the hold; but one of them I drove out of the ship, and the other I caught. This is how it was: for the first one with infinite pains I made a trap, looking to its capture and destruction; but the wily rodent, not to be deluded, took the hint and got ashore the day the thing was completed.

It is, according to tradition, a most reassuring sign to find rats coming to a ship, and I had a mind to abide the knowing one of Rodriguez; but a breach of discipline decided the matter against him. While I slept one night, my ship sailing on, he undertook to walk over me, beginning at the crown of my head, concerning which I am always sensitive. I sleep lightly. Before his impertinence had got him even to my nose I cried "Rat!" had him by the tail, and threw him out of the companionway into the sea.

As for the centiped, I was not aware of its presence till the wretched insect, all feet and venom, beginning, like the rat, at my head, wakened me by a sharp bite on the scalp. This also was more than I could tolerate. After a few applications of kerosene the poisonous bite, painful at first, gave me no further inconvenience.

From this on for a time no living thing disturbed my solitude; no insect even was present in my vessel, except the spider and his wife, from Boston, now with a family of young spiders. Nothing, I say, till sailing down the last stretch of the Indian Ocean, where mosquitos came by hundreds from rain-water poured out of the heavens. Simply a barrel of rain-water stood on deck five days, I think, in the sun, then music began. I knew the sound at once; it was the same as heard from Alaska to New Orleans.

Again at Cape Town, while dining out one day, I was taken with the song of a cricket, and Mr. Branscombe, my host, volunteered to capture a pair of them for me. They were sent on board next day in a box labeled, "Pluto and Scamp." Stowing them away in the binnacle in their own snug box, I left them there without food till I got to sea—a few days. I had never heard of a cricket eating anything. It seems that Pluto was a cannibal, for only the wings of poor Scamp were visible when I opened the lid, and they lay broken on the floor of the prison-box. Even with Pluto it had gone hard, for he lay on his back stark and stiff, never to chirrup again.

Ascension Island, where the goat was marooned, is called the Stone Frigate, R.N., and is rated "tender" to the South African Squadron. It lies in 7° 55′ south latitude and 14° 25′ west longitude, being in the very heart of the southeast trade-winds and about eight hundred and forty miles from the coast of Liberia. It is a mass of volcanic matter, thrown up from the bed of the ocean to the height of two thousand eight hundred and eighteen feet at the highest point above sea-level. It is a strategic point, and belonged to Great Britain before it got cold. In the limited but rich soil at the top of the island, among the clouds, vegetation has taken root, and a little scientific farming is carried on under the supervision of a gentleman from Canada. Also a few cattle and sheep are pastured there for the garrison mess. Water storage is made on a large scale. In a word, this heap of cinders and lava rock is stored and fortified, and would stand a siege.

Very soon after the *Spray* arrived I received a note from Captain Blaxland, the commander of the island, conveying his thanks for the royal mail brought from St. Helena, and inviting me to luncheon with him and his wife and sister at headquarters, not far away. It is hardly necessary to say that I availed myself of the captain's hospitality at once. A carriage was waiting at the jetty when I landed, and a sailor, with a broad grin, led the horse carefully up the hill to the captain's house, as if I were a lord of the admiralty, and a governor besides; and he led it as carefully down again when I returned. On the following day I visited the summit among the clouds, the same team being provided, and the same old sailor leading the horse. There was probably not a man on the island at that moment better able to walk than I. The sailor knew that. I finally suggested that we change places. "Let me take the bridle," I said, "and keep the horse from bolting." "Great Stone Frigate!" he exclaimed, as he burst into a laugh, "this 'ere 'oss wouldn't bolt no faster nor a turtle. If I didn't tow 'im 'ard we'd never get into port." I walked most of the way over the steep grades, whereupon my guide, every inch a sailor, became my friend. Arriving at the summit of the island, I met Mr. Schank, the farmer from Canada, and his sister, living very cozily in a house among the rocks, as snug as conies, and as safe. He showed me over the farm, taking me through a tunnel which led from one field to the other, divided by an inaccessible spur of mountain. Mr. Schank said that he had lost many cows and bullocks, as well as sheep, from breakneck over the steep cliffs and precipices. One cow, he said, would sometimes hook another right over a precipice to destruction, and go on feeding unconcernedly. It seemed that the animals on the island farm, like mankind in the wide world, found it all too small.

On the 26th of April, while I was ashore, rollers came in which rendered launching a boat impossible. However, the sloop being securely moored to a buoy in deep water outside of all breakers, she was safe, while I, in the best of quarters, listened to well-told stories among the officers of the Stone Frigate. On the evening of the 29th, the sea having gone down, I went on board and made preparations to start again on my voyage early next day, the boat-swain of the island and his crew giving me a hearty handshake as I embarked at the jetty.

For reasons of scientific interest, I invited in mid-ocean the most thorough investigation concerning the crew-list of the *Spray*. Very few had challenged it, and perhaps few ever will do so henceforth; but for the benefit of the few that may, I wished to clench beyond doubt the fact that it was not at all necessary in the expedition of a sloop around the world to have more than one man for the crew, all told, and that the *Spray* sailed with only one person on board. And so, by appointment, Lieutenant Eagles, the executive officer, in the morning, just as I was ready to sail, fumigated the sloop, rendering it impossible for a person to live concealed below, and proving that only one person was on board when she arrived. A certificate to this effect, besides the official documents from the many consulates, health offices, and custom-houses, will seem to many superfluous; but this story of the voyage may find its way into hands unfamiliar with the business of these offices and of their ways of seeing that a vessel's papers, and, above all, her bills of health, are in order.

The lieutenant's certificate being made out, the *Spray*, nothing loath, now filled away clear of the sea-beaten rocks, and the trade-winds, comfortably cool and bracing, sent her flying along on her course. On May 8, 1898, she crossed the track, homeward bound, that she had made October 2, 1895, on the voyage out. She passed Fernando de Noronha at night, going some miles south of it, and so I did not see the island. I felt a contentment in knowing that the *Spray* had encircled the globe, and even as an adventure alone I was in no way discouraged as to its utility, and said to myself, "Let what will happen, the voyage is now on record." A period was made.

Chapter 20

On May 10 there was a great change in the condition of the sea; there could be no doubt of my longitude now, if any had before existed in my mind. Strange and long-forgotten current ripples pattered against the sloop's sides in grateful music; the tune arrested the ear, and I sat quietly listening to it while the *Spray* kept on her course. By these current ripples I was assured that she was now off St. Roque and had struck the current which sweeps around that cape. The trade-winds, we old sailors say, produce this current, which, in its course from this point forward, is governed by the coast-line of Brazil, Guiana, Venezuela, and, as some would say, by the Monroe Doctrine.

The trades had been blowing fresh for some time, and the current, now at its height, amounted to forty miles a day. This, added to the sloop's run by the log, made the handsome day's work of one hundred and eighty miles on several consecutive days. I saw nothing of the coast of Brazil, though I was not many leagues off and was always in the Brazil current.

I did not know that war with Spain had been declared, and that I might be liable, right there, to meet the enemy and be captured. Many had told me at Cape Town that, in their opinion, war was inevitable, and they said: "The Spaniard will get you! The Spaniard will get you!" To all this I could only say that, even so, he would not get much. Even in the fever-heat over the disaster to the *Maine*

I did not think there would be war; but I am no politician. Indeed, I had hardly given the matter a serious thought when, on the 14th of May, just north of the equator, and near the longitude of the river Amazon, I saw first a mast, with the Stars and Stripes floating from it, rising astern as if poked up out of the sea, and then rapidly appearing on the horizon, like a citadel, the *Oregon!* As she came near I saw that the great ship was flying the signals "C B T," which read, "Are there any men-of-war about?" Right under these flags, and larger than the *Spray's* mainsail, so it appeared, was the yellowest Spanish flag I ever saw. It gave me nightmare some time after when I reflected on it in my dreams.

I did not make out the *Oregon's* signals till she passed ahead, where I could read them better, for she was two miles away, and I had no binoculars. When I had read her flags I hoisted the signal "No," for I had not seen any Spanish men-of-war; I had not been looking for any. My final signal, "Let us keep together for mutual protection," Captain Clark did not seem to regard as necessary. Perhaps my small flags were not made out; anyhow, the *Oregon* steamed on with a rush, looking for Spanish men-of-war, as I learned afterward. The *Oregon's* great flag was dipped beautifully three times to the *Spray's* lowered flag as she passed on. Both had crossed the line only a few hours before. I pondered long that night over the probability of a war risk now coming upon the *Spray* after she had cleared all, or nearly all, the dangers of the sea, but finally a strong hope mastered my fears.

On the 17th of May, the *Spray,* coming out of a storm at daylight, made Devil's Island, two points on the lee bow, not far off. The wind was still blowing a stiff breeze on shore. I could clearly see the dark-gray buildings on the island as the sloop brought it abeam. No flag or sign of life was seen on the dreary place.

Later in the day a French bark on the port tack, making for Cayenne, hove in sight, close-hauled on the wind. She was falling to leeward fast. The *Spray* was also closed-hauled, and was lugging on sail to secure an offing on the starboard tack, a heavy swell in the night having thrown her too near the shore, and now I considered the matter of supplicating a change of wind. I had already enjoyed my share of favoring breezes over the great oceans, and I asked myself if it would be right to have the wind turned now all into my sails while the Frenchman was bound the other way. A head current, which he stemmed, together with a scant wind, was bad enough for him. And so I could only say, in my heart, "Lord, let matters stand as they are, but do not help the Frenchman any more just now, for what would suit him well would ruin me!"

I remembered that when a lad I heard a captain often say in meeting that in answer to a prayer of his own the wind changed from southeast to northwest, entirely to his satisfaction. He was a good man, but did this glorify the Architect—the Ruler of the winds and the waves? Moreover, it was not a trade-wind, as I remember it, that changed for him, but one of the variables which will change when you ask it, if you ask long enough. Again, this man's brother maybe was not bound the opposite way, well content with a fair wind himself, which made all the difference in the world.[1]

On May 18, 1898, is written large in the *Spray's* log-book: "To-night, in latitude 7° 13′ N., for the first time in nearly three years I see the north star." The *Spray* on the day following logged one hundred and forty-seven miles. To this I add thirty-five miles for current sweeping her onward. On the 20th of May, about sunset, the island of Tobago, off the Orinoco, came into view, bearing west by north, distant twenty-two miles. The *Spray* was drawing rapidly toward her home destination. Later at night, while running free along the coast of Tobago, the wind still blowing fresh, I was startled by the sudden flash of breakers on the port bow and not far off. I luffed instantly offshore, and then tacked, heading in for the island. Finding myself, shortly after, close in with the land, I tacked again offshore, but without much altering the bearings of the danger. Sail whichever way I would, it seemed clear that if the sloop weathered the rocks at all it would be a close shave, and I watched with anxiety, while beating against the current, always losing ground. So the matter stood hour after hour, while I watched the flashes of light thrown up as regularly as the beats of the long ocean swells, and always they seemed just a little nearer. It was evidently a coral reef,—of this I had not the slightest doubt,—and a bad reef at that. Worse still, there might be other reefs ahead forming a bight into which the current would sweep me, and where I should be hemmed in and

[1] The Bishop of Melbourne (commend me to his teachings) refused to set aside a day of prayer for rain, recommending his people to husband water when the rainy season was on. In like manner, a navigator husbands the wind, keeping a weather-gage where practicable.

finally wrecked. I had not sailed these waters since a lad, and lamented the day I had allowed on board the goat that ate my chart. I taxed my memory of sea lore, of wrecks on sunken reefs, and of pirates harbored among coral reefs where other ships might not come, but nothing that I could think of applied to the island of Tobago, save the one wreck of Robinson Crusoe's ship in the fiction, and that gave me little information about reefs. I remembered only that in Crusoe's case he kept his powder dry. "But there she booms again," I cried, "and how close the flash is now! Almost aboard was that last breaker! But you'll go by, *Spray,* old girl! 'Tis abeam now! One surge more! and oh, one more like that will clear your ribs and keel!" And I slapped her on the transom, proud of her last noble effort to leap clear of the danger, when a wave greater than the rest threw her higher than before, and, behold, from the crest of it was revealed at once all there was of the reef. I fell back in a coil of rope, speechless and amazed, not distressed, but rejoiced. Aladdin's lamp! My fisherman's own lantern! It was the great revolving light on the island of Trinidad, thirty miles away, throwing flashes over the waves, which had deceived me! The orb of the light was now dipping on the horizon, and how glorious was the sight of it! But, dear Father Neptune, as I live, after a long life at sea, and much among corals, I would have made a solemn declaration to that reef! Through all the rest of the night I saw imaginary reefs, and not knowing what moment the sloop might fetch up on a real one, I tacked off and on till daylight, as nearly as possible in the same track, all for the want of a chart. I could have nailed the St. Helena goat's pelt to the deck.

My course was now for Grenada, to which I carried letters from Mauritius. About midnight of the 22d of May I arrived at the island, and cast anchor in the roads off the town of St. George, entering the inner harbor at daylight on the morning of the 23d, which made forty-two days' sailing from the Cape of Good Hope. It was a good run, and I doffed my cap again to the pilot of the *Pinta.*

Lady Bruce, in a note to the *Spray* at Port Louis, said Grenada was a lovely island, and she wished the sloop might call there on the voyage home. When the *Spray* arrived, I found that she had been fully expected. "How so?" I asked. "Oh, we heard that you were at Mauritius," they said, "and from Mauritius, after meeting Sir Charles Bruce, our old governor, we knew you would come to

Grenada." This was a charming introduction, and it brought me in contact with people worth knowing.

The *Spray* sailed from Grenada on the 28th of May, and coasted along under the lee of the Antilles, arriving at the island of Dominica on the 30th, where, for the want of knowing better, I cast anchor at the quarantine ground; for I was still without a chart of the islands, not having been able to get one even at Grenada. Here I not only met with further disappointment in the matter, but was threatened with a fine for the mistake I made in the anchorage. There were no ships either at the quarantine or at the commercial roads, and I could not see that it made much difference where I anchored. But a negro chap, a sort of deputy harbormaster, coming along, thought it did, and he ordered me to shift to the other anchorage, which, in truth, I had already investigated and did not like, because of the heavier roll there from the sea. And so instead of springing to the sails at once to shift, I said I would leave outright as soon as I could procure a chart, which I begged he would send and get for me. "But I say you mus' move befo' you gets anyt'ing't all," he insisted, and raising his voice so that all the people alongshore could hear him, he added, "An' jes now!" Then he flew into a towering passion when they on shore snickered to see the crew of the *Spray* sitting calmly by the bulwark instead of hoisting sail. "I tell you dis am quarantine," he shouted, very much louder than before. "That's all right, general," I replied; "I want to be quarantined anyhow." "That's right, boss," some one on the beach cried, "that's right; you get quarantined," while others shouted to the deputy to "make de white trash move 'long out o' dat." They were about equally divided on the island for and against me. The man who had made so much fuss over the matter gave it up when he found that I wished to be quarantined, and sent for an all-important half-white, who soon came alongside, starched from clue to earing. He stood in the boat as straight up and down as a fathom of pump-water—a marvel of importance. "Charts!" cried I, as soon as his shirt-collar appeared over the sloop's rail; "have you any charts?" "No, sah," he replied with much-stiffened dignity; "no, sah; cha'ts do'sn't grow on dis island." Not doubting the information, I tripped anchor immediately, as I had intended to do from the first, and made all sail for St. John, Antigua, where I arrived on the 1st of June, having sailed with great caution in midchannel all the way.

The *Spray*, always in good company, now fell in with the port officers' steam-launch at the harbor entrance, having on board Sir Francis Fleming, governor of the Leeward Islands, who, to the delight of "all hands," gave the officer in charge instructions to tow my ship into port. On the following day his Excellency and Lady Fleming, along with Captain Burr, R.N., paid me a visit. The courthouse was tendered free to me at Antigua, as was done also at Grenada, and at each place a highly intelligent audience filled the hall to listen to a talk about the seas the *Spray* had crossed, and the countries she had visited.

Chapter 21

On the 4th of June, 1898, the *Spray* cleared from the United States consulate, and her license to sail single-handed, even round the world, was returned to her for the last time. The United States consul, Mr. Hunt, before handing the paper to me, wrote on it, as General Roberts had done at Cape Town, a short commentary on the voyage. The document, by regular course, is now lodged in the Treasury Department at Washington, D. C.

On June 5, 1898, the *Spray* sailed for a home port, heading first direct for Cape Hatteras. On the 8th of June she passed under the sun from south to north; the sun's declination on that day was 22° 54', and the latitude of the *Spray* was the same just before noon. Many think it is excessively hot right under the sun. It is not necessarily so. As a matter of fact the thermometer stands at a bearable point whenever there is a breeze and a ripple on the sea, even exactly under the sun. It is often hotter in cities and on sandy shores in higher latitudes.

The *Spray* was booming joyously along for home now, making her usual good time, when of a sudden she struck the horse latitudes, and her sail flapped limp in a calm. I had almost forgotten this calm belt, or had come to regard it as a myth. I now found it real, however, and difficult to cross. This was as it should have been, for, after all of the dangers of the sea, the dust-storm on the coast of Africa, the "rain of blood" in Australia, and the war risk when nearing home, a natural experience would have been missing had the calm of the horse latitudes been left out. Anyhow, a philosophical turn of thought now was not amiss, else one's patience would have given out almost at the harbor entrance. The term of her probation was eight days. Evening after evening during this time I read by the light of a candle on deck. There was no wind at all, and the sea became smooth and monotonous. For three days I saw a full-rigged ship on the horizon, also becalmed.

Sargasso, scattered over the sea in bunches, or trailed curiously along down the wind in narrow lanes, now gathered together in great fields, strange sea-animals, little and big, swimming in and out, the most curious among them being a tiny sea-horse which I captured and brought home preserved in a bottle. But on the 18th of June a gale began to blow from the southwest, and the sargasso was dispersed again in windrows and lanes.

On this day there was soon wind enough and to spare. The same might have been said of the sea. The *Spray* was in the midst of the turbulent Gulf Stream itself. She was jumping like a porpoise over the uneasy waves. As if to make up for lost time, she seemed to touch only the high places. Under a sudden shock and strain her rigging began to give out. First the main-sheet strap was carried away, and then the peak halyard-block broke from the gaff. It was time to reef and refit, and so when "all hands" came on deck I went about doing that.

The 19th of June was fine, but on the morning of the 20th another gale was blowing, accompanied by cross-seas that tumbled about and shook things up with great confusion. Just as I was thinking about taking in sail the jibstay broke at the masthead, and fell, jib and all, into the sea. It gave me the strangest sensation to see the bellying sail fall, and where it had been suddenly to see only space. However, I was at the bows, with presence of mind to gather it in on the first wave that rolled up, before it was torn or trailed under the sloop's bottom. I found by the amount of work done in three minutes' or less time that I had by no means grown stiff-jointed on the voyage; anyhow, scurvy had not set in, and being now within a few degrees of home, I might complete the voyage, I thought, without the aid of a doctor. Yes, my health was still good, and I could skip about the decks in a lively manner, but could I climb? The great King Neptune tested me severely at this time, for the stay being gone, the mast itself switched about like a reed, and was not easy to climb; but a gun-tackle purchase was got up, and the stay set taut from the masthead, for I had spare blocks and rope on board with which to rig it, and the jib, with a reef in it, was soon pulling again like a "sodger" for home. Had the *Spray's* mast not been well stepped, however, it would have been "John Walker" when the stay broke. Good work in the building of my vessel stood me always in good stead.

On the 23d of June I was at last tired, tired, tired of baffling squalls and fretful cobble-seas. I had not seen a vessel for days and days, where I had expected the company of at least a schooner now and then. As to the whistling of the wind through the rigging, and the slopping of the sea against the sloop's sides, that was well enough in its way, and we could not have got on without it, the *Spray* and I; but there was so much of it now, and it lasted so long! At noon of that day a winterish storm was upon us from the nor'west. In the Gulf Stream, thus late in June, hailstones were pelting the *Spray*, and lightning was pouring down from the clouds, not in flashes alone, but in almost continuous streams. By slants, however, day and night I worked the sloop in toward the coast, where, on the 25th of June, off Fire Island, she fell into the tornado which, an hour earlier, had swept over New York city with lightning that wrecked buildings and sent trees flying about in splinters; even ships at docks had parted their moorings and smashed into other ships, doing great damage. It was the climax storm of the voyage, but I saw the unmistakable character of it in time to have all snug aboard and receive it under bare poles. Even so, the sloop shivered when it struck her, and she heeled over unwillingly on her beam ends; but rounding to, with a sea-anchor ahead, she righted and faced out the storm. In the midst of the gale I could do no more than look on, for what is a man in a storm like this? I had seen one electric storm on the voyage, off the coast of Madagascar, but it was unlike this one. Here the lightning kept on longer, and thunderbolts fell in the sea all about. Up to this time I was bound for New York; but when all was over I rose, made sail, and hove the sloop round from starboard to port tack, to make for a quiet harbor to think the matter over; and so, under short sail, she reached in for the coast of Long Island, while I sat thinking and watching the lights of coasting-vessels which now began to appear in sight. Reflections of the voyage so nearly finished stole in upon me now; many tunes I had hummed again and again came back once more. I found myself repeating fragments of a hymn often sung by a dear Christian woman of Fairhaven when I was rebuilding the *Spray*. I was to hear once more and only once, in profound solemnity, the metaphorical hymn:

> By waves and wind I'm tossed and driven.

And again:

> But still my little ship outbraves
> The blust'ring winds and stormy waves.

After this storm I saw the pilot of the *Pinta* no more.

The experiences of the voyage of the *Spray*, reaching over three years, had been to me like reading a book, and one that was more and more interesting as I turned the pages, till I had come now to the last page of all, and the one more interesting than any of the rest.

When daylight came I saw that the sea had changed color from dark green to light. I threw the lead and got soundings in thirteen fathoms. I made the land soon after, some miles east of Fire Island, and sailing thence before a pleasant breeze along the coast, made for Newport. The weather after the furious gale was remarkably fine. The *Spray* rounded Montauk Point early in the afternoon; Point Judith was abeam at dark; she fetched in at Beavertail next. Sailing on, she had one more danger to pass—Newport harbor was mined. The *Spray* hugged the rocks along where neither friend nor foe could come if drawing much water, and where she would not disturb the guard-ship in the channel. It was close work, but it was safe enough so long as she hugged the rocks close, and not the mines. Flitting by a low point abreast of the guard-ship, the dear old *Dexter*, which I knew well, some one on board of her sang out, "There goes a craft!" I threw up a light at once and heard the hail, "*Spray*, ahoy!" It was the voice of a friend, and I knew that a friend would not fire on the *Spray*. I eased off the main-sheet now, and the *Spray* swung off for the beacon-lights of the inner harbor. At last she reached port in safety, and there at 1 A.M. on June 27, 1898, cast anchor, after the cruise of more than forty-six thousand miles round the world, during an absence of three years and two months, with two days over for coming up.

Was the crew well? Was I not? I had profited in many ways by the voyage. I had even gained flesh, and actually weighed a pound more than when I sailed from Boston. As for aging, why, the dial of my life was turned back till my friends all said, "Slocum is young again." And so I was, at least ten years younger than the day I felled the first tree for the construction of the *Spray*.

My ship was also in better condition than when she sailed from Boston on her long voyage. She was still as sound as a nut, and as tight as the best ship afloat. She did not leak a drop—not one drop! The pump, which had been little used before reaching Australia, had not been rigged since that at all.

The first name on the *Spray's* visitors' book in the home port was written by the one who always said, "The *Spray* will come back." The *Spray* was not quite satisfied till I sailed her around to her birthplace, Fairhaven, Massachusetts, farther along. I had myself a desire to return to the place of the very beginning whence I had, as I have said, renewed my age. So on July 3, with a fair wind, she waltzed beautifully round the coast and up the Acushnet River to Fairhaven, where I secured her to the cedar spile driven in the bank to hold her when she was launched. I could bring her no nearer home.

If the *Spray* discovered no continents on her voyage, it may be that there were no more continents to be discovered; she did not seek new worlds, or sail to powwow about the dangers of the seas. The sea has been much maligned. To find one's way to lands already discovered is a good thing, and the *Spray* made the discovery that even the worst sea is not so terrible to a well-appointed ship. No king, no country, no treasury at all, was taxed for the voyage of the *Spray*, and she accomplished all that she undertook to do.

To succeed, however, in anything at all, one should go understandingly about his work and be prepared for every emergency. I see, as I look back over my own small achievement, a kit of not too elaborate carpenters' tools, a tin clock, and some carpet-tacks, not a great many, to facilitate the enterprise as already mentioned in the story. But above all to be taken into account were some years of schooling, where I studied with diligence Neptune's laws, and these laws I tried to obey when I sailed overseas; it was worth the while.

And now, without having wearied my friends, I hope, with detailed scientific accounts, theories, or deductions, I will only say that I have endeavored to tell just the story of the adventure itself. This, in my own poor way, having been done, I now moor ship, weather-bitt cables, and leave the sloop *Spray,* for the present, safe in port.

From a feeling of diffidence toward sailors of great experience, I refrained, in the preceding chapters as prepared for serial publication in the "Century Magazine," from entering fully into the details of the *Spray's* build, and of the primitive methods employed to sail her. Having had no yachting experience at all, I had no means of knowing that the trim vessels seen in our harbors and near the land could not all do as much, or even more, than the *Spray*, sailing, for example, on a course with the helm lashed.

I was aware that no other vessel had sailed in this manner around the globe, but would have been loath to say that another could not do it, or that many men had not sailed vessels of a certain rig in that manner as far as they wished to go. I was greatly amused, therefore, by the flat assertions of an expert that it could not be done.

The *Spray*, as I sailed her, was entirely a new boat, built over from a sloop which bore the same name, and which, tradition said, had first served as an oysterman, about a hundred years ago, on the coast of Delaware. There was no record in the custom-house of where she was built. She was once owned at Noank, Connecticut, afterward in New Bedford and when Captain Eben Pierce presented her to me, at the end of her natural life, she stood, as I have already described, propped up in a field at Fairhaven. Her lines were supposed to be those of a North Sea fisherman. In rebuilding timber by timber and plank by plank, I added to her freeboard twelve inches amidships, eighteen inches forward, and fourteen inches aft, thereby increasing her sheer, and making her, as I thought, a better deep-water ship. I will not repeat the history of the rebuilding of

374

the *Spray*, which I have detailed in my first chapter, except to say that, when finished, her dimensions were thirty-six feet nine inches over all, fourteen feet two inches wide, and four feet two inches deep in the hold, her tonnage being nine tons net, and twelve and seventy one-hundredths tons gross.

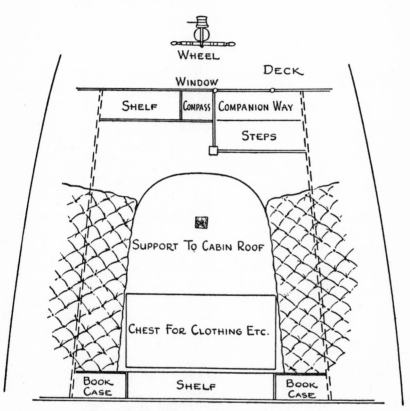

Plan of the After-cabin of the *Spray*

I gladly produce the lines of the *Spray*, with such hints as my really limited fore-and-aft sailing will allow, my seafaring life having been spent mostly in barks and ships. No pains have been spared to give them accurately. The *Spray* was taken from New York to Bridgeport, Connecticut, and, under the supervision of the Park City Yacht Club, was hauled out of water and very carefully measured in every way to secure a satisfactory result. Captain Robins produced the model. Our young yachtsmen, pleasuring in the "lilies of the sea," very naturally will not think favorably of my craft. They have a right to their opinion, while I stick to mine. They will take exceptions to her short ends, the advantage of these being most apparent in a heavy sea.

Some things about the *Spray's* deck might be fashioned differently without materially affecting the vessel. I know of no good reason why for a party-boat a cabin trunk might not be built amidships instead of far aft, like the one on her, which leaves a very narrow space between the wheel and the line of the companionway. Some even say that I might have improved the shape of her stern. I do not know about that. The water leaves her run sharp after bearing her to the last inch, and no suction is formed by undue cutaway.

Smooth-water sailors say, "Where is her overhang?" They never crossed the Gulf Stream in a nor'easter, and they do not know what is best in all weathers. For your life, build no fantail overhang on a craft going offshore. As a sailor judges his prospective ship by a "blow of the eye" when he takes interest enough to look her over at all, so I judged the *Spray,* and I was not deceived.

In a sloop-rig the *Spray* made that part of her voyage reaching from Boston through the Strait of Magellan, during which she experienced the greatest variety of weather conditions. The yawl-rig then adopted was an improvement only in that it reduced the size of a rather heavy mainsail and slightly improved her steering qualities on the wind. When the wind was aft the jigger was not in use; invariably it was then furled. With her boom broad off and with the wind two points on the quarter the *Spray* sailed her truest course. It never took long to find the amount of helm, or angle of rudder, required to hold her on her course, and when that was found I lashed the wheel with it at that angle. The mainsail then drove her, and the main-jib, with its sheet boused flat amidships or a little to one side or the other, added greatly to the steadying power. Then if the wind was even strong or squally I would sometimes set a flying-jib also, on a pole rigged out on the bow-sprit, with the sheets hauled flat amidships, which was a safe thing to do, even in a gale of wind. A stout downhaul on the gaff was a necessity, because without it the mainsail might not have come down when I wished to lower it in a breeze. The amount of helm required varied according to the amount of wind and its direction. These points are quickly gathered from practice.

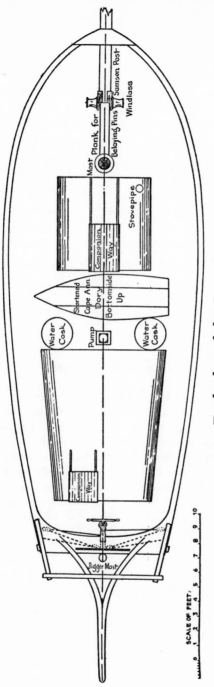

Deck-plan of the *Spray*

SCALE OF FEET: 0 1 2 3 4 5 6 7 8 9 10

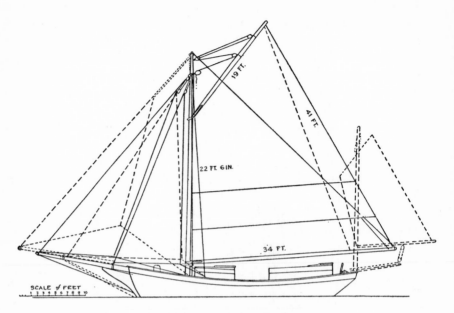

Sail-plan of the *Spray*

The solid lines represent the sail-plan of the *Spray* on starting for the long voyage. With it she crossed the Atlantic to Gibraltar, and then crossed again southwest to Brazil. In South American waters the bowsprit and boom were shortened and the jigger-sail added to form the yawl-rig with which the rest of the trip was made, the sail-plan of which is indicated by the dotted lines. The extreme sail forward is a flying jib occasionally used, set to a bamboo stick fastened to the bowsprit. The manner of setting and bracing the jigger-mast is not indicated in this drawing, but may be partly observed in the drawings for the Deck-plan of the *Spray* and the Steering-gear of the *Spray*.

Briefly I have to say that when close-hauled in a light wind under all sail she required little or no weather helm. As the wind increased I would go on deck, if below, and turn the wheel up a spoke more or less, relash it, or, as sailors say, put it in a becket, and then leave it as before.

To answer the questions that might be asked to meet every contingency would be a pleasure, but it would overburden my book. I can only say here that much comes to one in practice, and that, with such as love sailing, mother-wit is the best teacher, after experience. Labor-saving appliances? There were none. The sails were hoisted by hand; the halyards were rove through ordinary ships' blocks with common patent rollers. Of course the sheets were all belayed aft.

The windlass used was in the shape of a winch, or crab, I think it is called. I had three anchors, weighing forty pounds, one hundred pounds, and one hundred and eighty pounds respectively. The windlass and the forty-pound anchor, and the "fiddle-head," or carving, on the end of the cutwater, belonged to the original *Spray*. The ballast, concrete cement, was stanchioned down securely. There was no iron or lead or other weight on the keel.

If I took measurements by rule I did not set them down, and after sailing even the longest voyage in her I could not tell offhand the length of her mast, boom, or gaff. I did not know the center of effort in her sails, except as it hit me in practice at sea, nor did I care a rope yarn about it. Mathematical calculations, however, are all right in a good boat, and the *Spray* could have stood them. She was easily balanced and easily kept in trim.

Some of the oldest and ablest shipmasters have asked how it was possible for her to hold a true course before the wind, which was just what the *Spray* did for weeks together. One of these gentlemen, a highly esteemed shipmaster and friend, testified as government expert in a famous murder trial in Boston, not long since, that a ship would not hold her course long enough for the steersman to leave the helm to cut the captain's throat. Ordinarily it would be so. One might say that with a square-rigged ship it would always be so. But the *Spray*, at the moment of the tragedy in question, was sailing around the globe with no one at the helm, except at intervals more or less rare. However, I may say here that this would have had no bearing on the murder case in Boston. In all probability Justice laid her hand on the true rogue. In other words, in the case of a model and rig similar to that of the tragedy ship, I should myself testify as did the nautical experts at the trial.

But see the run the *Spray* made from Thursday Island to the Keeling Cocos Islands, twenty-seven hundred miles distant, in twenty-three days, with no one at the helm in that time, save for

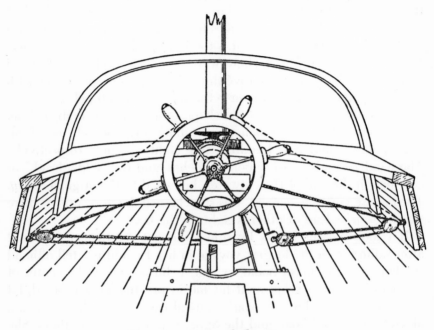

Steering-gear of the *Spray*

The dotted lines are the ropes used to lash the wheel. In practice the loose ends were belayed, one over the other, around the top spokes of the wheel.

about one hour, from land to land. No other ship in the history of the world ever performed, under similar circumstances, the feat on so long and continuous a voyage. It was, however, a delightful midsummer sail. No one can know the pleasure of sailing free over the great oceans save those who have had the experience. It is not necessary, in order to realize the utmost enjoyment of going around the globe, to sail alone, yet for once and the first time there was a great deal of fun in it. My friend the government expert, and saltest of salt sea-captains, standing only yesterday on the deck of the *Spray*, was convinced of her famous qualities, and he spoke enthusiastically of selling his farm on Cape Cod and putting to sea again.

To young men contemplating a voyage I would say go. The tales of rough usage are for the most part exaggerations, as also are the stories of sea danger. I had a fair schooling in the so-called "hard ships" on the hard Western Ocean, and in the years there I do not remember having once been "called out of my name." Such recol-

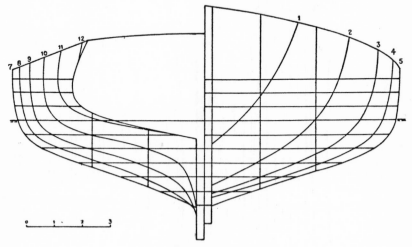

Body-plan of the *Spray*

lections have endeared the sea to me. I owe it further to the officers of all the ships I ever sailed in as boy and man to say that not one ever lifted so much as a finger to me. I did not live among angels, but among men who could be roused. My wish was, though, to please the officers of my ship wherever I was, and so I got on. Dangers there are, to be sure, on the sea as well as on the land, but the intelligence and skill God gives to man reduce these to a minimum. And here comes in again the skilfully modeled ship worthy to sail the seas.

To face the elements is, to be sure, no light matter when the sea is in its grandest mood. You must then know the sea, and know that you know it, and not forget that it was made to be sailed over.

I have given in the plans of the *Spray* the dimensions of such a ship as I should call seaworthy in all conditions of weather and on all seas. It is only right to say, though, that to insure a reasonable

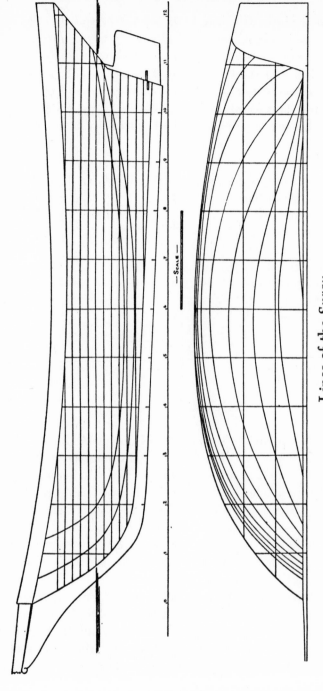

Lines of the *Spray*

measure of success, experience should sail with the ship. But in order to be a successful navigator or sailor it is not necessary to hang a tar-bucket about one's neck. On the other hand, much thought concerning the brass buttons one should wear adds nothing to the safety of the ship.

I may some day see reason to modify the model of the dear old *Spray*, but out of my limited experience I strongly recommend her wholesome lines over those of pleasure-fliers for safety. Practice in a craft such as the *Spray* will teach young sailors and fit them for the more important vessels. I myself learned more seamanship, I think, on the *Spray* than on any other ship I ever sailed, and as for patience, the greatest of all the virtues, even while sailing through the reaches of the Strait of Magellan, between the bluff mainland and dismal Fuego, where through intricate sailing I was obliged to steer, I learned to sit by the wheel, content to make ten miles a day beating against the tide, and when a month at that was all lost, I could find some old tune to hum while I worked the route all over again, beating as before. Nor did thirty hours at the wheel, in storm, overtax my human endurance, and to clap a hand to an oar and pull into or out of port in a calm was no strange experience for the crew of the *Spray*. The days passed happily with me wherever my ship sailed.

A Note About "Rescue of Some Gilbert Islanders"

In 1882, when Slocum commanded the *Northern Light,* he picked up in mid-Pacific a small company of Gilbert Islanders who had been caught in an open boat by a storm and blown hundreds of miles from home. He then wrote an account of the incident which, some years later, he appended to the first edition of *Voyage of the Liberdade,* perhaps to fill out the signature. In the introductory "Greeting" to that book, composed after Virginia's death and after the *Aquidneck* had come to grief, he said:

> In addition to the voyage of the Liberdade and history of what led to it, is related the rescue of the Gilbert Islanders, on that other memorable voyage in the lofty, noble ship, the Northern Light.
>
> Often and often, in the hour of great distress and bitter sufferings, the story of the Islanders has come in my thoughts, and I have said: "My state is not yet so bad as was theirs, nor my condition so woeful as that of the stricken sailors on the pest-ridden bark, upon the inhospitable coast, told in the story."

Both *Rescue* and the paragraphs above were deleted when Roberts Brothers reissued *Voyage of the Liberdade* in 1894.

Rescue of Some Gilbert Islanders

This narrative, relating the wonderful adventures of a small band of South Sea Islanders, who were driven to sea by a storm and finally rescued and restored to health and taken to their home in the GREAT PACIFIC, was gathered in part from the natives themselves, and by the assistance of books in the Polynesian language, sixty-two volumes of which were in their boat when picked up, mostly school books and religious works.

Comparing their geography with mine, for instance, I found that Buckiroro, their kingdom, was what we know to be the Gilbert Islands. Taiban corresponded to Japan, etc. By comparing their Bible with mine, chapter and verse, I soon learned something of their language so that in this way and with a few words of English which they could speak the following story was learned:

Early in October, the season when the darting bill-fish are not dangerous to voyagers, the king of the Gilbert Group of Islands in Polynesia, observing that the sea was smooth, sent from the Island of Apamana twelve natives on a business errand over to the neighboring Island of Nanouti. They started in the morning when the wind was fair and reached their destination on the following afternoon, making the voyage in an open boat which was 21 feet long, 7 feet wide and about 3 feet deep, and was sharp at both ends.

They remained on Nanouti about two weeks and set out on the return trip.

Rescue of Some Gilbert Islanders

This was about the end of October. They were overtaken by a storm and driven to leeward of their archipelago, and continued to be drifted about from north to south, and east to west, at the scant mercy of a changing monsoon, until Sunday, the 10th of the following December, when the *Northern Light* picked up the surviving five, about six hundred miles from their island home. Seven of their number had by this time perished, the first to succumb being a woman. The supply of food they were possessed of was limited to a small quantity of dry pulverized banana, and their stock of water could not in the beginning have exceeded twelve gallons as their utensils would not have held more, and one of these, a five-gallon jar, was broken the second day out on their terrible adventure. A few bottles of cocoanut oil completed their stock of provisions. All above this that they had to subsist on was the uncertain flying-fish that occasionally fell in their boat as manna from heaven. Their condition told us a story that words could not express, and their mute wonder was the greatest appeal to our deepest sympathy.

Speaking of these people as natives of a "South Sea Island," would not, I think, convey to the most of the Christian world a proper conception of the class of people, a few of whom we had been fortunate enough to rescue from inconceivable horrors. A more devout band of Christians I never met. When first hauled out of their cheerless cockleshell of a boat, more dead than alive, and placed safely on board our comfortable ship, a man who appeared to be a leader gave thanks to the Almighty with becoming reverence. They then fell on the deck in utter exhaustion. Brandy and other stimulants were administered. Warm tea seemed to agree very well with one or two who refused brandy on the plea that they were Christians. They all smoked, however, I could then see some good even in tobacco. When the woman, poor thing, had finished her light meal and smoked a few whiffs from a pipe, she reached out her hand for our infant son, Garfield, beckoned him to come, but before he could go to her, she was away in the land of visions, dreaming, probably, of being ceaselessly tossed on the remorseless sea, without hope other than her hope in heaven, among the dead and the dying, waiting only for death to end her own sufferings. The remainder soon followed the example of the woman, and on waking they seemed much bewildered, looked around the ship, then aloft at the cloud of white canvas. Their own craft had, in the meantime, been thoroughly

387

cleaned, propped upright, a tent-like roof made over her; all their little trinkets and scanty clothing washed and spread out to dry in a tropical sun, which, for the two days previous, had been darkened by tempest and rain, which made their condition hapless indeed.

"Allah is great!" would have exclaimed the famous Sinbad. Whaggie,* the youngest of the three young men, to my surprise, now addressed me in broken English, "Captain, where ship bound?" I informed him that we were bound for Japan. "Ship no stop Apamana?" To this query I replied it was possible we might touch at his island, if winds prevailed from the west, and if we had easterly winds we should touch at Ponape,—in any event they should be cared for as well as circumstances would permit. "Captain," said Whaggie, "I thank you." Not one on board our ship, I am sure, but would have rendered the unfortunates any assistance which lay in his power, thinking of the day perhaps, that might sometime come when he would be glad of merciful treatment himself. For my own part I had but to go back a short way in my career to remember being succored by islanders of less pretensions to Christianity than many who would not do so much; and it seemed as if I heard the voice of these simple people continually saying, "Show us the mercy which we to others show."

The change in their fortune soon began to tell on these waifs of the sea, three of whom were young men whose physique and manly form could not be matched by any three men among my crew. The fourth was an elderly man, the husband of the surviving woman, and a brighter eye than twinkled in his old head it would be hard to find. It was he who refused brandy, repeating his only words of English, "Me missionary!" † pointing at himself and then upwards. We readily comprehended his meaning. The poor old fellow seemed quite reconciled in the belief that his time was about up. When we were removing him into regular quarters along with the rest, Whaggie looked at him and shook his head, saying, "Tabboo!" ‡ We laughed them out of this idea, and told them that among "white" missionaries there was no "tabboo." The old man did not at first place much

* Spelling is phonetic.
† Missionary signifies believer in the Christian faith; the word is used in this sense throughout the South Sea Islands.
‡ "Tabboo" is a fatalistic exclamation, meaning it is finished—the end is come, and supply is cut off.

faith in what I said, but later on we became great friends. I never visited their quarters but he asked me by signs and gestures to sit down, invariably, too, alongside of his wife. What man could ask for greater mark of confidence!

Poor thing, it was not amiss, that a white sister was at hand who could extend to her needful help. I fully expected when she came round, to have her pay the same compliments to my good wife that her husband had heaped upon me, but she did not, for what reason I know not, except that women are possibly more inclined to jealousy than men.

About a week on board and prospects looked like landing our proteges on their own island. We reached within forty-five miles, and I fully expected to make the land early next morning. On learning this the islanders set to rejoicing. I came on deck, in the middle watch, and found the three young men arm in arm, walking the decks, singing sacred hymns.

Our disappointment next day was great when we found by observation that we had struck the equatorial current and had been set far to the westward. With a light easterly wind it was not practicable to pursue the course longer. The disappointment to them must have been very great. I felt conscience-smitten for having held out such high expectations, but it really looked like a sure thing to me at the time.

Thence we shaped our course for Ebon Island, which also lay in our track. We made it at night, a dark, boisterous night, and not the time to be hovering about coral reefs in a heavy ship. So from this we took our departure for Baring Island, expecting to sight it early next day. We sailed fairly over the site next day, but found no island. From where Baring Island was supposed to be I now shaped a course for Ponape, and had sailed fifteen miles when the mast-head lookout hailed, "Land, ho! nearly ahead!" This I made out to be Baring Island, thirty miles to the west of its assigned position on the charts.

Our island friends were in doubt if they would be kindly received by the inhabitants of this land; they were in doubt of its being inhabited by others than cannibals, and as night and stormy weather were again upon us, communication with the shore was cut off. Whaggie, to avoid being landed in the strange country, stowed himself away in the ship. I did not feel justified in simply giving them provisions and sending them off in their boat to an almost unknown island and perhaps extremely unkind people. They were all evidently alarmed at the idea of being thus turned away, and I considered I had no more right to turn them adrift than I would have with people of any other nation thrown on our hospitality. Northeast trades now fairly opened out on us and my mind was soon made up. Calling our visitors to me I acquainted them with what I thought best for all concerned. "Taiban" (Japan) was the word, and I assure you their faces at once brightened up and a load was taken off my mind.

The next morning, as our ship fairly danced along toward Japan, Whaggie asked if I thought they should ever see Apamana again. I looked at their situation now in a new aspect, and determined that they should see their home and friends again if my efforts could bring this about. I made light of their fears and told them, as best I could, that one of our many warships cruising the ocean would very likely carry them back, boat and all. Whaggie intimated that the king of Apamana would be pleased enough to "pay money, give plenty cobre, etc." Perhaps he would have knighted me into the bargain, who knows? My opportunity was probably lost by being met with foul currents, otherwise I might now be known as Lord Bukiroro instead of plain S— or still better, perhaps as Governor of an island! As for goods or money payment we could not entertain a thought of it. For, was it not so with Sinbad, the sailor, when he proffered goods to the owner of the ship instrumental in his escape from the mountain? Was he not told: "We take nothing from any one, and when we behold a ship-wrecked person on the shore of the sea, or on an island (or in a boat), we take him with us and feed him and give him drink, and if he be naked we clothe him, and when we arrive at the port of safety we give him something of our property as a present, and act toward him with kindness and favor for the sake of God whose name be exalted?" This sentiment, I think, is worth being kept in mind. I would fain add that "the inhabitants of the port of safety to which the ship arrives also act kindly toward him." It is right that we should not be outdone by an Arab.

We arrived safely in Yokohama on the 15th of January; thirty odd days on the *Northern Light* with all the comforts of a home afloat had restored our strange passengers again to health; the keen winter winds, however, biting cold to them, racked their joints with pain.

Upon nearing the coast of Japan, our islanders who had never before witnessed other than coral islands and balmy climes beheld now a great country before them, clad in snow; and the beauty of hoar Fusiama, lofty, glistening in the sun, surpassed their dreams. Convulsed with agitation the castaways peered long and anxiously over the rail of the ship at this strange land robed in white, to which their genii had sent them; and the old man exhausting his English, exclaimed, "Oh, big island! big island!" and Whaggie said, "Uh, hot!" when he meant uh, cold; for the wind was from north and that in Japan in the middle of winter we all know means cold.

I was at a loss to know what to do with these waifs of the ocean or how to provide for them when they landed in Yokohama where clearly they were as lost and helpless as were the "Babes in the Wood." Had they been shipped on the articles the protection of our government would then have been amply provided; nevertheless, their story raised a warm sympathy for them in the hearts of the kind residents and private help came in from all directions, from ministers and merchants. Our American Minister at Tokio, Hon. Judge Bingham gave liberally from a private purse where he could not extend the aid of government; also the generous British Minister, Sir Harry Parks, contributed clothing and money; in fact, more funds were sent in than the original estimate, to supply their wants until they reached their home, so much so that I advertised that no more was necessary; above this, the Pacific Mail Steam Ship Co. gave them a free passage, boat and all, to San Francisco.

The mention, later, that the money raised in Japan was sufficient to provide food for them all the time they were here (in Honolulu) and something left! was reassuring, if indeed there had been any doubt of it.

Friends in Japan had the pleasure of knowing that there was enough for them while at Honolulu; and as one finger poi costs but a trifle more than the thinner kind which requires two fingers to convey it, they have every reason to believe that the Islanders enjoyed the best of food and were happy the few weeks they were there. It was the wish of their benefactors in Japan that they should return home like princes carrying with them good accounts of the white man's hospitality and religion at home.

What became of the boat after it left Yokohama I'm sure I don't know, but have no doubt that it was carried back to its owner, the King of Buckiroro.

I saw them off for San Francisco in the *City of Tokio*. In due time they arrived at that place and were kindly taken care of; their photograph was taken there in a group, a woodcut of the same can be seen in the Sailors' Magazine. A bank credit of ample means went with them. From San Francisco they were taken to Honolulu where they again fell into good hands, for the same kind treatment awaited them there which had followed them from Japan.

But Whaggie, I find now, when so earnestly assuring me that his King would be pleased, would pay money, would pay plenty cobre, etc., for their return home—had told only half of the story; for here at Honolulu he met a betrothed who had watched and waited the coming back of her lover in the boat; months having passed, however with no tidings from the sea, the little crew was given up as lost; then the maid of Apamana had retired forlorn to Oahu, where, rejoicing at last she met her Whaggie on the lee; then the broken plight was mended by marriage vow.

Passage was secured for the little band of survivors to their native home in the mission ship *Morning Star;* and Whaggie took his happy bride along home with him. Thus, after a tour of peculiar adventures of many, many thousands of miles our interesting Whaggie brought home a wife to the surprise of his long wondering neighbors.

Thus we have another illustration of the devious course of human life in the which we find "Truth stranger than Fiction."

A Check List of Published Work of Captain Joshua Slocum

BOOKS

Voyage of the Liberdade—Description of a Voyage "Down to the Sea." Boston: Press of Robinson & Stephenson, 1890. Includes "Rescue of Some Gilbert Islanders" and "Extracts from Letters and Newspapers" commenting on the voyage.

Voyage of the Liberdade. Boston: Roberts Brothers, 1894. This edition offered the buyer a choice of color of binding: red, blue, or yellow.

Voyage of the Destroyer from New York to Brazil. Boston: Press of Robinson Printing Company, 1894. Victor Slocum wrote that his father had 500 copies printed.

Sailing Alone Around the World. Illustrated by Thomas Fogarty and George Varian. New York: The Century Company, 1900. There were reprintings in 1900, 1901, 1905, 1907, 1911, 1917, 1919, 1923, 1925, 1927, 1930, 1934, 1935, 1936, 1937, 1941, all of them small, for a total of 27,474 copies. In 1930, and for a period of three years thereafter, Blue Ribbon Books, Inc., using the original plates, issued three printings of a lower priced edition, a total of 16,200 copies. Further printings from the original plates were made in 1954 by Sheridan House, Inc., and in 1956 by Grosset & Dunlap, Inc. In the latter year the book entered the public domain.

Sailing Alone Around the World was first published in London in 1900 by Sampson Low, Marston & Company. In 1948, it became No. 1 in the "Mariners Library" series brought out by Rupert Hart-Davis. The Reprint Society edition appeared in 1949; and Pan Books, Ltd., paperbound, in 1950.

Around the World in the Sloop Spray—"A Geographical Reader Describing Captain Slocum's Voyage Alone Around the World." New York: Charles Scribner's Sons, 1903. This abridgment of *Sailing Alone Around the World* was made by Edward R. Shaw and includes a brief preface

393

by Slocum. There were two editions, one printed by the Scribner Press for inclusion in the "Scribner Series of School Reading," the other by the Caxton Press. Both were for school use.

NEWSPAPERS

Travel letters from the *Spray* appeared in the *Boston Globe* on three Mondays: 14 October 1895, p. 6; 21 October 1895, p. 5; 11 November 1895, p. 4. Each was signed Joshua Slocum and copyrighted by Roberts Brothers.

PERIODICALS

Sailing Alone Around the World. The Century Illustrated Monthly Magazine, September 1899-March 1900.

Voyage of the Destroyer from New York to Brazil. McClure's, March 1900. An abridged and edited version of the book.

The Voyage of the Aquidneck and its Varied Adventures in South American Waters. Outing, November 1902-April 1903. This is *Voyage of the Liberdade* with a new introductory paragraph and minor changes.

"Bully Hayes, the Last Buccaneer." *Outing,* March 1906. The by-line on this piece is "Written from Data Supplied by Captain Joshua Slocum." Internal evidence confirms the suggestion that Slocum had no hand in its writing.

TRANSLATIONS

En världsomsegling på egen hand. Translated by Hugo Gyllander. Uppsala: Lindblad, 1921. Other editions in 1944 and 1953 (illustrated).

Sam jeden żaglowcem naokoło świata. Translated by Ludwik Szwykowski. Warszawa: Główna Ksiegarnia Wojskowa, 1930.

Seul autour du monde sur un voilier de 11 mètres. Paris: Chiron, 1936.

Erdumseglung—ganz allein. Leipzig: Brockhaus, 1936.

Ensam seglare jorden runt och Liberdades resa. Introduction by Sigfrid Siwertz. Translated by Lisbeth and Louis Renner. Illustrated. Stockholm: Bonnier, 1952.

Alleen in een kotter de wereld rond—De tocht van de Spray. Amsterdam: Uitgeverij V/H C. De Boer Jr., 1955.

MISCELLANEOUS

Sloop Spray Souvenir. Arranged and Supplied with Notes by Henrietta E. Slocum. The Gilliss Press. Copyright 1901 by Joshua Slocum. It is obvious that Slocum himself is the arranger and supplier of notes for this 48-page booklet which he sold at the Pan American Exposition and thereafter. "A collection of reviews of the Spray's famous voyage around the world, from leading journals, with something tangible of the Spray herself—namely, a piece of her original mainsail, which was torn, beyond repair, in the gale off Cape Horn. . . . Admiring friends of the Spray, visiting her with jack-knives, first and last, by their keen appreciation of souvenirs, suggested the preparation of this memento. . . ."

A *Note on Sources*

In addition to what Joshua Slocum tells of himself in his books, my best sources of information were letters, photographs, newspaper accounts, and the recollections of persons who had known him. Had I not begun inquiring when I did, much that illuminates the man and his work might have fallen by the way or been lost altogether.

I have already said that in July 1952, in West Tisbury, Massachusetts, I called on the Hettie of the saga. She was then Mrs. Ulysses E. Mayhew, and had been for thirty years. Before she died, only three months later, she put me in touch with her first husband's three surviving children.

In September 1952, I began a correspondence with B. Aymar Slocum, then seventy-nine; also with Jessie Slocum Joyce, seventy-seven, who invariably signed her letters "The Captain's Daughter"; and with J. Garfield Slocum, who was seventy-one. B. Aymar Slocum, with whom I twice visited as well as corresponded, furnished photographs of his parents, their marriage certificate, two letters written by his father, and vivid recollections of his mother. Jessie Slocum Joyce also wrote of her mother and sent a photograph of her father taken in Washington, D.C., in 1888-89 by Mathew B. Brady. Garfield—he asked me to address him so—was in his last illness. While in bed, he wrote notes on 3 x 5 pieces of paper which his wife then clipped together and sent me. He died in January 1955.

Victor, the captain's oldest son, had died in 1949. However, a niece, Catherine Woodruff, had preserved his papers pertaining to his father and granted me the use of them, and they, too, were helpful. Two of the captain's cousins, Grace Murray Brown and Lorimer

B. Slocum, whose assistance I acknowledged in *The Search for Captain Slocum,* have since died.

It was Lorimer Slocum who directed me to his former teacher of American literature at Princeton, J. Duncan Spaeth. Professor Spaeth had been so impressed by the literary qualities of *Sailing Alone,* as well as by its author's accomplishments as navigator and sailor, that he went to see the captain at Gloucester sometime after 1900. A year before he died, Spaeth wrote me about that visit—and then wrote a second time as further memories returned.

I cannot say how many letters I sent in pursuit of material, or how many persons I saw. I did not keep a record, and perhaps it does not matter. What was very moving was that, almost without exception, people were eager to do whatever they could. It was characteristic of all classes of persons who had seen or spoken with the captain to know and feel certain he was an uncommon man.

A few words concerning an informant may suggest what some of the research was like and how narrow the margin of time which remained. For a couple of seasons at Martha's Vineyard I had asked about Slocum, written of him, and given a talk on him in a local chapel. Then, one day, a citizen of West Tisbury told me that I ought to see one, George G. Gifford. For fifty years Gifford had kept store and been town clerk in West Tisbury, but by this time he was living off-island, as Vineyarders say, in an old folks home. A relative then supplied the address—East Providence, Rhode Island—and I wrote, but no answer came. I waited a while, then wrote again, but with the same results. A year went by until, on another trip to New England, I made an excursion to East Providence and located Mr. Gifford's home. I knocked on the door, was let in and asked to wait while an attendant went to announce me. Presently he returned bringing with him a truly old man. It was George Gifford; he was blind. My letters had been read aloud, but he had not felt like troubling anyone to write out his reply. He said he thought I would stop by sooner or later. His sentences came slowly but perfectly clearly. There and then I took down what he had to say about Slocum as he had known him in West Tisbury. Mr. Gifford is no longer living.

Through the columns of the *New York Times,* the *New York Herald Tribune,* the *Sydney Morning Herald,* and *The Age,* Melbourne, which published my letters of inquiry, I reached perhaps a dozen other persons who had the sort of firsthand knowledge, or documents, or photographs I was looking for.

Slocum's letters pertaining to the *Aquidneck* addressed to various government officials are in the records of the Department of State (Record Group 59) in the National Archives, Washington, D.C. His letters to Roberts Brothers and Eugene Hardy are in the Library of the Peabody Museum, Salem, Massachusetts. Those to editors of the *Century* magazine are in the Century Collection, Manuscript Room of the New York Public Library.

The Smithsonian Institution, Washington, D.C., owns six letters, one pasted in the front of a presentation copy of *Sailing Alone* in the Library, and five in the records of the Department of Engineering and Industries. I have acquired four more letters: four pages to John W. Edmonds, New York, 3 May 1890; one page to Frank J. Donovan, Esq., Manly, New South Wales, 11 November 1896; six pages to Joseph B. Gilder, Keeling-Cocos Islands, 20 August 1897; one page to Francis J. Underhill, Esq., Newport, Rhode Island, 29 August 1900. I also have photostats or transcripts of eight others not in any of the collections mentioned above. Seven have been published in whole or part in *The Search for Captain Slocum* and/or *The Voyages of Joshua Slocum*.

The main newspaper sources were the *New York Times*, indexed and on microfilm, the *New York Herald*, the *New York Tribune*, the *Boston Globe*, the *Boston Herald*, the *Vineyard Gazette*, Edgartown, the *New Bedford Standard, Evening Times*, and *Mercury*, the *New Era of Riverton and Palmyra, New Jersey*, the *Mount Holly News*, and the *New Jersey Mirror* of Mt. Holly, New Jersey. Also, a number of unidentified clippings were loaned or are in my possession.

All the earlier photographs, and a few of the later ones as well, came from members of the Slocum family.

The photographs taken by the writer and illustrator, Clifton Johnson, when he visited Slocum and Hettie at their West Tisbury home in 1902, were lent by his widow, the late Anna M. Johnson, formerly of South Hadley, Massachusetts.

Winfield Scott Clime, of Old Lyme, Connecticut, lent the only set of prints he still owned of pictures taken of Slocum in the summer of 1907. Clime, in those days, was a young man in government service, also a painter and photographer. He looked for his subjects on the Potomac River waterfront, and there, of course, he found the captain and *Spray*.

The latest photograph, the *Spray* hauled out in Miami in the winter of 1907-1908, Slocum standing on deck, was sent by another eye-witness, Vincent Gilpin, of West Chester, Pennsylvania.

Selected Bibliography

There are, as yet, few published references to Joshua Slocum which are critically interesting or factually accurate. I list below only those which I feel illuminate, much or little, human character or social and literary history.

Robert Greenhalgh Albion, article on Joshua Slocum in the *Dictionary of American Biography*.

W. S. Barclay, *The Land of Magellan*. London: Methuen, n.d.

Van Wyck Brooks, *The Confident Years, 1885-1915*. New York: Dutton, 1951.

Thomas Fleming Day, "On Capt. Joshua Slocum." *Rudder*. Reprinted in *The Rudder Treasury*, Tom Davin (ed.), New York, Sheridan, 1953.

Clifton Johnson, "Captain Joshua Slocum—The Man Who Sailed Around the World in a Thirty-Seven-Foot-Boat." *Outing*, October 1902.

——, "The Cook Who Sailed Alone." *Good Housekeeping*, February 1903.

Charmian London, *Book of Jack London*. New York: Century, 1921. 2 vols.

Jack London, *The Cruise of the Snark*. New York: Macmillan, 1911.

Frederick C. Matthews, *American Merchant Ships*, Series Two, Salem, Mass., 1931.

Elting E. Morison (ed.), *The Letters of Theodore Roosevelt*, Volume V: *Big Stick, 1905-1909*. Cambridge: Harvard University Press, 1952.

Major J. B. Pond, *Eccentricities of Genius—Memories of Famous Men and Women of the Platform and Stage*. New York, 1900.

Arthur Ransome, introduction to *Sailing Alone Around the World*. Mariners Library No. 1. London: Rupert Hart-Davis, 1948.

Felix Riesenberg, *Cape Horn*. New York: Dodd, Mead, 1939.

Charles Elihu Slocum, M.D., *A Short History of the Slocum, Slocumb and Slocomb Families 1637-1908*. Defiance, Ohio: Vol. I, 1882; Vol. II, 1908.

Selected Bibliography

Victor Slocum, *Captain Joshua Slocum—The Life and Voyages of America's Best Known Sailor.* New York: Sheridan, 1950.

Walter Magnes Teller, "Any Word of Captain Slocum?" *Vineyard Gazette,* 19 June 1953.

——— Introduction to *Sailing Alone Around the World.* New York: Sheridan, 1954. The same in Great Adventure Library, New York: Grosset and Dunlap, 1956.

——— *The Search for Captain Slocum: A Biography.* New York: Scribner's, 1956.

——— "Postscripts to *The Search for Captain Slocum.*" *American Neptune,* July 1958.